Recently, I haven't been exercising at all!! And so now, when I bike up even a slight incline, I get muscle cramps...And not just in my legs, but in my arms, too! Why?

—*Masashi Kishimoto, 2003*

岸本斉史

Author/artist Masashi Kishimoto was born in 1974 in rural Okayama Prefecture, Japan. After spending time in art college, he won the Hop Step Award for new manga artists with his manga **Karakuri** (Mechanism). Kishimoto decided to base his next story on traditional Japanese culture. His first version of **Naruto**, drawn in 1997, was a one-shot story about fox spirits; his final version, which debuted in **Weekly Shonen Jump** in 1999, quickly became the most popular ninja manga in Japan.

NARUTO VOL. 17
SHONEN JUMP Manga Edition

This volume contains material that was originally published in English in **SHONEN JUMP** #58. Artwork in the magazine may have been slightly altered from that presented here.

STORY AND ART BY MASASHI KISHIMOTO

Translation & English Adaptation/Mari Morimoto
Touch-Up Art & Lettering/Annaliese Christman
Design/Yvonne Cai
Editor/Joel Enos

Printed in the U.S.A.

Published by VIZ Media, LLC
P.O. Box 77010
San Francisco, CA 94107

12
First printing, September 2007
Twelfth printing, January 2022

VIZ MEDIA
viz.com

ratings.viz.com

PARENTAL ADVISORY
NARUTO is rated T for Teen and is recommended for ages 13 and up. This volume contains realistic and fantasy violence.

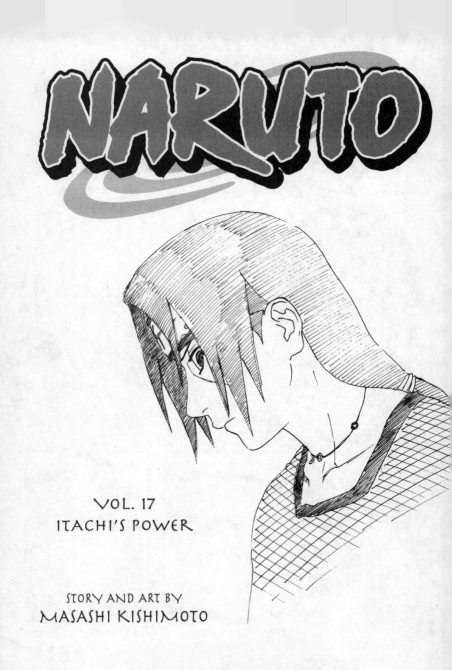

NARUTO

VOL. 17
ITACHI'S POWER

STORY AND ART BY
MASASHI KISHIMOTO

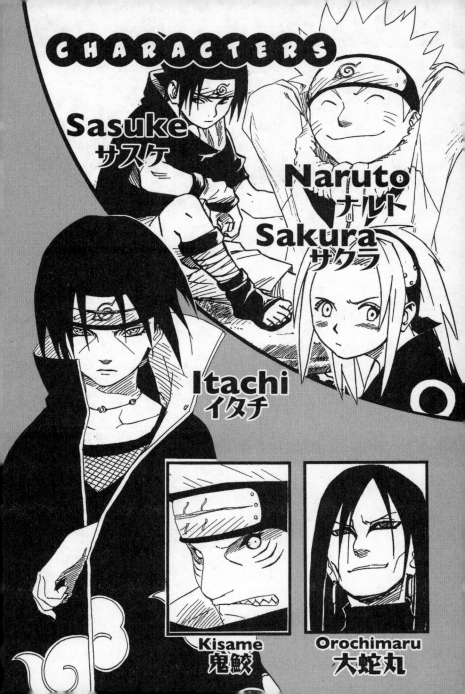

CHARACTERS

Sasuke
サスケ

Naruto
ナルト

Sakura
サクラ

Itachi
イタチ

Kisame
鬼鮫

Orochimaru
大蛇丸

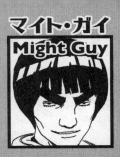

マイト・ガイ

Might Guy

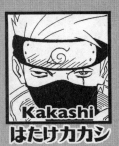

Kakashi

はたけカカシ

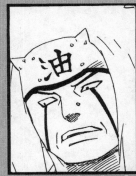

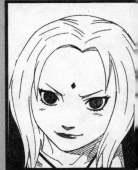

Jiraiya 自来也

Tsunade 綱手

The Story So Far…

Twelve years ago a destructive nine-tailed fox spirit attacked the ninja village of Konohagakure. The Hokage, or village champion, defeated the fox by sealing its soul into the body of a baby boy. Now that boy, Uzumaki Naruto, has grown up to be a ninja-in-training, learning the art of ninjutsu with his teammates Sakura and Sasuke.

Naruto and company take on the Chûnin Selection Exams but suffer a sudden attack from Orochimaru in the Forest of Death. Orochimaru leaves a curse mark on Sasuke's body and vanishes, only to return during the final round to launch *Operation Destroy Konoha!*

While Naruto battles Gaara, the Third Hokage sacrifices himself to defeat Orochimaru. Konohagakure is saved, and Jiraiya and Naruto set out to hunt down the elusive Tsunade to fill the position of Fifth Hokage, but they are pursued by two menacing shadows…

NARUTO

VOL. 17
ITACHI'S POWER

CONTENTS

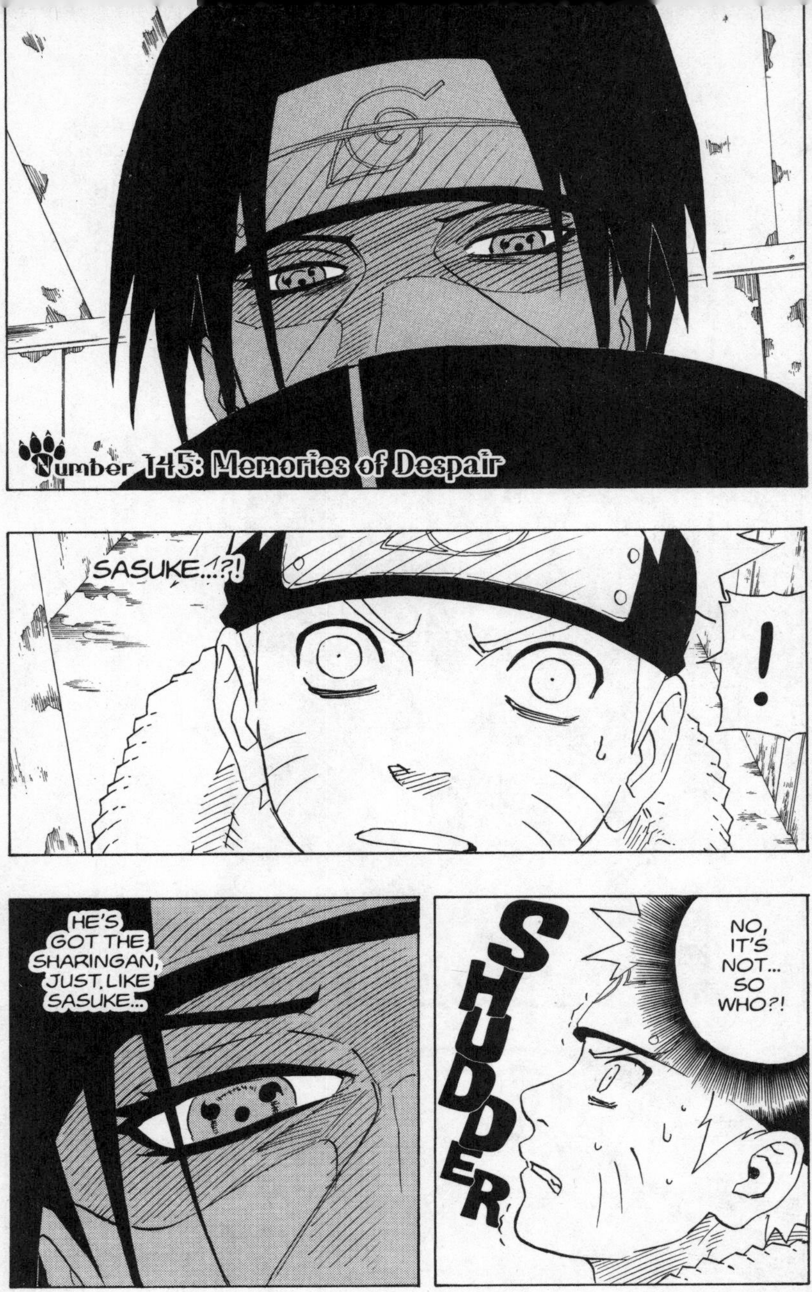
Number 145: Memories of Despair
SASUKE...!?!
!
NO, IT'S NOT... SO WHO?!
SHUDDER
HE'S GOT THE SHARINGAN, JUST LIKE SASUKE...

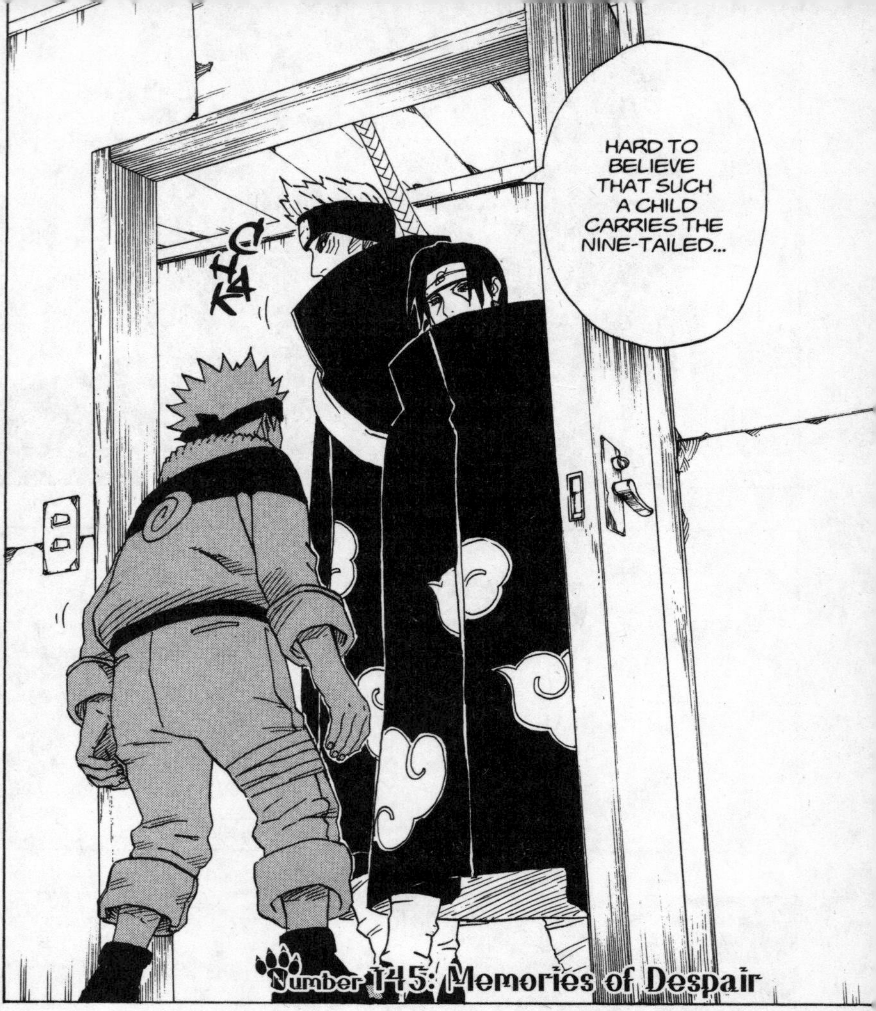
HARD TO BELIEVE THAT SUCH A CHILD CARRIES THE NINE-TAILED...
CHAK
Number 145: Memories of Despair

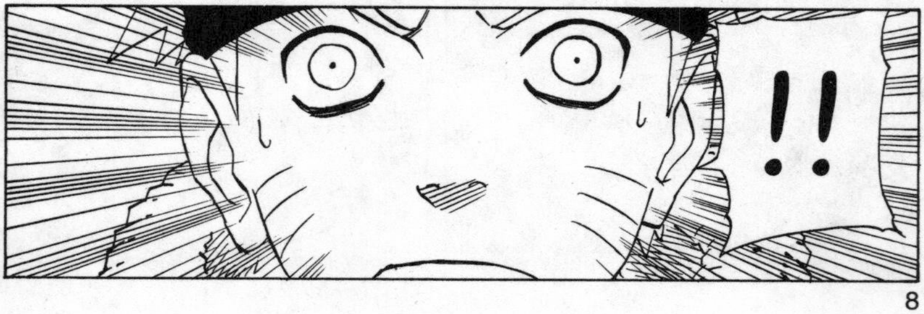
!!

READ THIS WAY

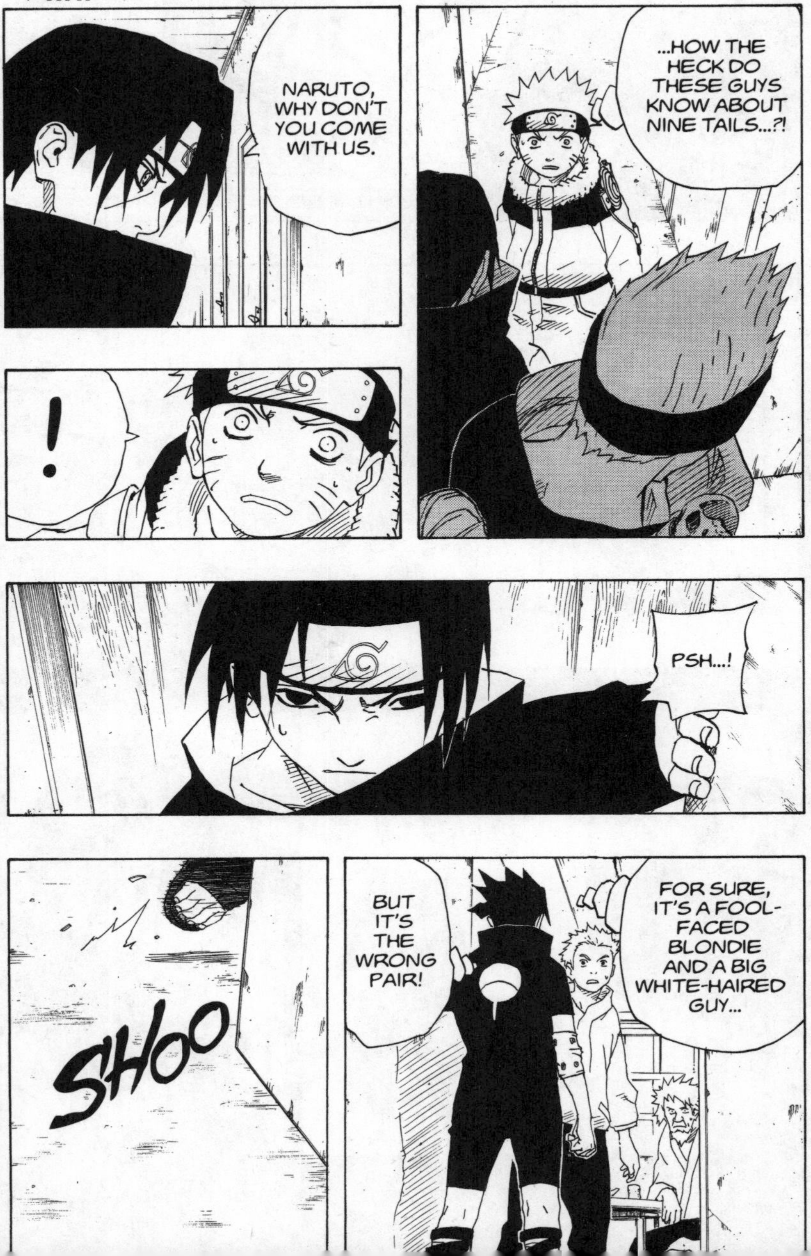
...HOW THE HECK DO THESE GUYS KNOW ABOUT NINE TAILS...?!
NARUTO, WHY DON'T YOU COME WITH US.
!
PSH...!
FOR SURE, IT'S A FOOL-FACED BLONDIE AND A BIG WHITE-HAIRED GUY...
BUT IT'S THE WRONG PAIR!
SHOO

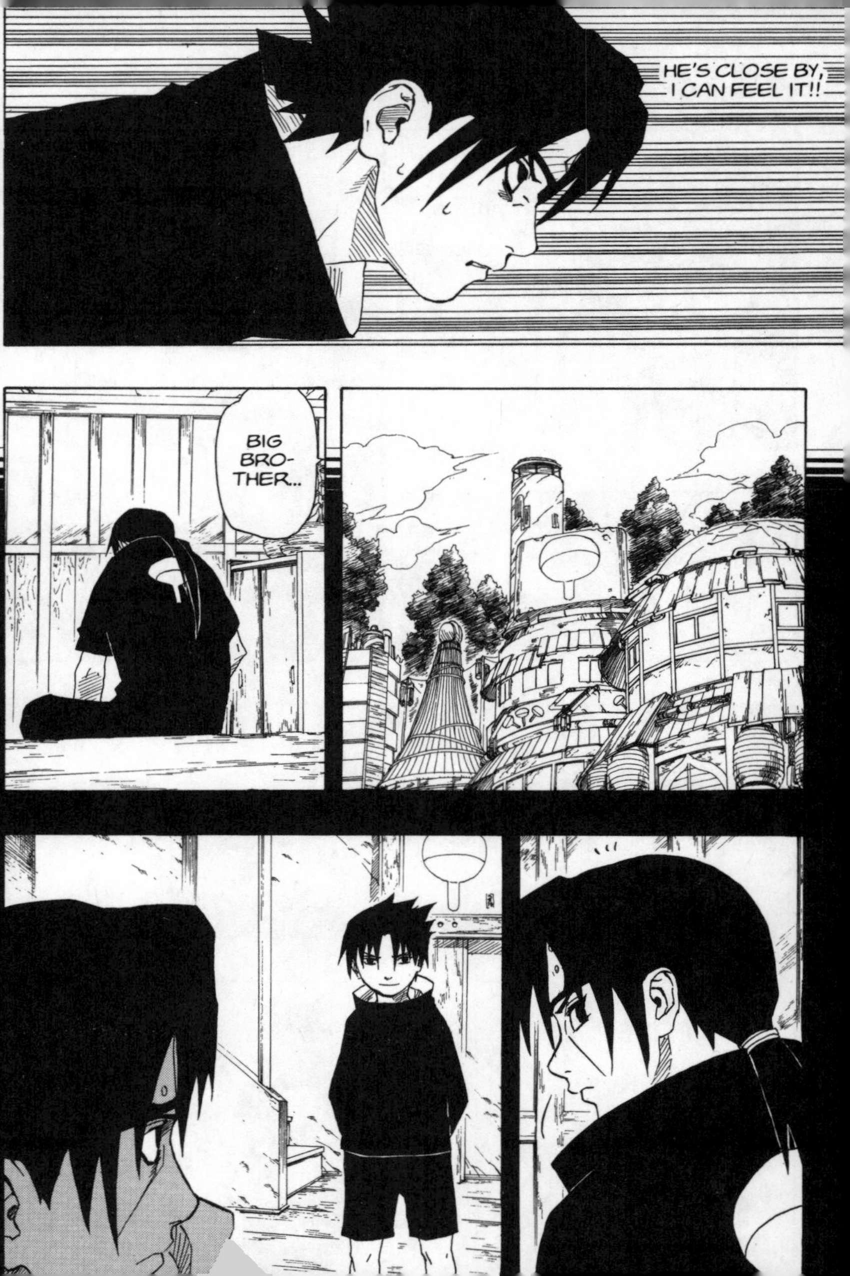
HE'S CLOSE BY, I CAN FEEL IT!!
BIG BRO- THER...

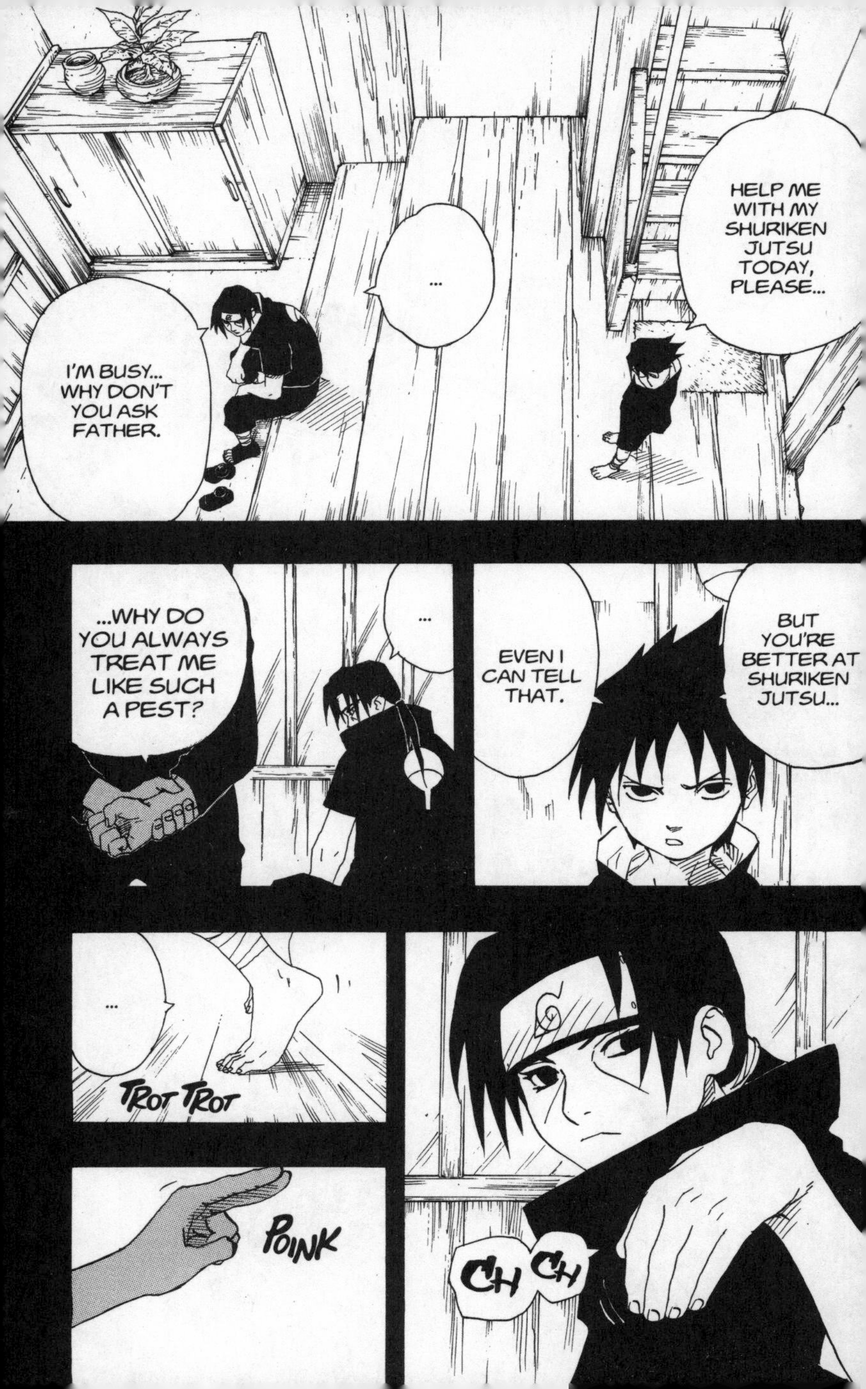
HELP ME WITH MY SHURIKEN JUTSU TODAY, PLEASE...
...
I'M BUSY... WHY DON'T YOU ASK FATHER.
BUT YOU'RE BETTER AT SHURIKEN JUTSU...
EVEN I CAN TELL THAT.
...
...WHY DO YOU ALWAYS TREAT ME LIKE SUCH A PEST?
CH CH
...
TROT TROT
POINK

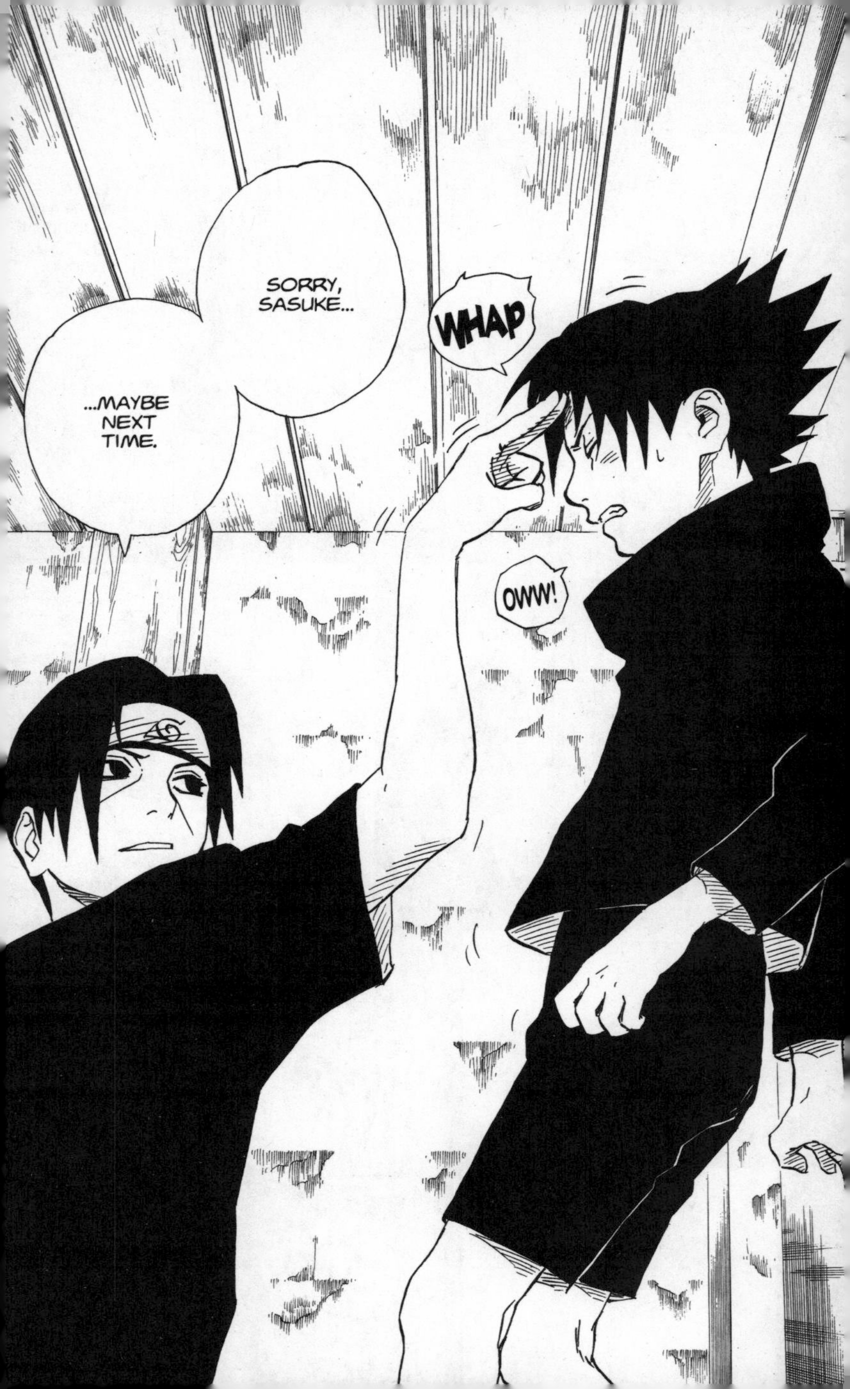
SORRY, SASUKE...
...MAYBE NEXT TIME.
WHAP
OWW!

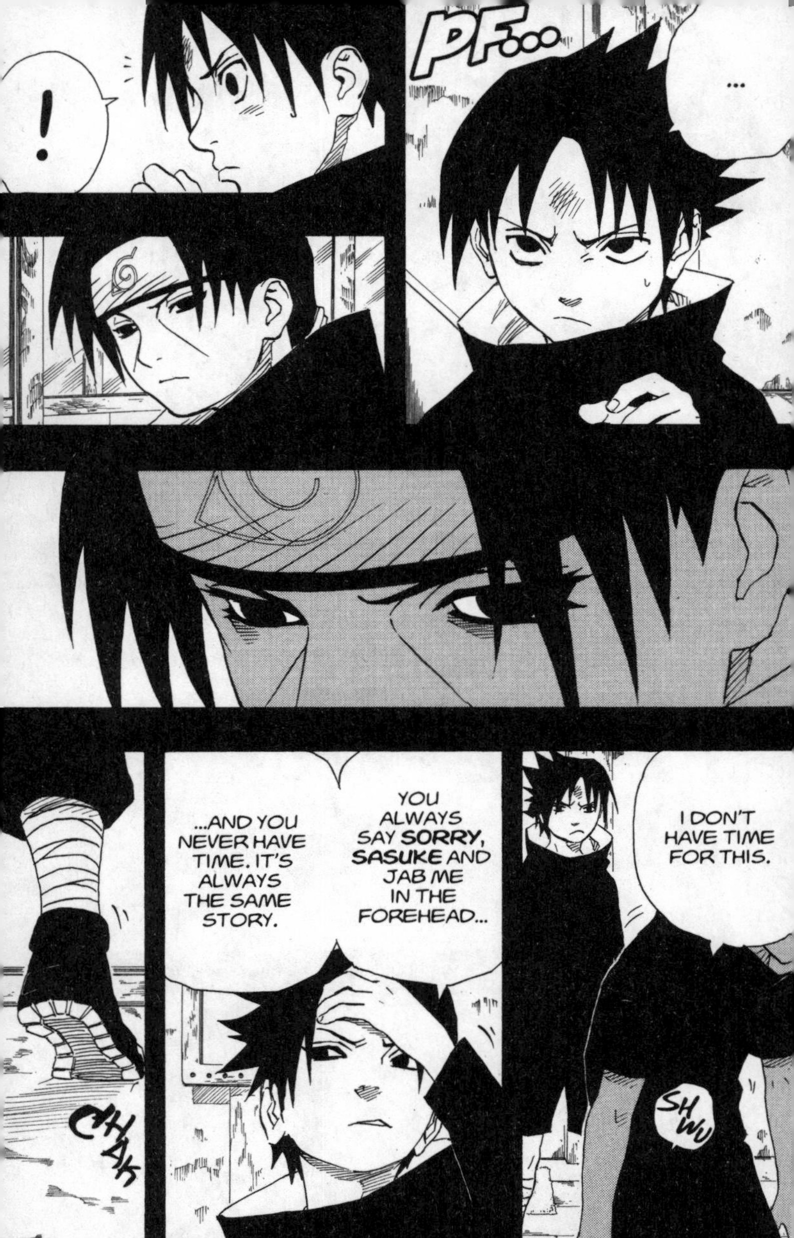

PF...
...
!
I DON'T HAVE TIME FOR THIS.
SHWU
YOU ALWAYS SAY **SORRY, SASUKE** AND JAB ME IN THE FOREHEAD...
...AND YOU NEVER HAVE TIME. IT'S ALWAYS THE SAME STORY.
CHAK

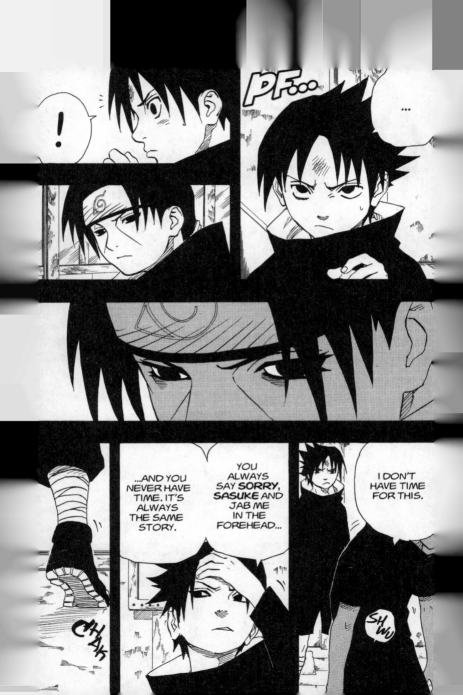

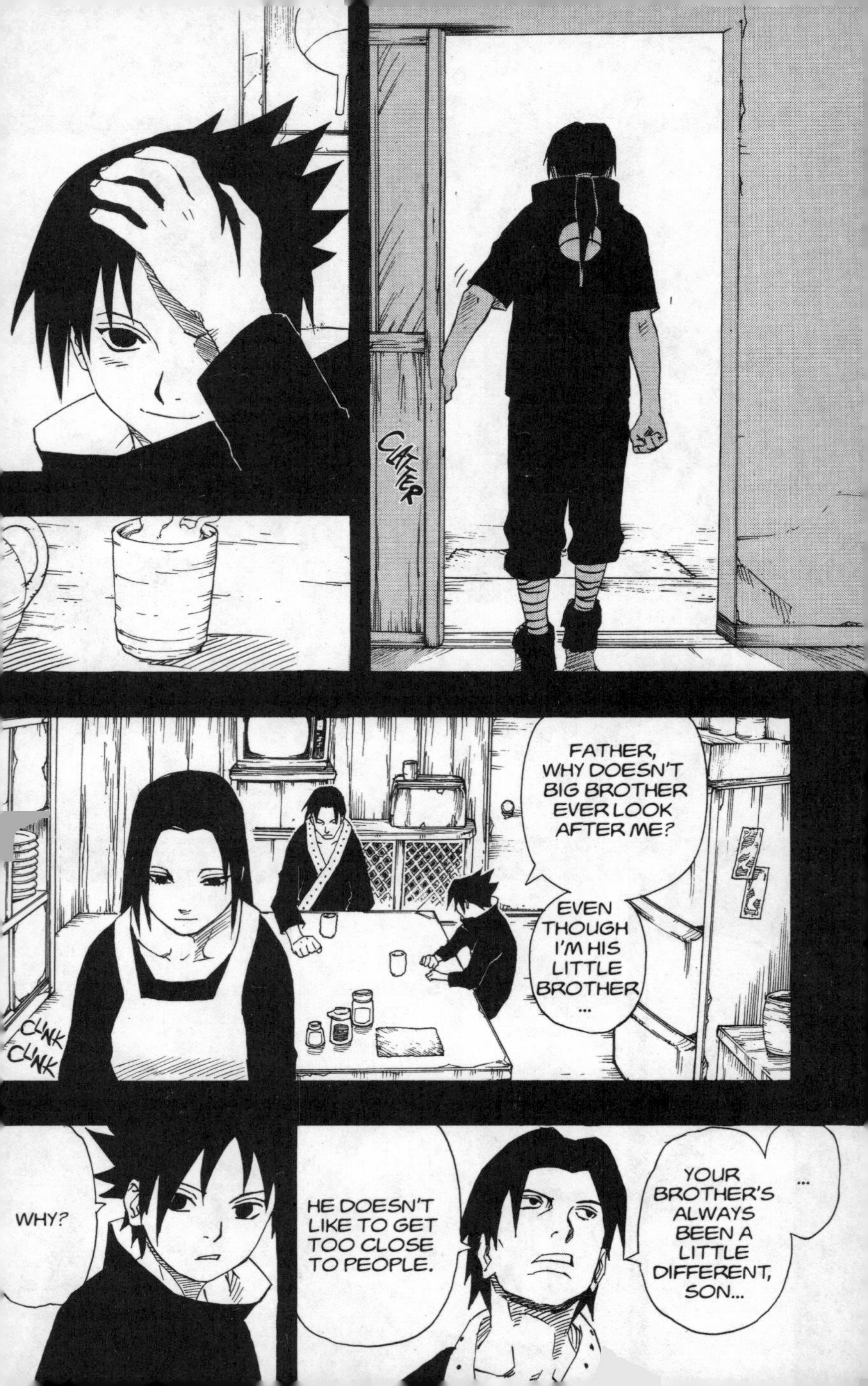
CLATTER
FATHER, WHY DOESN'T BIG BROTHER EVER LOOK AFTER ME?
EVEN THOUGH I'M HIS LITTLE BROTHER ...
CLINK CLINK
...
YOUR BROTHER'S ALWAYS BEEN A LITTLE DIFFERENT, SON...
HE DOESN'T LIKE TO GET TOO CLOSE TO PEOPLE.
WHY?

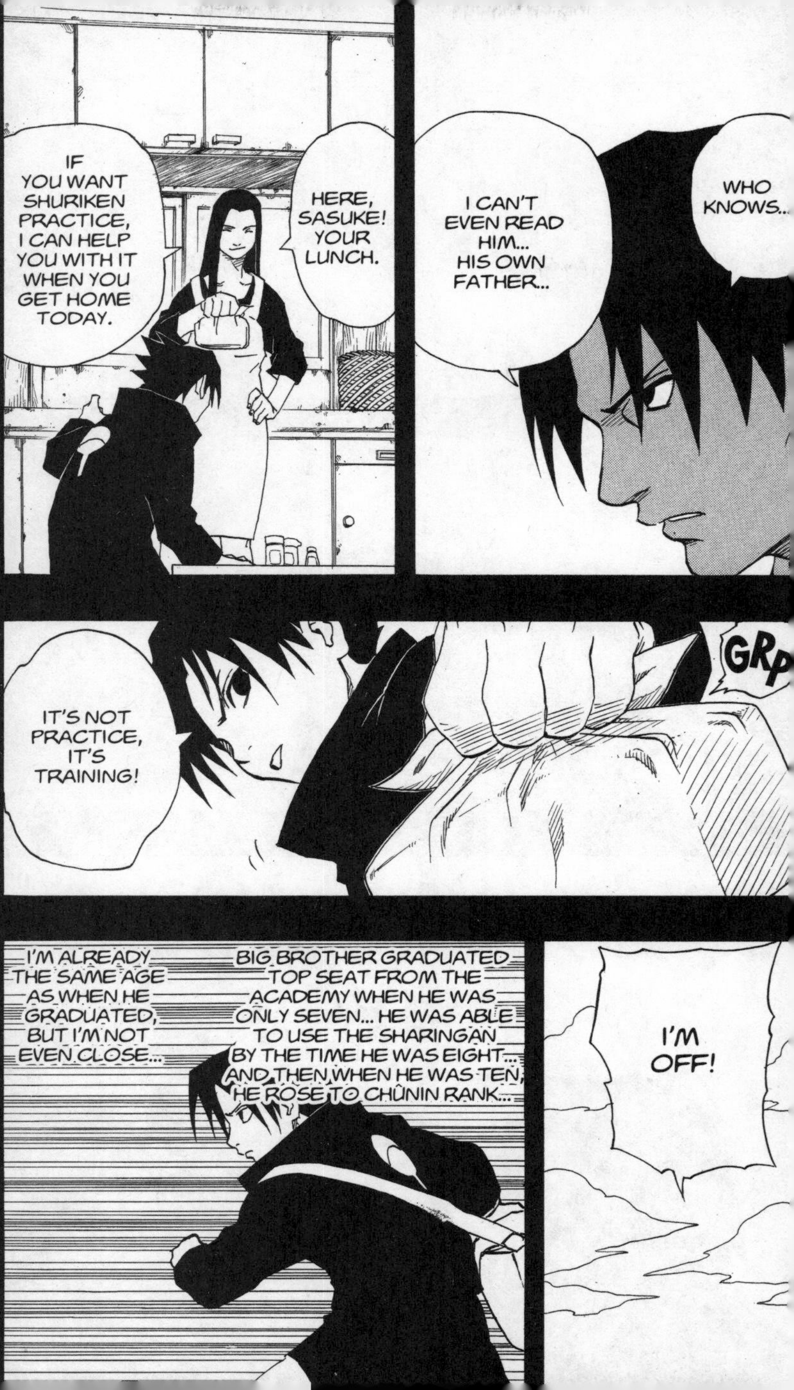
WHO KNOWS...
I CAN'T EVEN READ HIM... HIS OWN FATHER...
HERE, SASUKE! YOUR LUNCH.
IF YOU WANT SHURIKEN PRACTICE, I CAN HELP YOU WITH IT WHEN YOU GET HOME TODAY.
GRP
IT'S NOT PRACTICE, IT'S TRAINING!
I'M OFF!
BIG BROTHER GRADUATED TOP SEAT FROM THE ACADEMY WHEN HE WAS ONLY SEVEN... HE WAS ABLE TO USE THE SHARINGAN BY THE TIME HE WAS EIGHT... AND THEN WHEN HE WAS TEN, HE ROSE TO CHÛNIN RANK...
I'M ALREADY THE SAME AGE AS WHEN HE GRADUATED, BUT I'M NOT EVEN CLOSE...

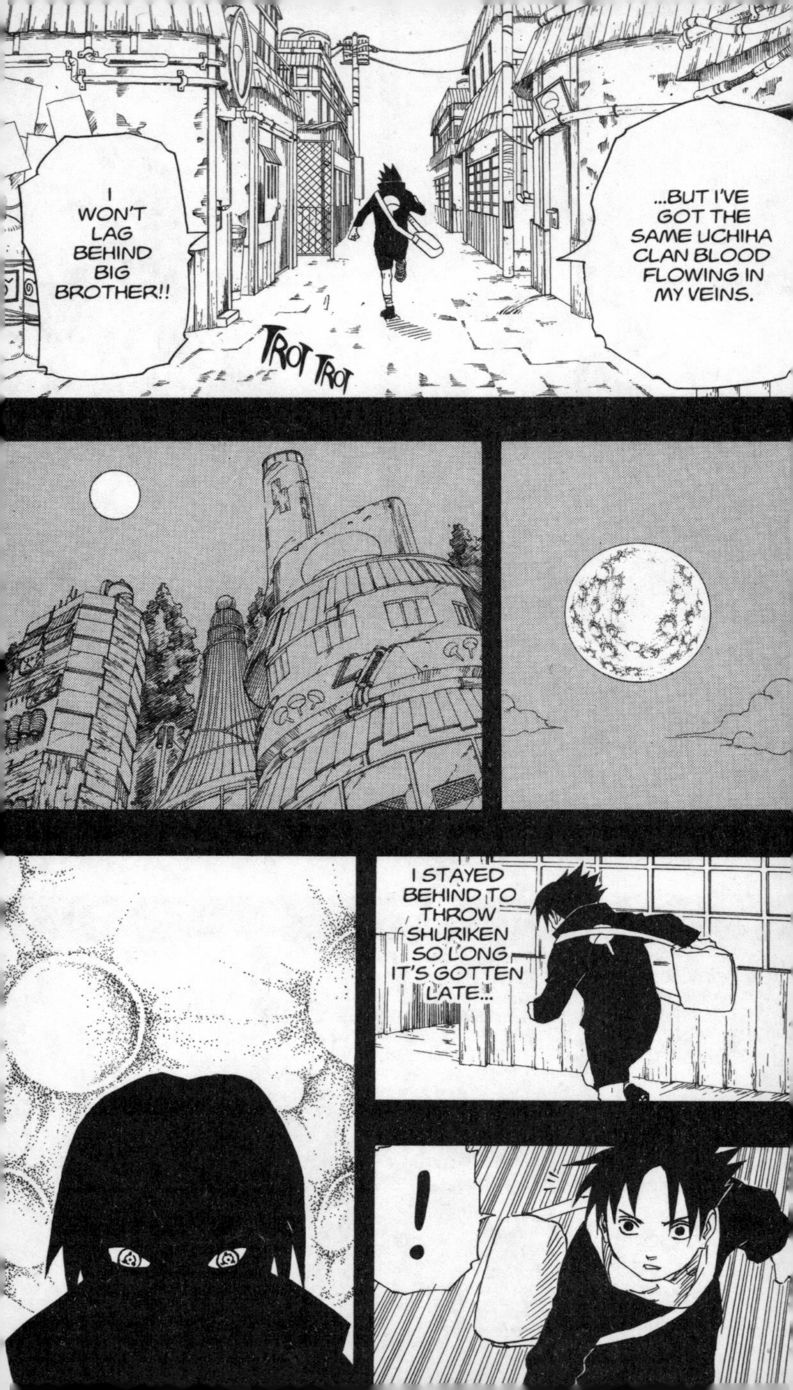
...BUT I'VE GOT THE SAME UCHIHA CLAN BLOOD FLOWING IN MY VEINS.
I WON'T LAG BEHIND BIG BROTHER!!
TROT TROT
I STAYED BEHIND TO THROW SHURIKEN SO LONG IT'S GOTTEN LATE...
!

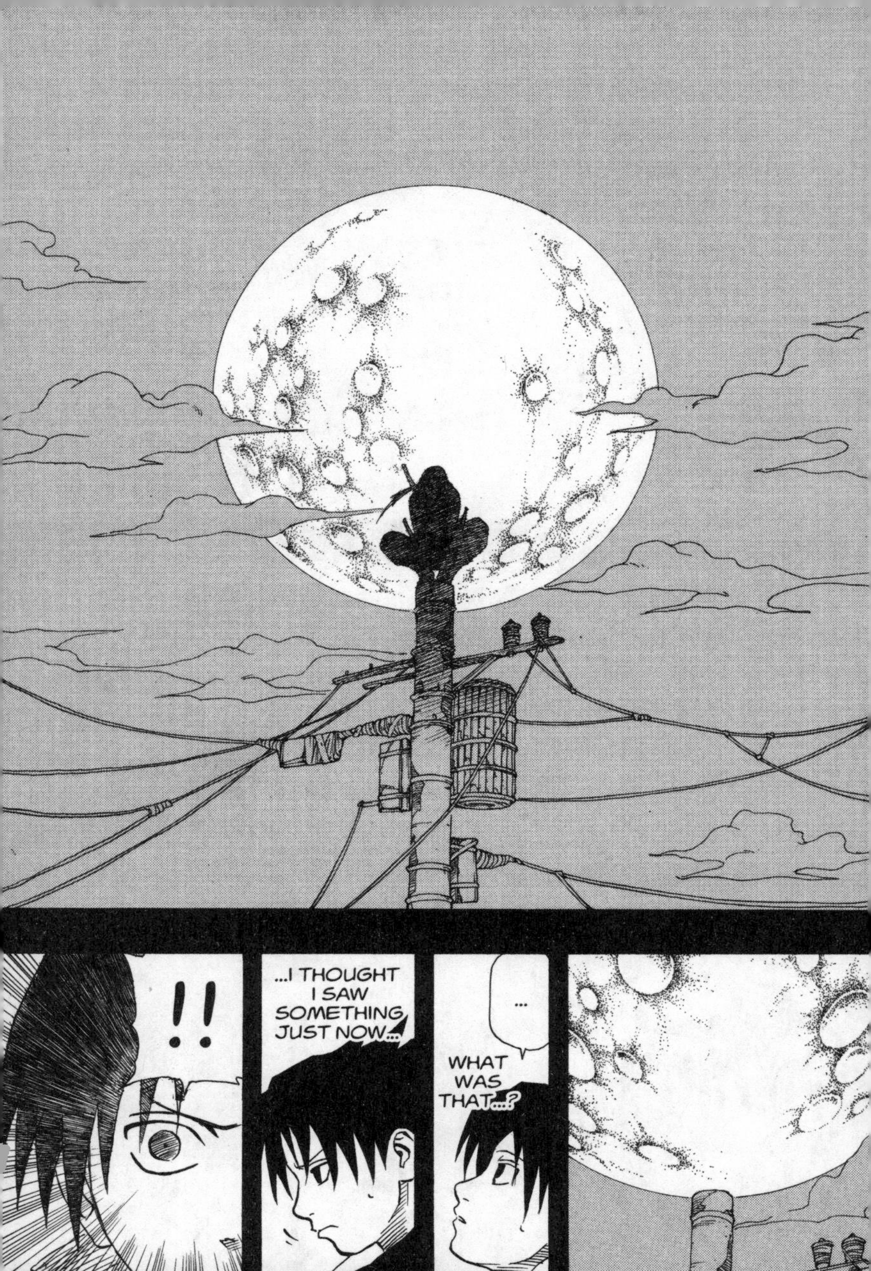
...
WHAT WAS THAT...?
...I THOUGHT I SAW SOMETHING JUST NOW...
!!

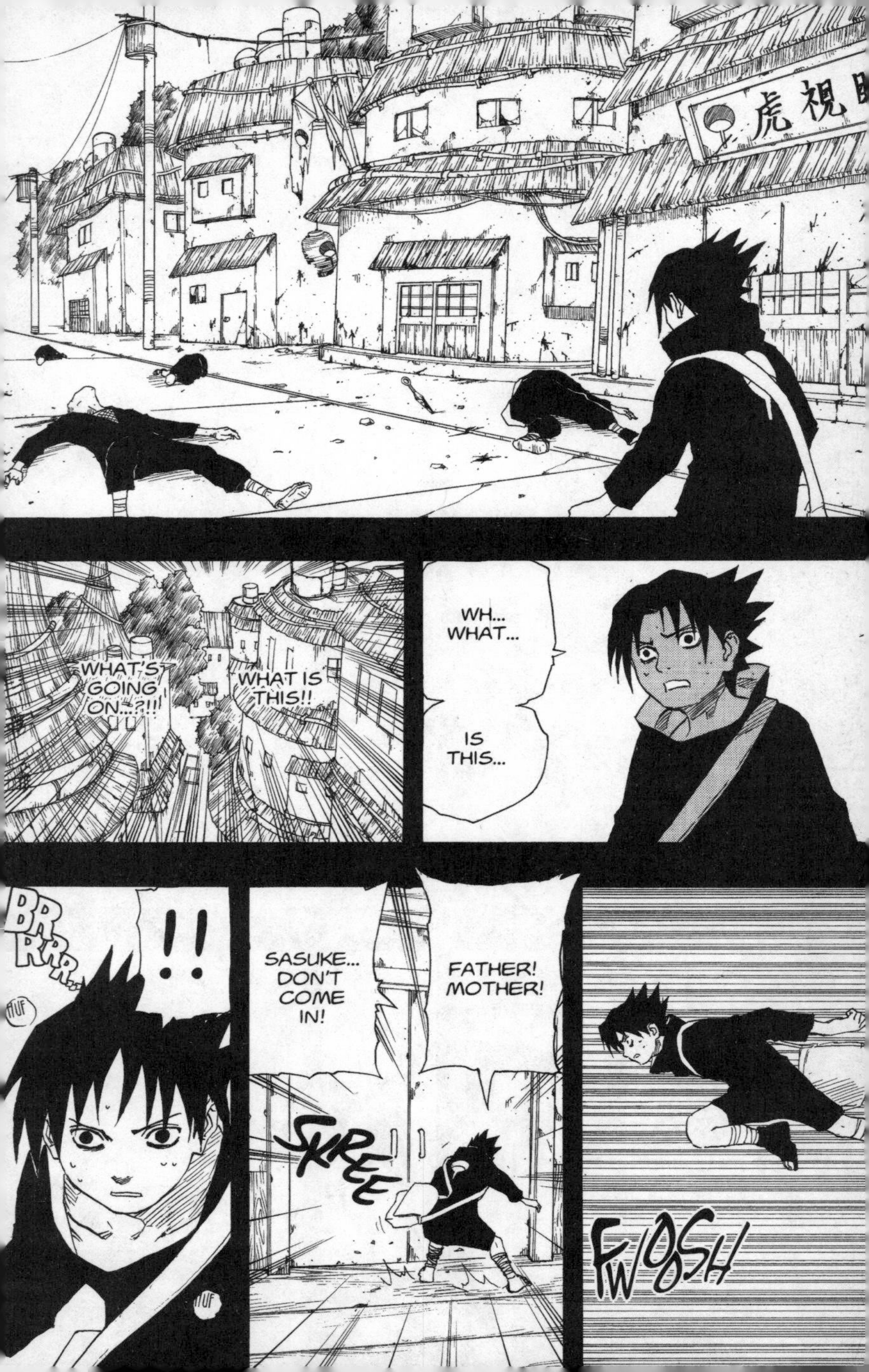
虎視
WH... WHAT...
IS THIS...
WHAT IS THIS!!
WHAT'S GOING ON...?!!!
FWOOSH
FATHER! MOTHER!
SASUKE... DON'T COME IN!
SKREE
!!
BRRRRR...
HUF
HUF

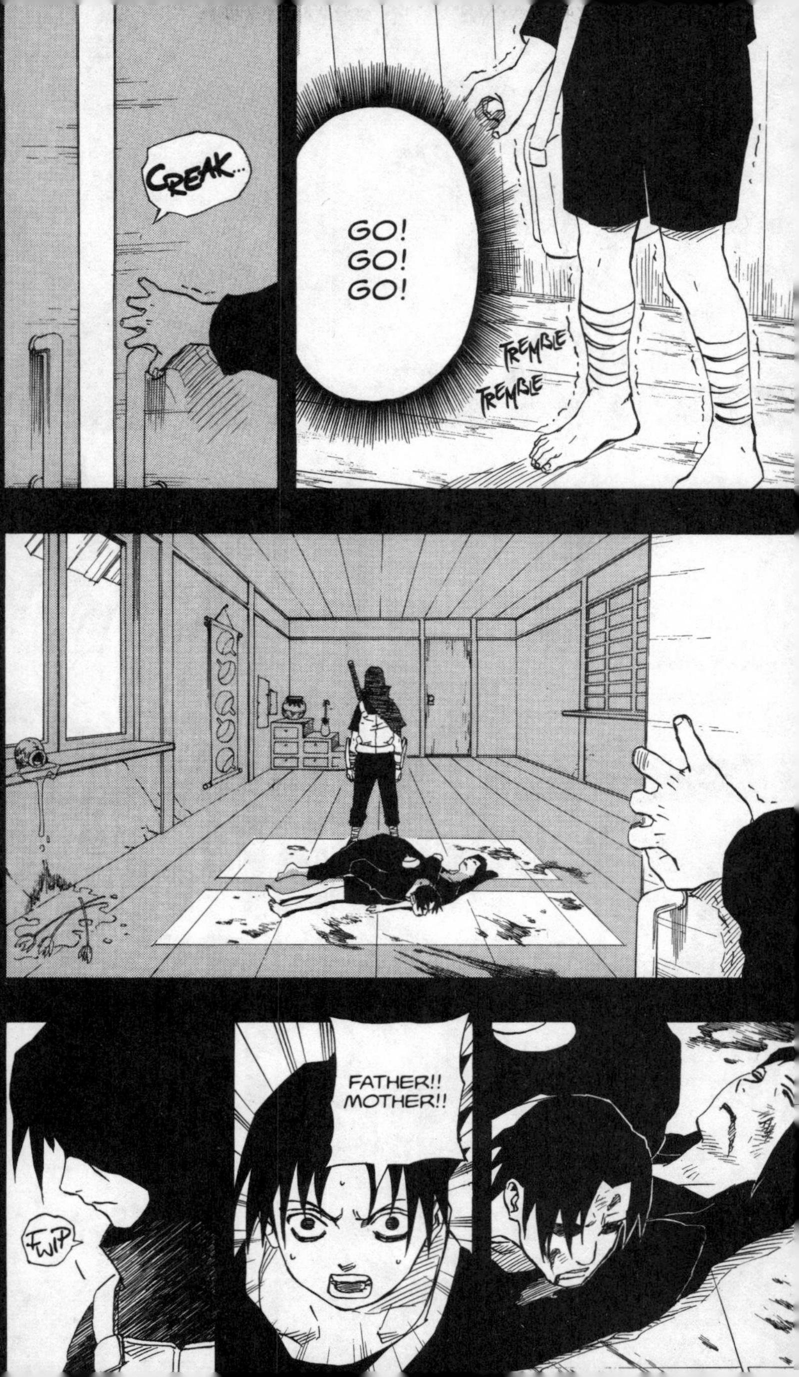
GO! GO! GO!
TREMBLE
TREMBLE
CREAK...
FATHER!! MOTHER!!
FWIP

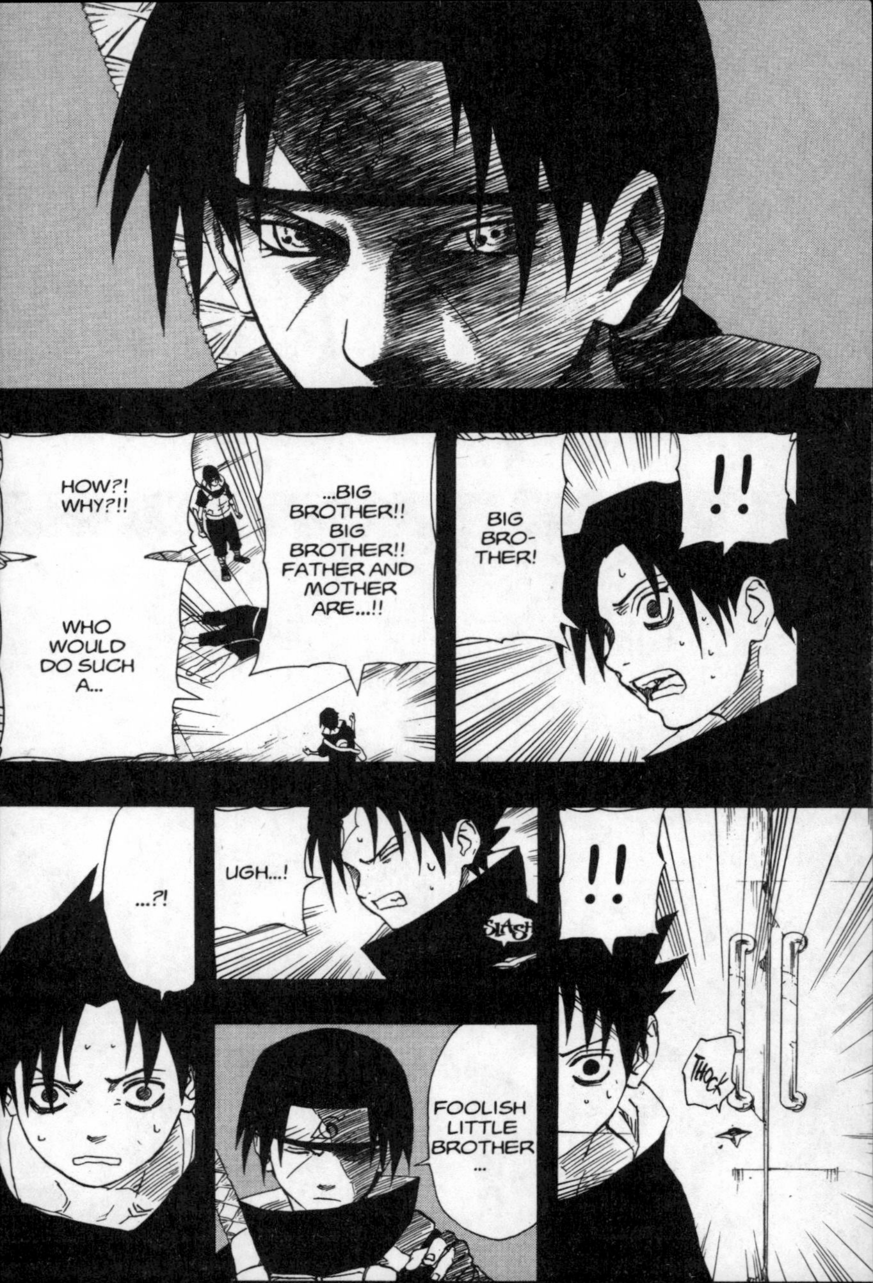
!!
BIG BRO- THER!
...BIG BROTHER!! BIG BROTHER!! FATHER AND MOTHER ARE...!!
HOW?! WHY?!!
WHO WOULD DO SUCH A...
!!
THOCK
UGH...!
SLASH
FOOLISH LITTLE BROTHER ...
...?!

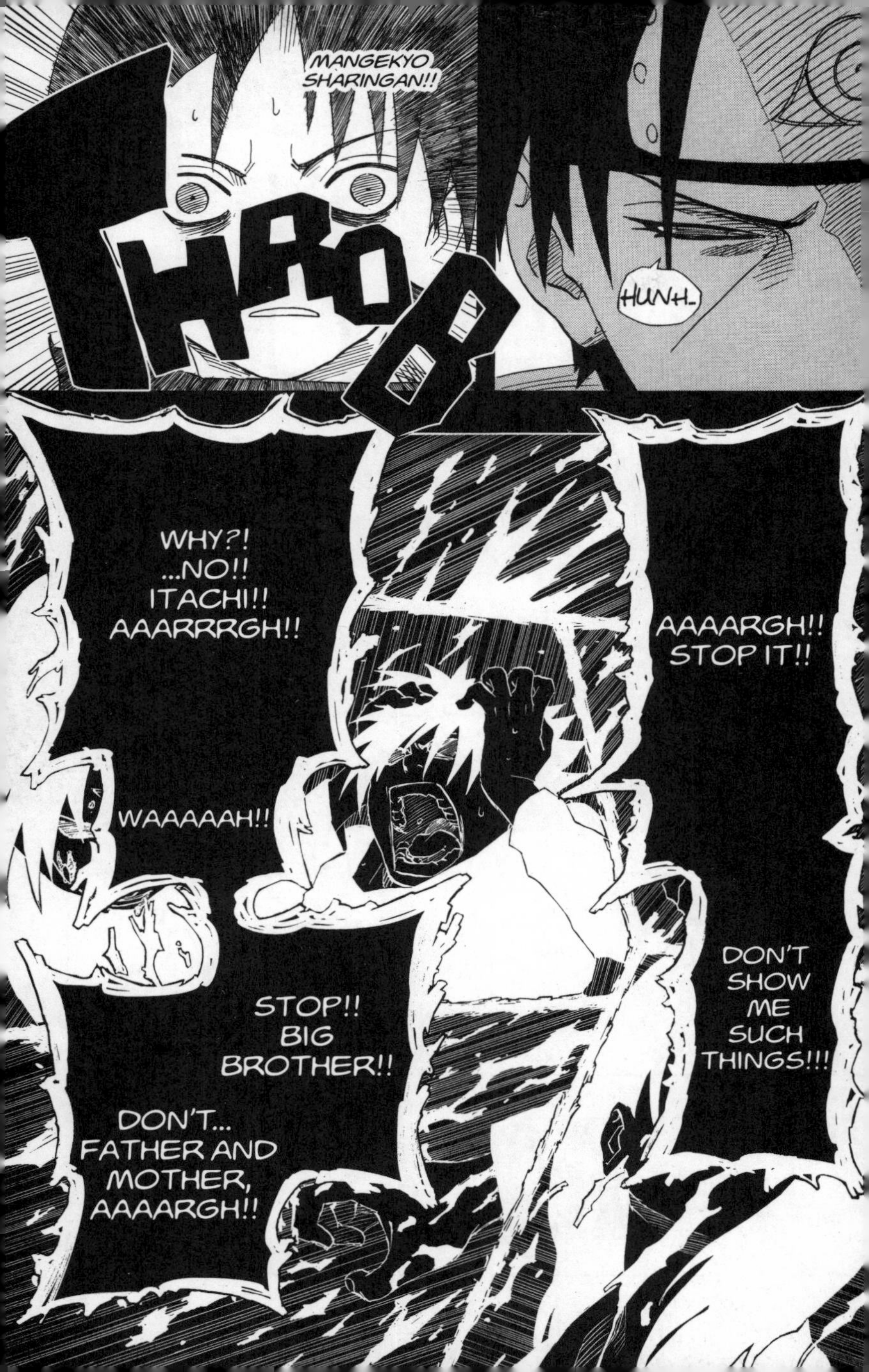
HUNH...
MANGEKYO SHARINGAN!!
THROB
AAAARGH!! STOP IT!!
WHY?! ...NO!! ITACHI!! AAARRRGH!!
WAAAAAH!!
DON'T SHOW ME SUCH THINGS!!!
STOP!! BIG BROTHER!!
DON'T... FATHER AND MOTHER, AAAARGH!!

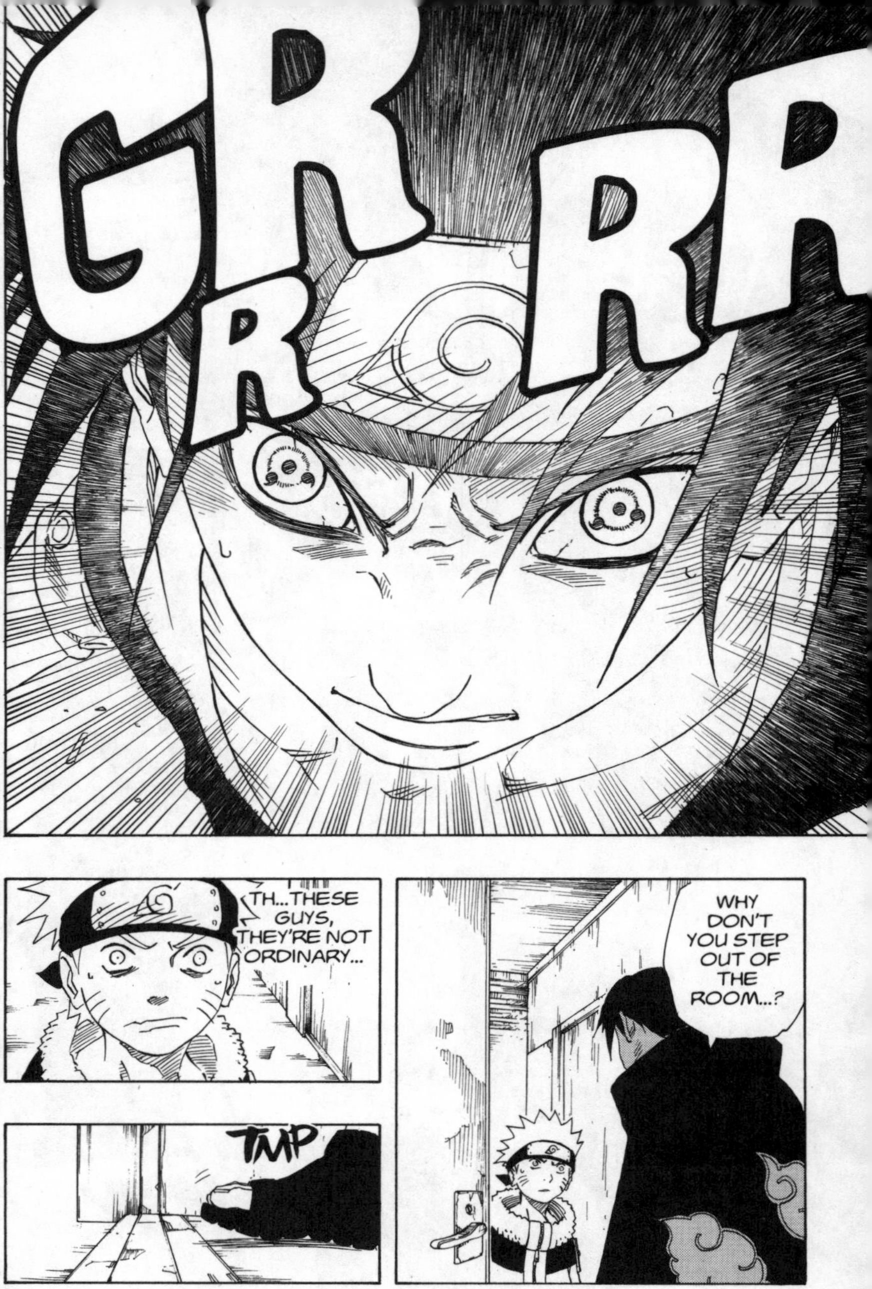
CRRRR
WHY DON'T YOU STEP OUT OF THE ROOM...?
TH...THESE GUYS, THEY'RE NOT ORDINARY...
TMP

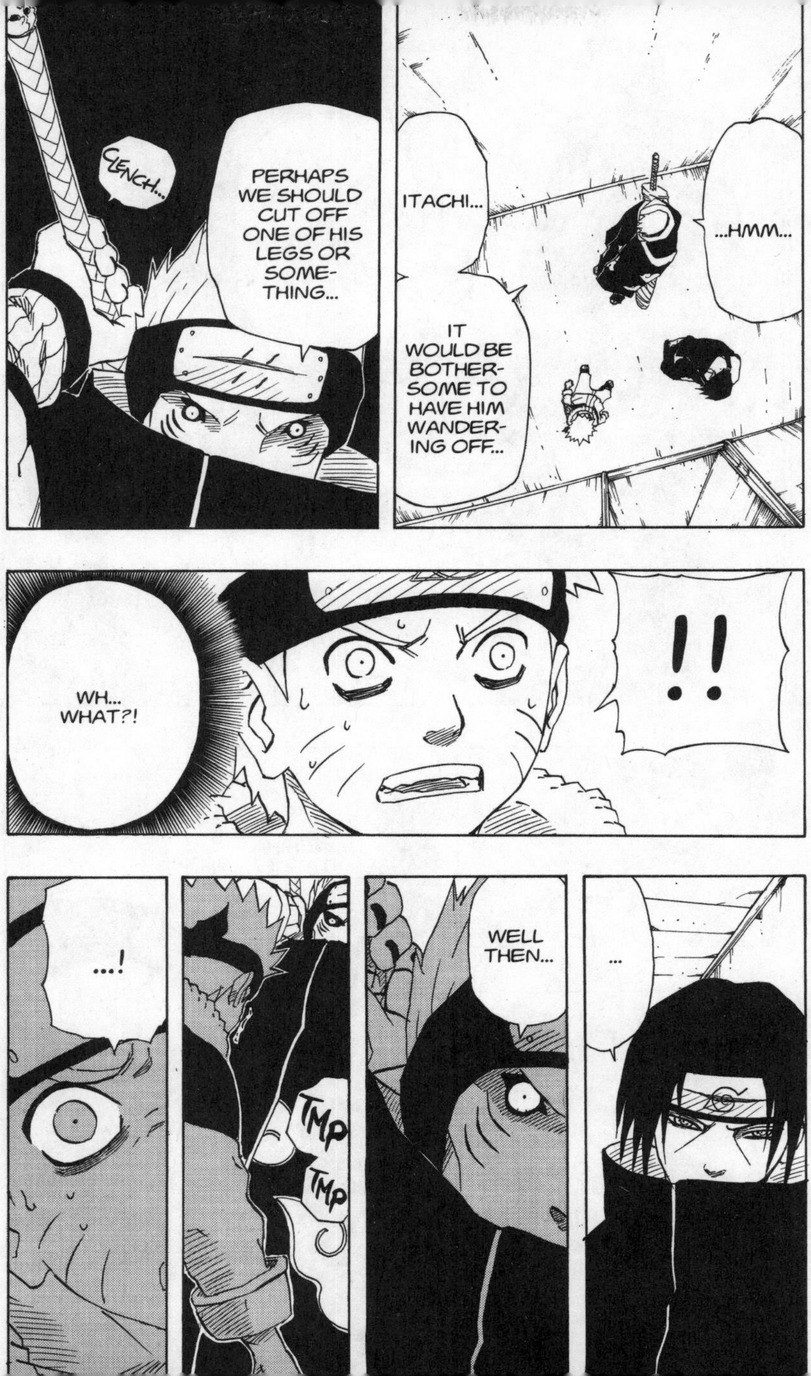
...HMM...
ITACHI...
IT WOULD BE BOTHER-SOME TO HAVE HIM WANDER-ING OFF...
CLENCH...
PERHAPS WE SHOULD CUT OFF ONE OF HIS LEGS OR SOME-THING...
!!
WH... WHAT?!
...
WELL THEN...
TMP
TMP
...!

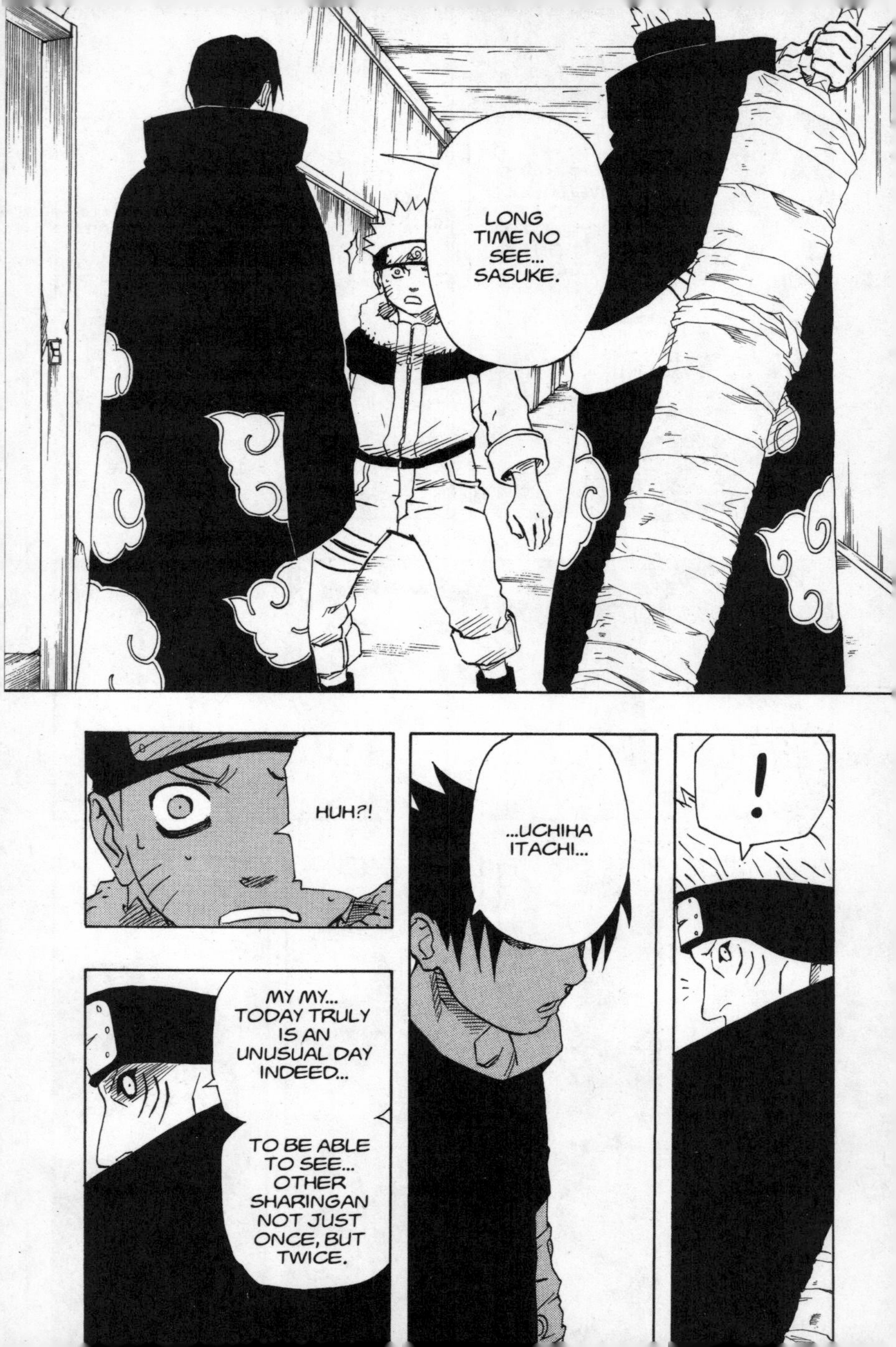
LONG TIME NO SEE... SASUKE.
!
...UCHIHA ITACHI...
HUH?!
MY MY... TODAY TRULY IS AN UNUSUAL DAY INDEED...
TO BE ABLE TO SEE... OTHER SHARINGAN NOT JUST ONCE, BUT TWICE.

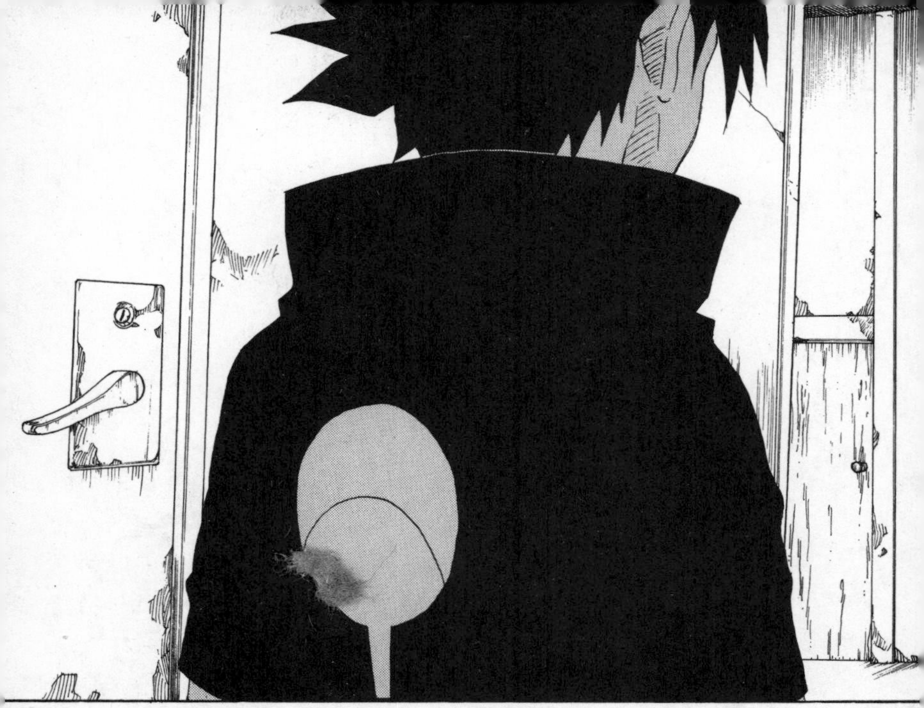
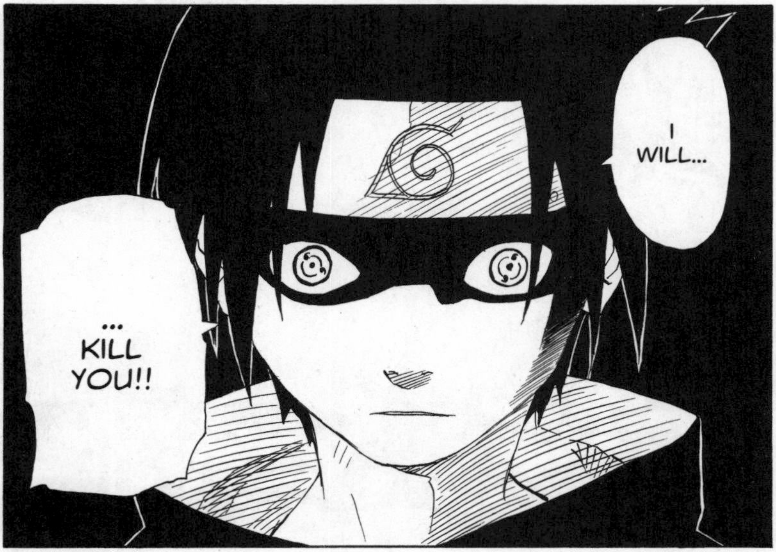
I WILL...
... KILL YOU!!

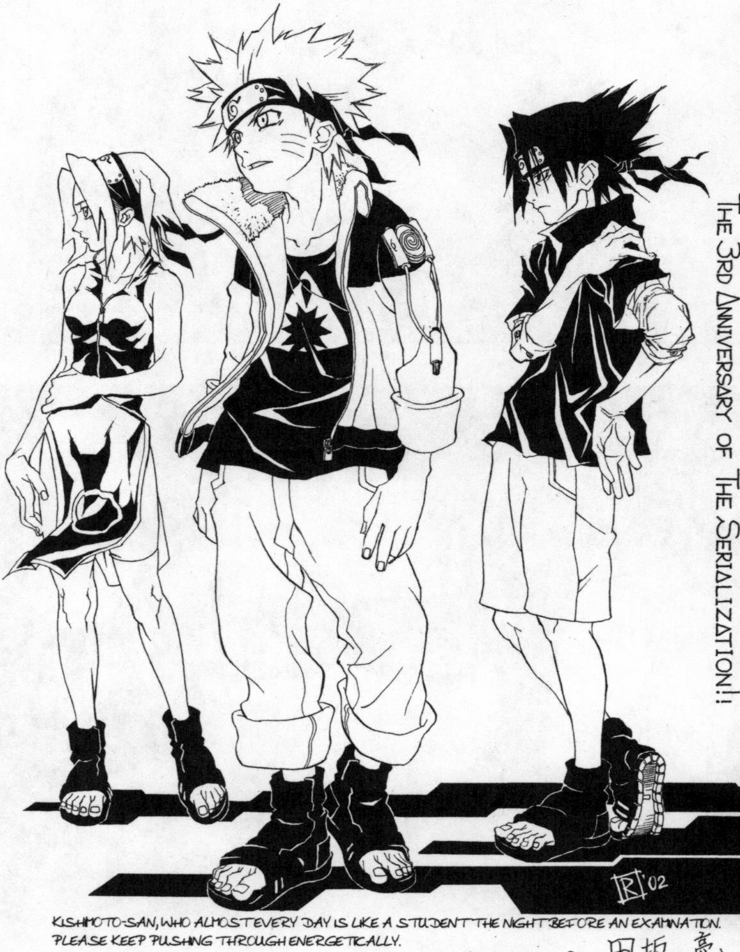

CONGRATULATONS!!
THE 3RD ANNIVERSARY OF THE SERIALIZATION!!
祝・3周年。

KISHIMOTO-SAN, WHO ALMOST EVERY DAY IS LIKE A STUDENT THE NIGHT BEFORE AN EXAMINATON.
PLEASE KEEP PUSHING THROUGH ENERGETICALLY.

NOVEMBER . 8 . 田坂亮
RYO TASAKA

Number 146: Along with Hatred...!!

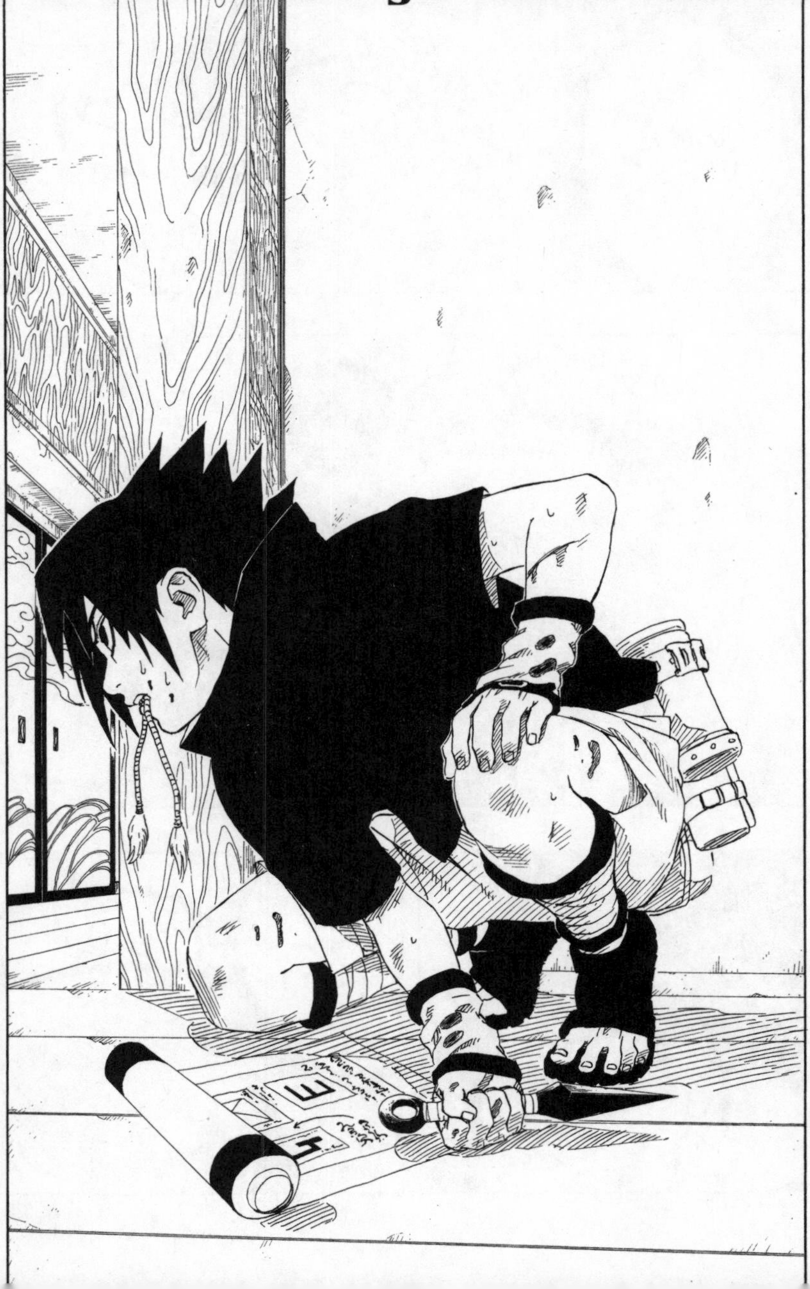

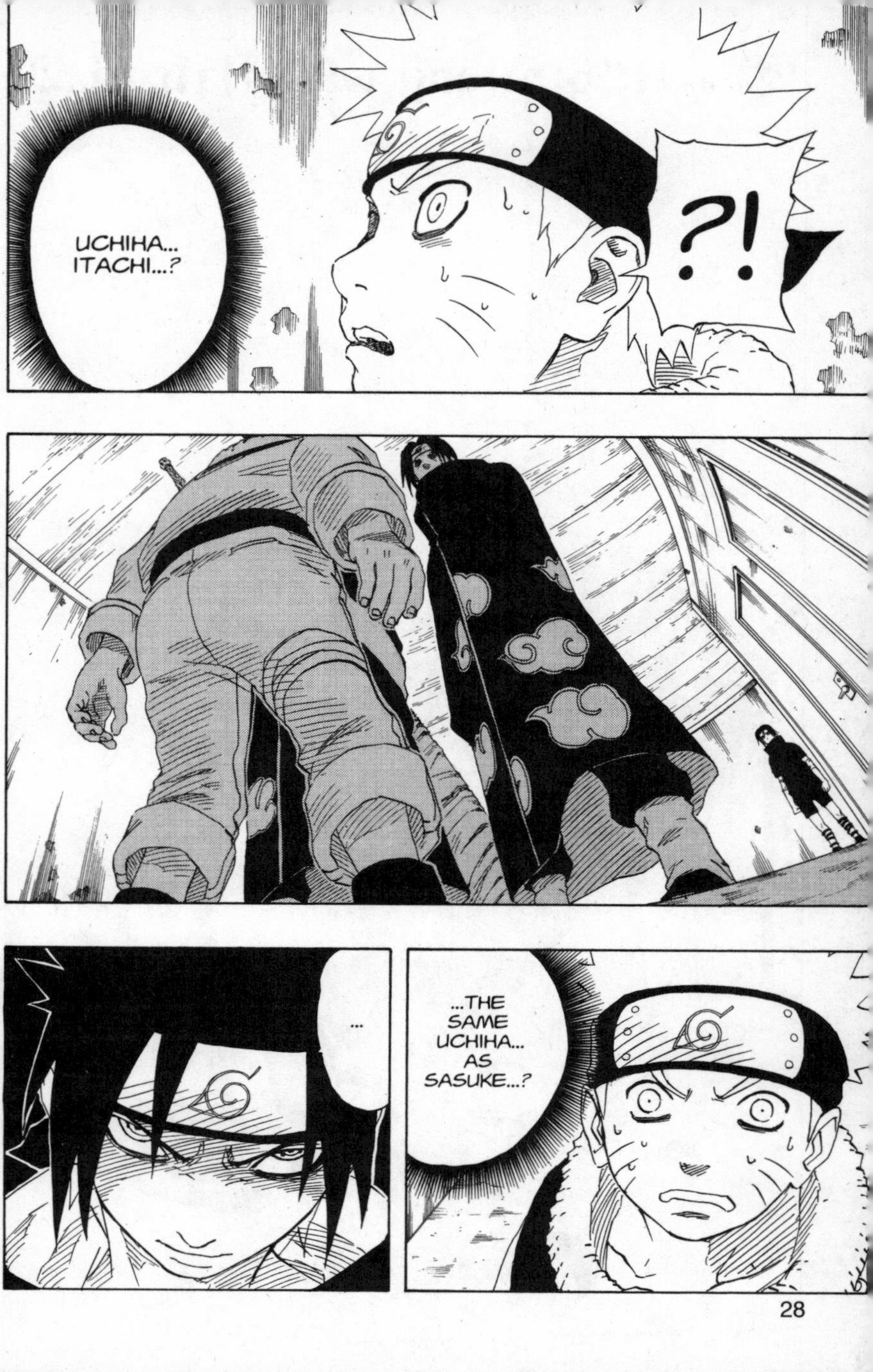
?!
UCHIHA... ITACHI...?
...THE SAME UCHIHA... AS SASUKE...?
...

READ THIS WAY

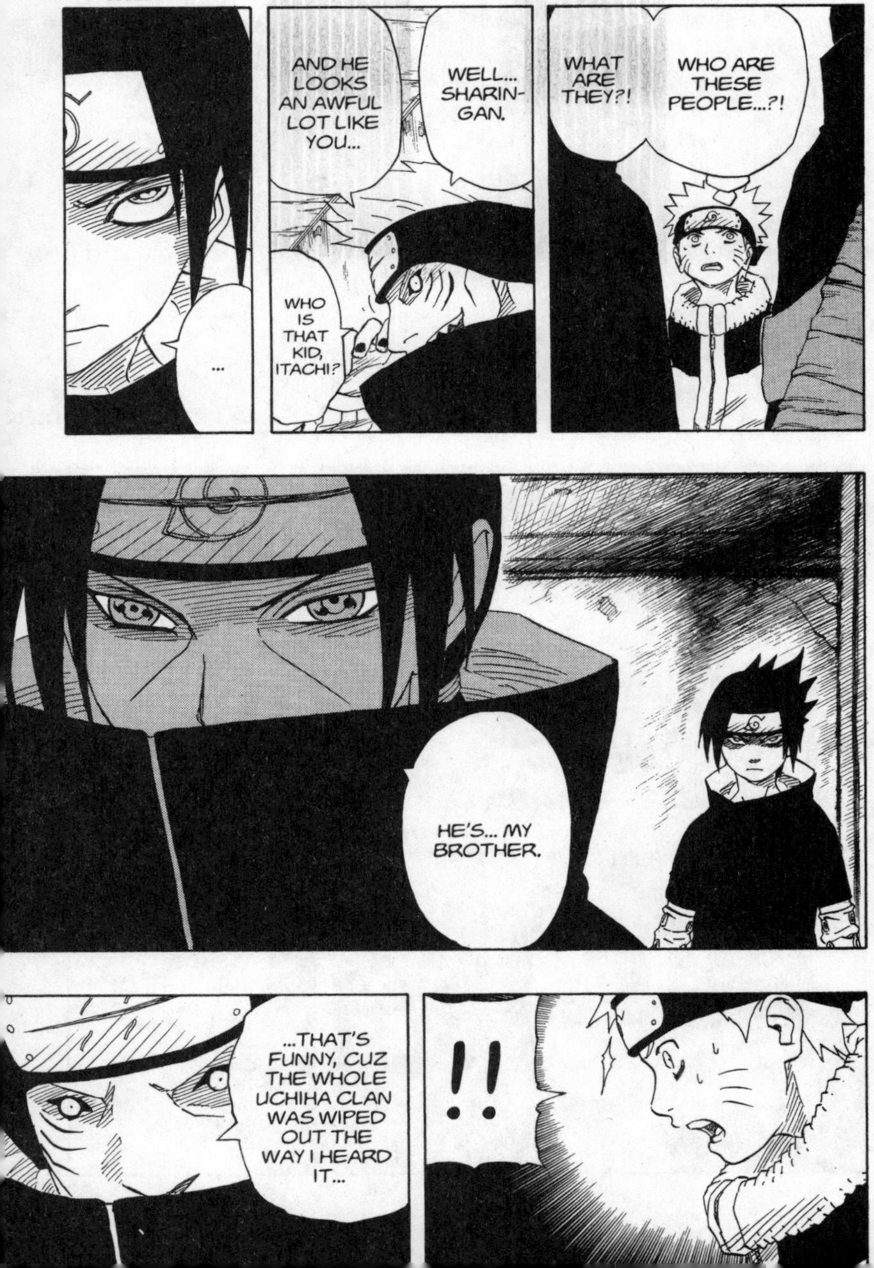
WHO ARE THESE PEOPLE...?!
WHAT ARE THEY?!
WELL... SHARIN-GAN.
AND HE LOOKS AN AWFUL LOT LIKE YOU...
WHO IS THAT KID, ITACHI?
...
HE'S... MY BROTHER.
!!
...THAT'S FUNNY, CUZ THE WHOLE UCHIHA CLAN WAS WIPED OUT THE WAY I HEARD IT...

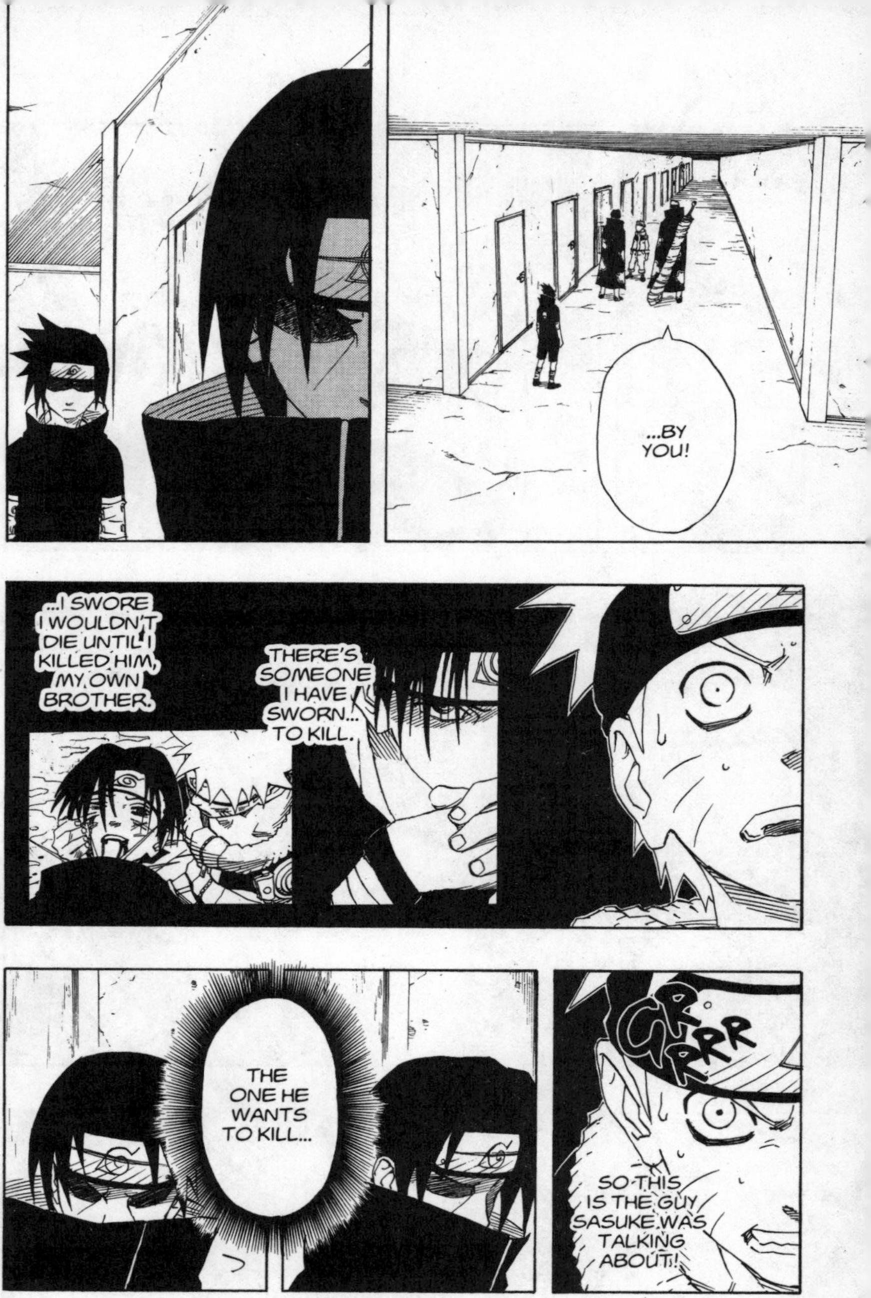
...BY YOU!
THERE'S SOMEONE I HAVE SWORN... TO KILL.
...I SWORE I WOULDN'T DIE UNTIL I KILLED HIM, MY OWN BROTHER.
GRRRR
SO THIS IS THE GUY SASUKE WAS TALKING ABOUT!
THE ONE HE WANTS TO KILL...

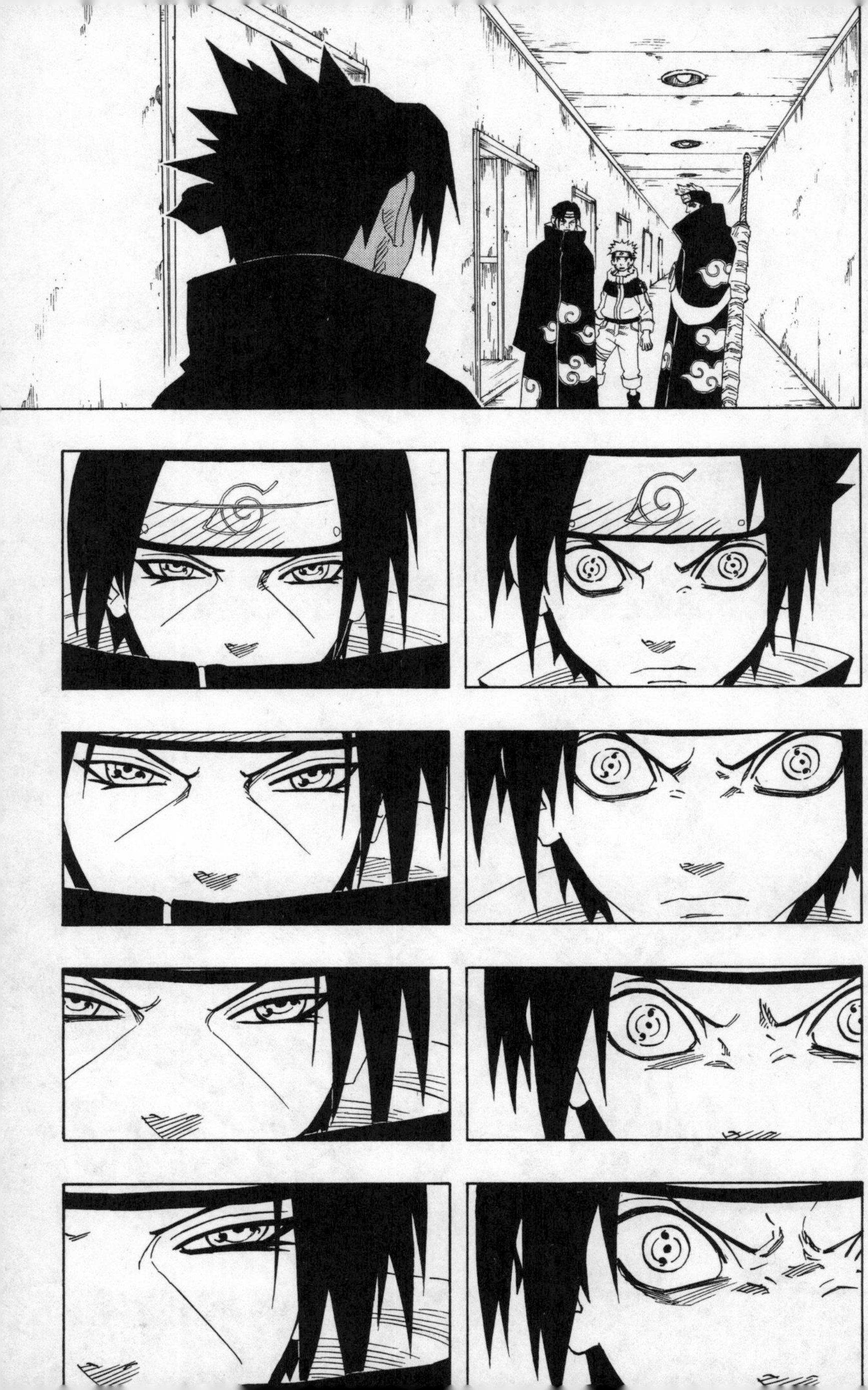

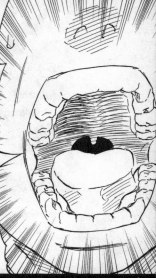

AAAAARGH!!

A...
AAAAH!!

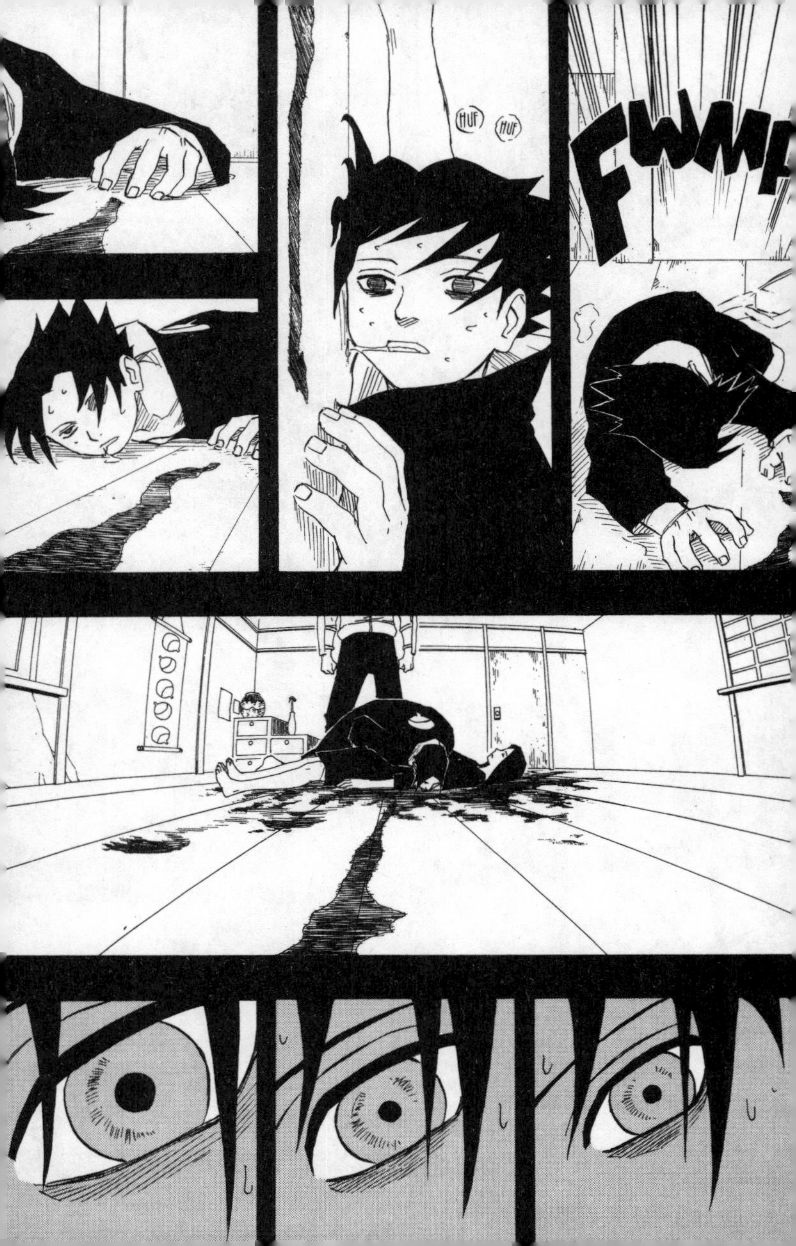
FWMP
HUF HUF

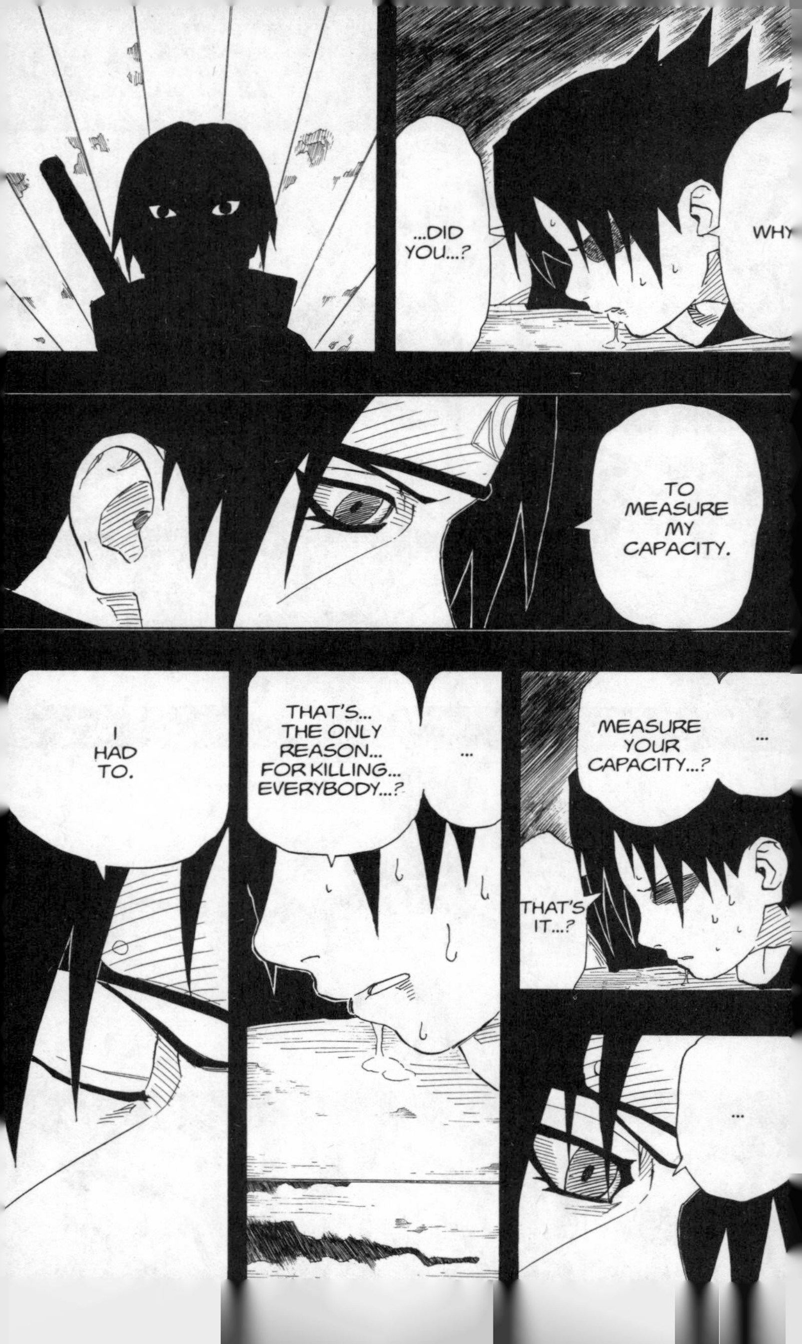
WHY
...DID YOU...?
TO MEASURE MY CAPACITY.
...
MEASURE YOUR CAPACITY...?
THAT'S IT...?
...
...
THAT'S... THE ONLY REASON... FOR KILLING... EVERYBODY...?
I HAD TO.

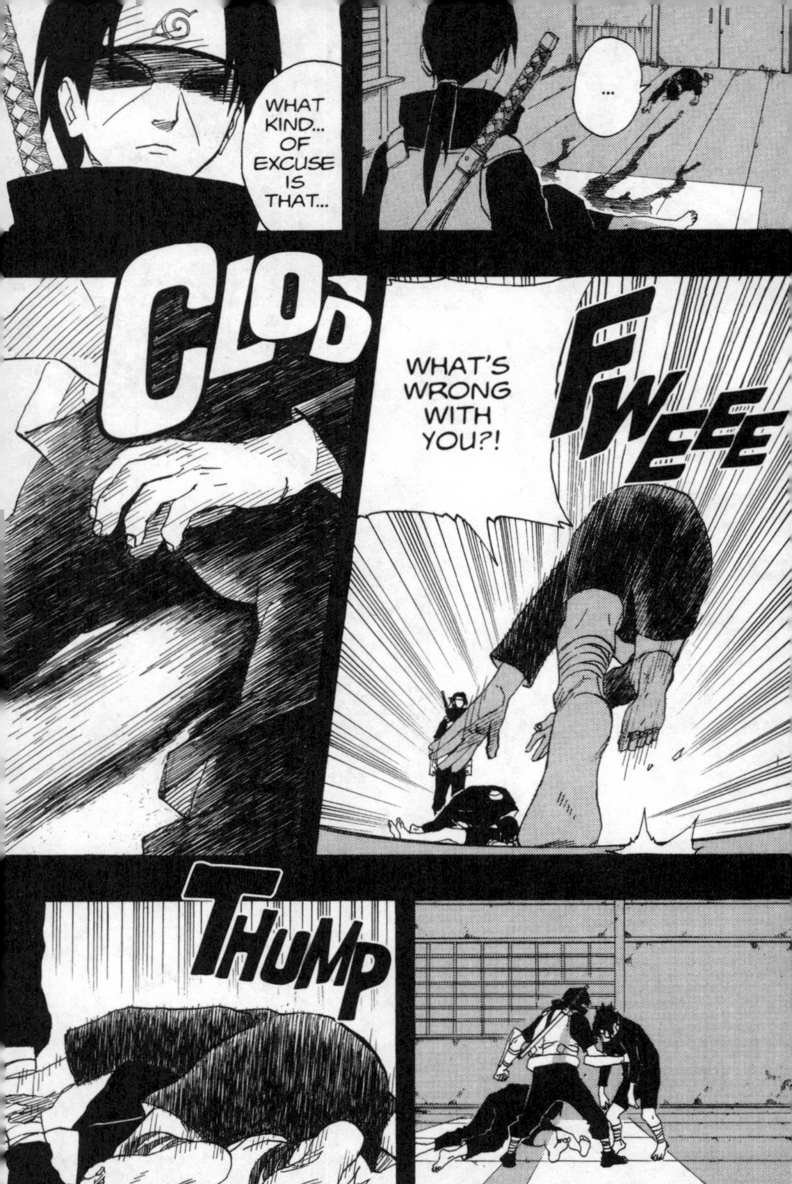
...
WHAT KIND... OF EXCUSE IS THAT...
FWEEE
WHAT'S WRONG WITH YOU?!
CLOD
THUMP

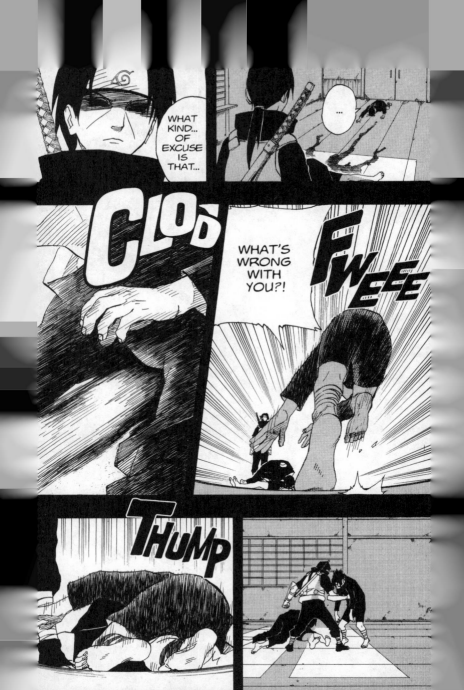

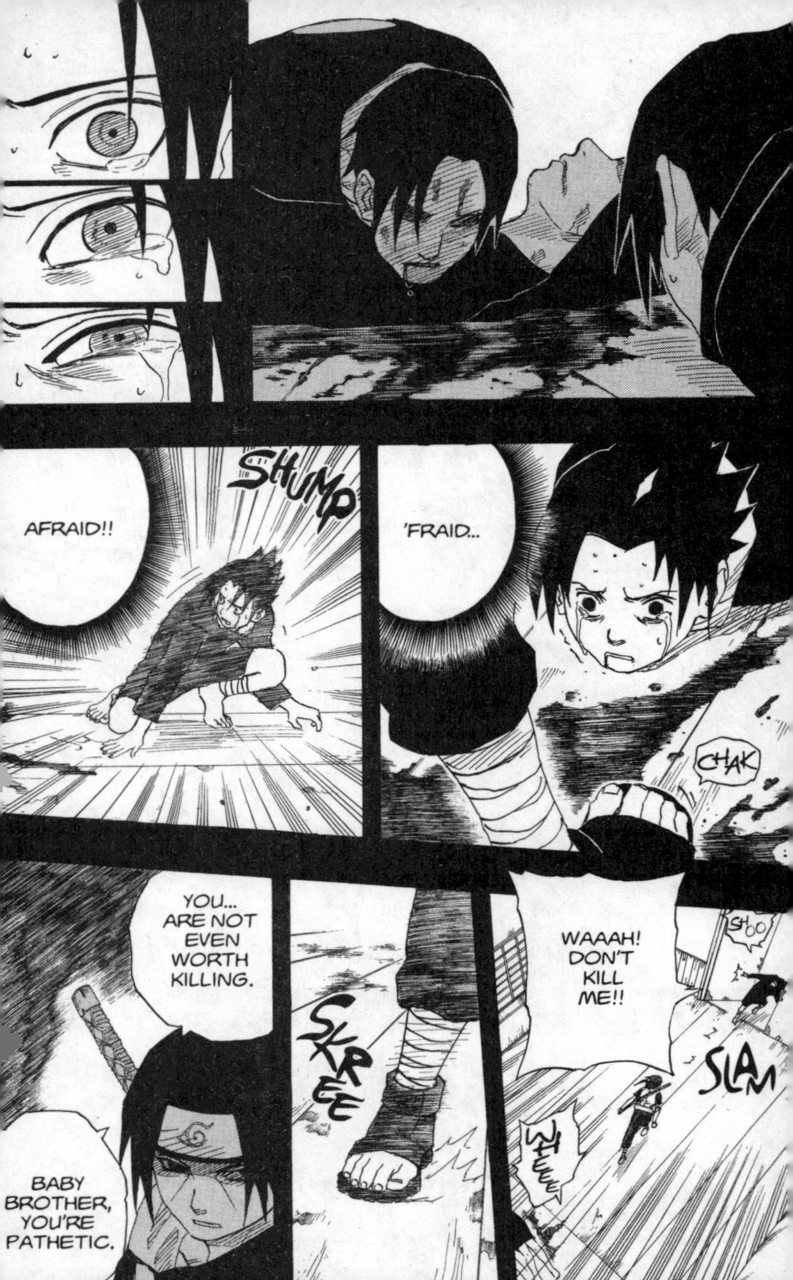
'FRAID...
CHAK
AFRAID!!
SHUMP
WAAAH! DON'T KILL ME!!
SHOO
SLAM
WHEEE
SKREE
YOU... ARE NOT EVEN WORTH KILLING.
BABY BROTHER, YOU'RE PATHETIC.

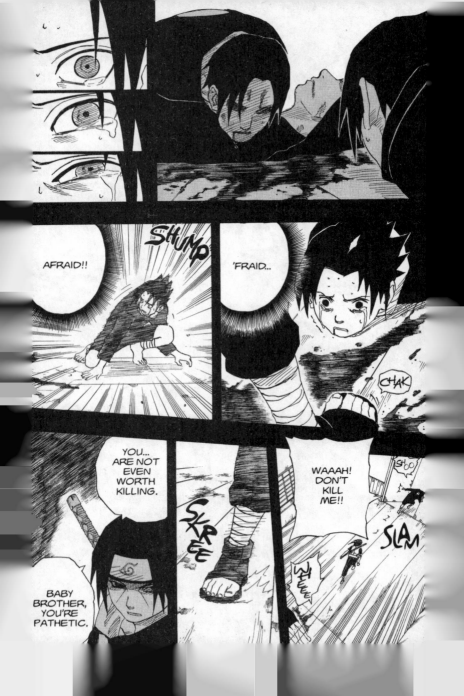

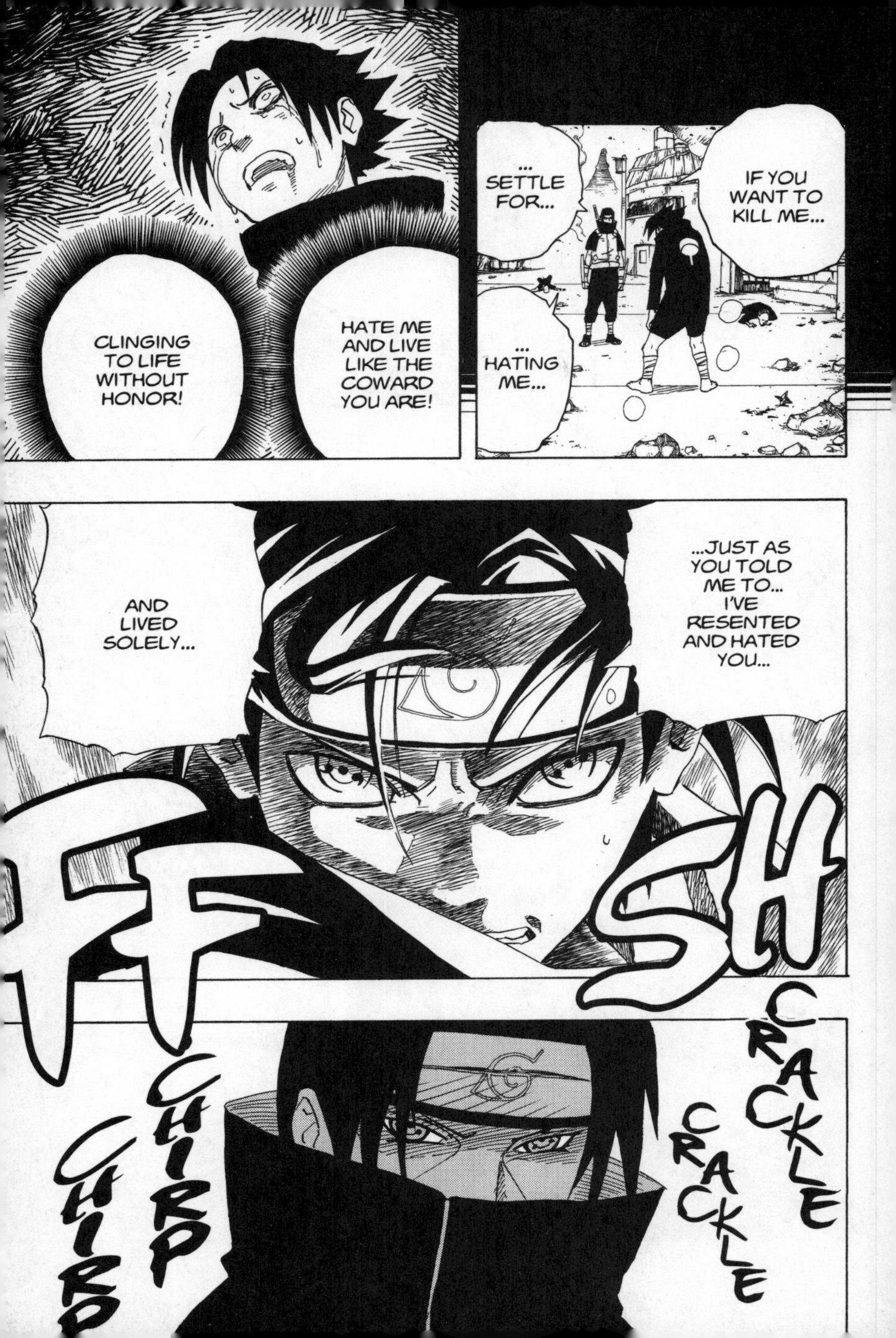
IF YOU WANT TO KILL ME...
... SETTLE FOR...
... HATING ME...
HATE ME AND LIVE LIKE THE COWARD YOU ARE!
CLINGING TO LIFE WITHOUT HONOR!
...JUST AS YOU TOLD ME TO... I'VE RESENTED AND HATED YOU...
AND LIVED SOLELY...
SH
FF
CRACKLE
CRACKLE
CHIRP
CHIRP

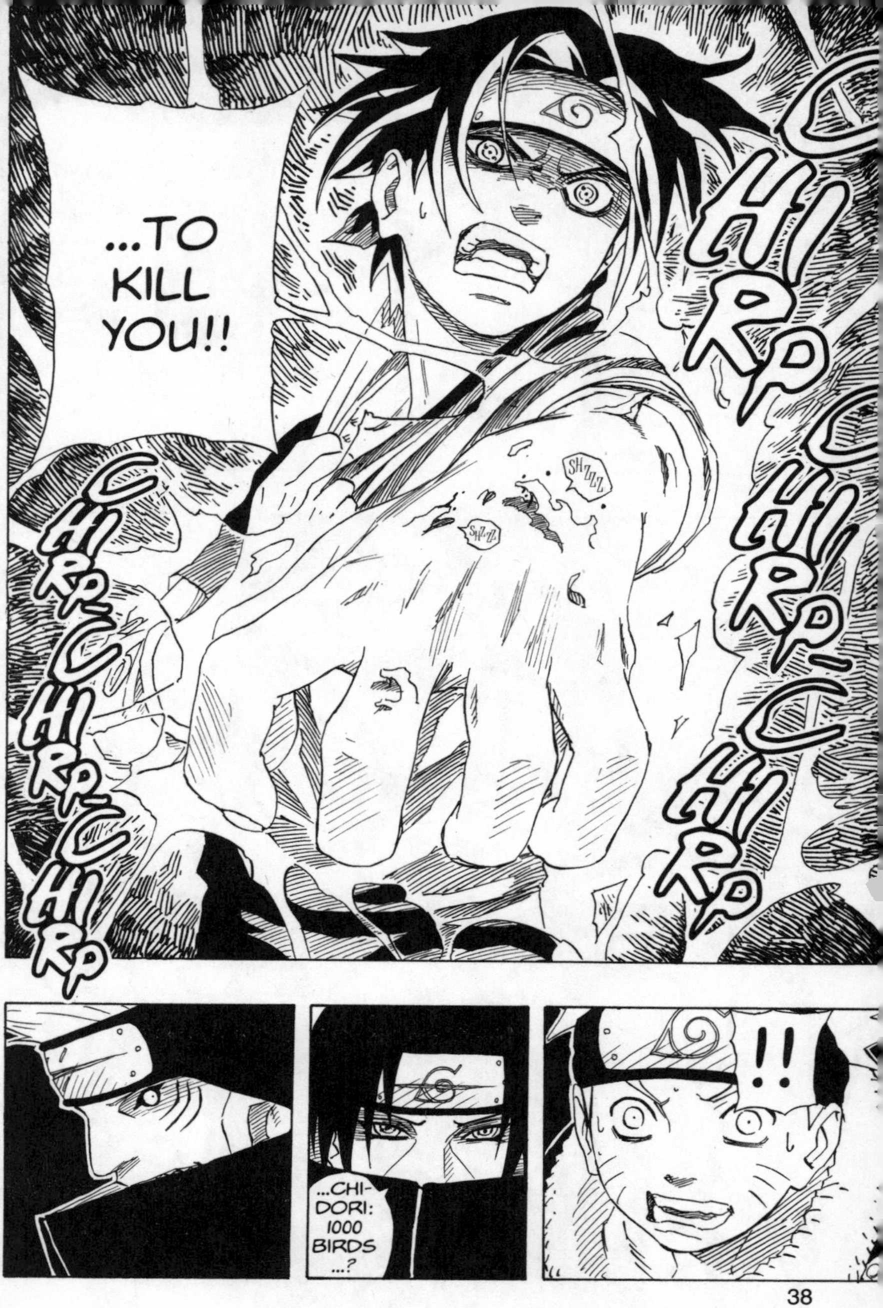
CHIRP-CHIRP-CHIRP
...TO KILL YOU!!
SHZZZ
SHZZZ
CHIRP-CHIRP-CHIRP
!!
...CHIDORI: 1000 BIRDS ...?

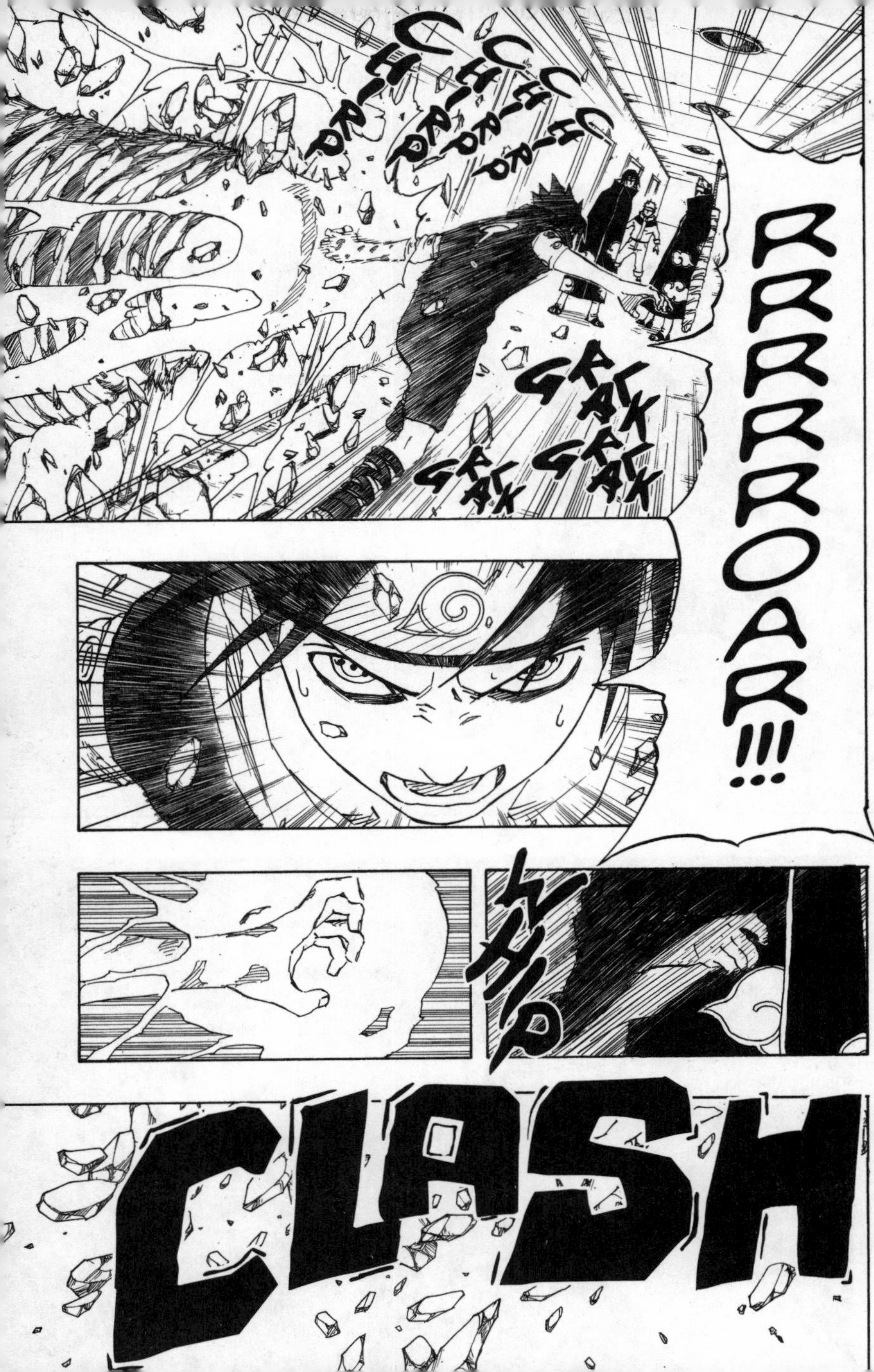
CHI-RRP-RRP
CHI-RRP
CHI-RRP
RRRRROAR!!!
GRACK GRACK
GRACK
CLASH

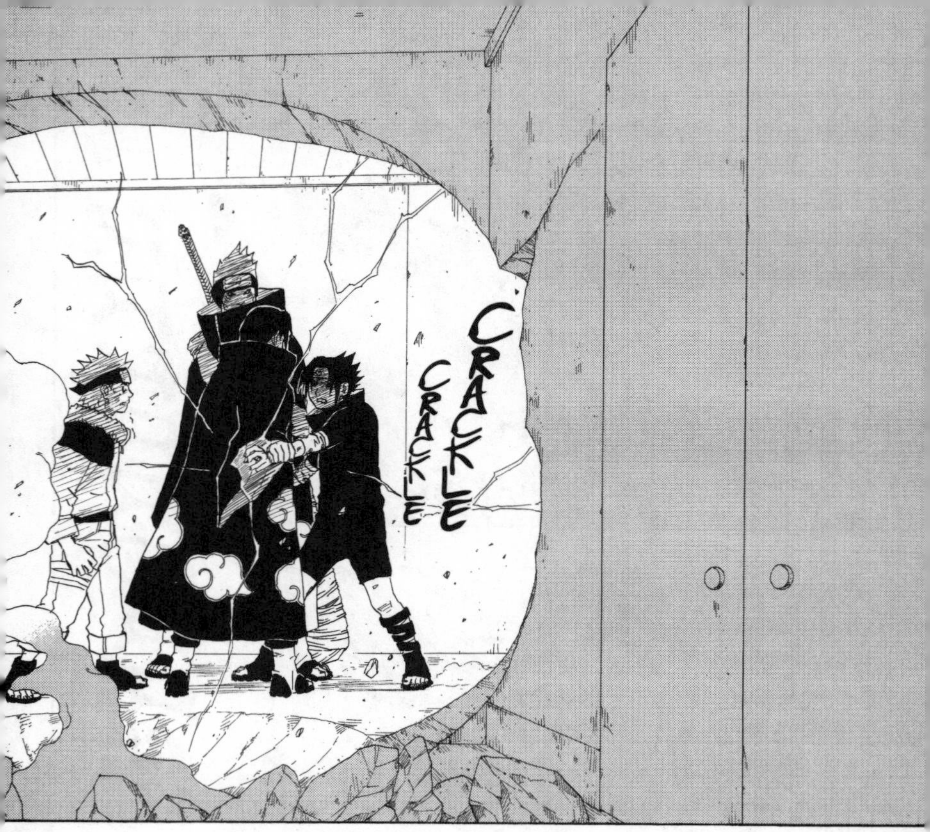
CRACKLE
CRACKLE
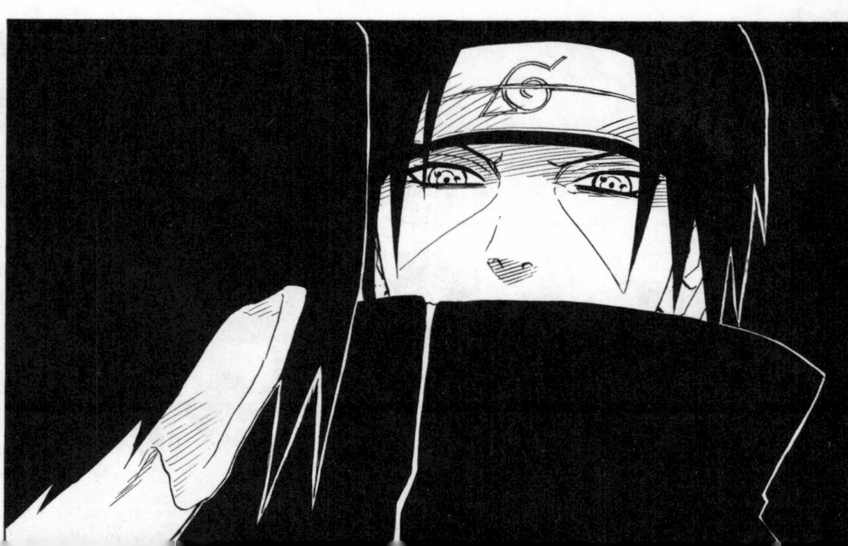

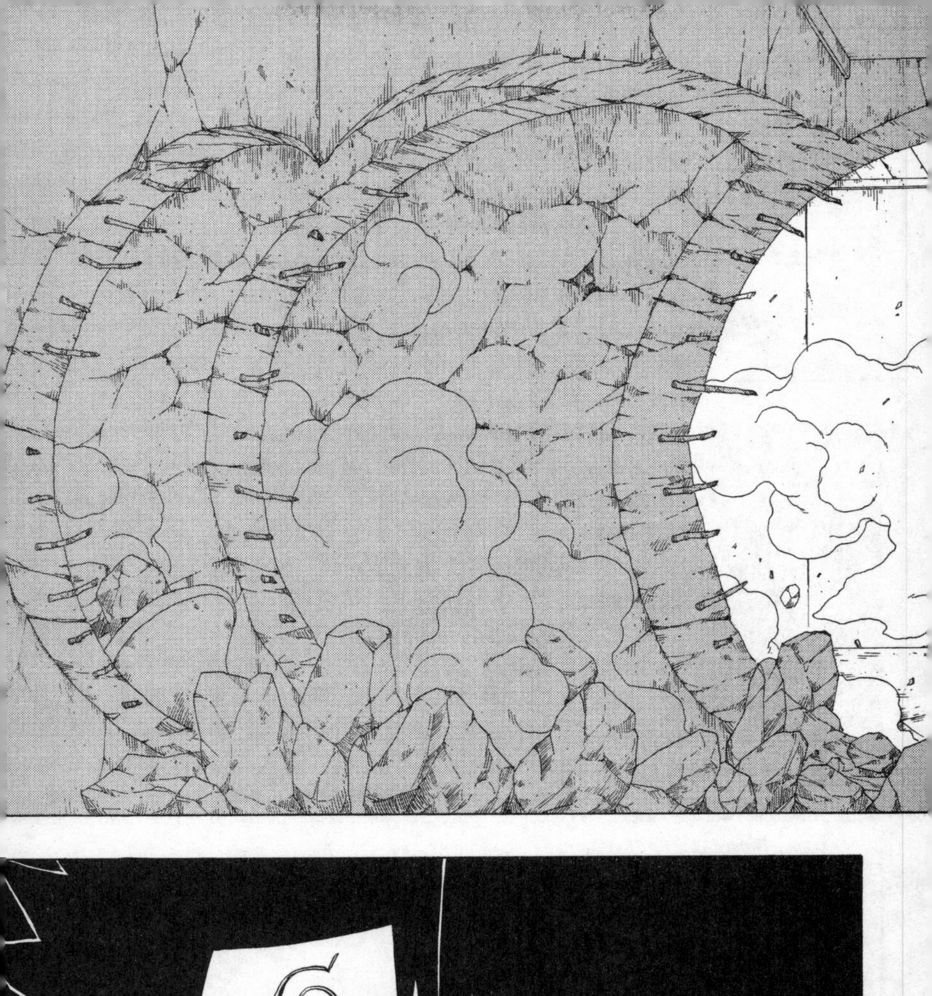

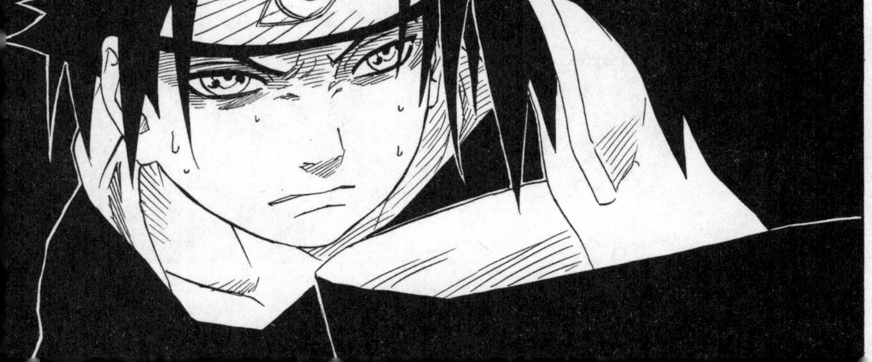

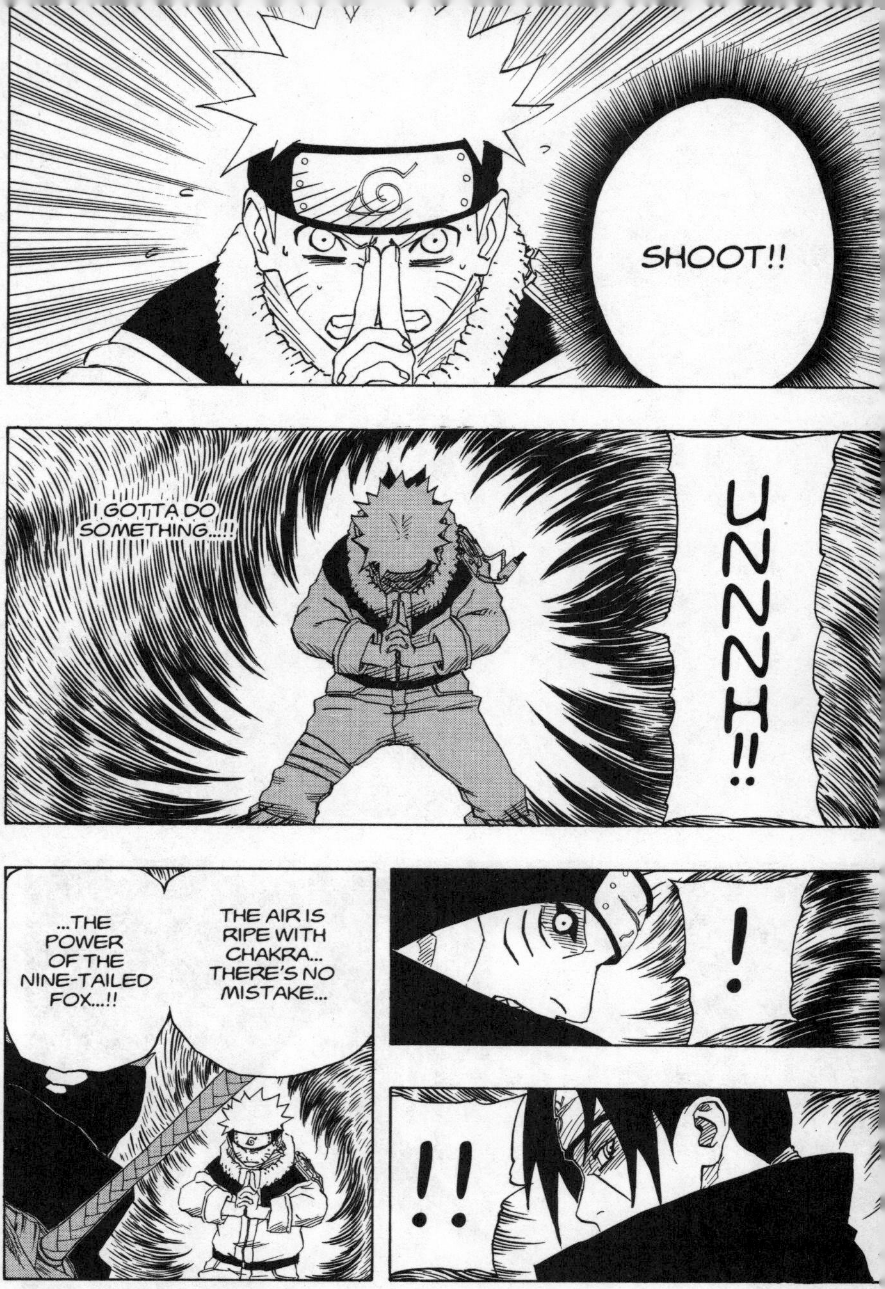
SHOOT!!
UNNNH!!
I GOTTA DO SOMETHING...!!
!
!!
THE AIR IS RIPE WITH CHAKRA... THERE'S NO MISTAKE...
...THE POWER OF THE NINE-TAILED FOX...!!

READ THIS WAY

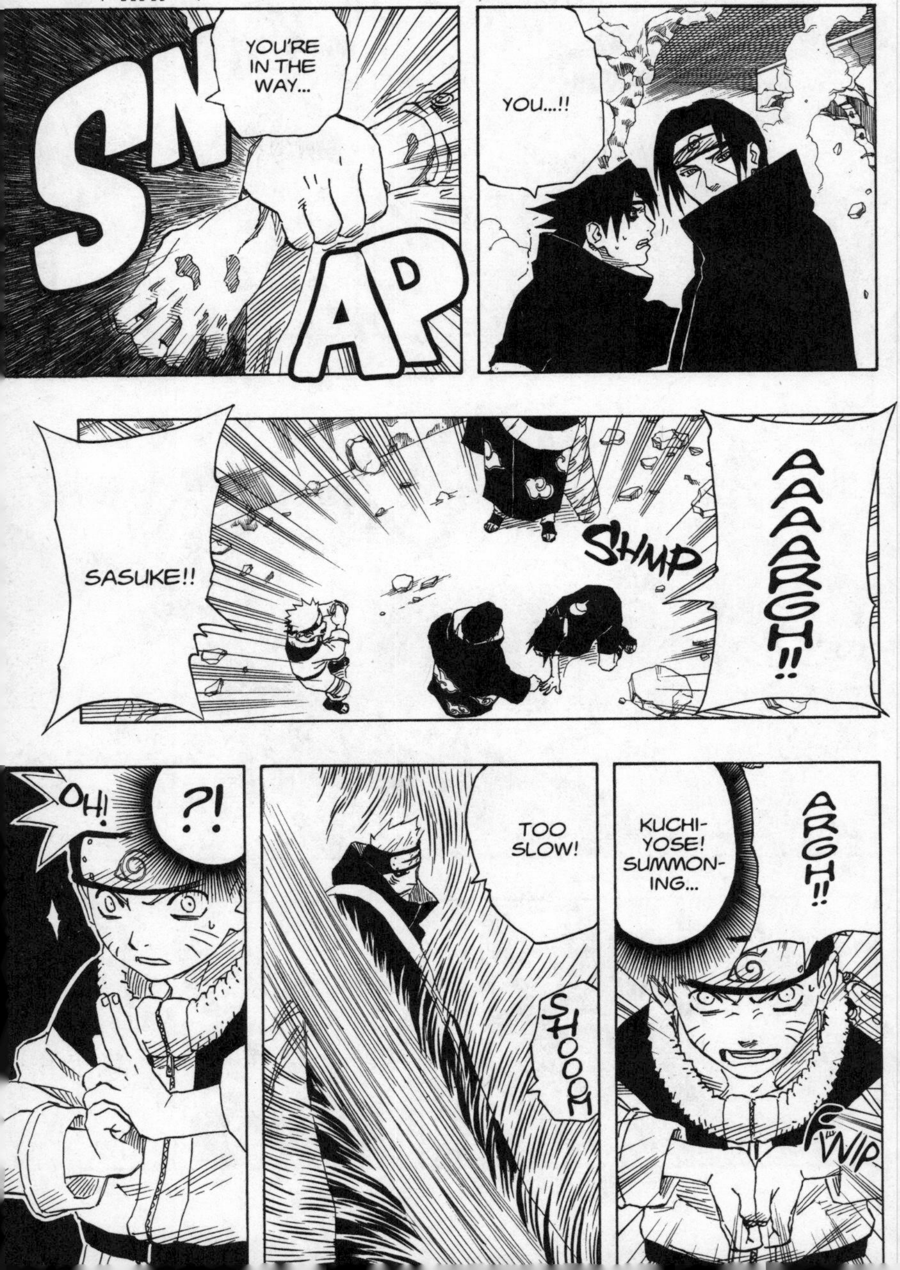
YOU...!!
YOU'RE IN THE WAY...
SNAP
AAAARGH!!
SHMP
SASUKE!!
ARGH!!
KUCHI-YOSE! SUMMONING...
WIP
TOO SLOW!
SHOOOM
?!
OH!

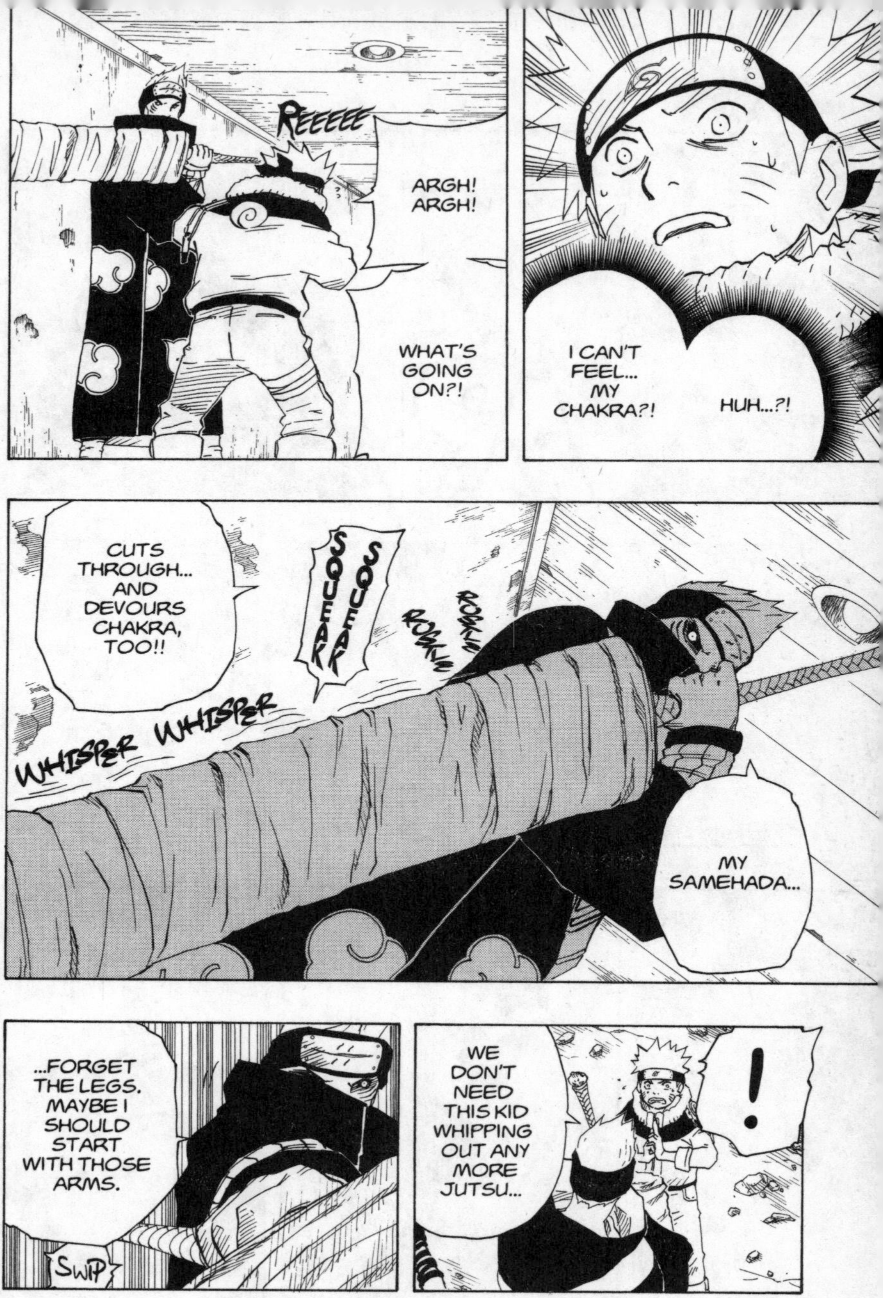
HUH...?!
I CAN'T FEEL... MY CHAKRA?!
REEEEEE
ARGH! ARGH!
WHAT'S GOING ON?!
MY SAMEHADA...
ROSKLE ROSKLE
SQUEAK SQUEAK
CUTS THROUGH... AND DEVOURS CHAKRA, TOO!!
WHISPER WHISPER
!
WE DON'T NEED THIS KID WHIPPING OUT ANY MORE JUTSU...
...FORGET THE LEGS. MAYBE I SHOULD START WITH THOSE ARMS.
SWIP

READ THIS WAY

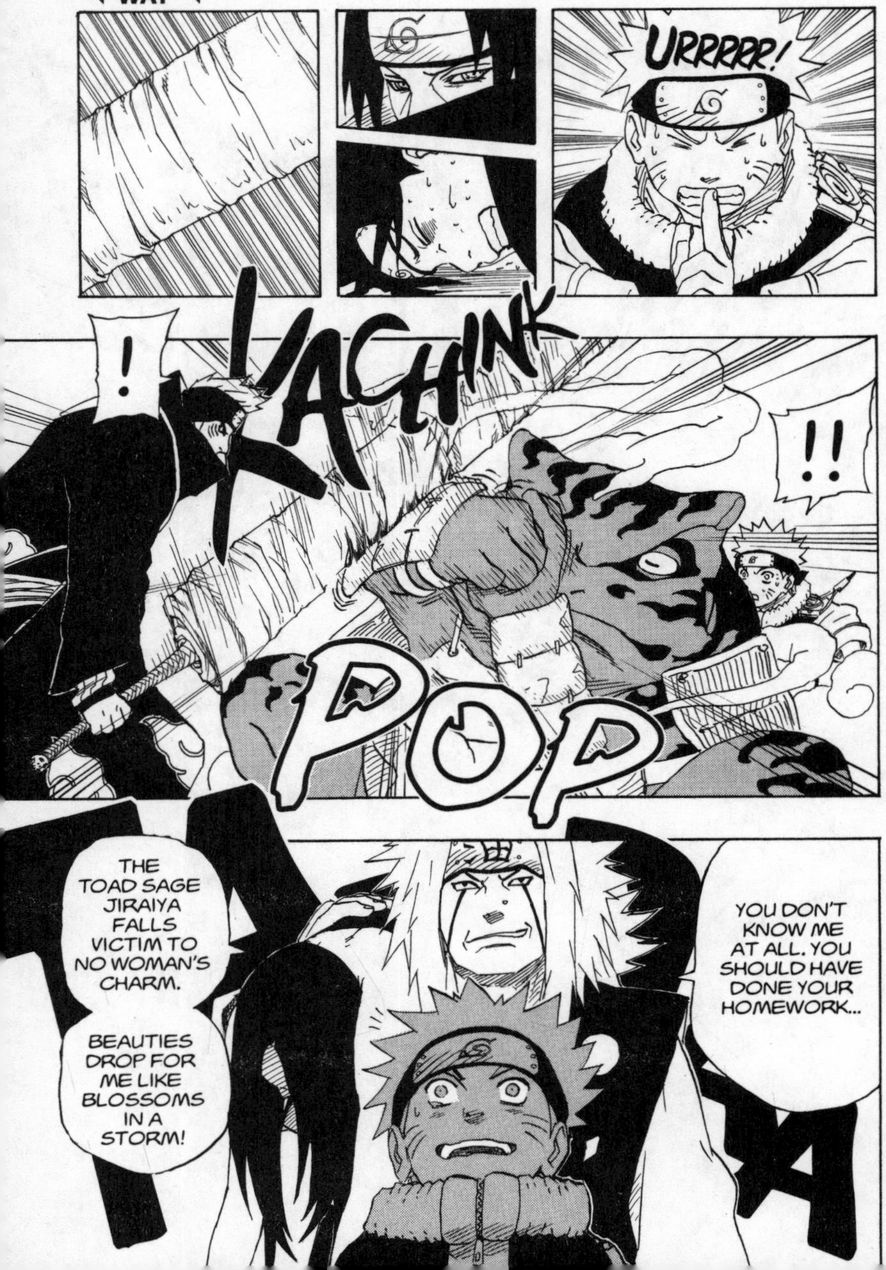
URRRRR!
VACHINK
!!
!
POP
YOU DON'T KNOW ME AT ALL. YOU SHOULD HAVE DONE YOUR HOMEWORK...
THE TOAD SAGE JIRAIYA FALLS VICTIM TO NO WOMAN'S CHARM.
BEAUTIES DROP FOR ME LIKE BLOSSOMS IN A STORM!

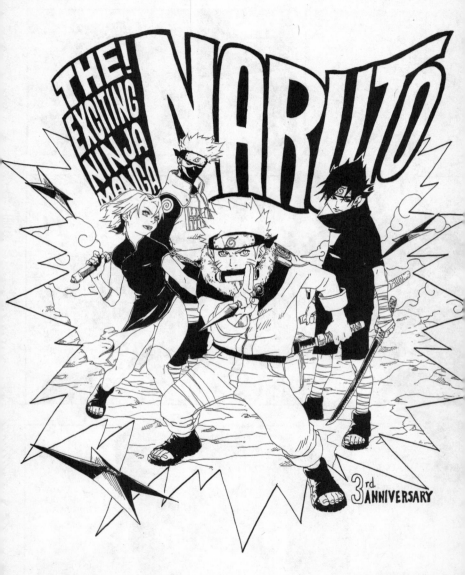

THE!
EXCITING
NINJA
MANGA

NARUTO

3rd. ANNIVERSARY

池本幹雄
MIKIO IKEMOTO

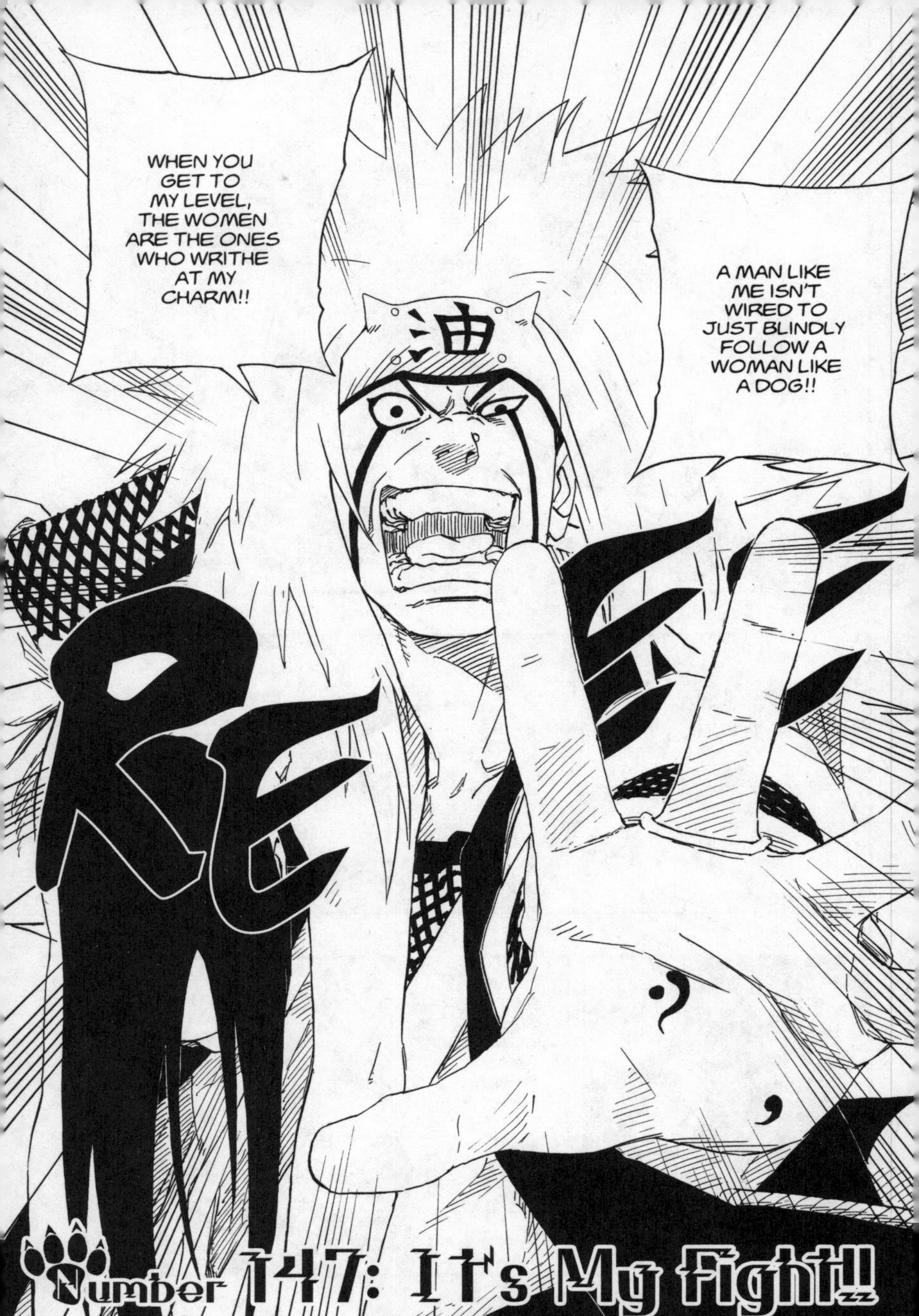
A MAN LIKE ME ISN'T WIRED TO JUST BLINDLY FOLLOW A WOMAN LIKE A DOG!!
WHEN YOU GET TO MY LEVEL, THE WOMEN ARE THE ONES WHO WRITHE AT MY CHARM!!

Number 147: It's My Fight!!

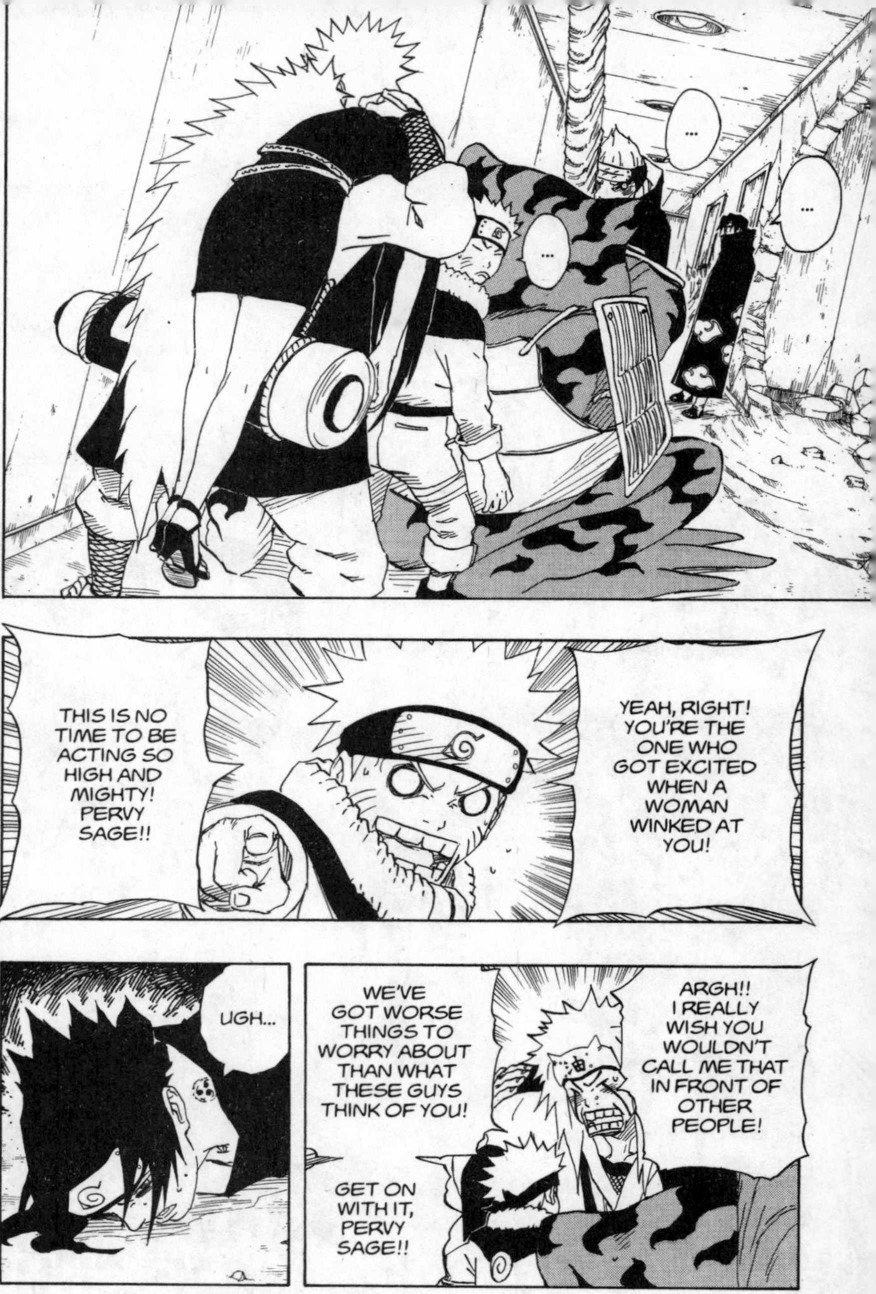
...
...
...
YEAH, RIGHT! YOU'RE THE ONE WHO GOT EXCITED WHEN A WOMAN WINKED AT YOU!
THIS IS NO TIME TO BE ACTING SO HIGH AND MIGHTY! PERVY SAGE!!
ARGH!! I REALLY WISH YOU WOULDN'T CALL ME THAT IN FRONT OF OTHER PEOPLE!
WE'VE GOT WORSE THINGS TO WORRY ABOUT THAN WHAT THESE GUYS THINK OF YOU!
GET ON WITH IT, PERVY SAGE!!
UGH...

READ THIS WAY

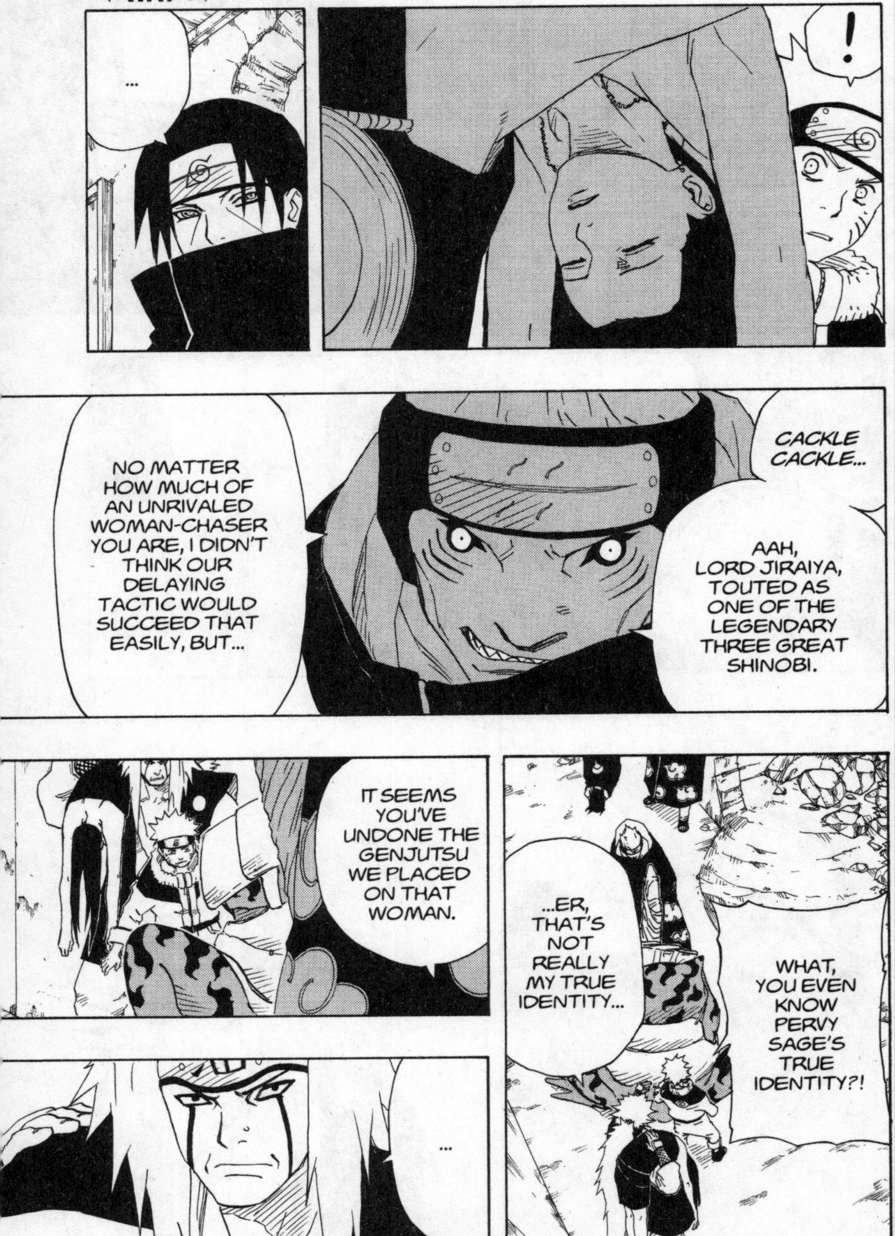
!
...
CACKLE CACKLE...
AAH, LORD JIRAIYA, TOUTED AS ONE OF THE LEGENDARY THREE GREAT SHINOBI.
NO MATTER HOW MUCH OF AN UNRIVALED WOMAN-CHASER YOU ARE, I DIDN'T THINK OUR DELAYING TACTIC WOULD SUCCEED THAT EASILY, BUT...
WHAT, YOU EVEN KNOW PERVY SAGE'S TRUE IDENTITY?!
...ER, THAT'S NOT REALLY MY TRUE IDENTITY...
IT SEEMS YOU'VE UNDONE THE GENJUTSU WE PLACED ON THAT WOMAN.
...

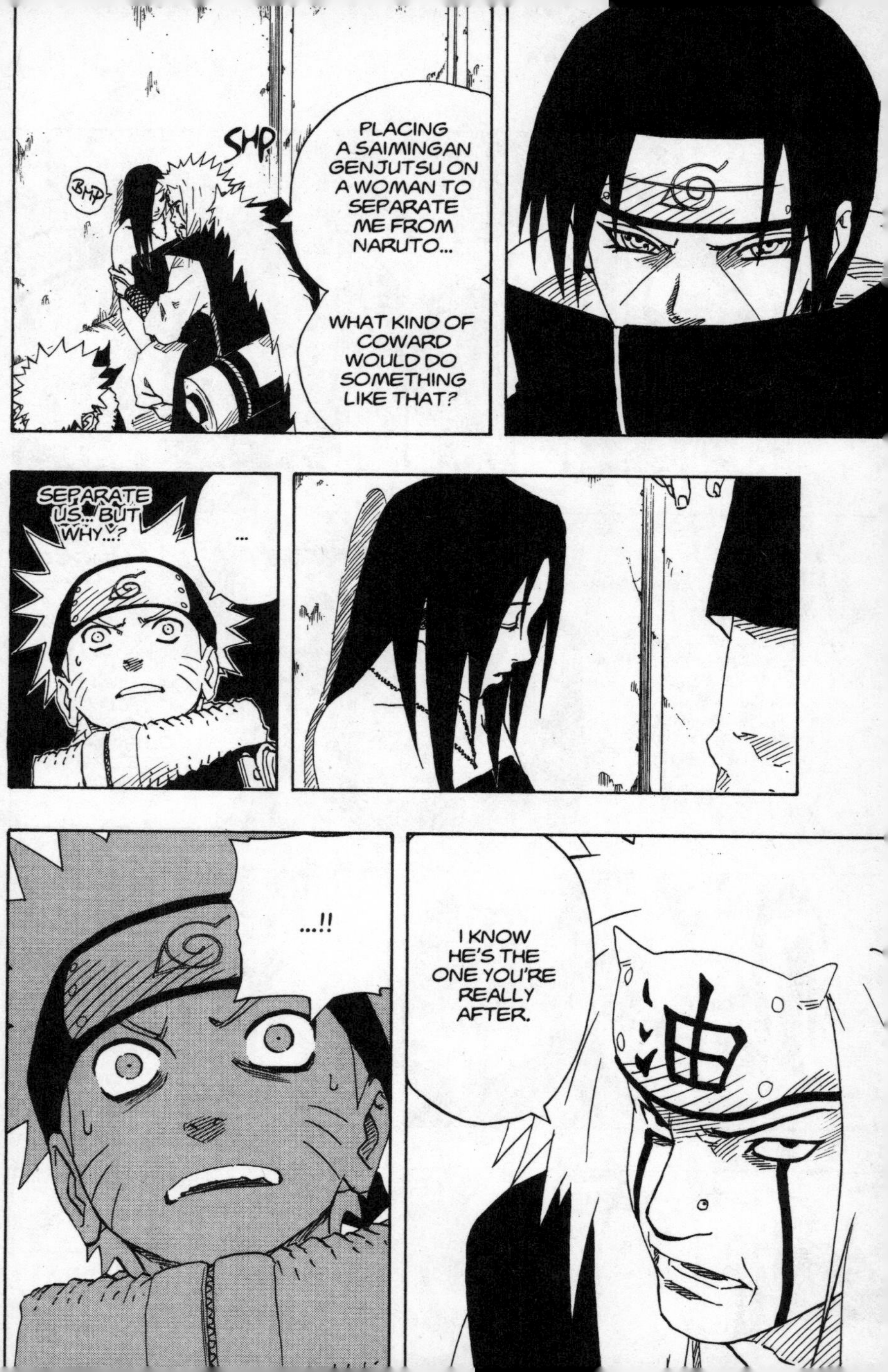
PLACING A SAIMINGAN GENJUTSU ON A WOMAN TO SEPARATE ME FROM NARUTO...
WHAT KIND OF COWARD WOULD DO SOMETHING LIKE THAT?
SHP
BMP
...
SEPARATE US... BUT WHY...?
I KNOW HE'S THE ONE YOU'RE REALLY AFTER.
...!!

READ THIS WAY

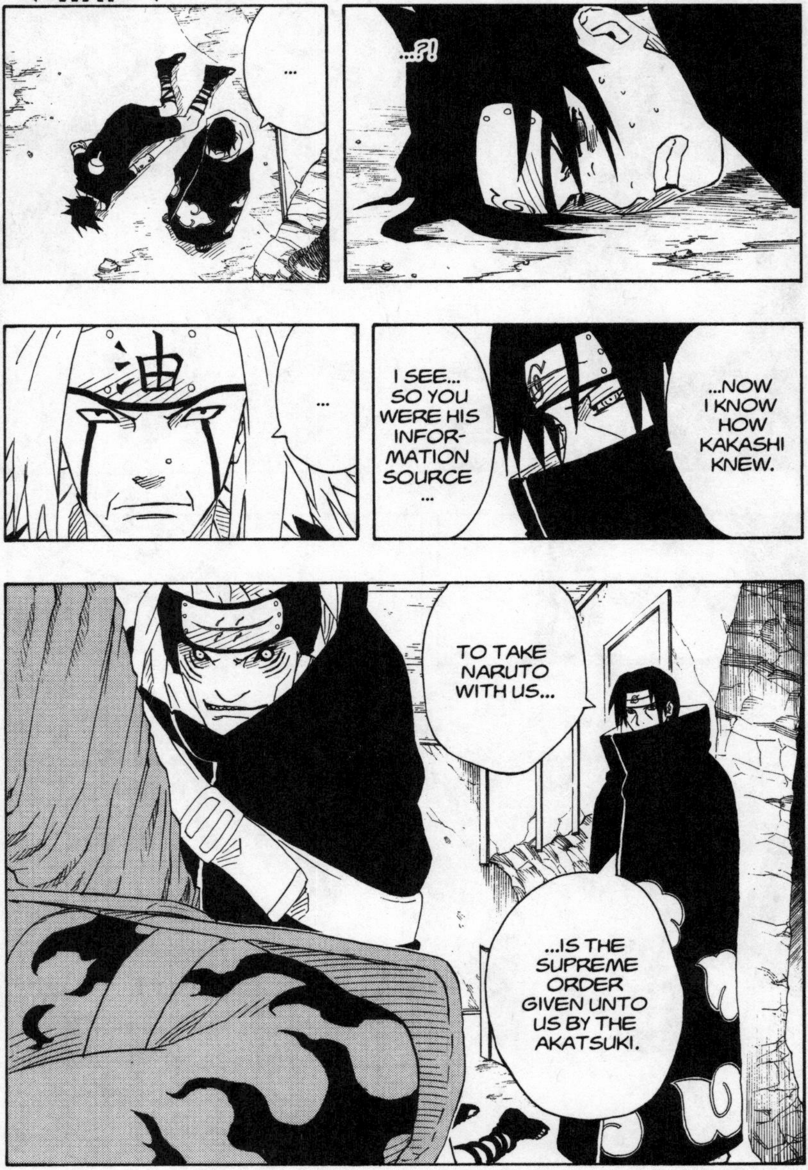

...?!
...
...NOW I KNOW HOW KAKASHI KNEW.
I SEE... SO YOU WERE HIS INFORMATION SOURCE...
...
TO TAKE NARUTO WITH US...
...IS THE SUPREME ORDER GIVEN UNTO US BY THE AKATSUKI.

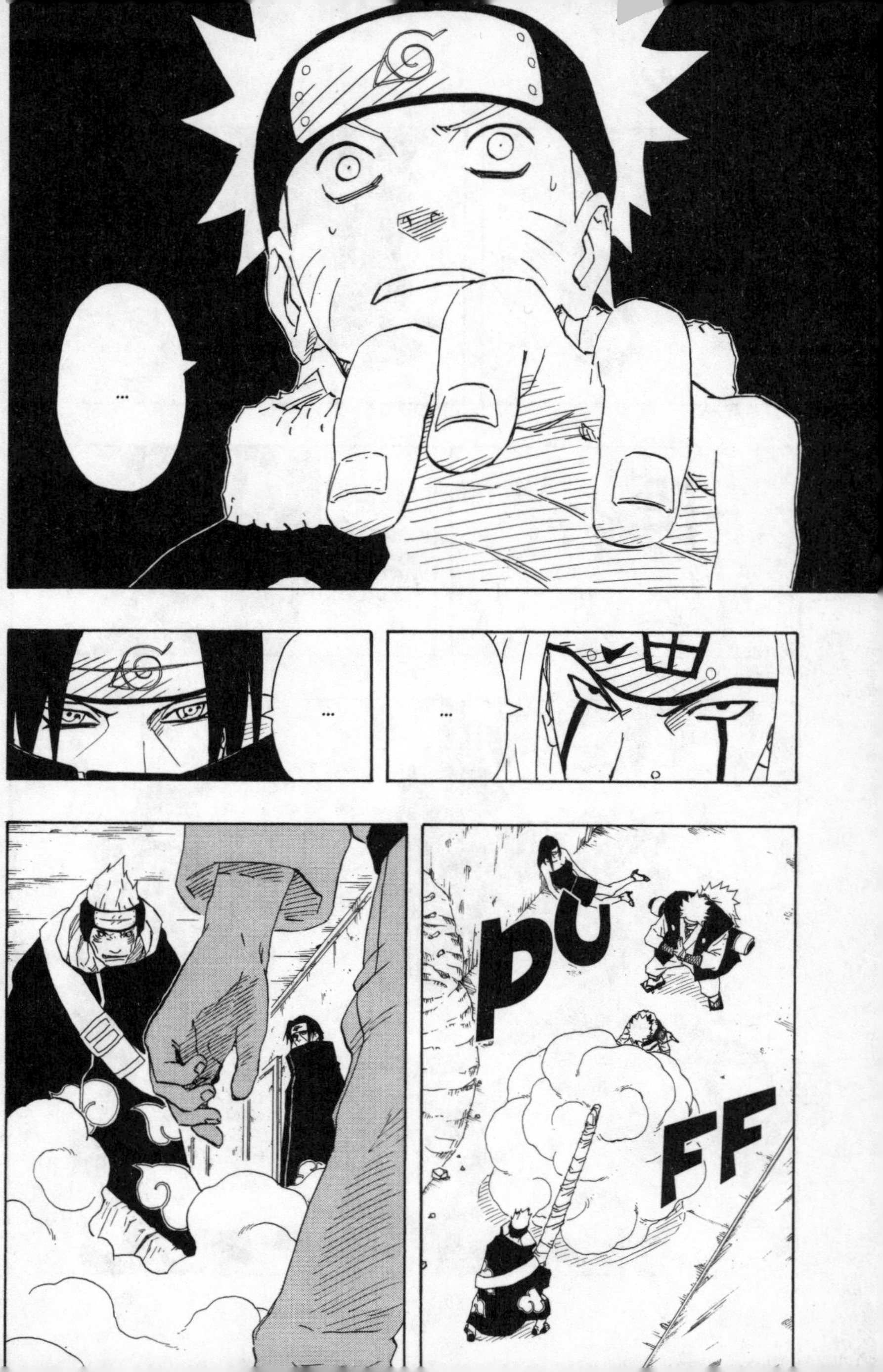
...
...
...
PUFF

READ THIS WAY

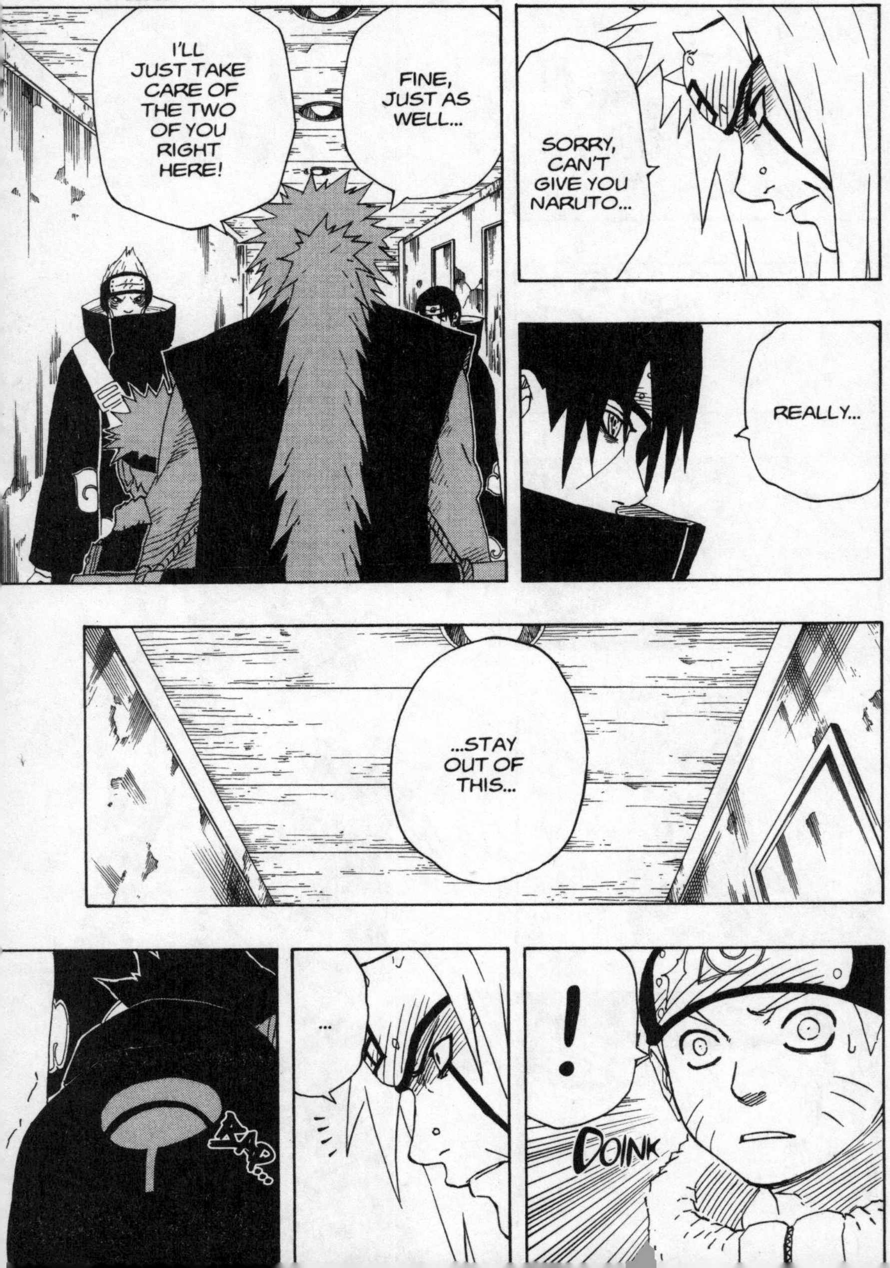

SORRY, CAN'T GIVE YOU NARUTO...
REALLY...
FINE, JUST AS WELL...
I'LL JUST TAKE CARE OF THE TWO OF YOU RIGHT HERE!
...STAY OUT OF THIS...
!
DOINK
...
BAP...

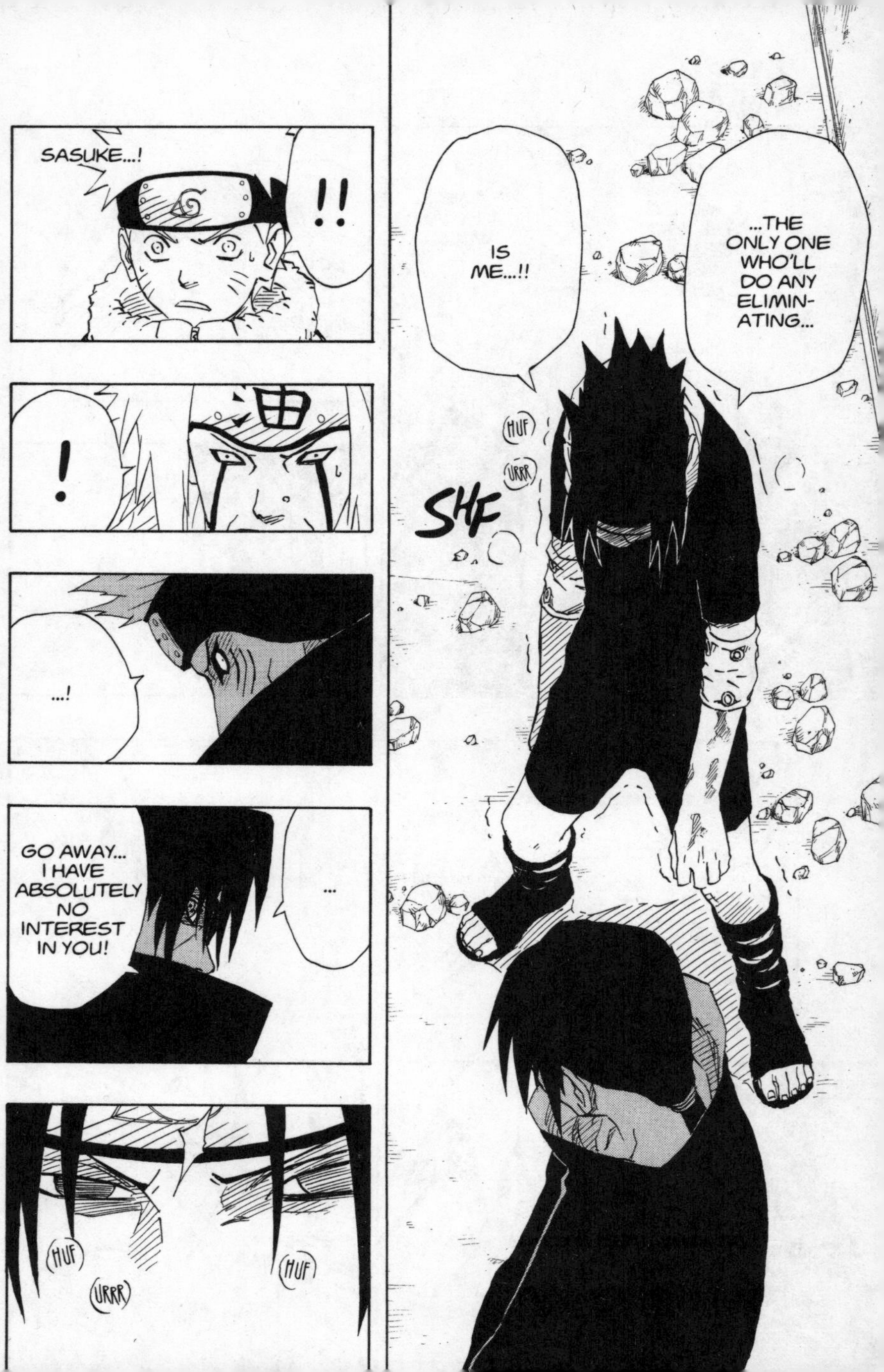
...THE ONLY ONE WHO'LL DO ANY ELIMIN-ATING...
IS ME...!!
HUF
URRR
SHF
SASUKE...!
!!
!
...!
...
GO AWAY... I HAVE ABSOLUTELY NO INTEREST IN YOU!
HUF
HUF
URRR

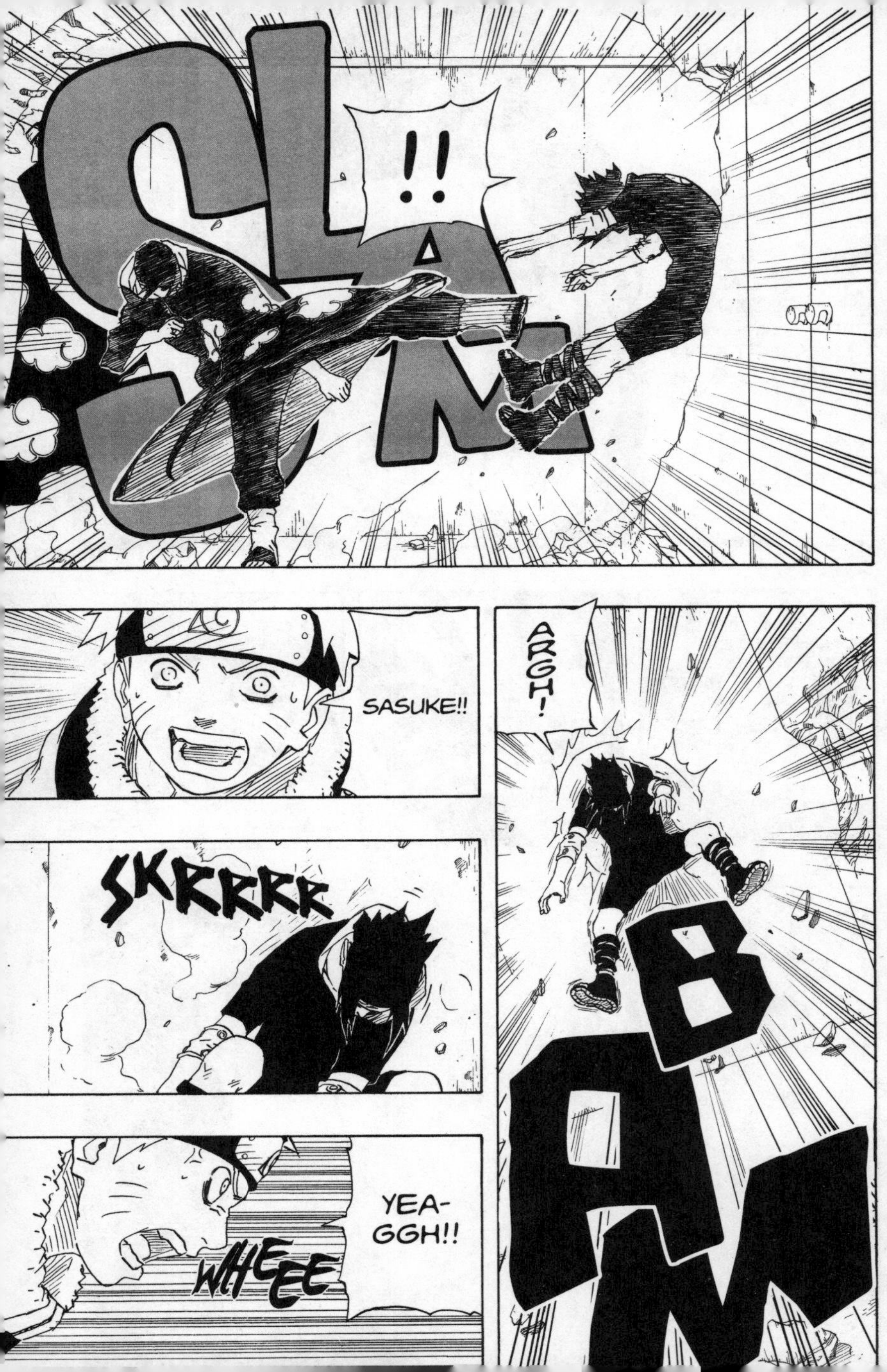
!!
SLAM
ARGH!
BAM
SASUKE!!
SKRRRR
YEA-GGH!!
WHEEE

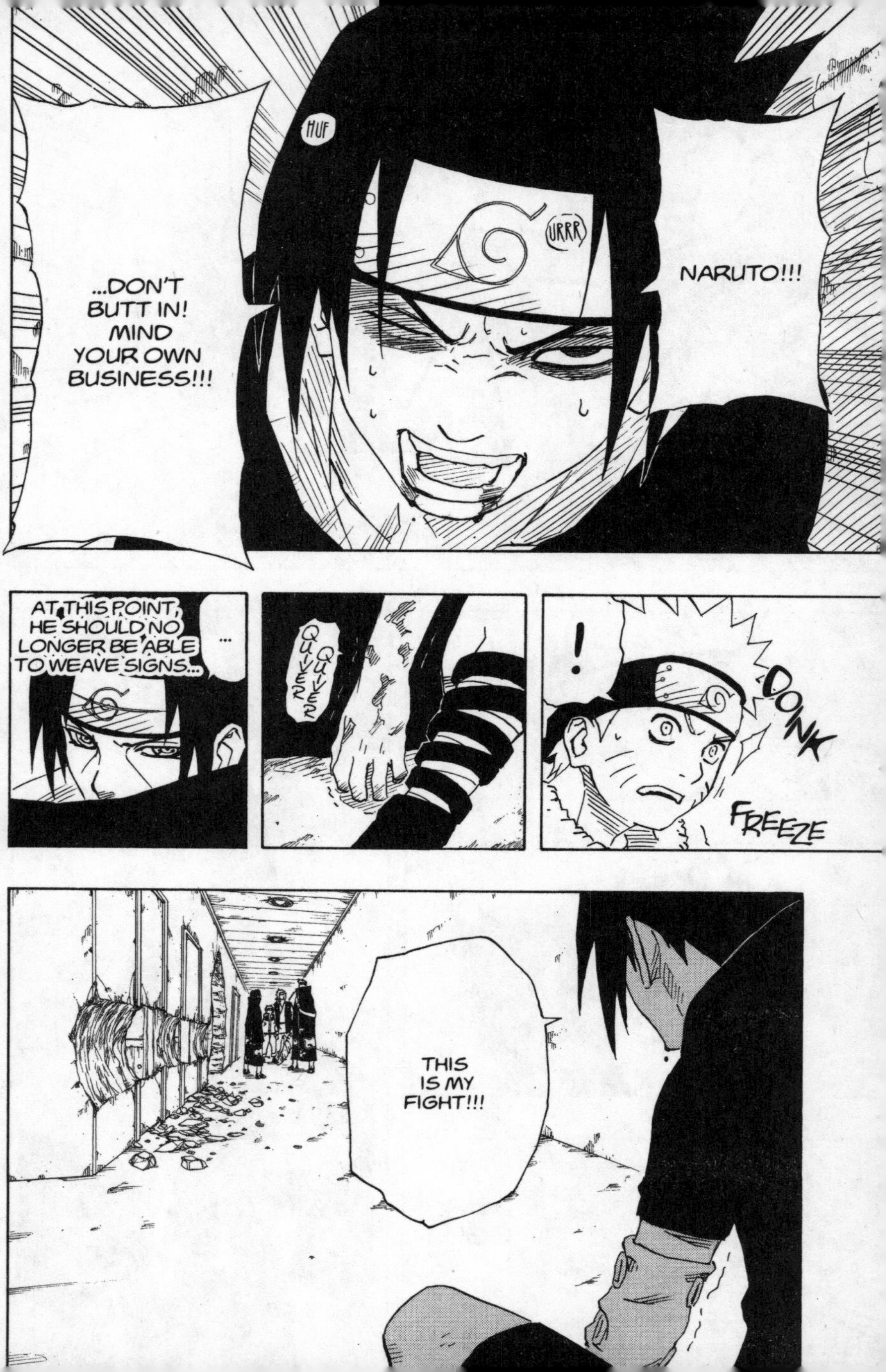
NARUTO!!!
URRR
HUF
...DON'T BUTT IN! MIND YOUR OWN BUSINESS!!!
!
DONK
FREEZE
QUIVER QUIVER
...
AT THIS POINT, HE SHOULD NO LONGER BE ABLE TO WEAVE SIGNS...
THIS IS MY FIGHT!!!

READ THIS WAY

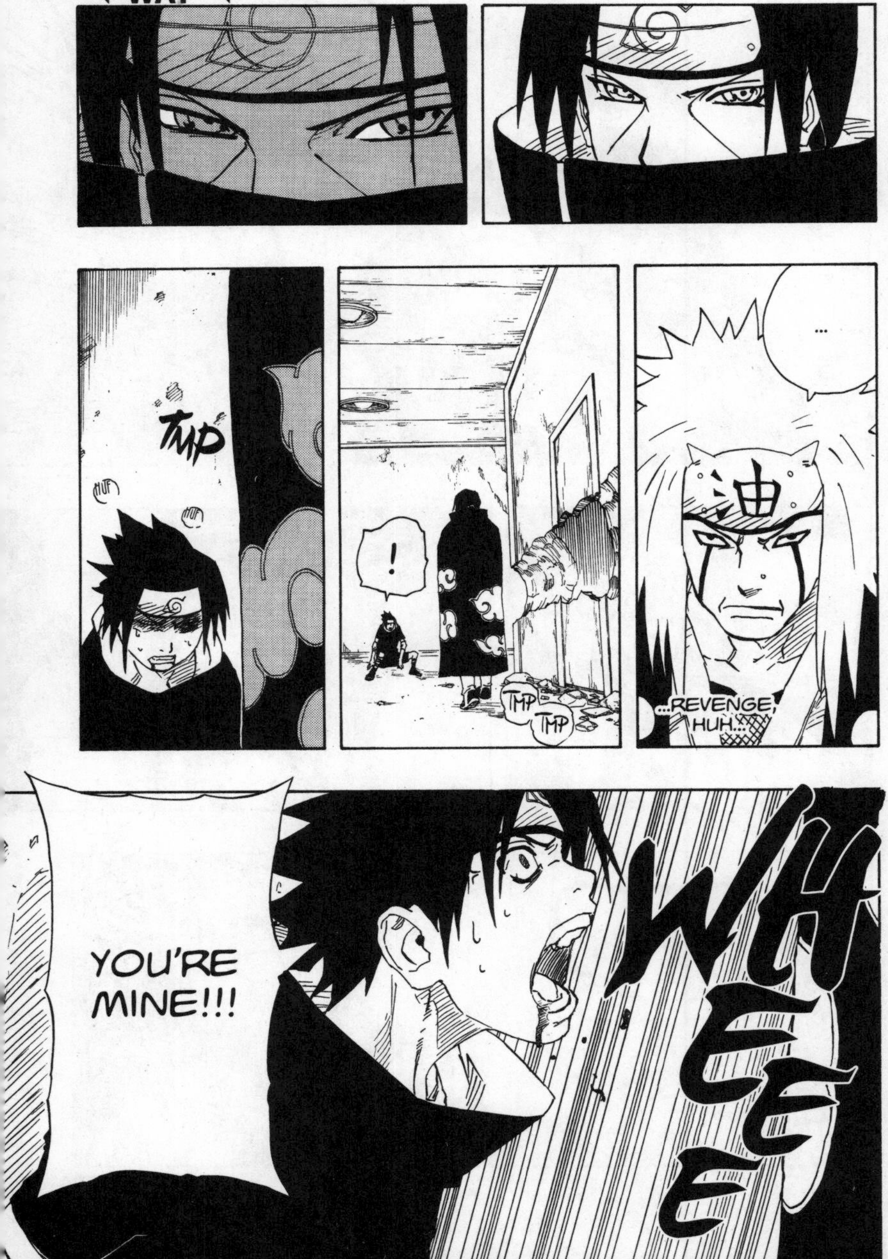
...
...REVENGE, HUH...
!
TMP
TMP
TMP
HUF
HUF
WHEEEE
YOU'RE MINE!!!

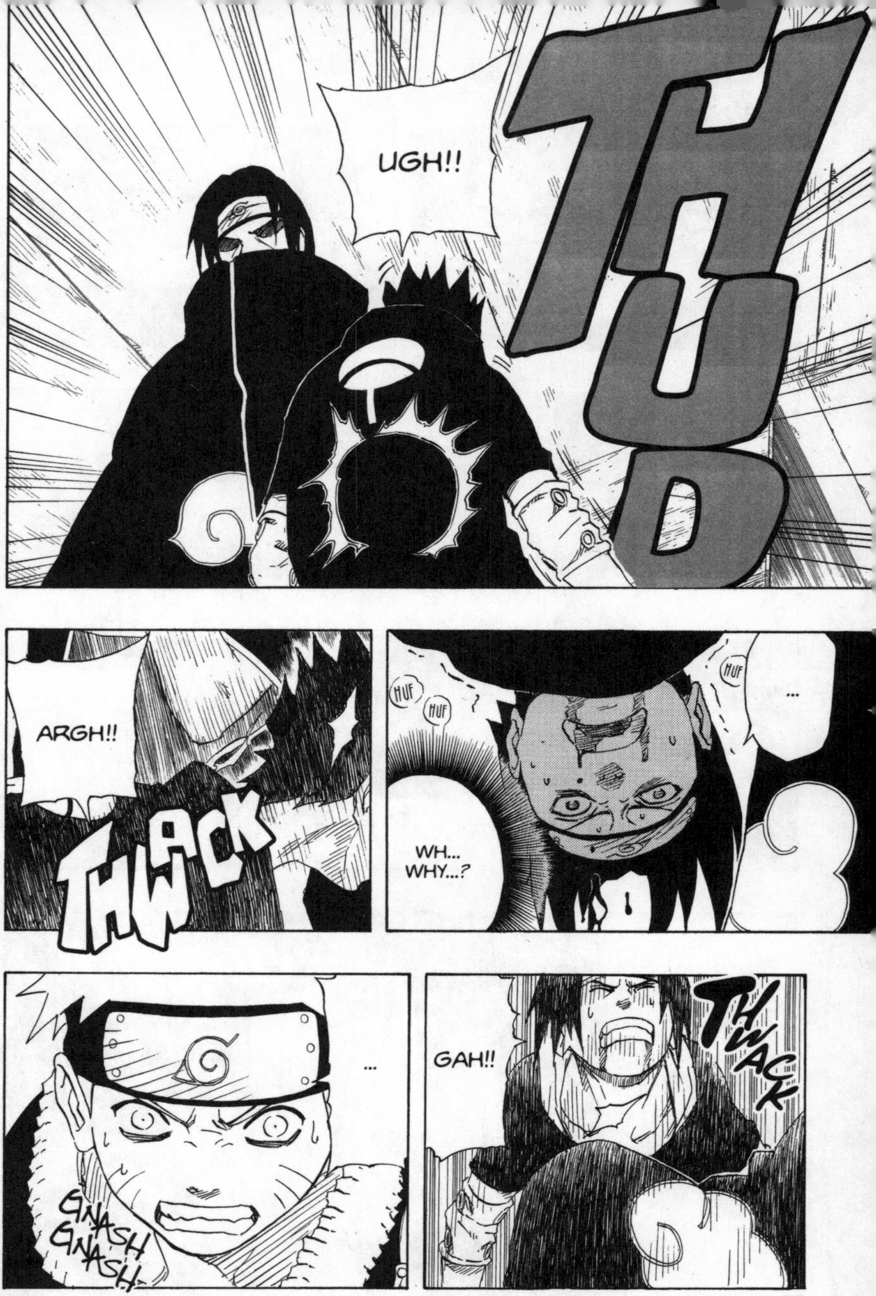
THUD
UGH!!
HUF
...
HUF
HUF
WH... WHY...?
ARGH!!
THWACK
THWACK
GAH!!
...
GNASH
GNASH

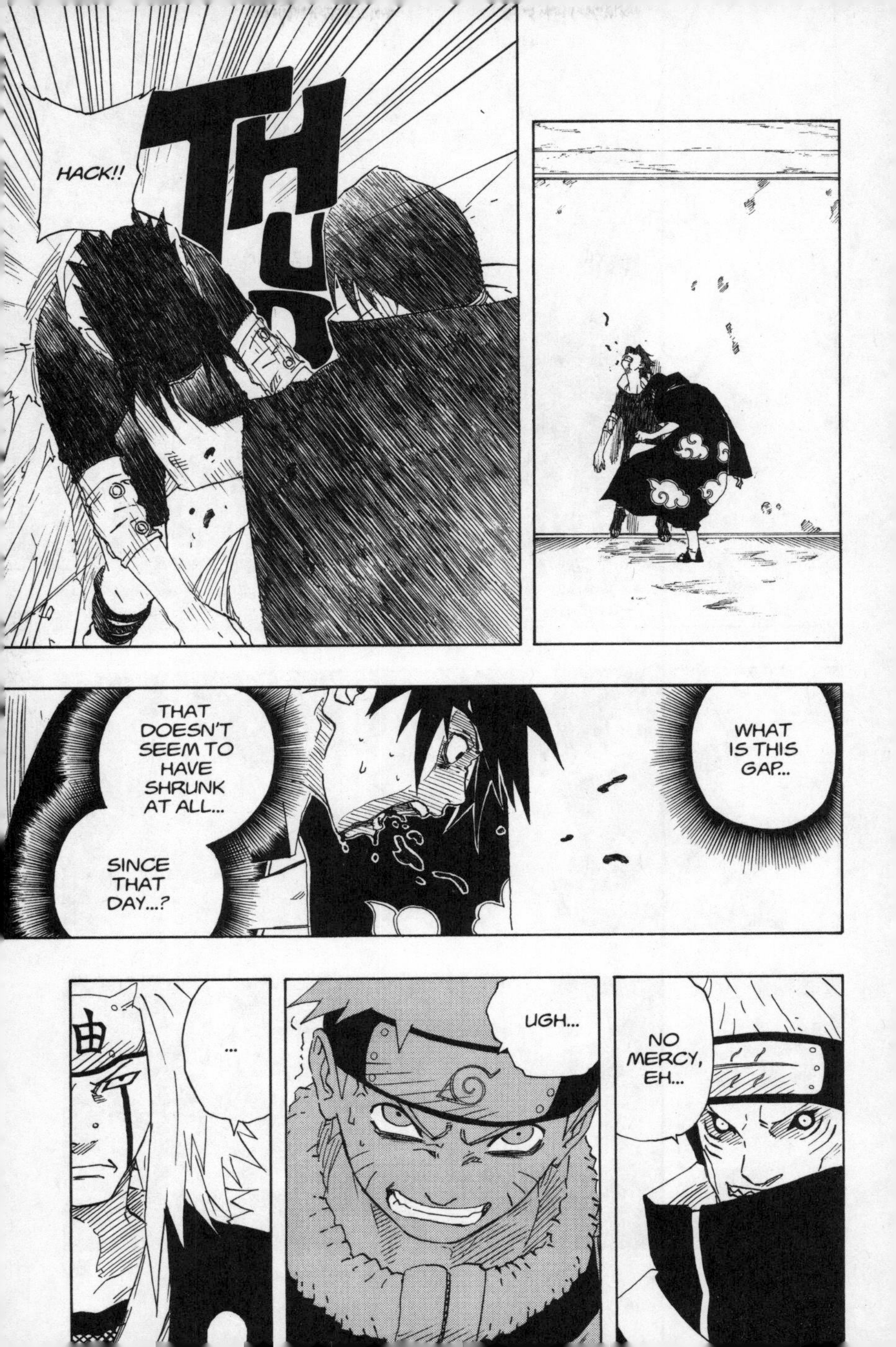
HACK!!
THUD
WHAT IS THIS GAP...
THAT DOESN'T SEEM TO HAVE SHRUNK AT ALL...
SINCE THAT DAY...?
NO MERCY, EH...
UGH...
...

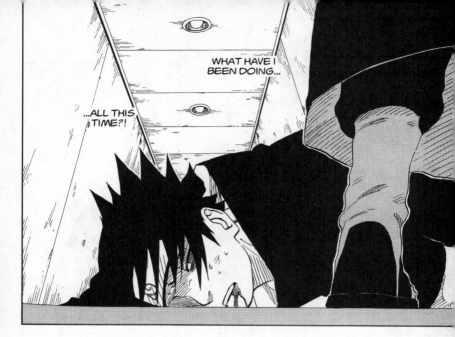

WHAT HAVE I
BEEN DOING...

...ALL THIS
TIME?!

CHOK!!

THOK

HUNH...

...WHAT...

...IN
THE
WORLD..

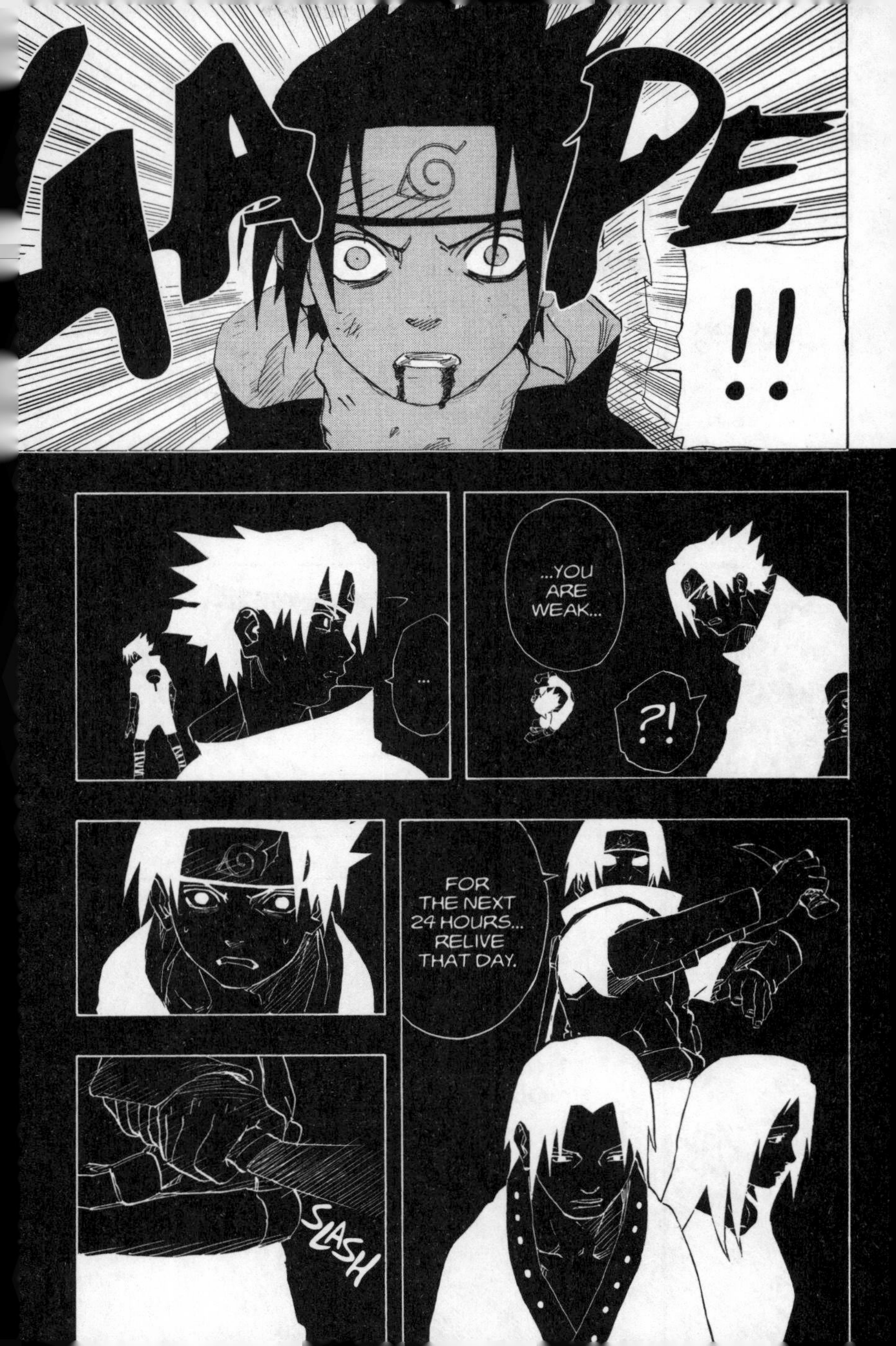
...YOU ARE WEAK...
?!
...
FOR THE NEXT 24 HOURS... RELIVE THAT DAY.
SLASH

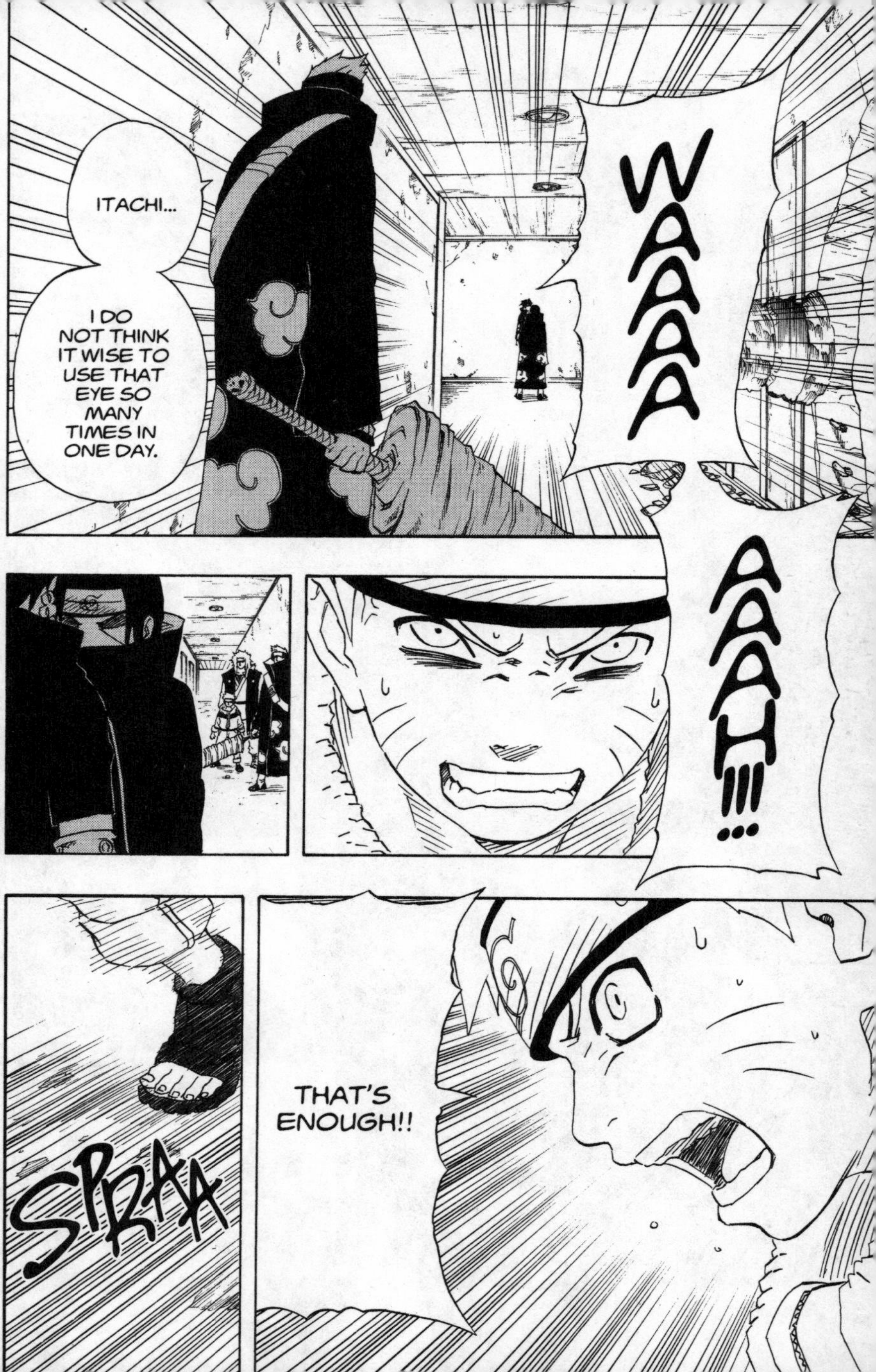
WAAAA
AAAH!!!
ITACHI...
I DO NOT THINK IT WISE TO USE THAT EYE SO MANY TIMES IN ONE DAY.
THAT'S ENOUGH!!
SPRAA

READ THIS WAY

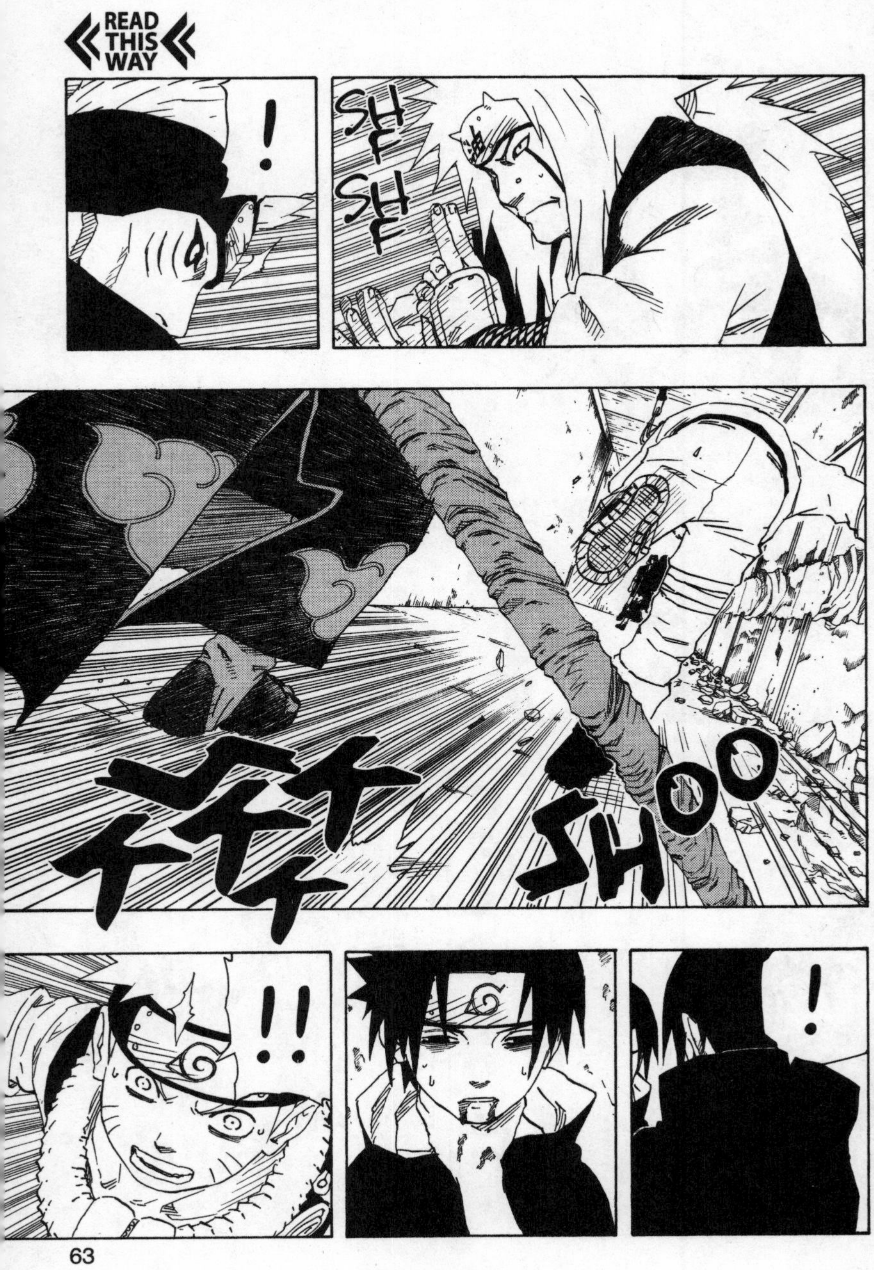
SHF SHF
!
SHOO
!
!!

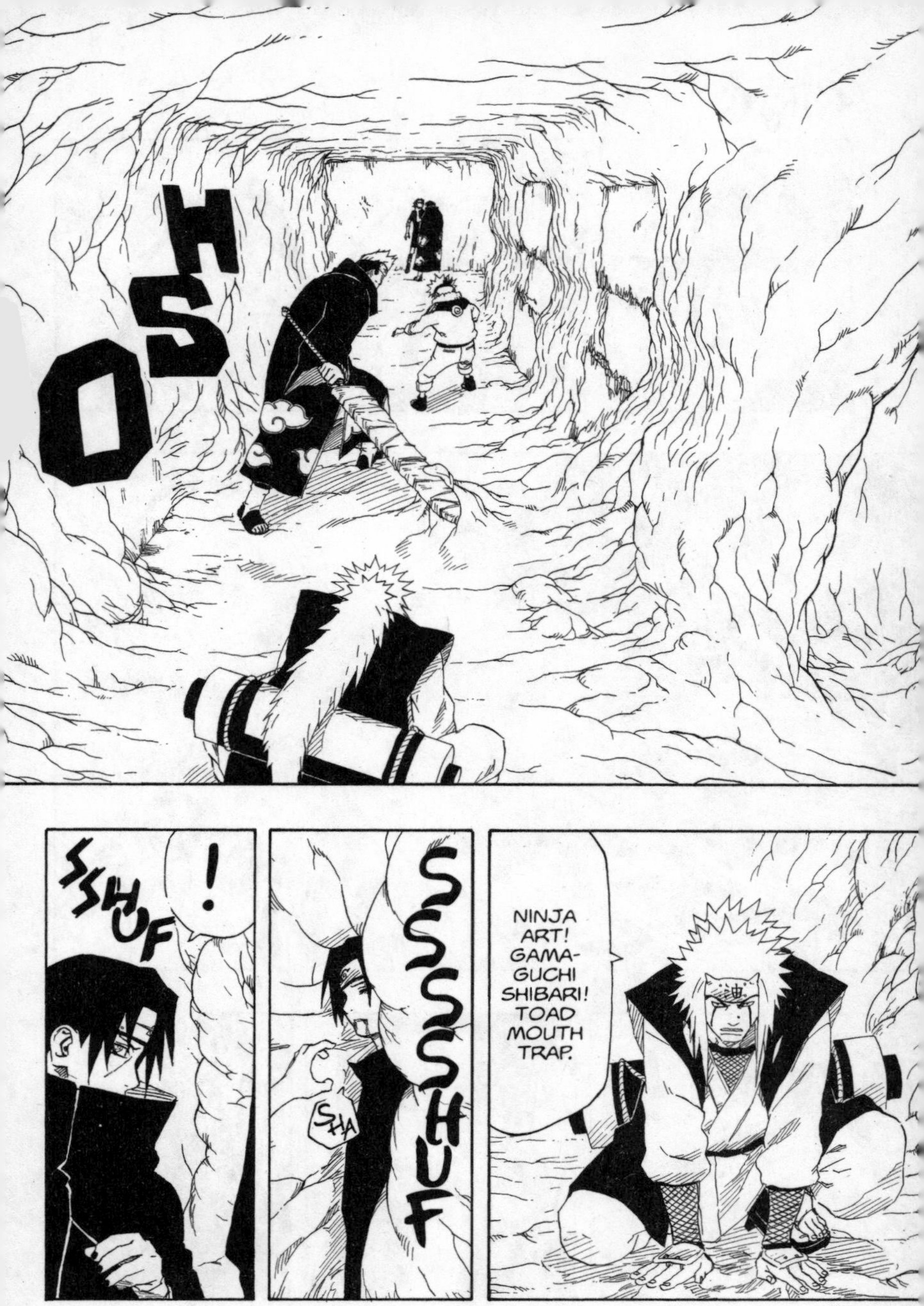
OSH
NINJA ART! GAMA-GUCHI SHIBARI! TOAD MOUTH TRAP.
SSSHUF
SHA
!
SSHUF

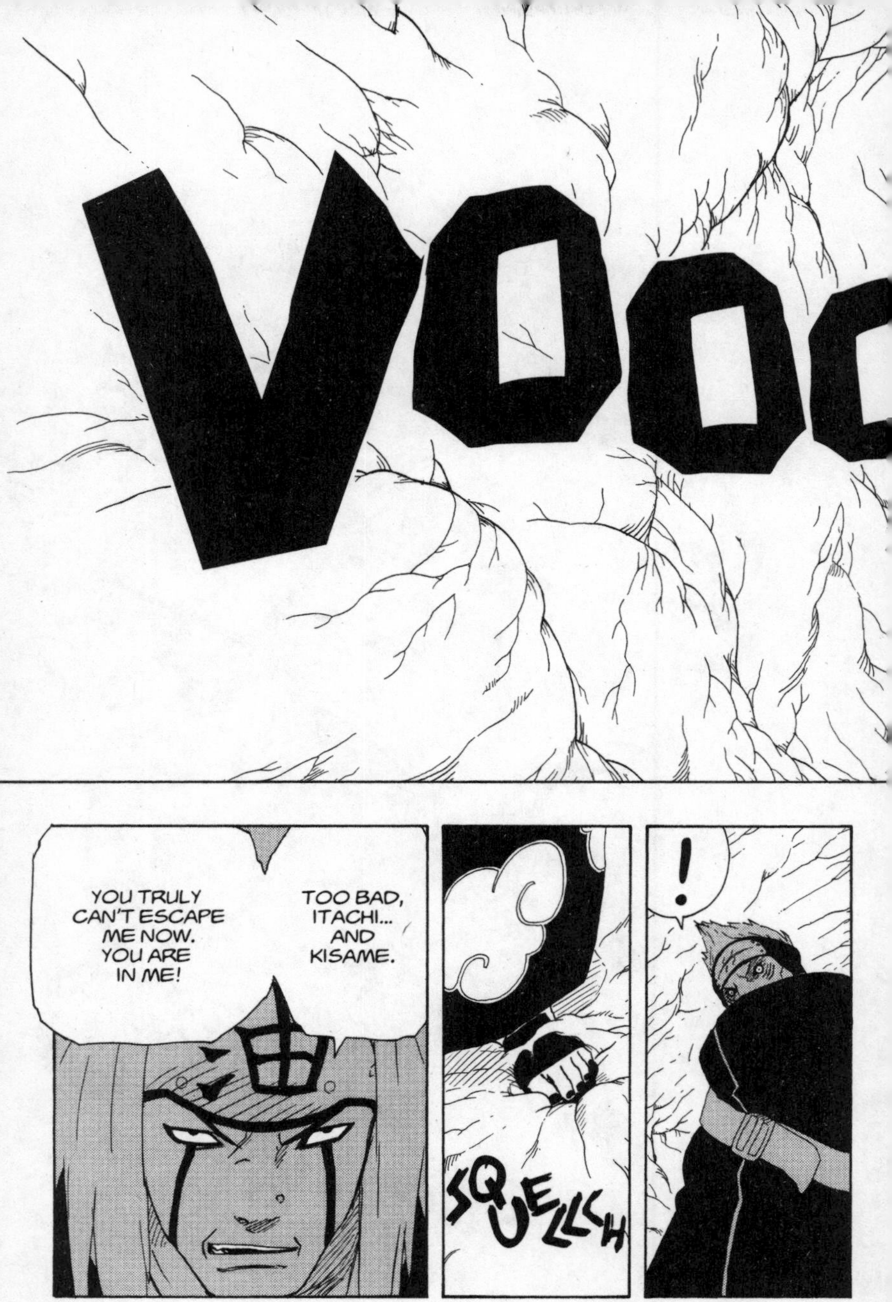
VOOO
!
SQUELLCH
TOO BAD, ITACHI... AND KISAME.
YOU TRULY CAN'T ESCAPE ME NOW. YOU ARE IN ME!

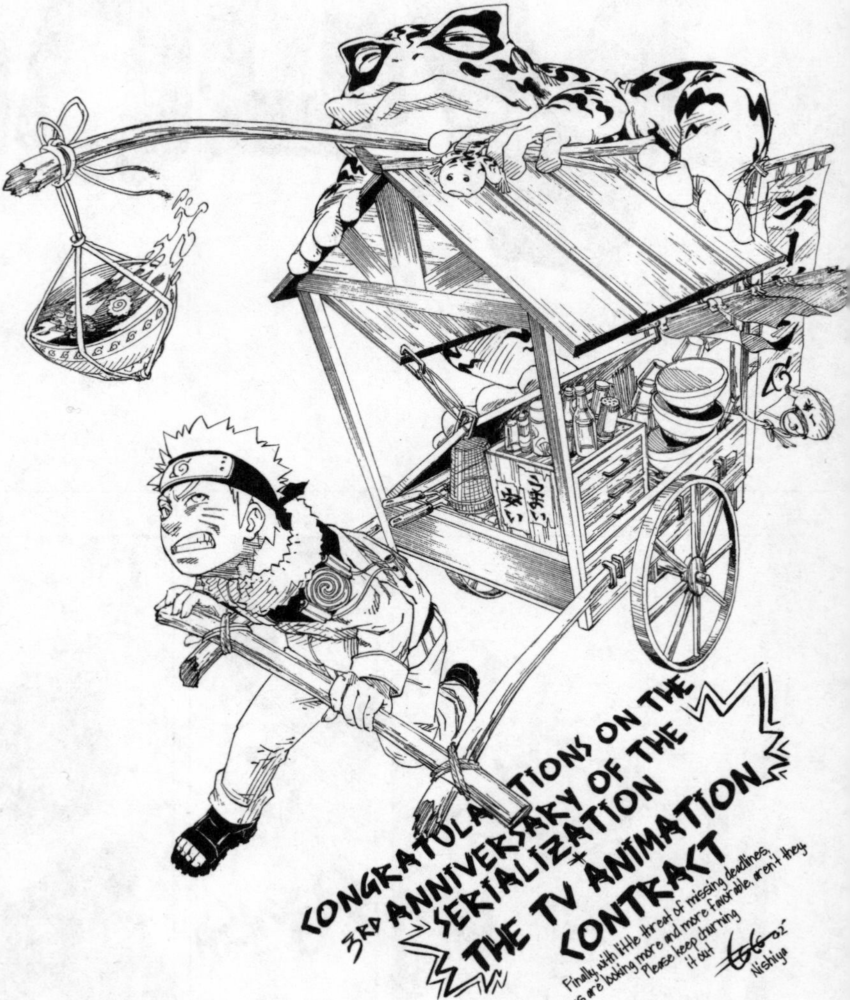
CONGRATULATIONS ON THE
3RD ANNIVERSARY OF THE
SERIALIZATION
+
THE TV ANIMATION
CONTRACT
Finally with little threat of missing deadlines,
things are looking more and more favorable, aren't they
Please keep churning
it out
'02
Nishiya

Number 148: Itachi's Power!!

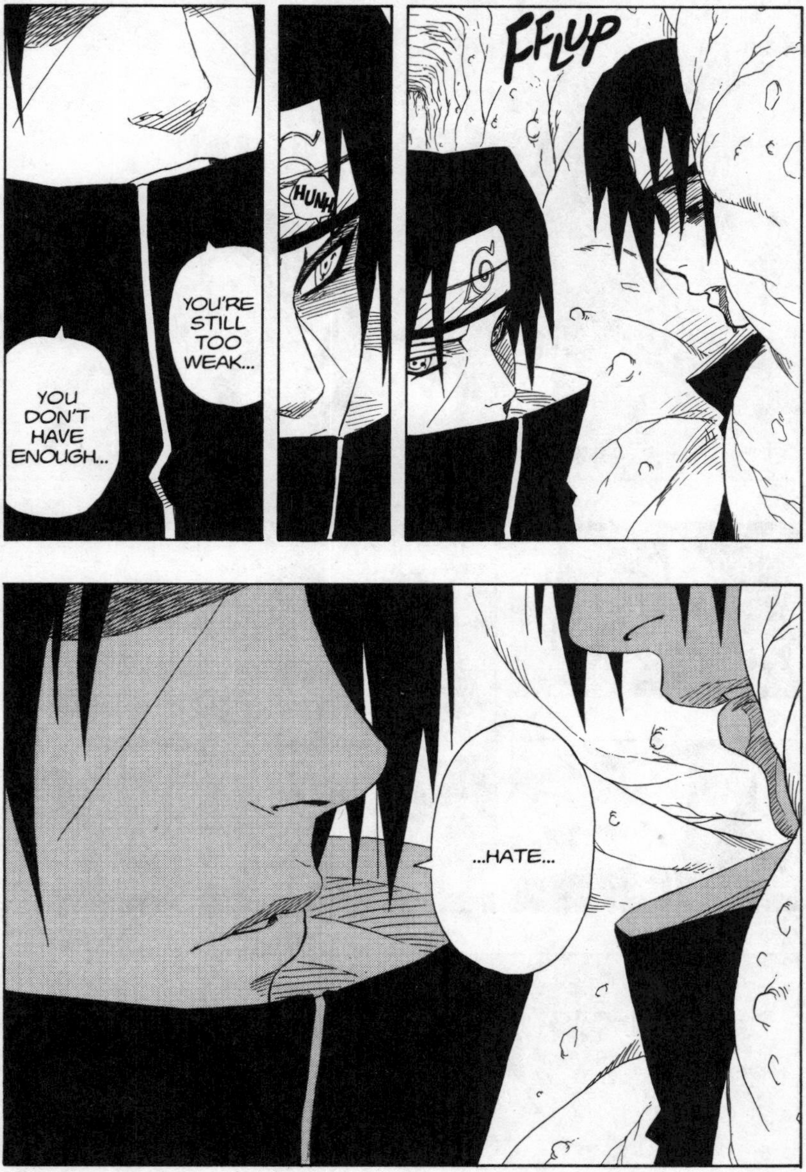
FFLUP
HUNH
YOU'RE STILL TOO WEAK...
YOU DON'T HAVE ENOUGH...
...HATE...

Number 148: Itachi's Power!!

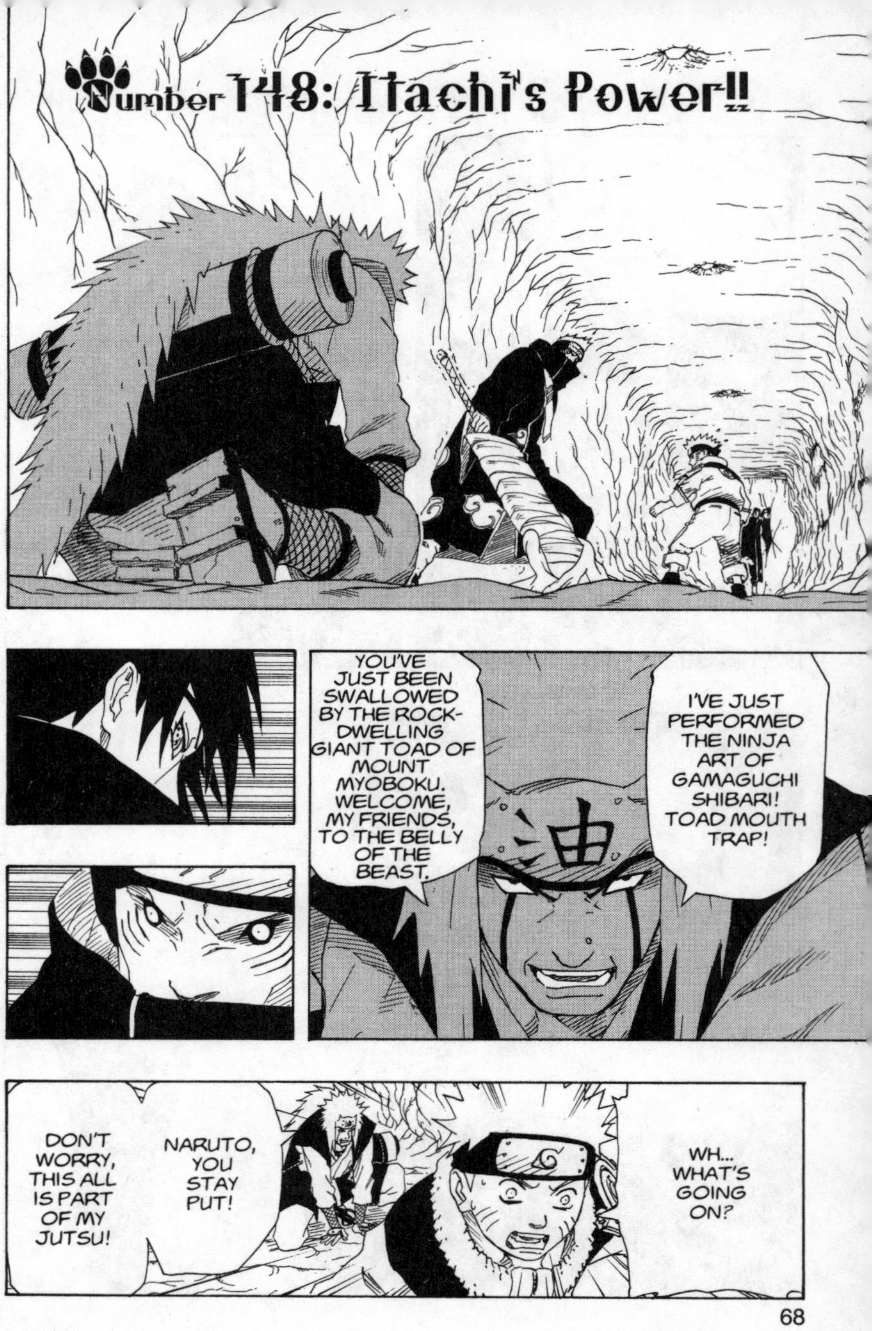
I'VE JUST PERFORMED THE NINJA ART OF GAMAGUCHI SHIBARI! TOAD MOUTH TRAP!
YOU'VE JUST BEEN SWALLOWED BY THE ROCK-DWELLING GIANT TOAD OF MOUNT MYOBOKU. WELCOME, MY FRIENDS, TO THE BELLY OF THE BEAST.
WH... WHAT'S GOING ON?
NARUTO, YOU STAY PUT!
DON'T WORRY, THIS ALL IS PART OF MY JUTSU!

READ THIS WAY

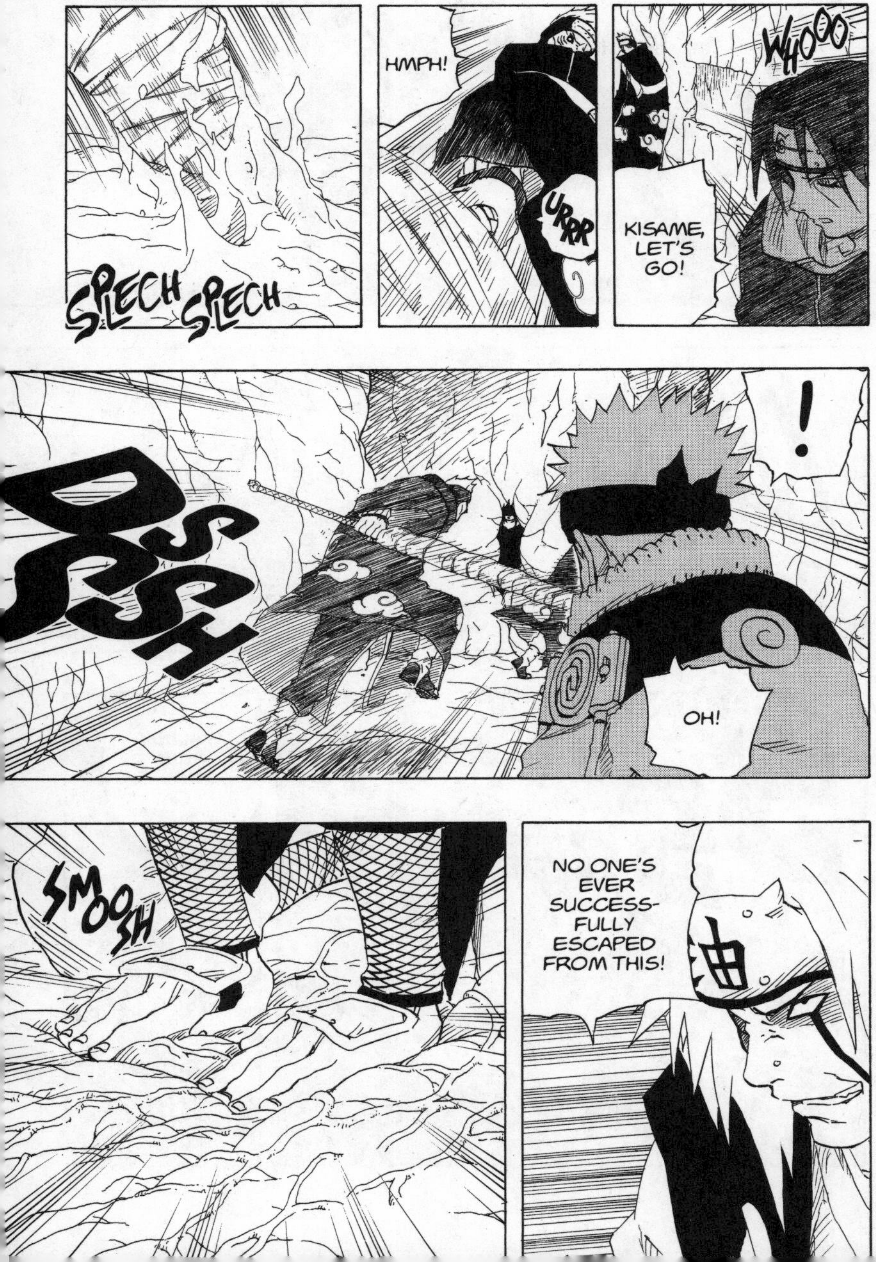
WHOOO
KISAME, LET'S GO!
HMPH!
URRR
SPLECH SPLECH
!
OH!
DASH
NO ONE'S EVER SUCCESS-FULLY ESCAPED FROM THIS!
SMOOSH

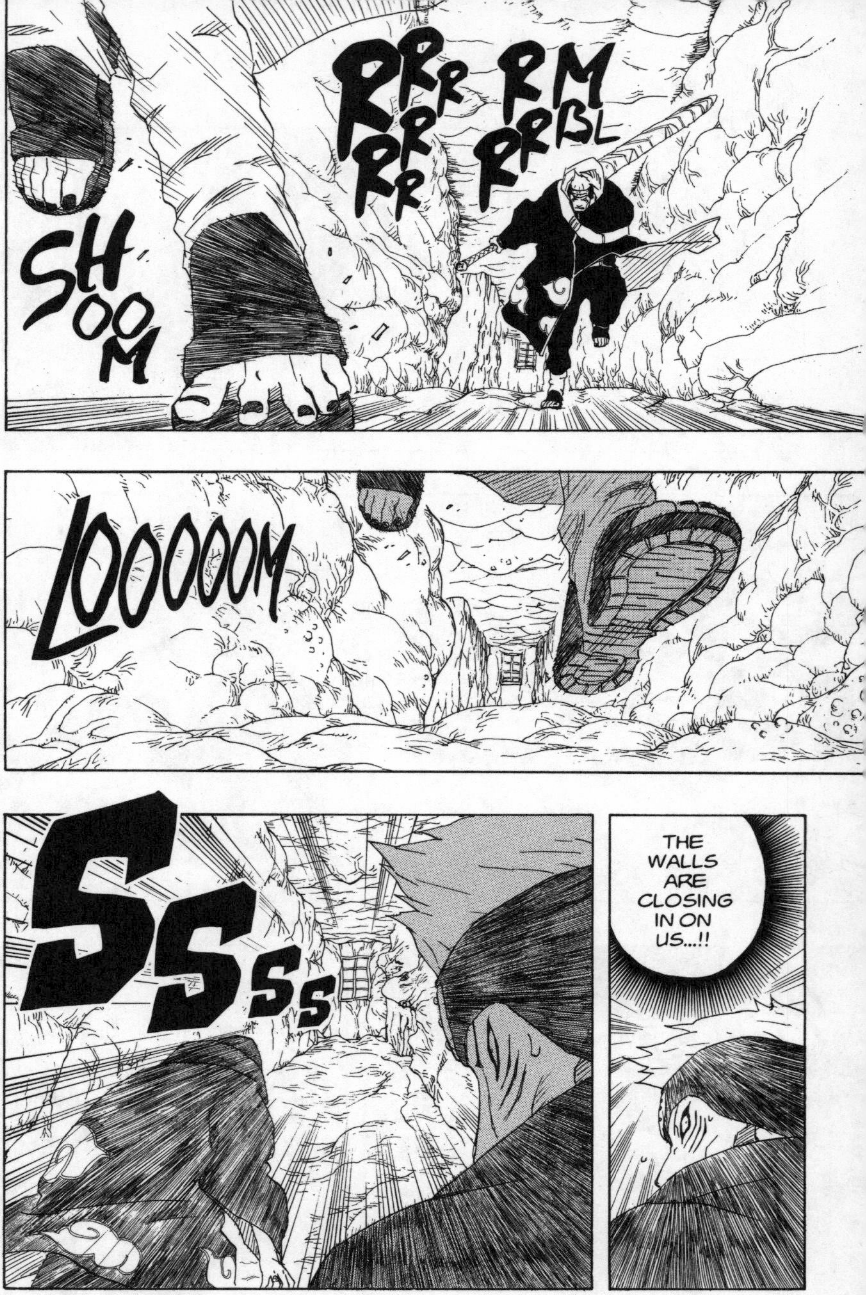
RRRRRR RM RRRBL
SHOOOM
LOOOOOM
THE WALLS ARE CLOSING IN ON US...!!
SSSS

READ THIS WAY

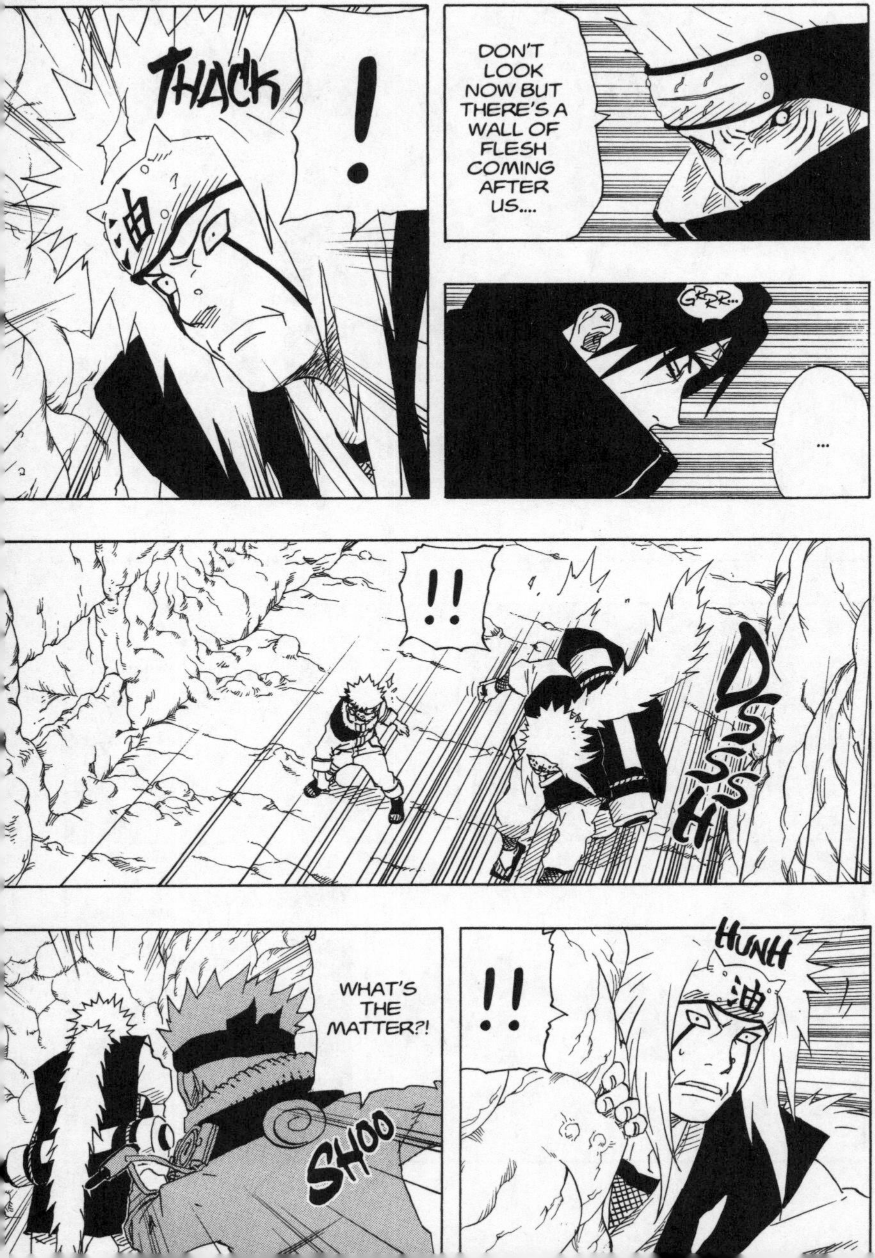
DON'T LOOK NOW BUT THERE'S A WALL OF FLESH COMING AFTER US....
GRRR...
...
THACK
!
!!
DSSSH
HUNH
!!
WHAT'S THE MATTER?!
SHOO

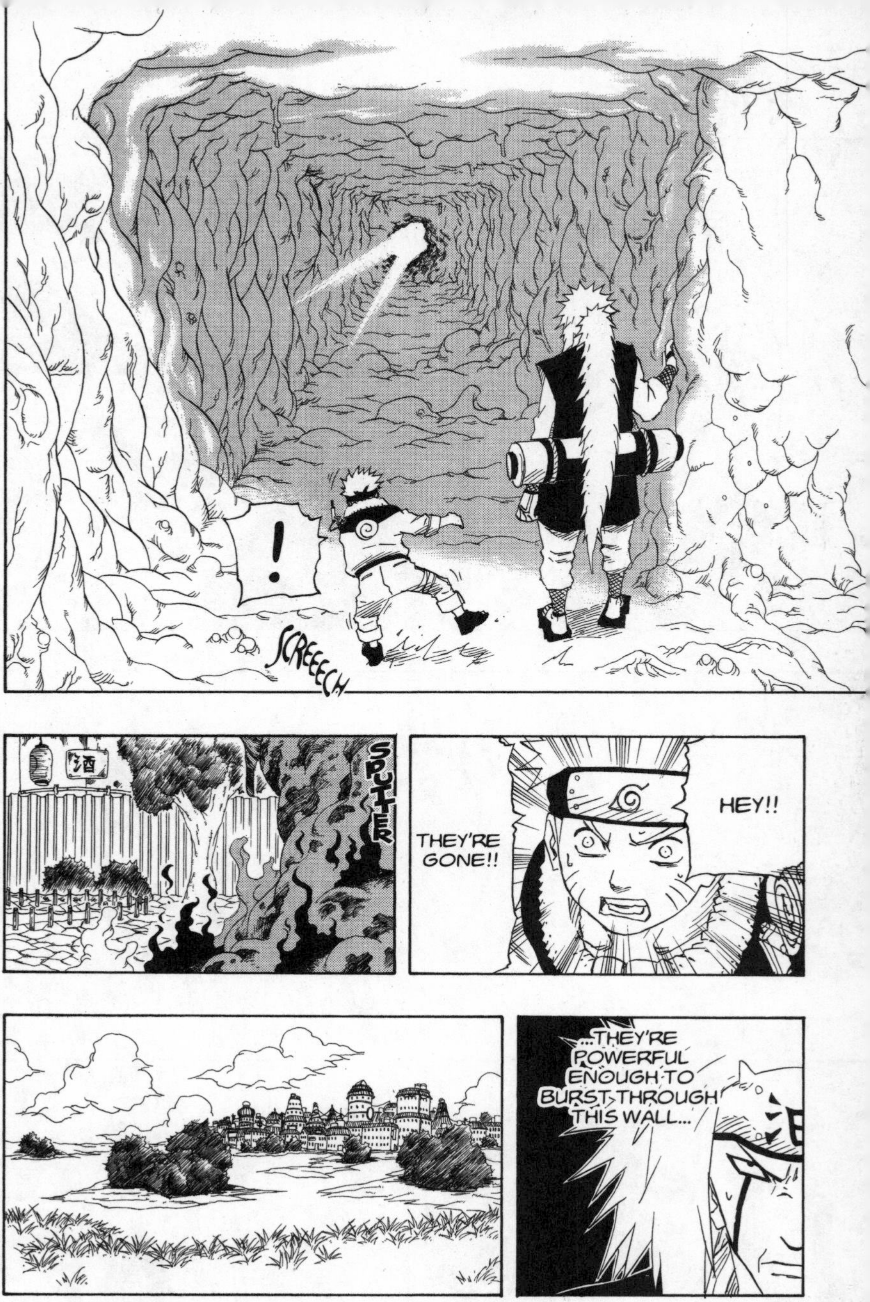
!
SCREEECH
HEY!!
THEY'RE GONE!!
SPUTTER
酒
...THEY'RE POWERFUL ENOUGH TO BURST THROUGH THIS WALL...

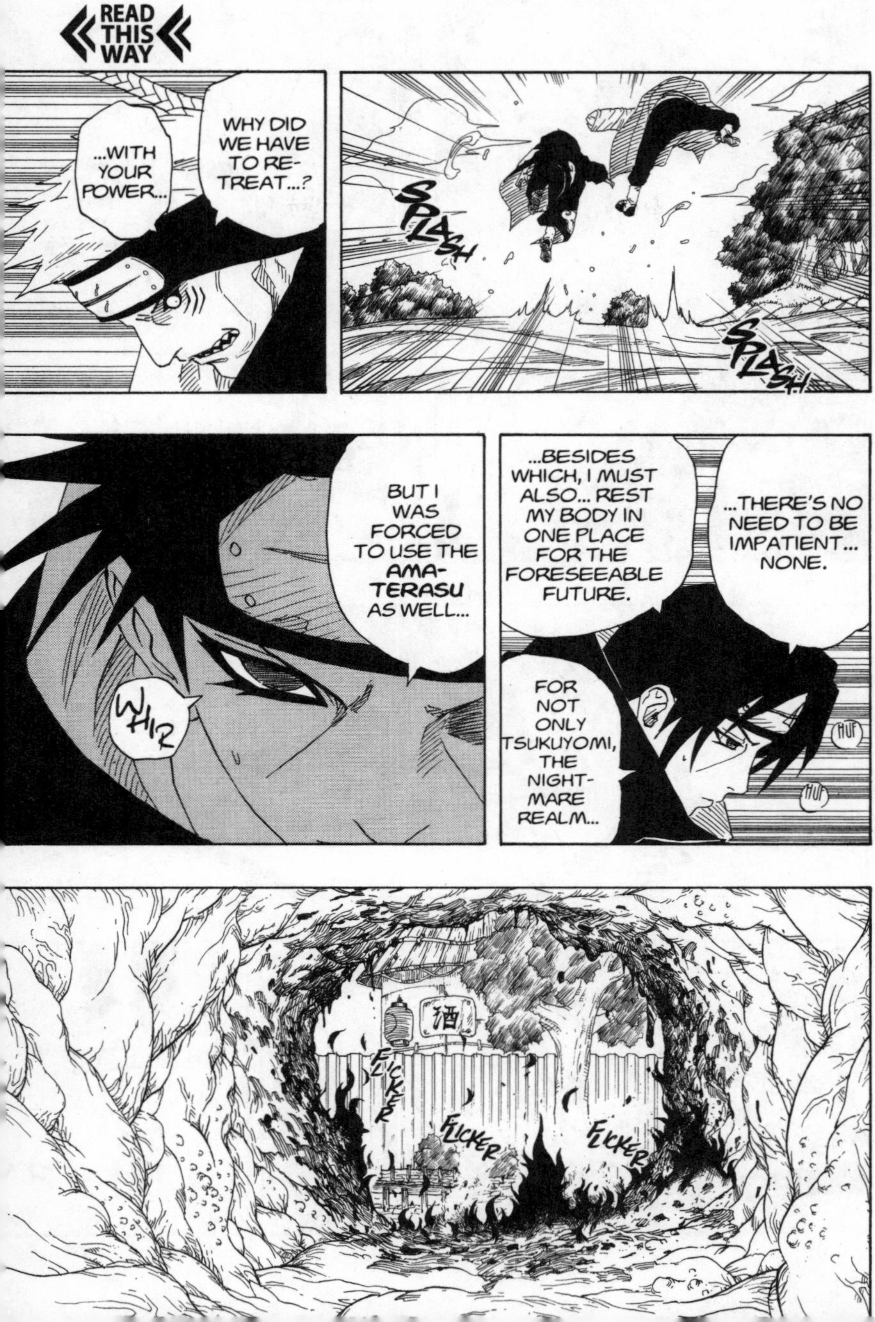
READ THIS WAY
SPLASH
SPLASH
WHY DID WE HAVE TO RE-TREAT...?
...WITH YOUR POWER...
...THERE'S NO NEED TO BE IMPATIENT... NONE.
...BESIDES WHICH, I MUST ALSO... REST MY BODY IN ONE PLACE FOR THE FORESEEABLE FUTURE.
FOR NOT ONLY TSUKUYOMI, THE NIGHT-MARE REALM...
HUF
HUF
BUT I WAS FORCED TO USE THE AMA-TERASU AS WELL...
WHIR
酒
FLICKER
FLICKER
FLICKER

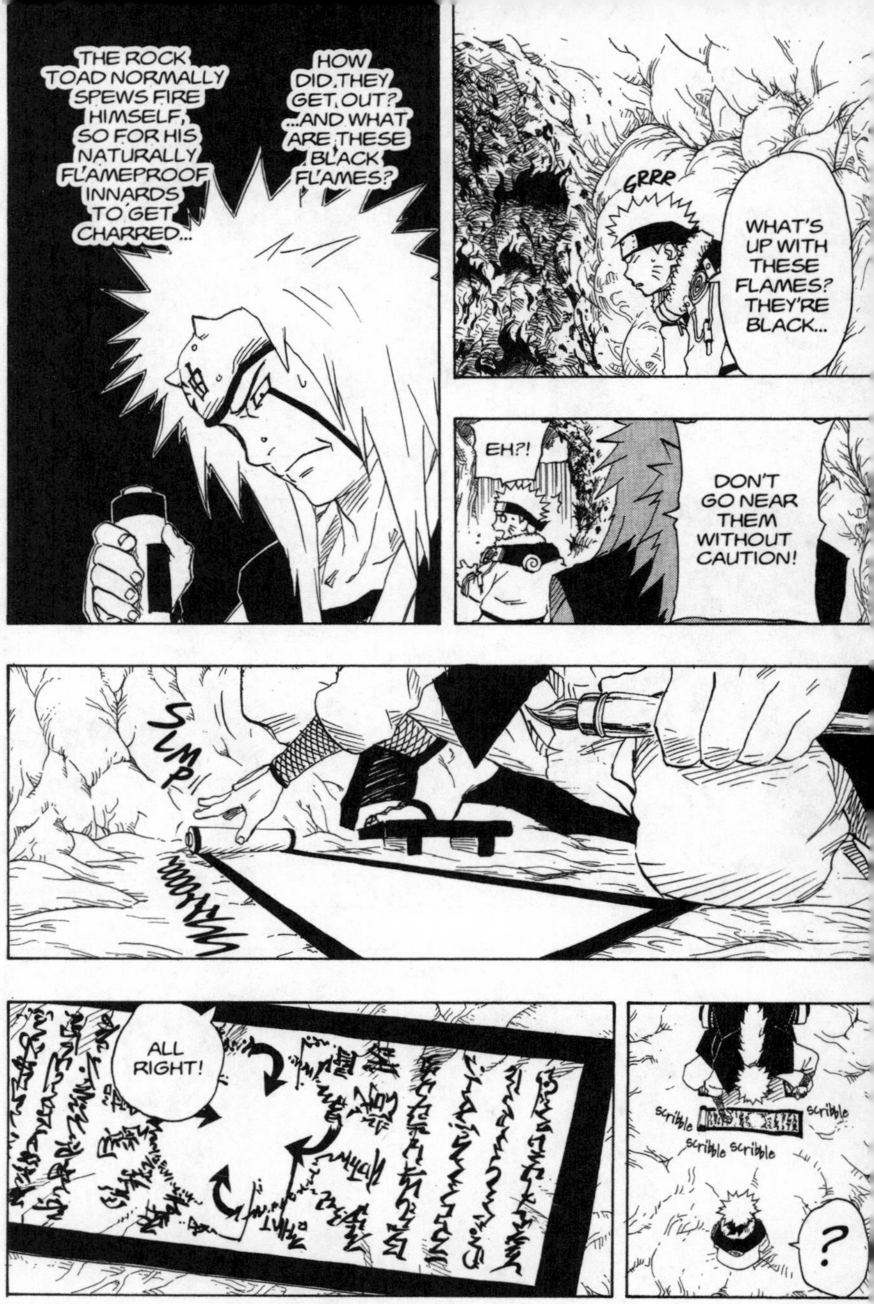
GRRR
WHAT'S UP WITH THESE FLAMES? THEY'RE BLACK...
DON'T GO NEAR THEM WITHOUT CAUTION!
EH?!
HOW DID THEY GET OUT? ...AND WHAT ARE THESE BLACK FLAMES?
THE ROCK TOAD NORMALLY SPEWS FIRE HIMSELF, SO FOR HIS NATURALLY FLAMEPROOF INNARDS TO GET CHARRED...
SLMP
scribble
scribble
scribble
scribble
?
ALL RIGHT!

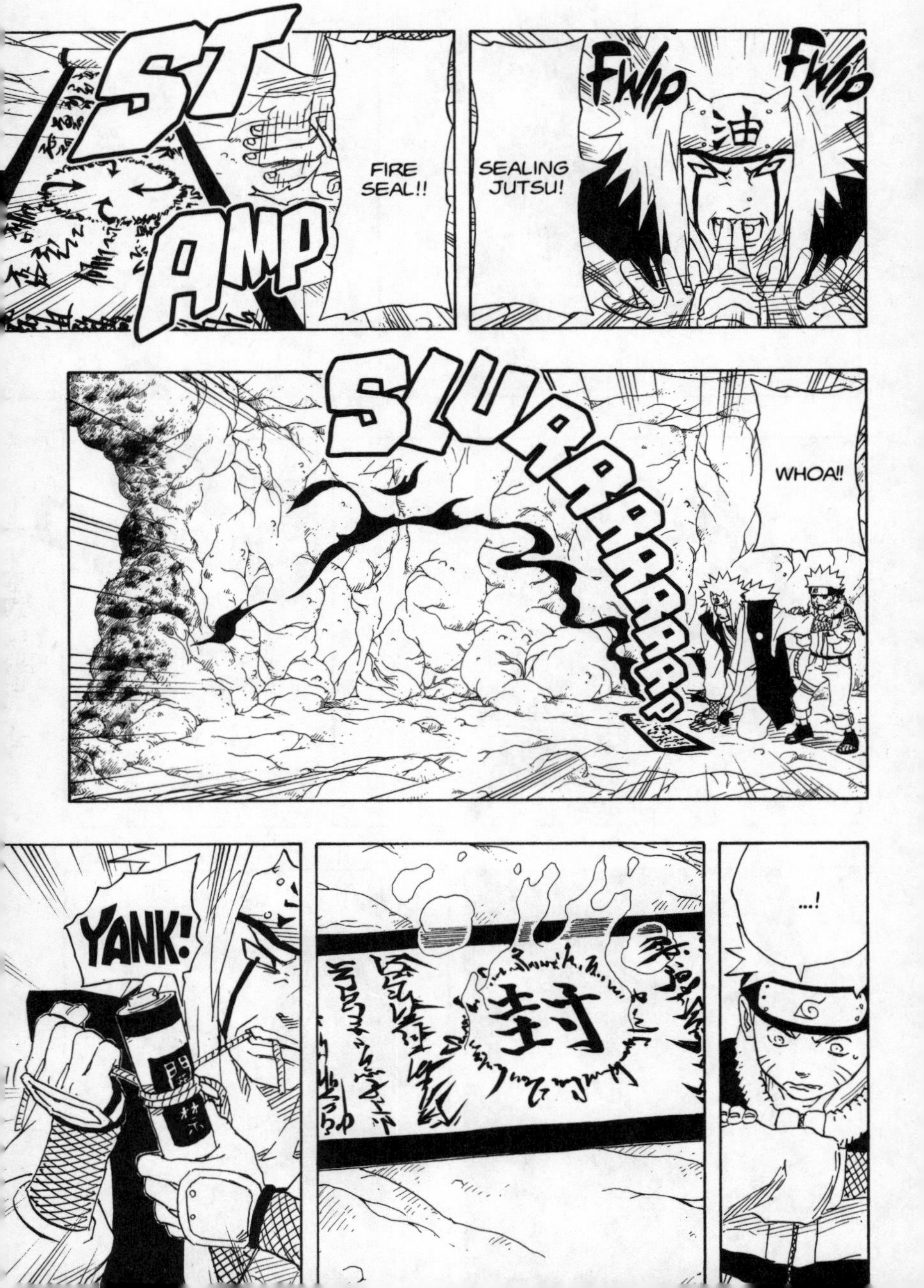
FWIP
FWIP
SEALING JUTSU!
FIRE SEAL!!
STAMP
WHOA!!
SLURRRRRRP
...!
YANK!

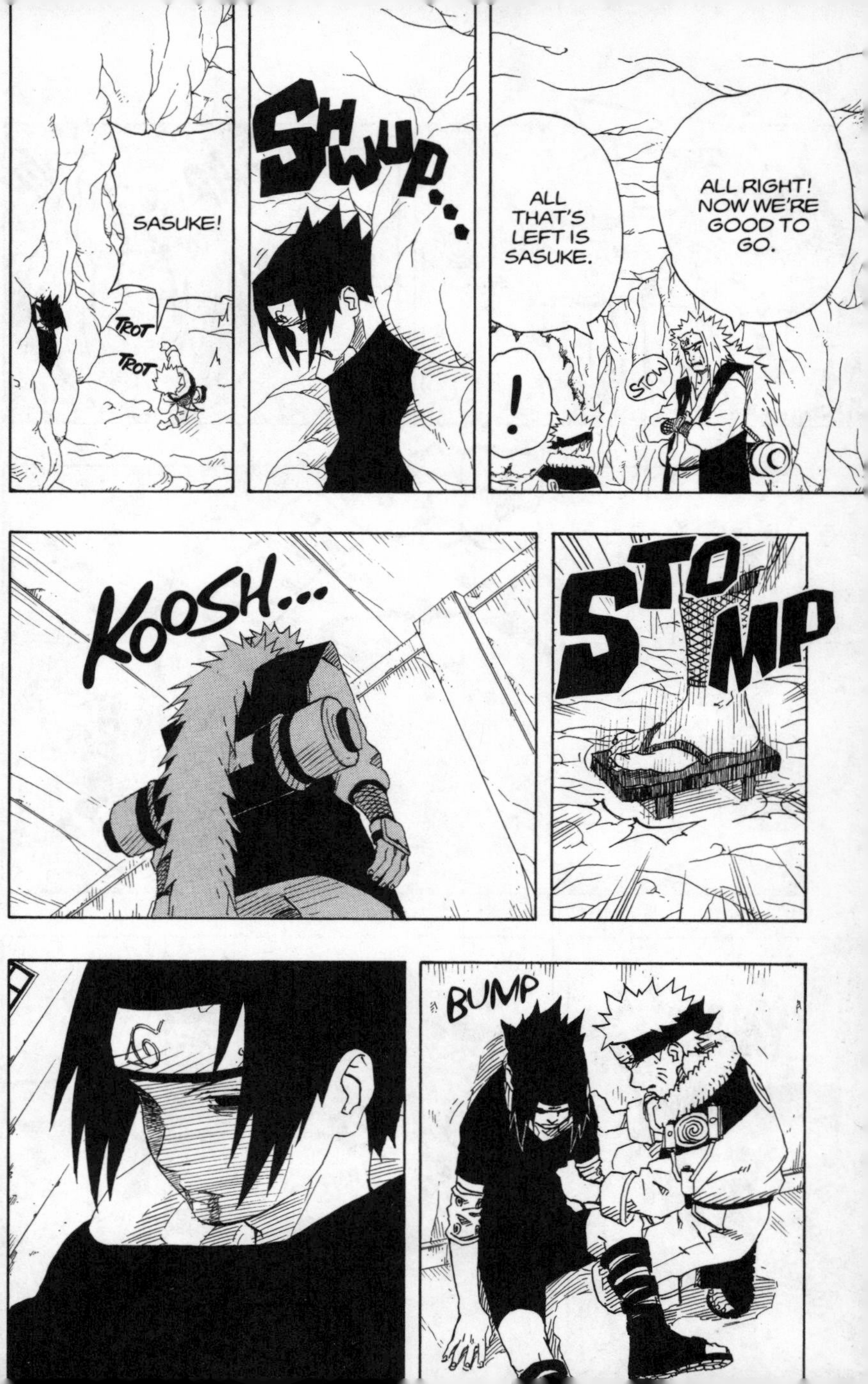
ALL RIGHT! NOW WE'RE GOOD TO GO.
STOW
ALL THAT'S LEFT IS SASUKE.
!
SHWUP...
SASUKE!
TROT
TROT
STOMP
KOOSH...
BUMP

READ THIS WAY

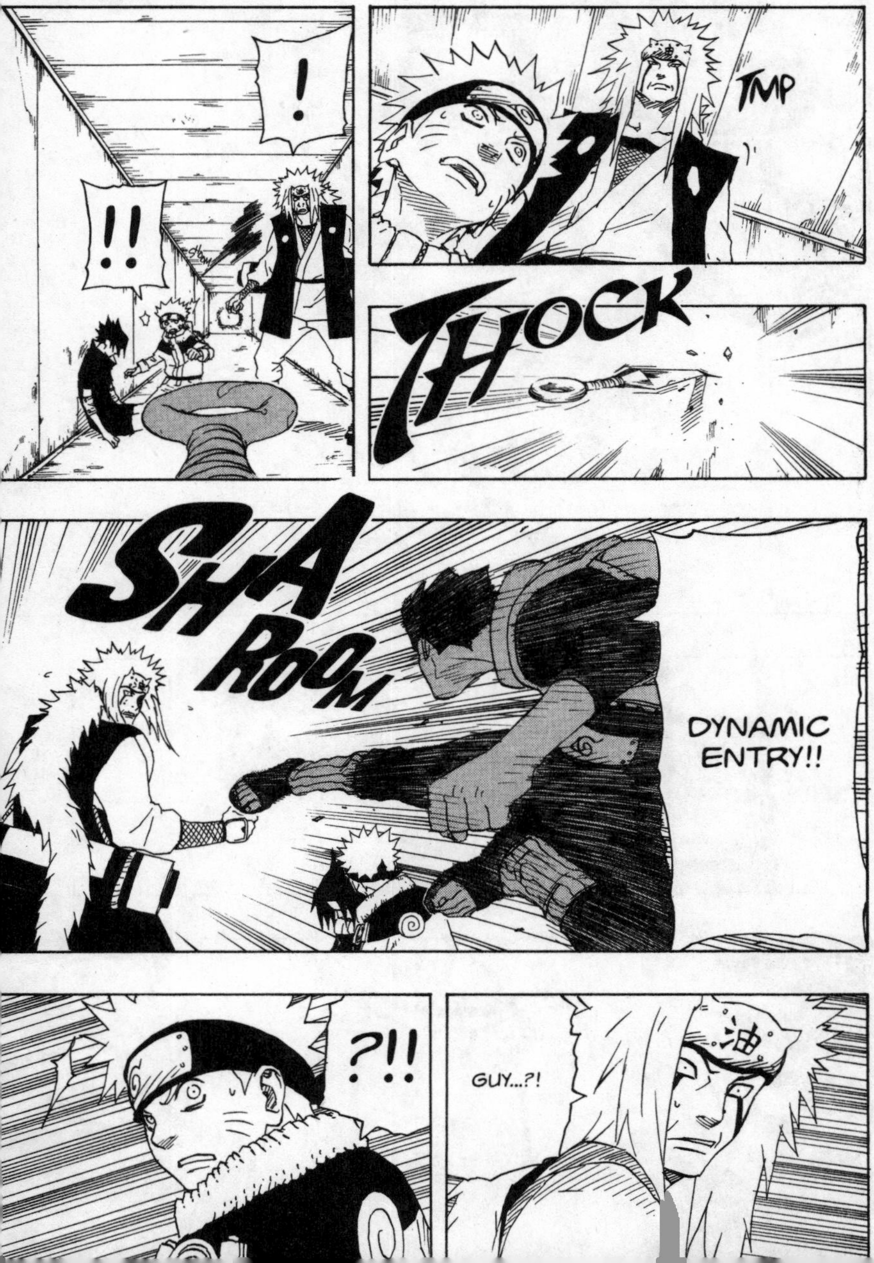
TMP
THOCK
!
!!
SHA ROOM
DYNAMIC ENTRY!!
GUY...?!
?!!

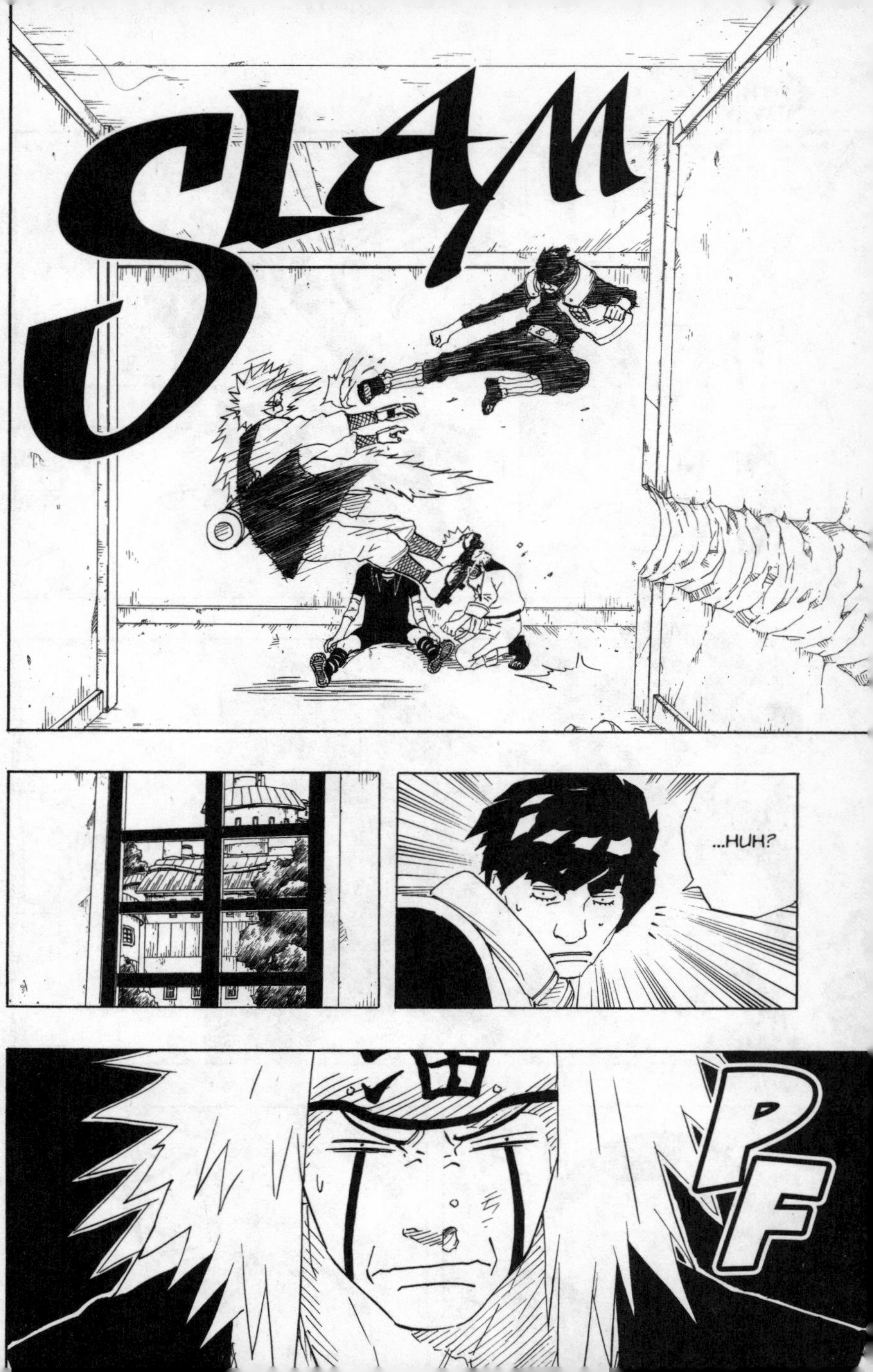
SLAM
...HUH?
PF

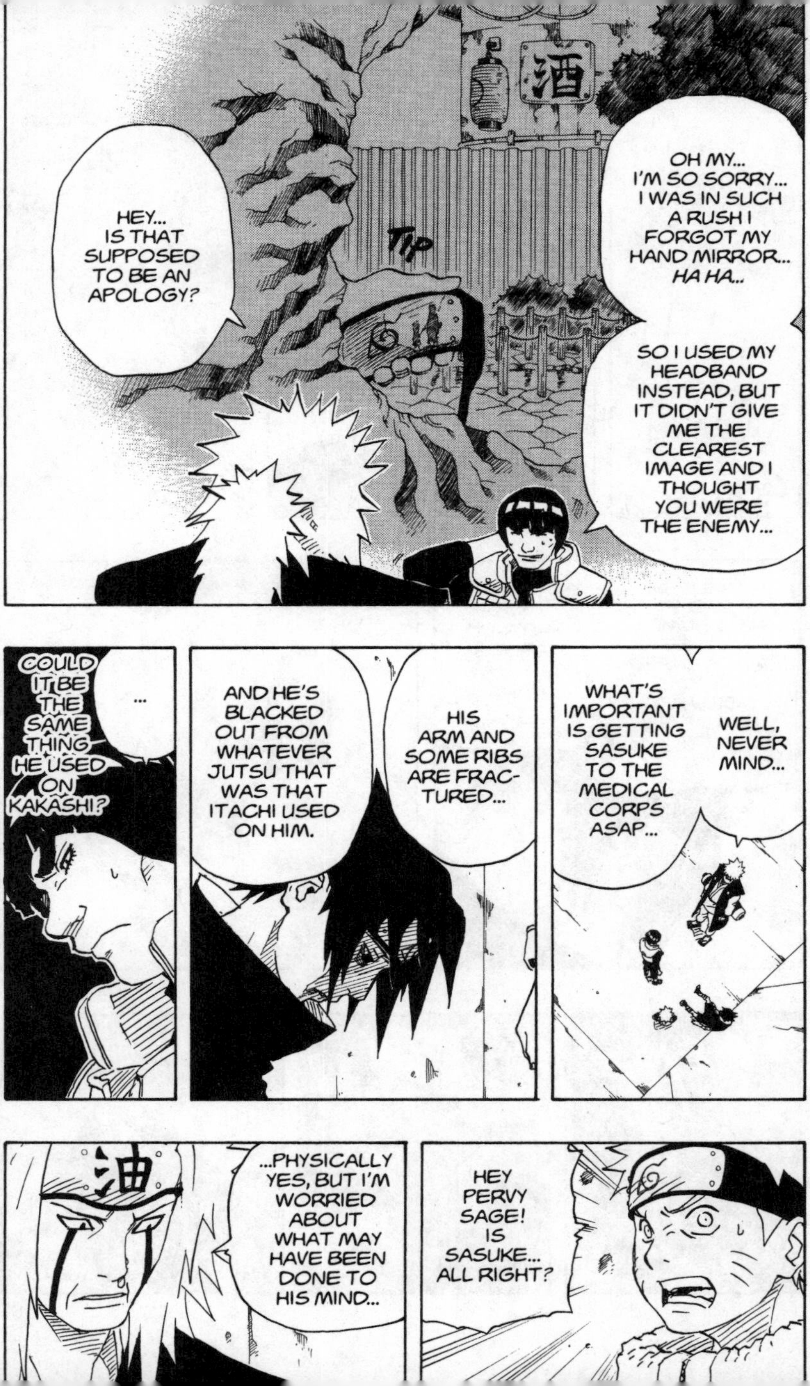
酒
OH MY... I'M SO SORRY... I WAS IN SUCH A RUSH I FORGOT MY HAND MIRROR... *HA HA...*
SO I USED MY HEADBAND INSTEAD, BUT IT DIDN'T GIVE ME THE CLEAREST IMAGE AND I THOUGHT YOU WERE THE ENEMY...
TIP
HEY... IS THAT SUPPOSED TO BE AN APOLOGY?
WELL, NEVER MIND...
WHAT'S IMPORTANT IS GETTING SASUKE TO THE MEDICAL CORPS ASAP...
HIS ARM AND SOME RIBS ARE FRAC-TURED...
AND HE'S BLACKED OUT FROM WHATEVER JUTSU THAT WAS THAT ITACHI USED ON HIM.
...
COULD IT BE THE SAME THING HE USED ON KAKASHI?
HEY PERVY SAGE! IS SASUKE... ALL RIGHT?
油
...PHYSICALLY YES, BUT I'M WORRIED ABOUT WHAT MAY HAVE BEEN DONE TO HIS MIND...

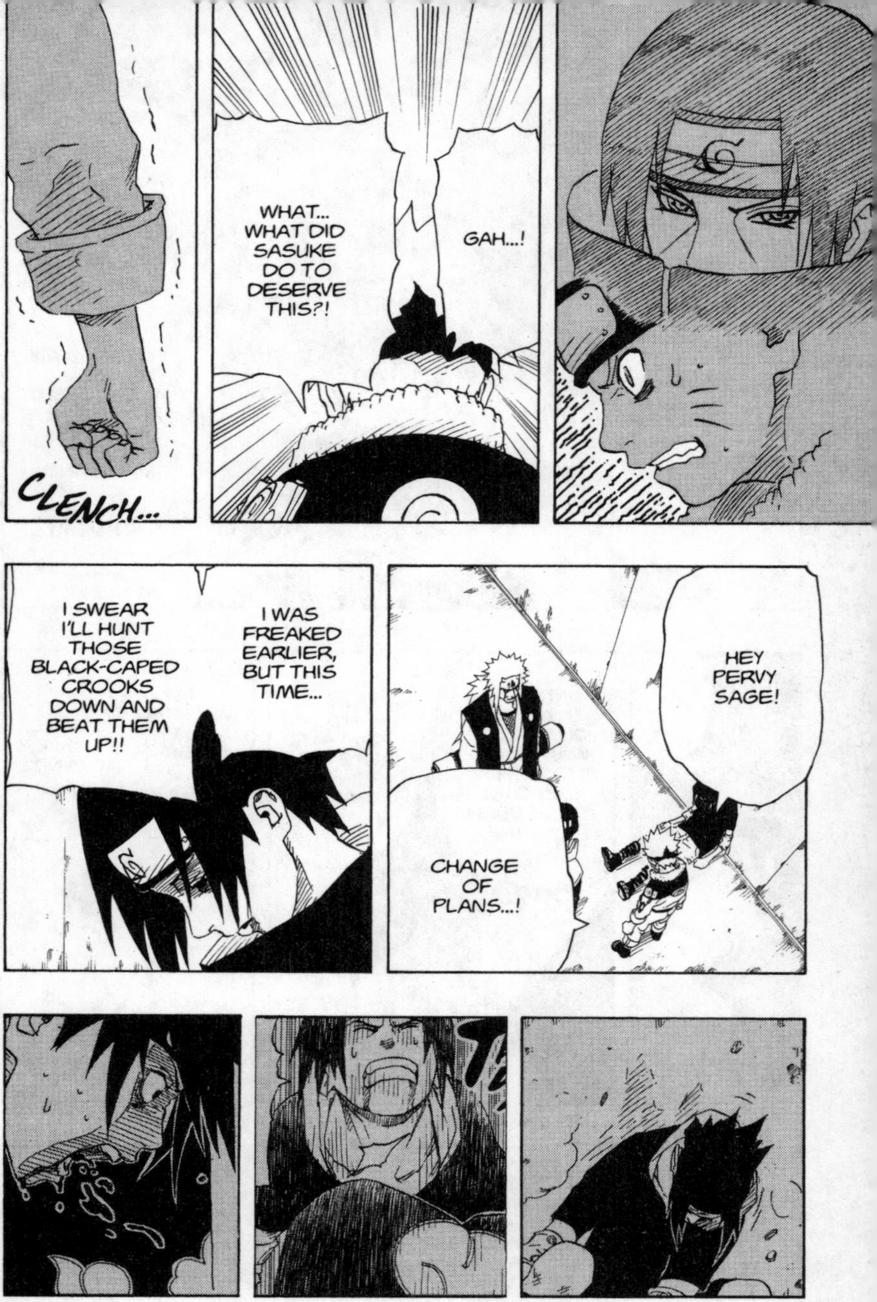
GAH...!
WHAT... WHAT DID SASUKE DO TO DESERVE THIS?!
CLENCH...
HEY PERVY SAGE!
CHANGE OF PLANS...!
I WAS FREAKED EARLIER, BUT THIS TIME...
I SWEAR I'LL HUNT THOSE BLACK-CAPED CROOKS DOWN AND BEAT THEM UP!!

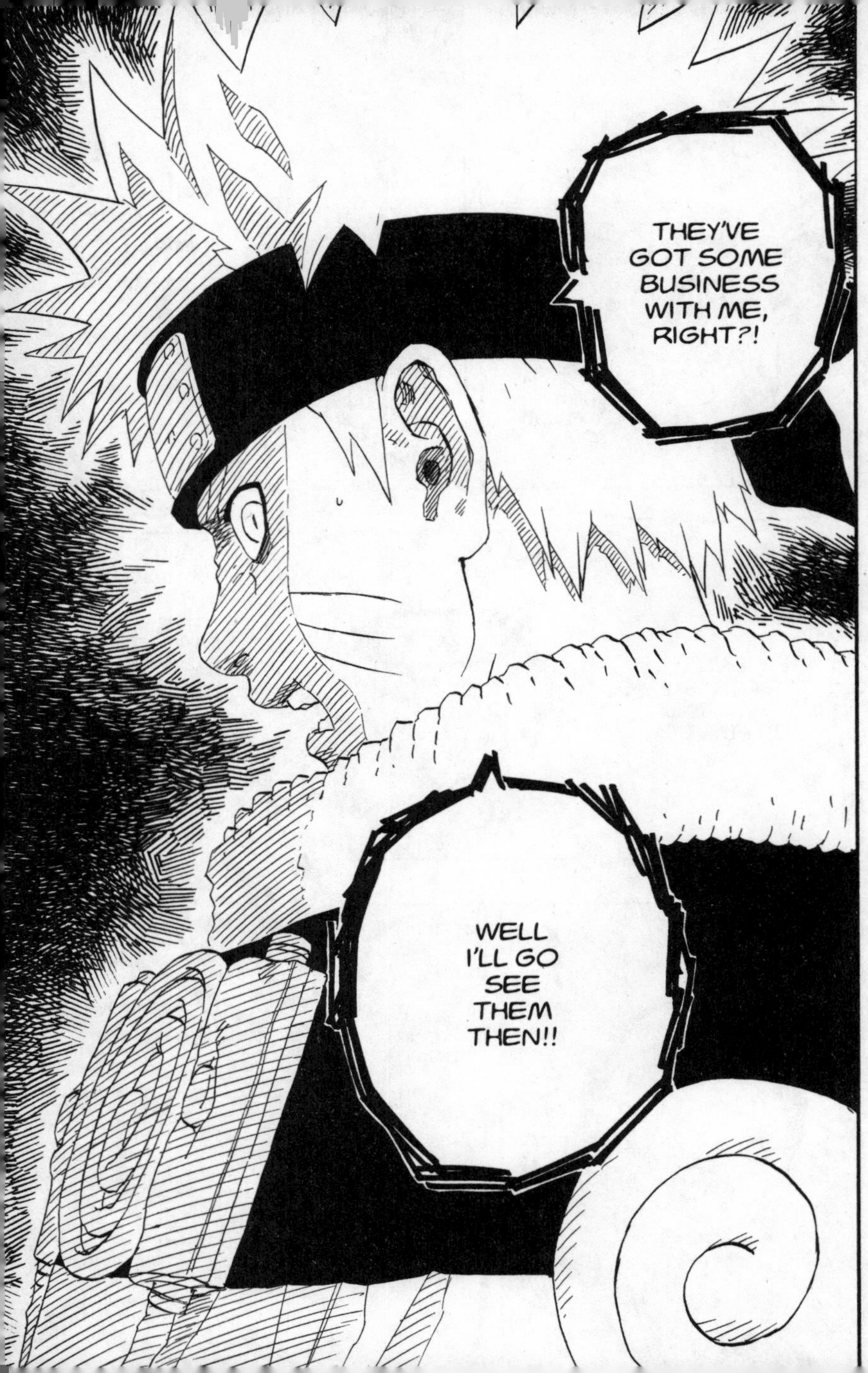
THEY'VE GOT SOME BUSINESS WITH ME, RIGHT?!
WELL I'LL GO SEE THEM THEN!!

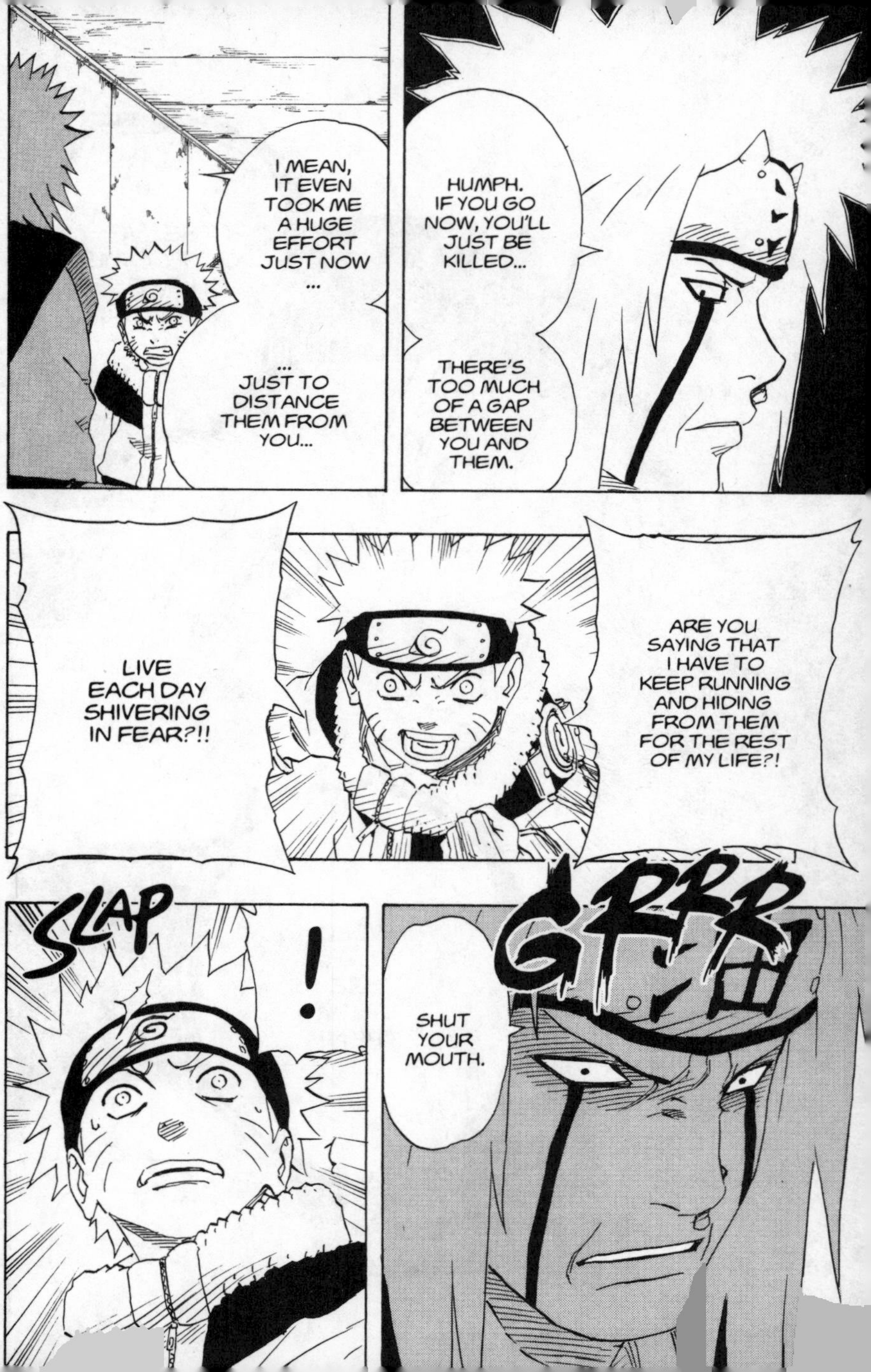
HUMPH. IF YOU GO NOW, YOU'LL JUST BE KILLED...
THERE'S TOO MUCH OF A GAP BETWEEN YOU AND THEM.
I MEAN, IT EVEN TOOK ME A HUGE EFFORT JUST NOW ...
... JUST TO DISTANCE THEM FROM YOU...
ARE YOU SAYING THAT I HAVE TO KEEP RUNNING AND HIDING FROM THEM FOR THE REST OF MY LIFE?!
LIVE EACH DAY SHIVERING IN FEAR?!!
GRRR
SHUT YOUR MOUTH.
SLAP
!

READ THIS WAY

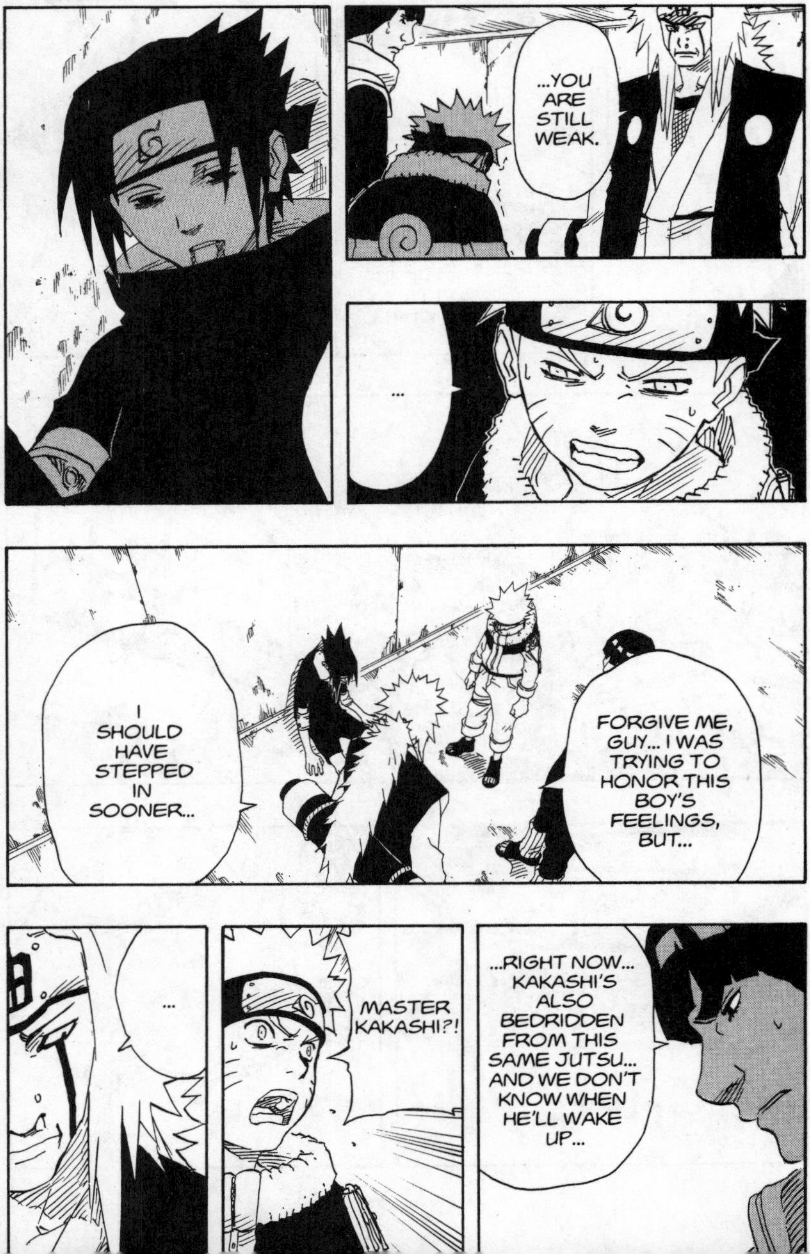
...YOU ARE STILL WEAK.
...
FORGIVE ME, GUY... I WAS TRYING TO HONOR THIS BOY'S FEELINGS, BUT...
I SHOULD HAVE STEPPED IN SOONER...
...RIGHT NOW... KAKASHI'S ALSO BEDRIDDEN FROM THIS SAME JUTSU... AND WE DON'T KNOW WHEN HE'LL WAKE UP...
MASTER KAKASHI?!
...

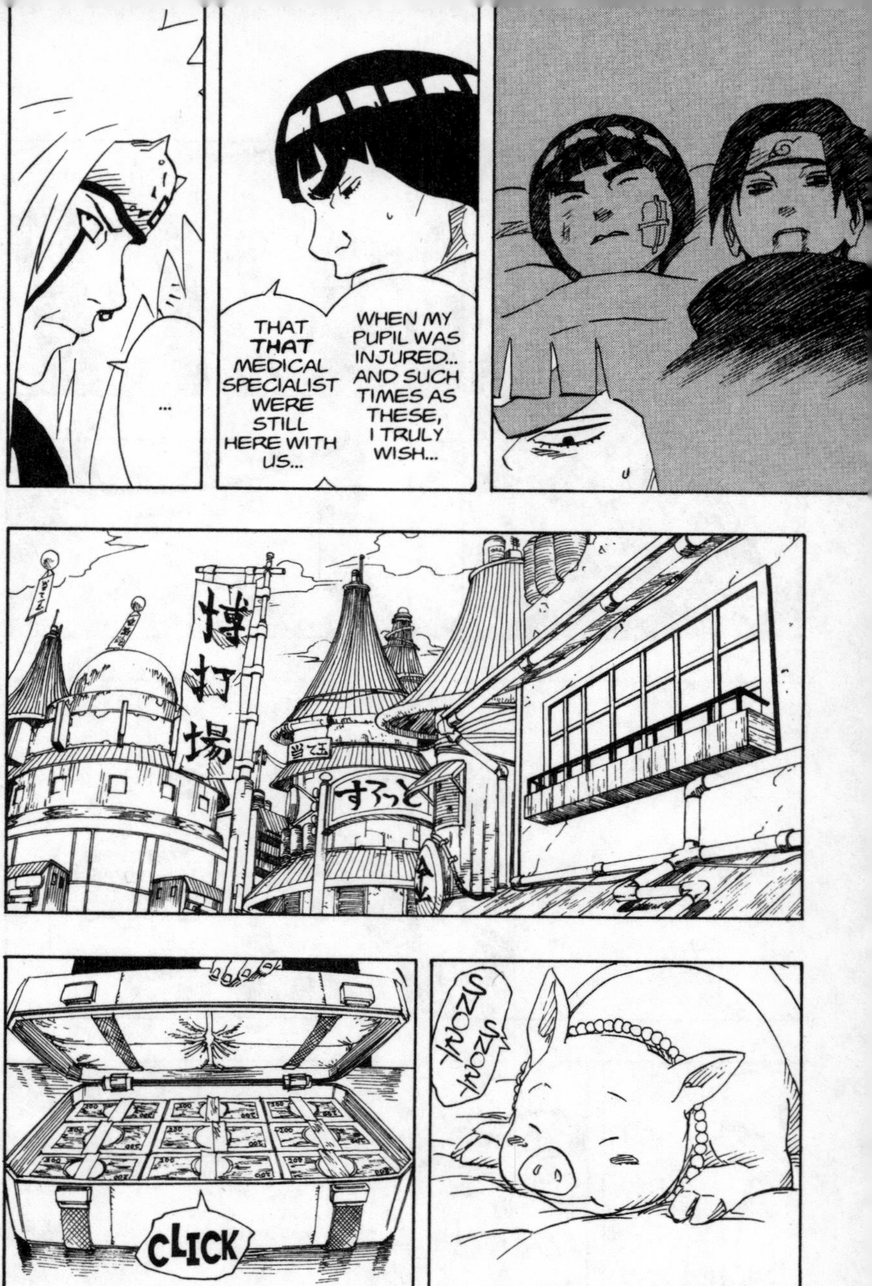
WHEN MY PUPIL WAS INJURED... AND SUCH TIMES AS THESE, I TRULY WISH...
THAT THAT MEDICAL SPECIALIST WERE STILL HERE WITH US...
...
博打場
すろっと
SNORT SNORT
CLICK

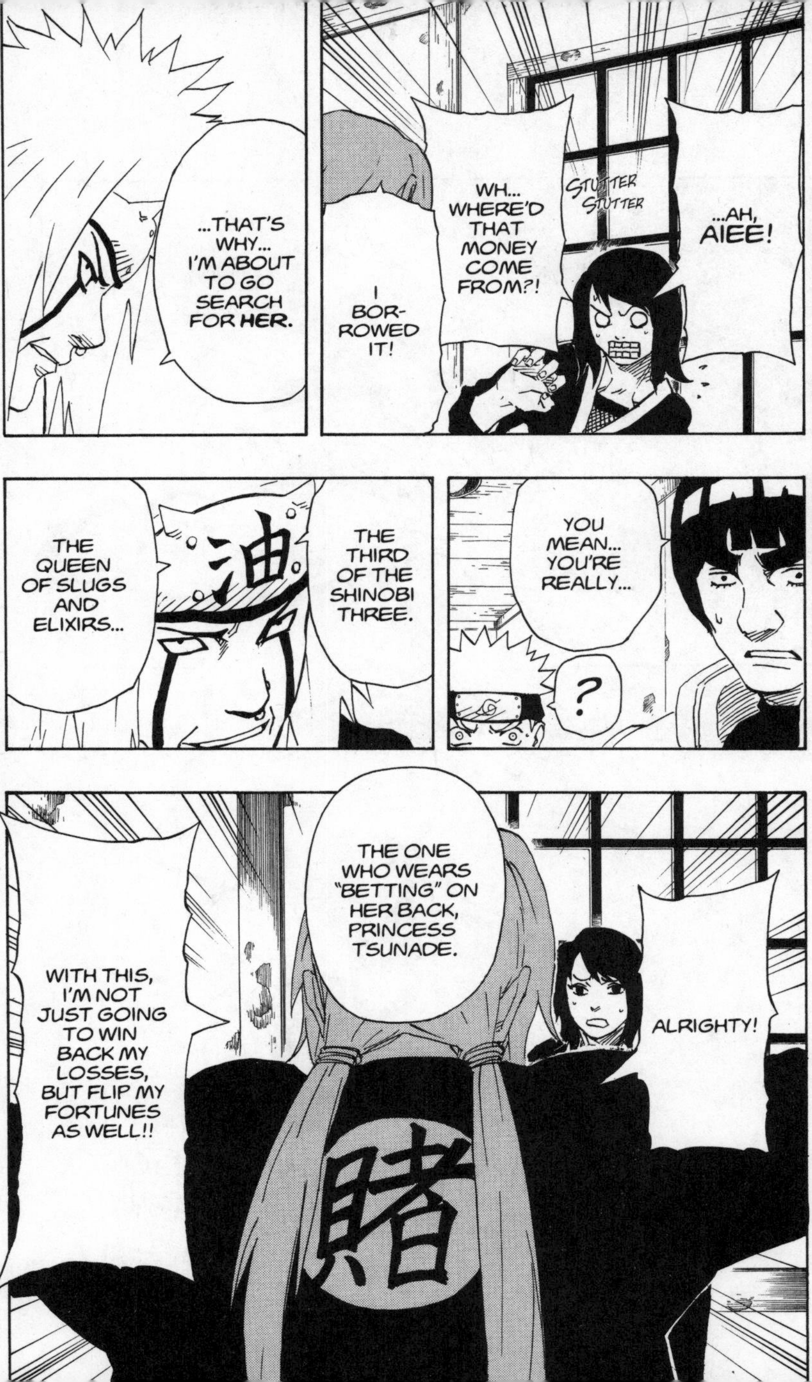

...AH, AIEE!
STUTTER STUTTER
WH... WHERE'D THAT MONEY COME FROM?!
I BOR-ROWED IT!
...THAT'S WHY... I'M ABOUT TO GO SEARCH FOR **HER**.
YOU MEAN... YOU'RE REALLY...
?
THE THIRD OF THE SHINOBI THREE.
THE QUEEN OF SLUGS AND ELIXIRS...
ALRIGHTY!
THE ONE WHO WEARS "BETTING" ON HER BACK, PRINCESS TSUNADE.
WITH THIS, I'M NOT JUST GOING TO WIN BACK MY LOSSES, BUT FLIP MY FORTUNES AS WELL!!

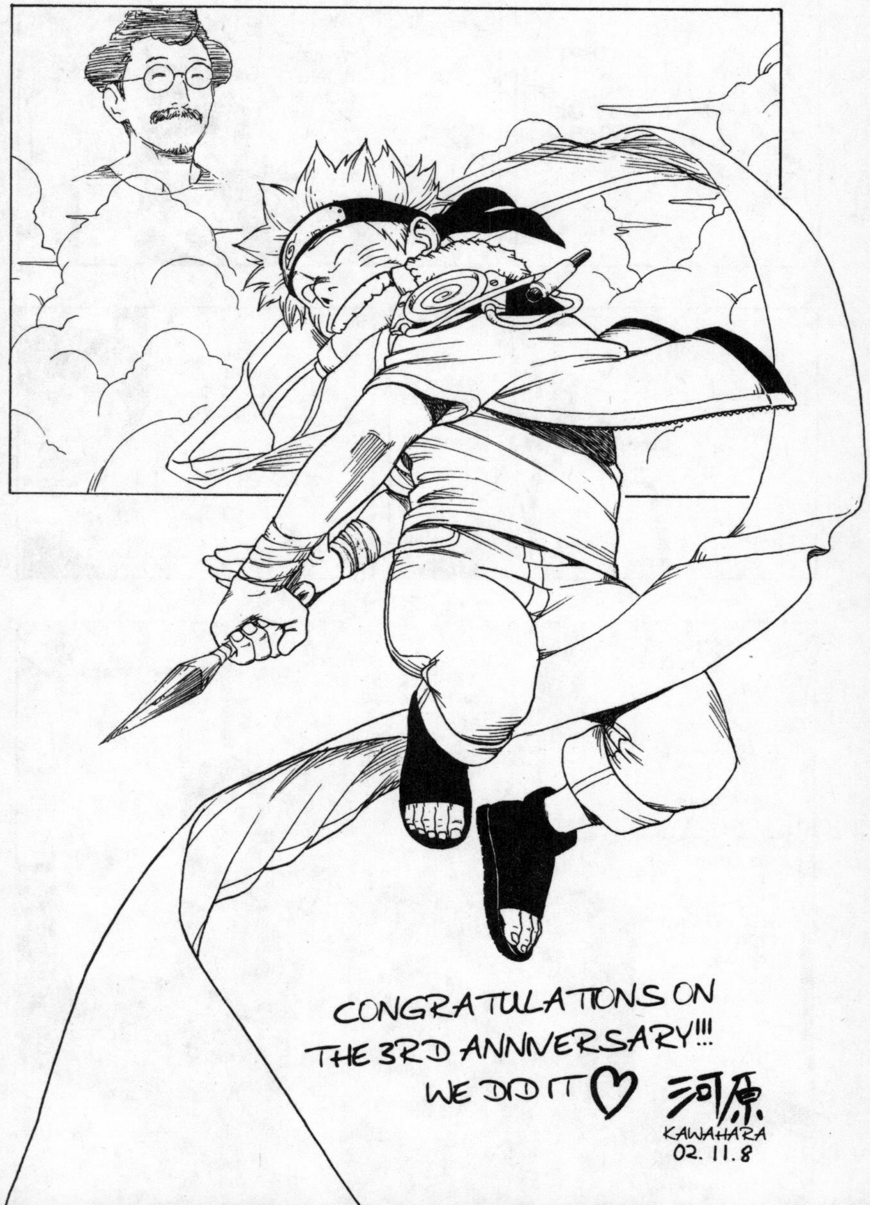
CONGRATULATIONS ON
THE 3RD ANNIVERSARY!!!
WE DID IT ♡
河原
KAWAHARA
02. 11. 8

Number 149: The Legendary...!!

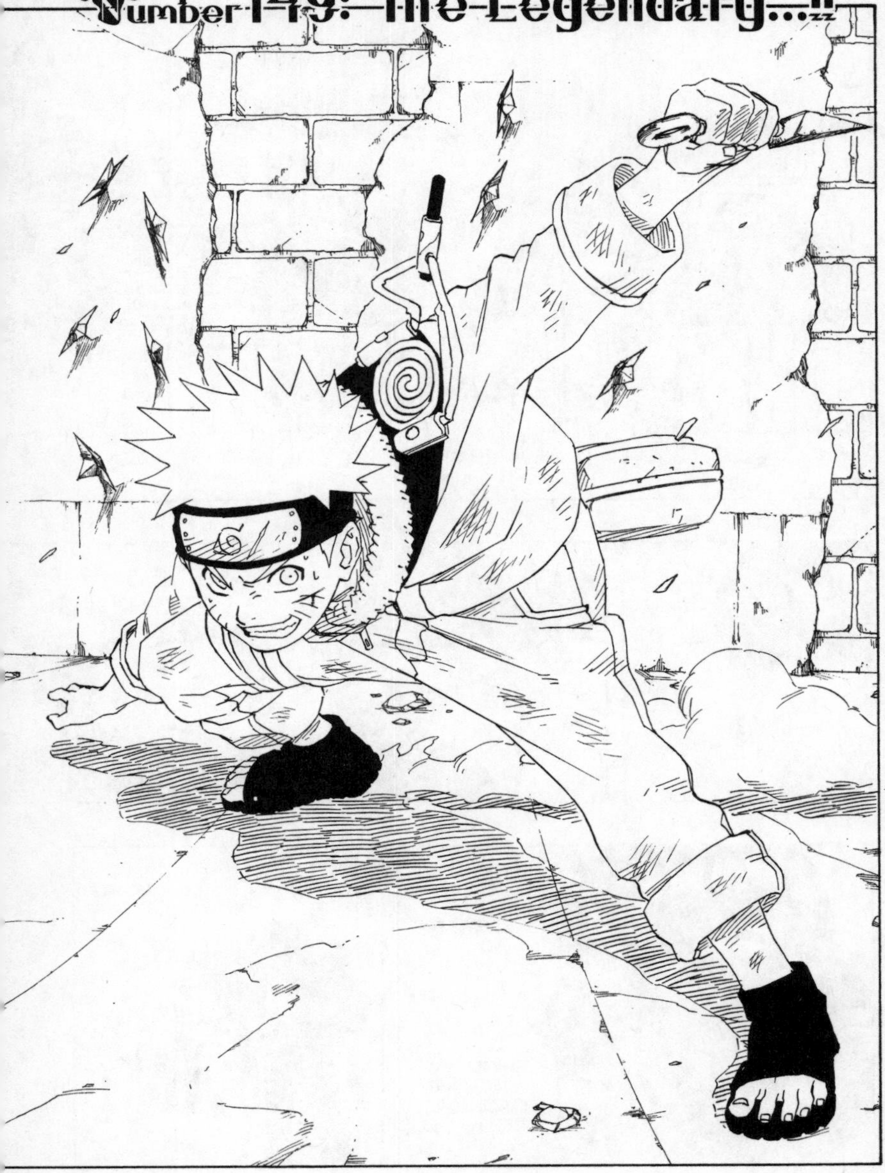

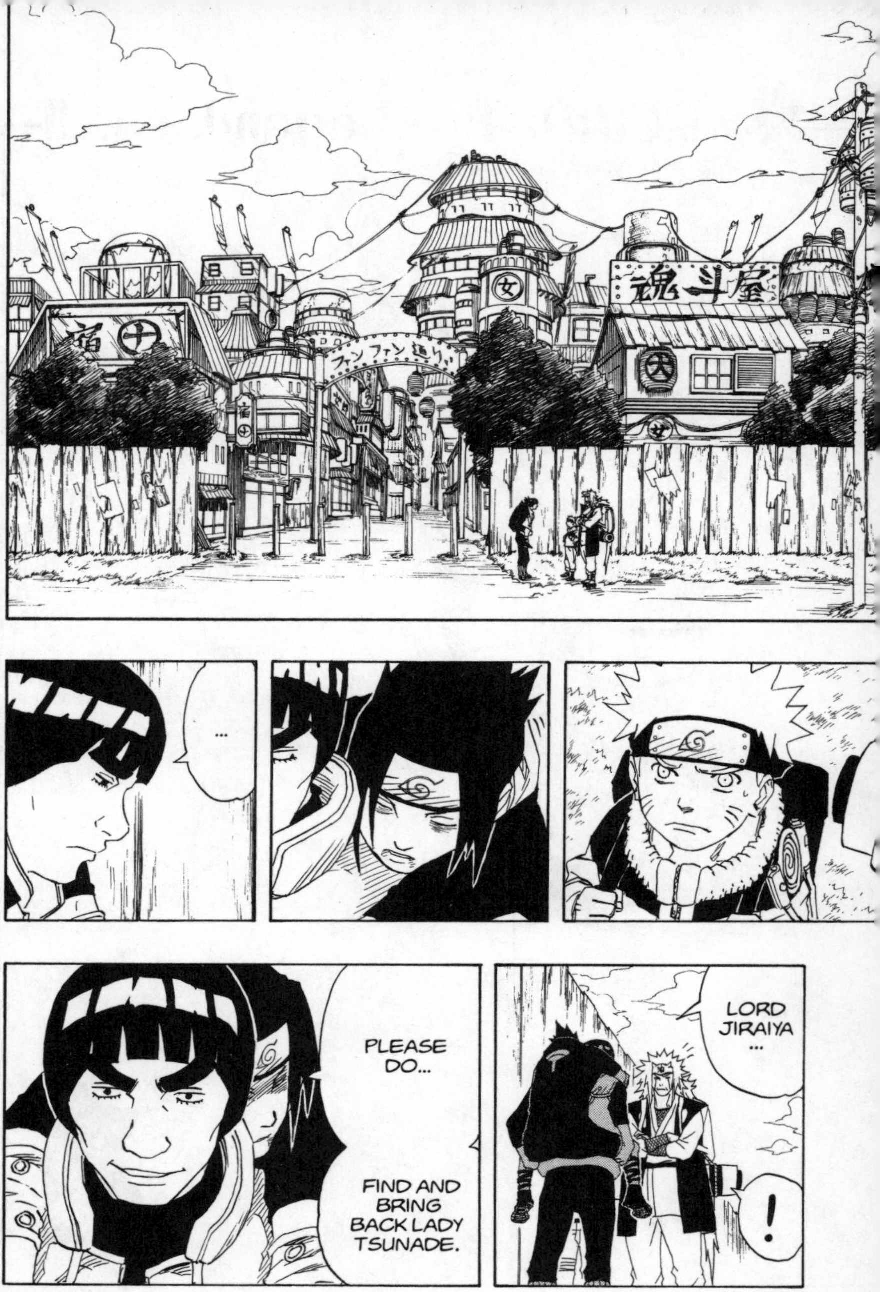
...
LORD JIRAIYA ...
!
PLEASE DO...
FIND AND BRING BACK LADY TSUNADE.

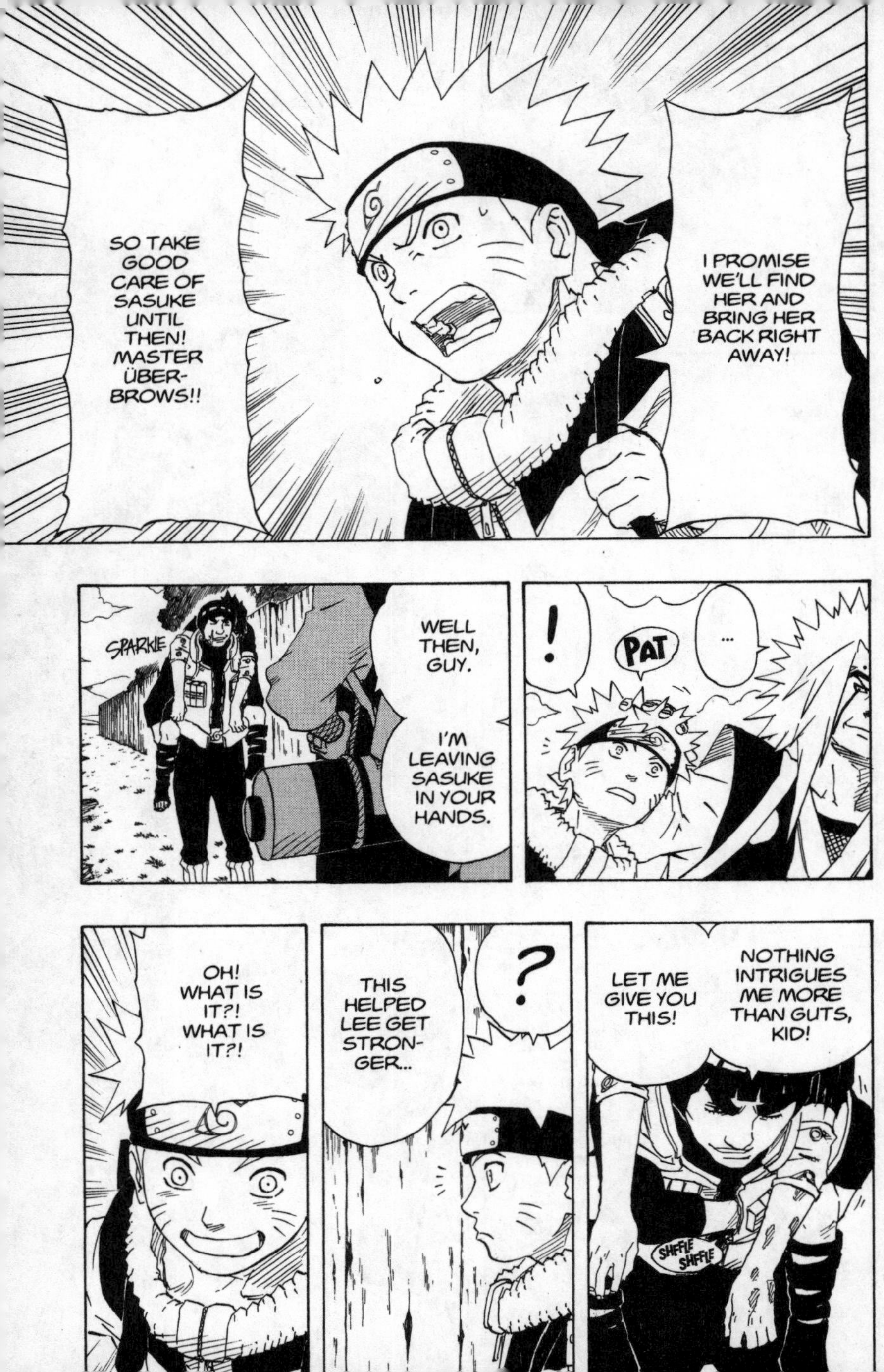
I PROMISE WE'LL FIND HER AND BRING HER BACK RIGHT AWAY!
SO TAKE GOOD CARE OF SASUKE UNTIL THEN! MASTER ÜBER-BROWS!!
...
!
PAT
WELL THEN, GUY.
I'M LEAVING SASUKE IN YOUR HANDS.
SPARKLE
NOTHING INTRIGUES ME MORE THAN GUTS, KID!
LET ME GIVE YOU THIS!
SHFFLE SHFFLE
?
THIS HELPED LEE GET STRONGER...
OH! WHAT IS IT?! WHAT IS IT?!

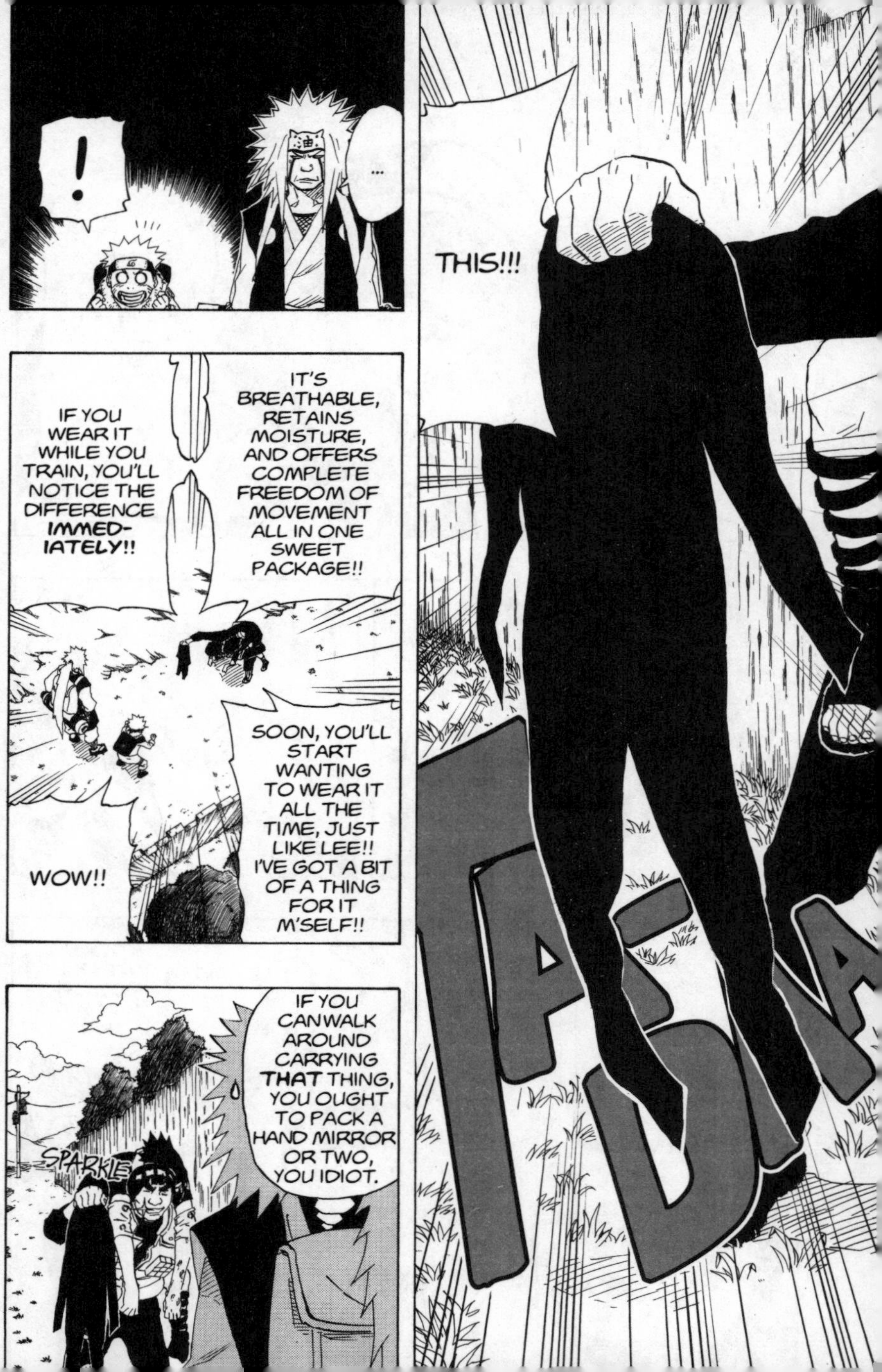
THIS!!!
TA-DA
!
...
IT'S BREATHABLE, RETAINS MOISTURE, AND OFFERS COMPLETE FREEDOM OF MOVEMENT ALL IN ONE SWEET PACKAGE!!
IF YOU WEAR IT WHILE YOU TRAIN, YOU'LL NOTICE THE DIFFERENCE **IMMED-IATELY**!!
SOON, YOU'LL START WANTING TO WEAR IT ALL THE TIME, JUST LIKE LEE!! I'VE GOT A BIT OF A THING FOR IT M'SELF!!
WOW!!
IF YOU CANWALK AROUND CARRYING **THAT** THING, YOU OUGHT TO PACK A HAND MIRROR OR TWO, YOU IDIOT.
SPARKLE

READ THIS WAY

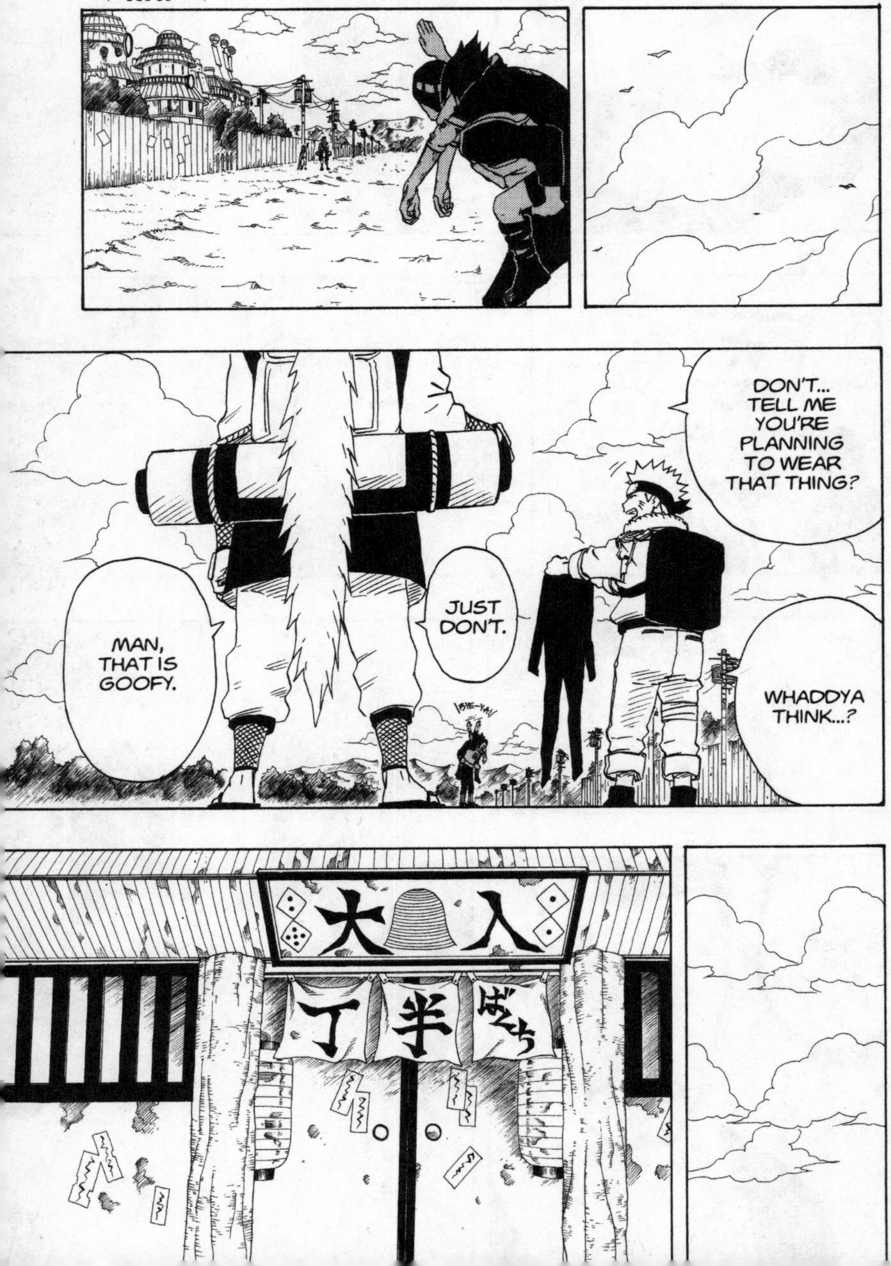
DON'T... TELL ME YOU'RE PLANNING TO WEAR THAT THING?
WHADDYA THINK...?
JUST DON'T.
BYE-YA!
MAN, THAT IS GOOFY.
大入
丁半
ばくち

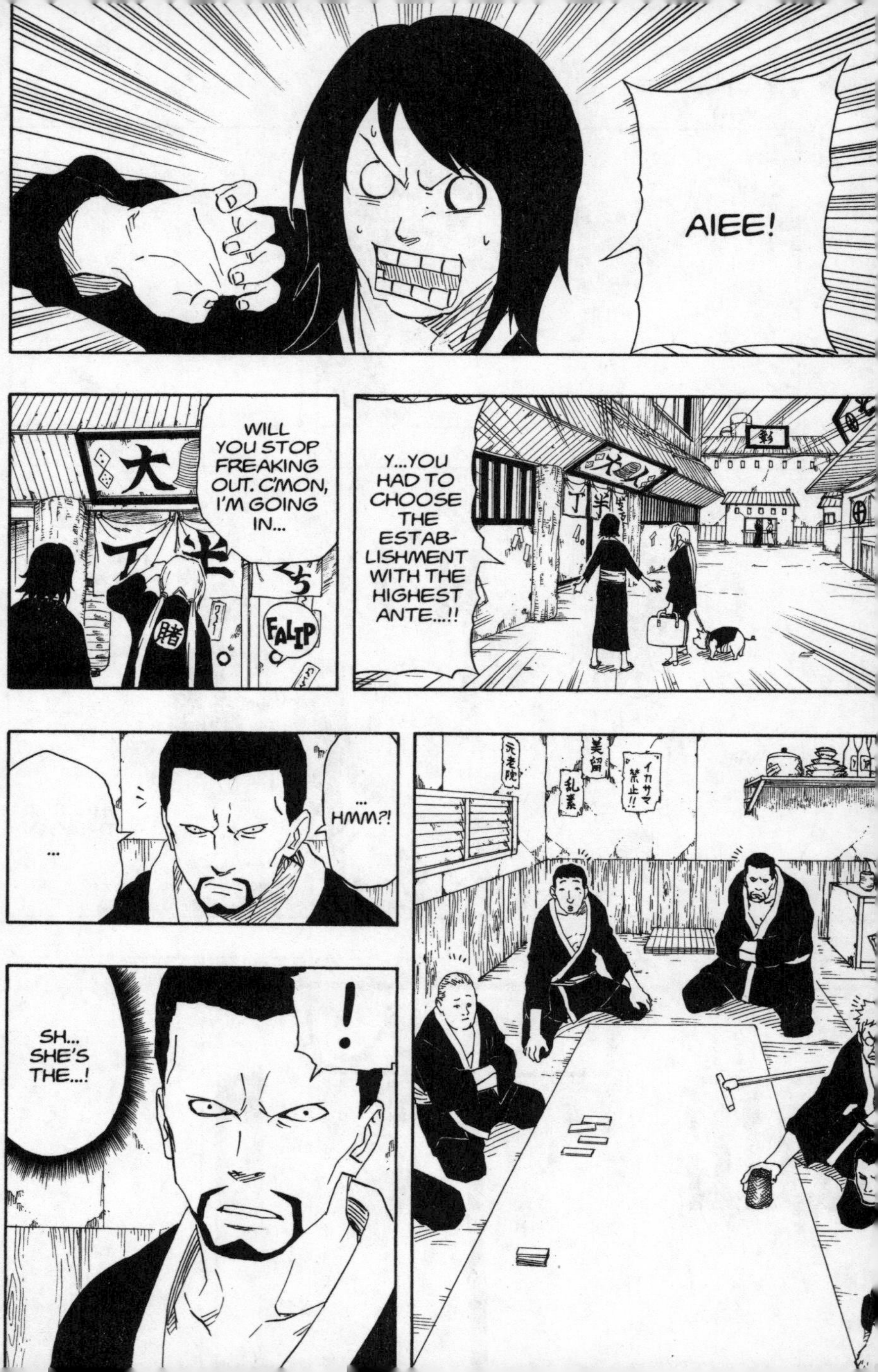
AIEE!
Y...YOU HAD TO CHOOSE THE ESTABLISHMENT WITH THE HIGHEST ANTE...!!
WILL YOU STOP FREAKING OUT. C'MON, I'M GOING IN...
FALIP
イカサマ禁止!!
...HMM?!
...
!
SH... SHE'S THE...!

READ THIS WAY

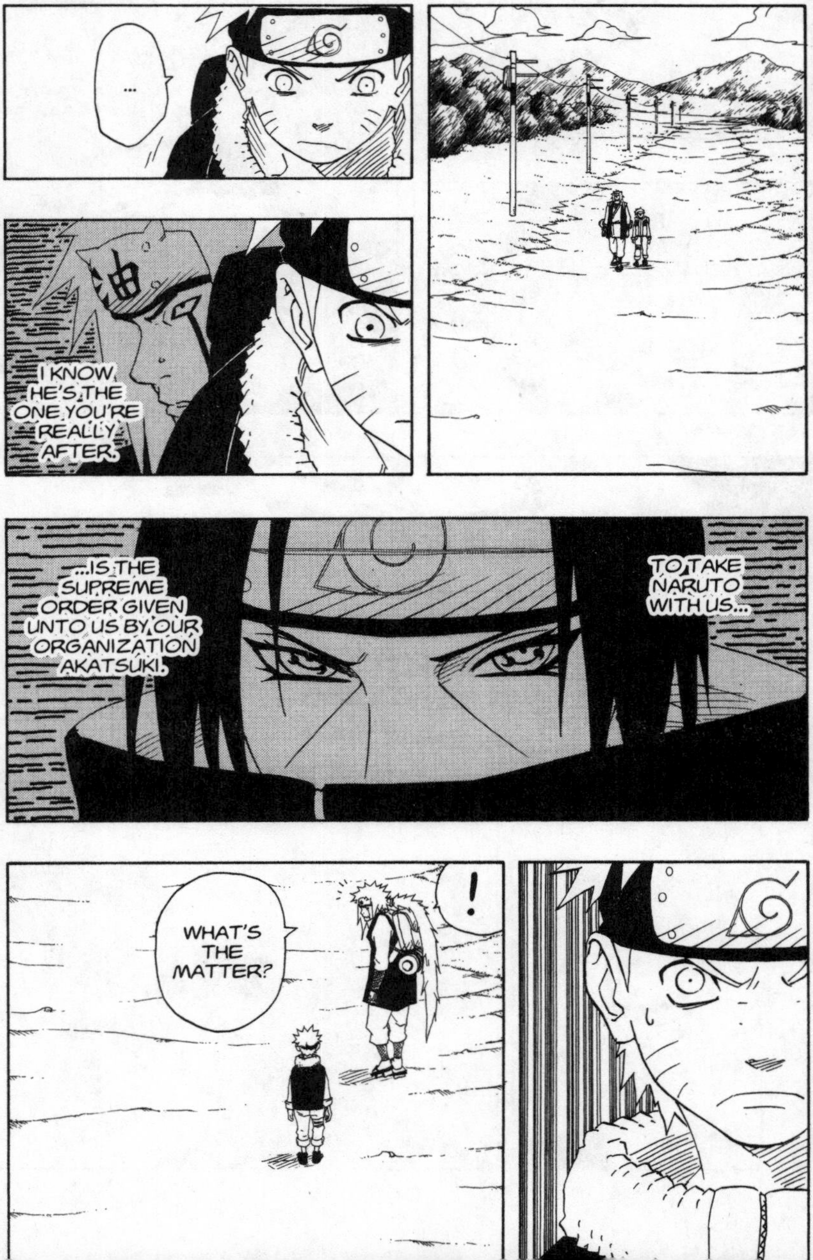
...
I KNOW HE'S THE ONE YOU'RE REALLY AFTER.
TO TAKE NARUTO WITH US...
...IS THE SUPREME ORDER GIVEN UNTO US BY OUR ORGANIZATION AKATSUKI.
!
WHAT'S THE MATTER?

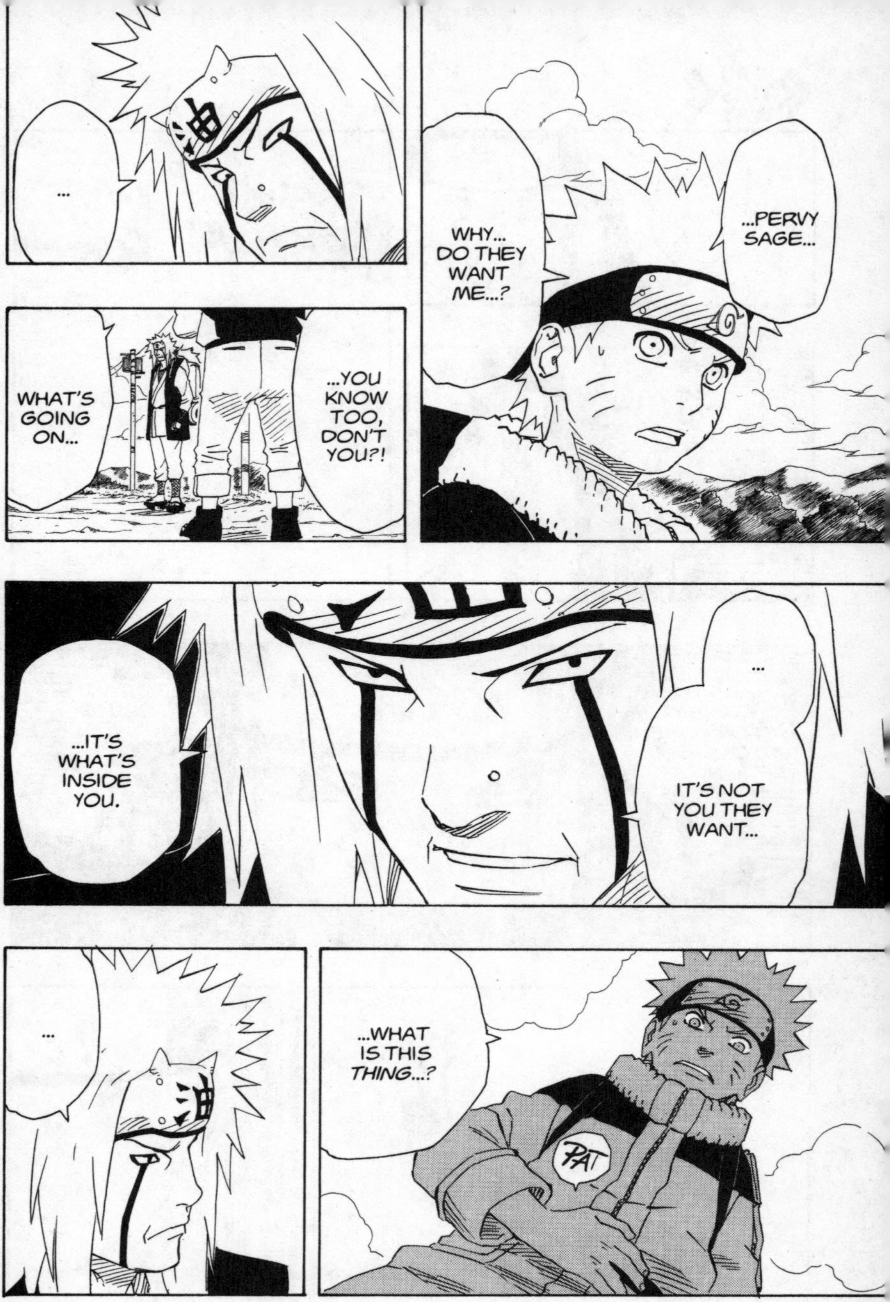
...PERVY SAGE...
WHY... DO THEY WANT ME...?
...
...YOU KNOW TOO, DON'T YOU?!
WHAT'S GOING ON...
...
IT'S NOT YOU THEY WANT...
...IT'S WHAT'S INSIDE YOU.
...WHAT IS THIS *THING*...?
PAT
...

READ THIS WAY

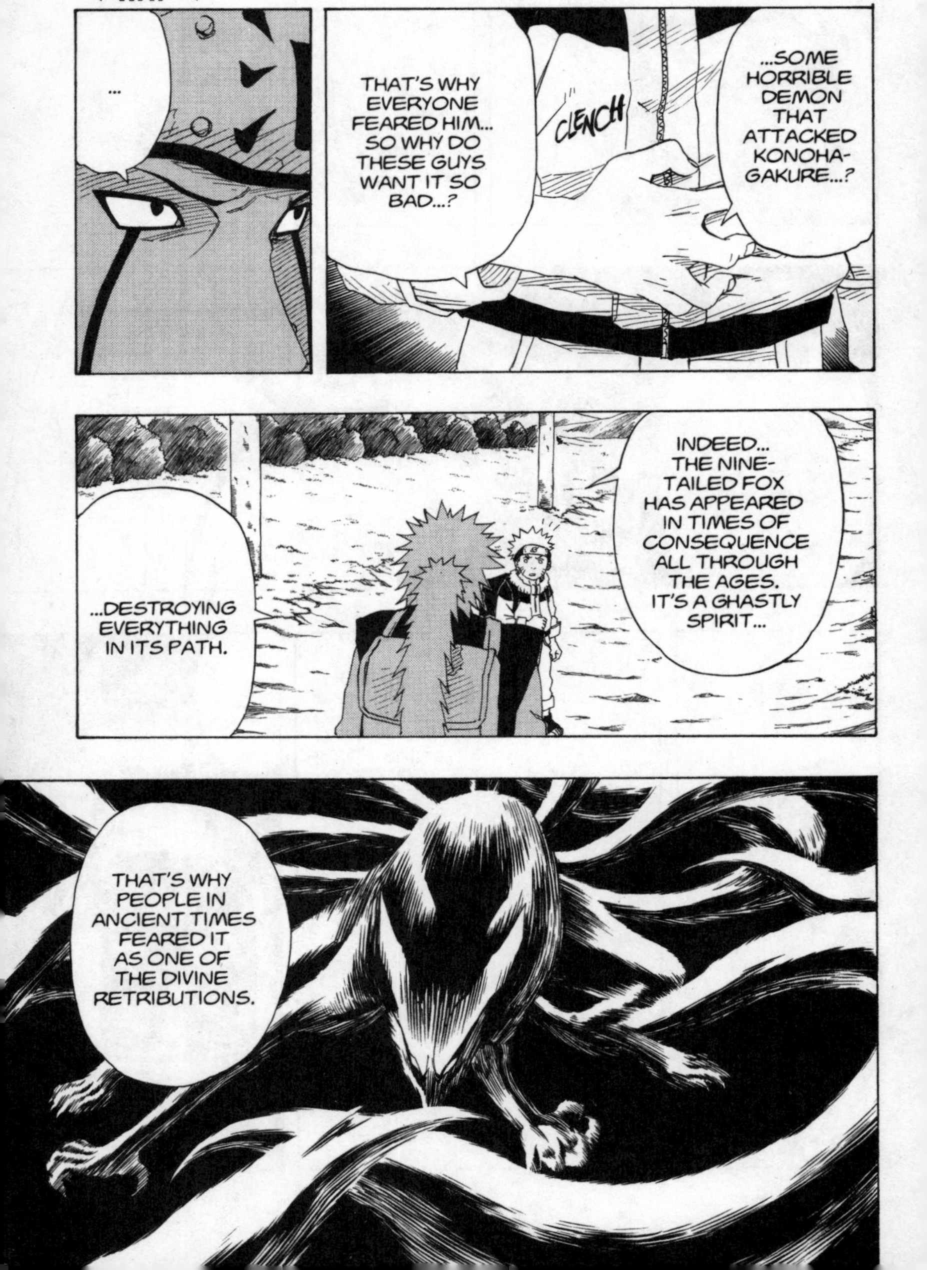
...SOME HORRIBLE DEMON THAT ATTACKED KONOHAGAKURE...?
CLENCH
THAT'S WHY EVERYONE FEARED HIM... SO WHY DO THESE GUYS WANT IT SO BAD...?
...
INDEED... THE NINE-TAILED FOX HAS APPEARED IN TIMES OF CONSEQUENCE ALL THROUGH THE AGES. IT'S A GHASTLY SPIRIT...
...DESTROYING EVERYTHING IN ITS PATH.
THAT'S WHY PEOPLE IN ANCIENT TIMES FEARED IT AS ONE OF THE DIVINE RETRIBUTIONS.

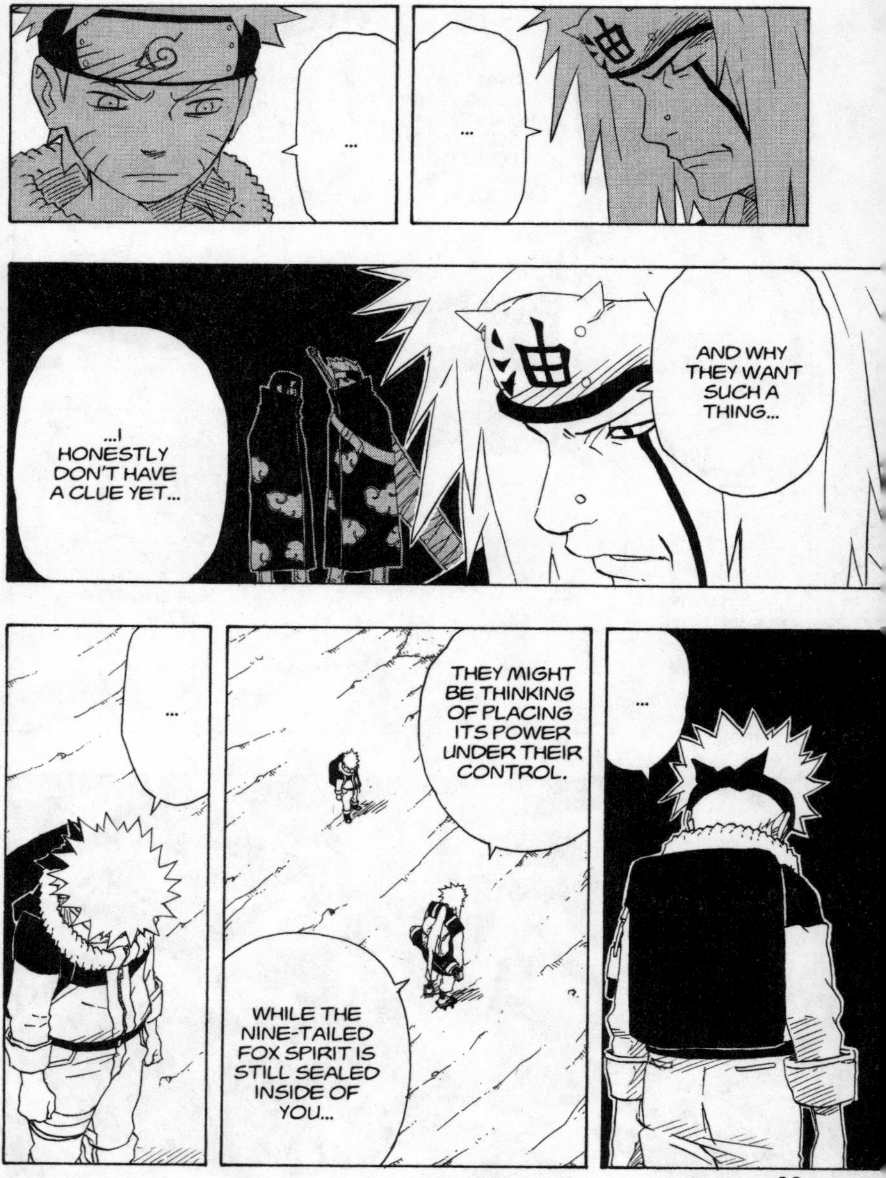
...
...
AND WHY THEY WANT SUCH A THING...
...I HONESTLY DON'T HAVE A CLUE YET...
...
THEY MIGHT BE THINKING OF PLACING ITS POWER UNDER THEIR CONTROL.
WHILE THE NINE-TAILED FOX SPIRIT IS STILL SEALED INSIDE OF YOU...
...

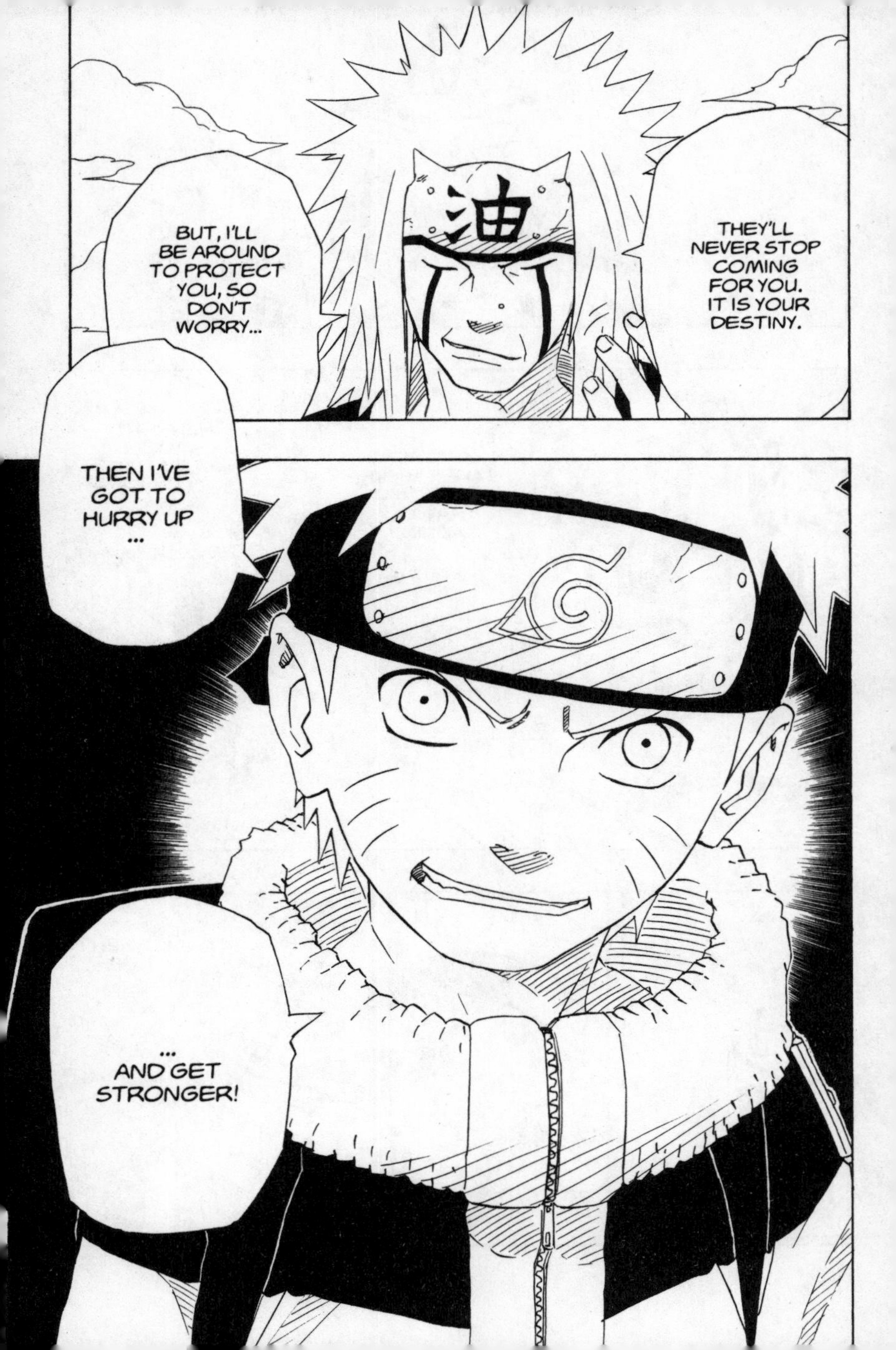
THEY'LL NEVER STOP COMING FOR YOU. IT IS YOUR DESTINY.
BUT, I'LL BE AROUND TO PROTECT YOU, SO DON'T WORRY...
THEN I'VE GOT TO HURRY UP ...
... AND GET STRONGER!

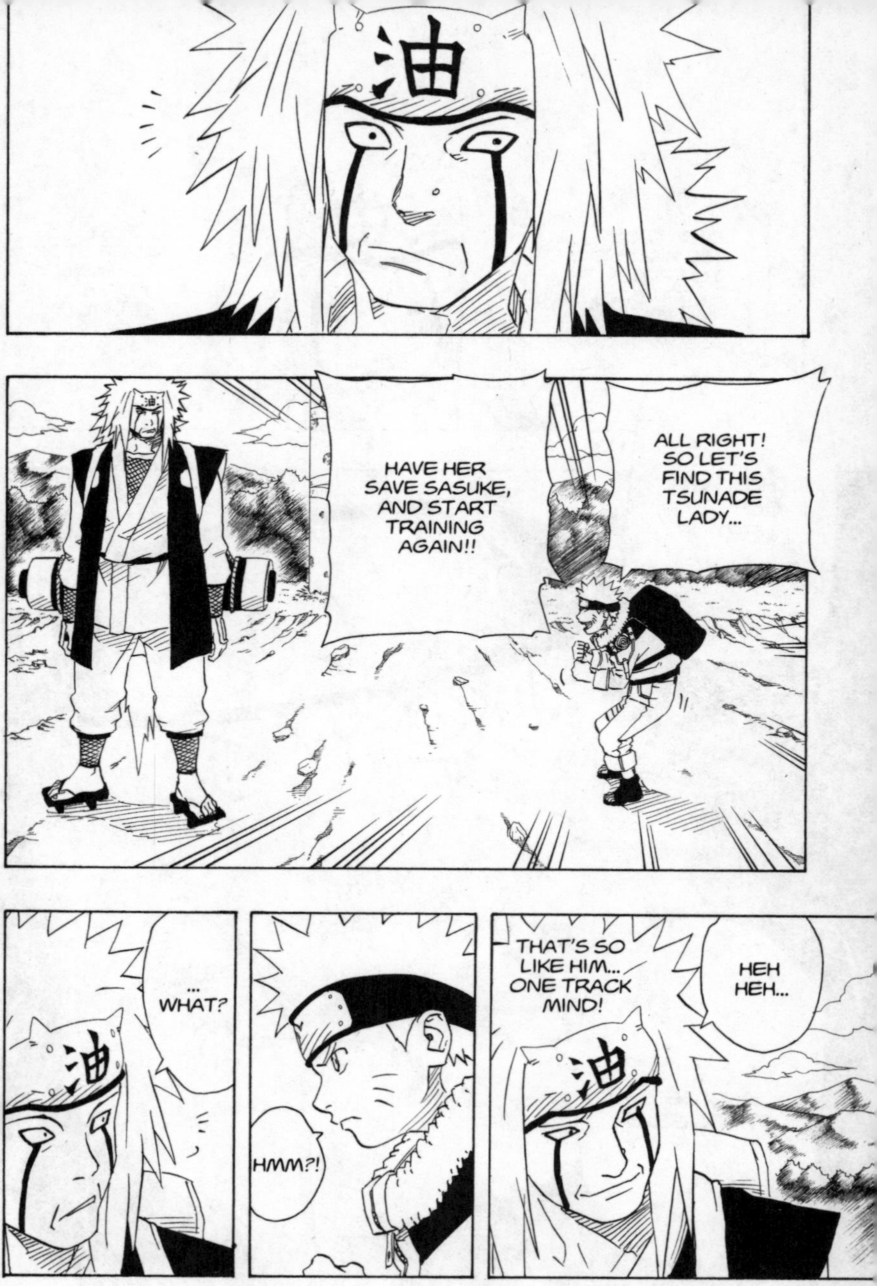

ALL RIGHT! SO LET'S FIND THIS TSUNADE LADY...
HAVE HER SAVE SASUKE, AND START TRAINING AGAIN!!
HEH HEH...
THAT'S SO LIKE HIM... ONE TRACK MIND!
HMM?!
... WHAT?

READ THIS WAY

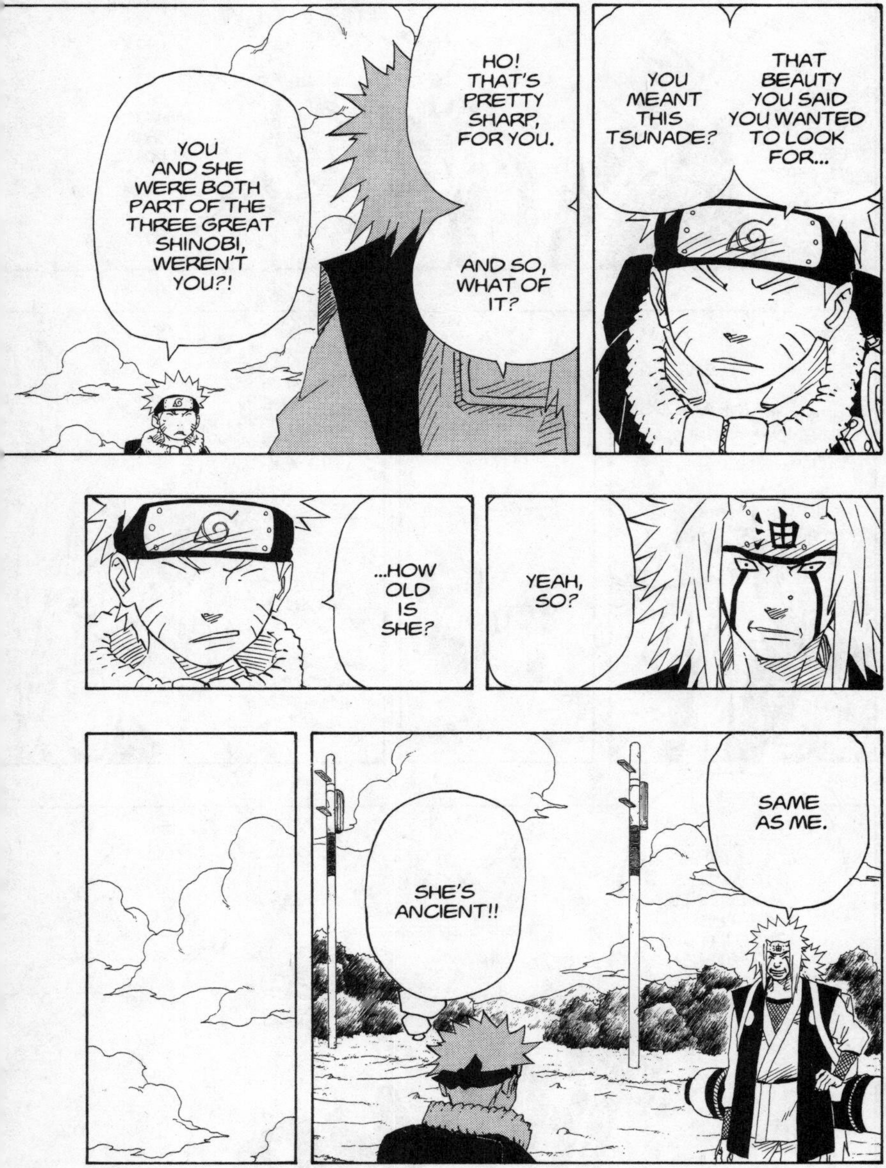
THAT BEAUTY YOU SAID YOU WANTED TO LOOK FOR...
YOU MEANT THIS TSUNADE?
HO! THAT'S PRETTY SHARP, FOR YOU.
AND SO, WHAT OF IT?
YOU AND SHE WERE BOTH PART OF THE THREE GREAT SHINOBI, WEREN'T YOU?!
YEAH, SO?
...HOW OLD IS SHE?
SAME AS ME.
SHE'S ANCIENT!!

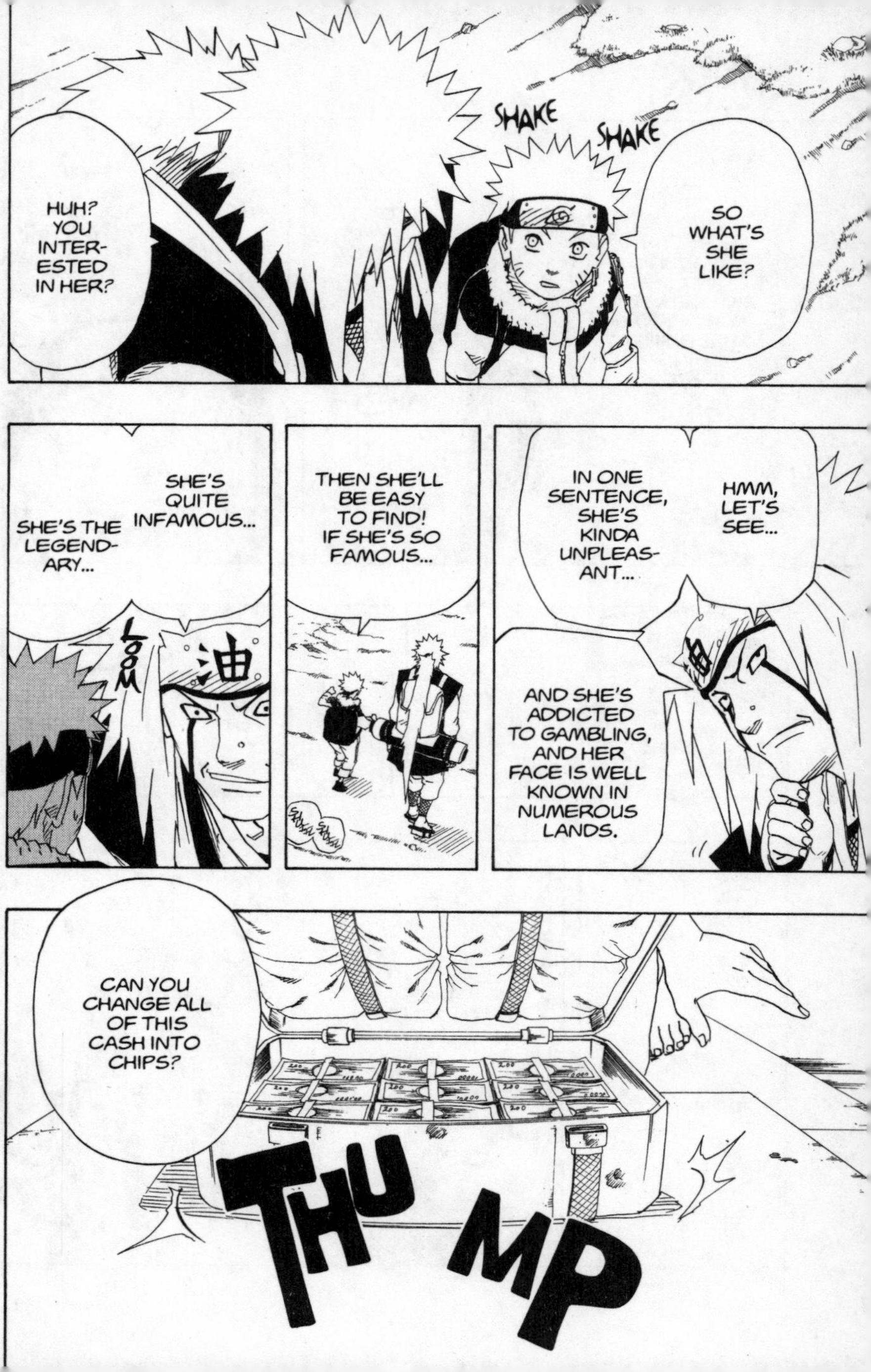
SO WHAT'S SHE LIKE?
SHAKE
SHAKE
HUH? YOU INTERESTED IN HER?
HMM, LET'S SEE...
IN ONE SENTENCE, SHE'S KINDA UNPLEASANT...
AND SHE'S ADDICTED TO GAMBLING, AND HER FACE IS WELL KNOWN IN NUMEROUS LANDS.
THEN SHE'LL BE EASY TO FIND! IF SHE'S SO FAMOUS...
SHE'S QUITE INFAMOUS...
SHE'S THE LEGENDARY...
LOOM
CAN YOU CHANGE ALL OF THIS CASH INTO CHIPS?
THUMP

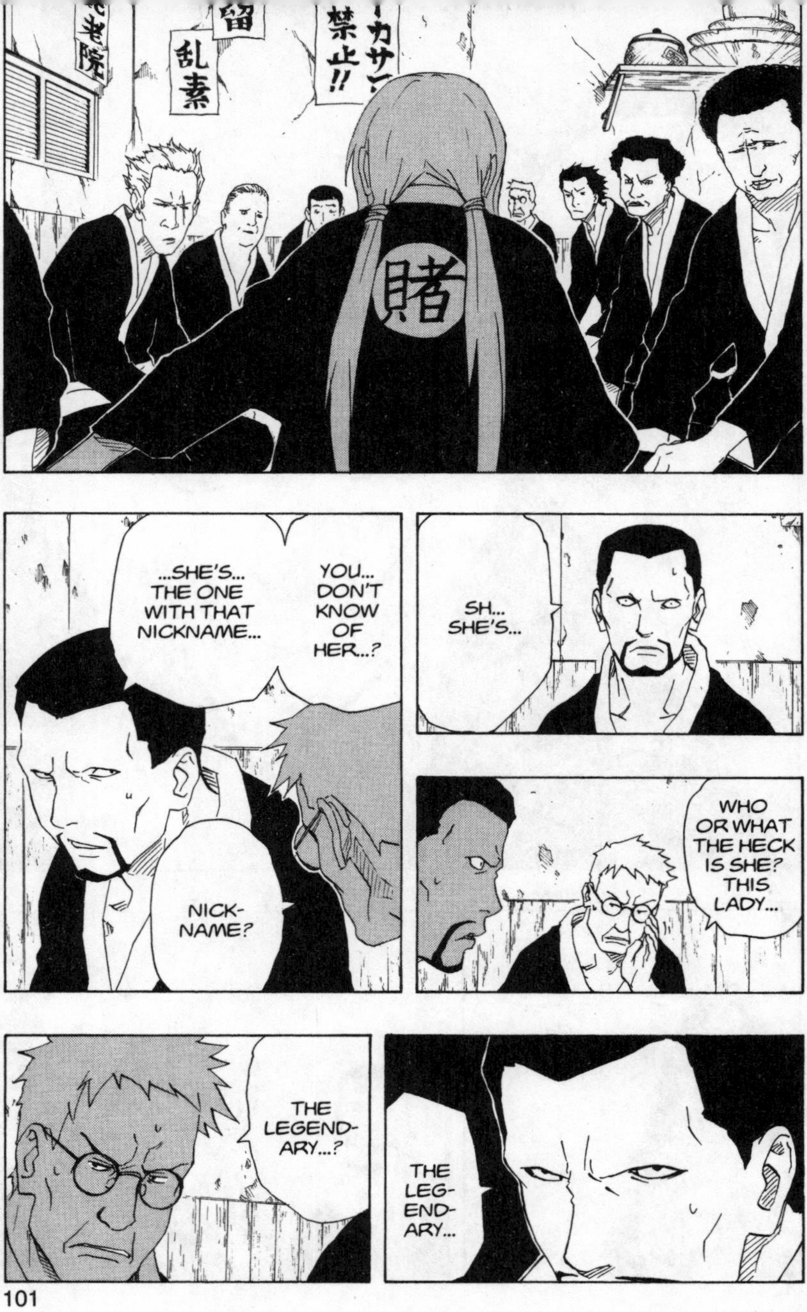
留
禁止!!
賭
SH... SHE'S...
WHO OR WHAT THE HECK IS SHE? THIS LADY...
YOU... DON'T KNOW OF HER...?
...SHE'S... THE ONE WITH THAT NICKNAME...
NICK-NAME?
THE LEG-END-ARY...
THE LEGEND-ARY...?

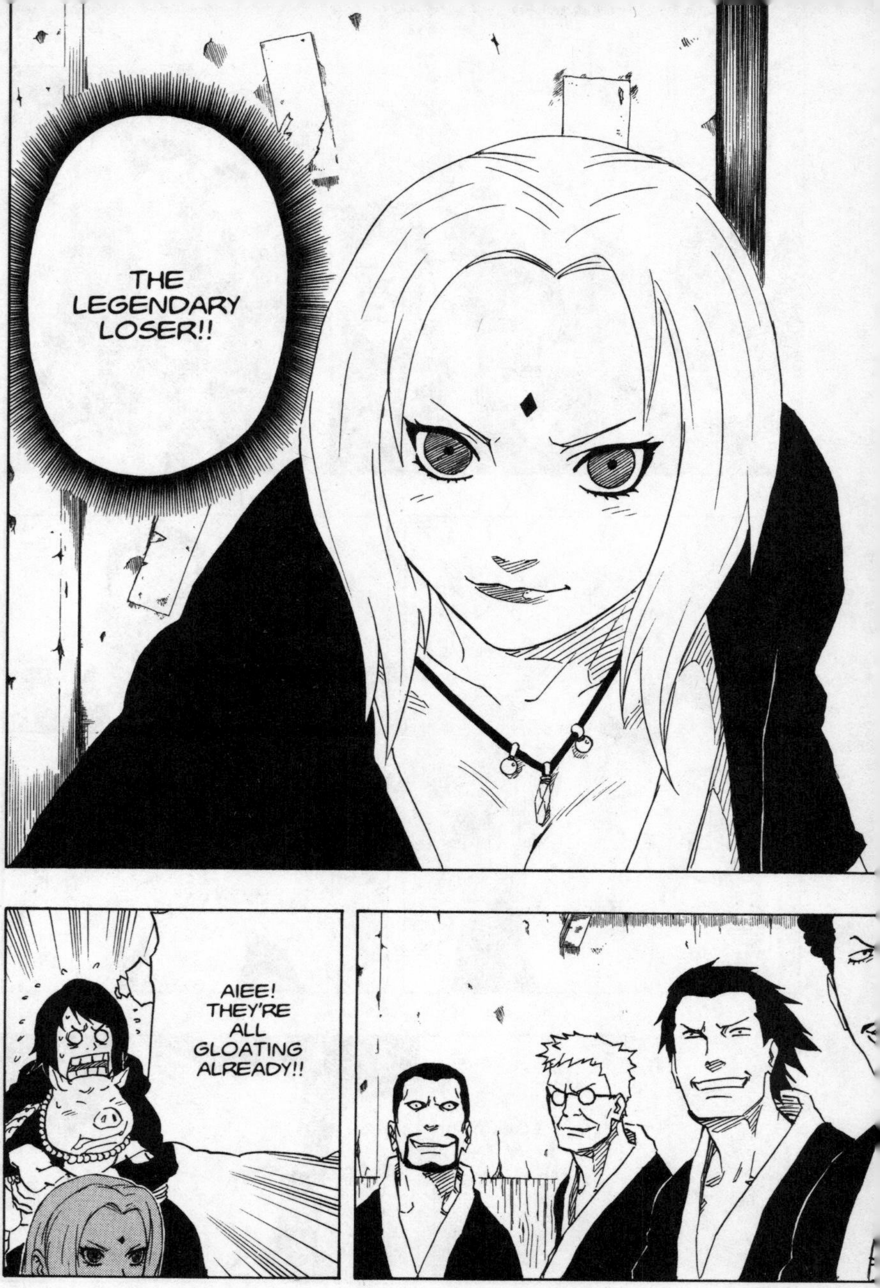
THE LEGENDARY LOSER!!
AIEE! THEY'RE ALL GLOATING ALREADY!!

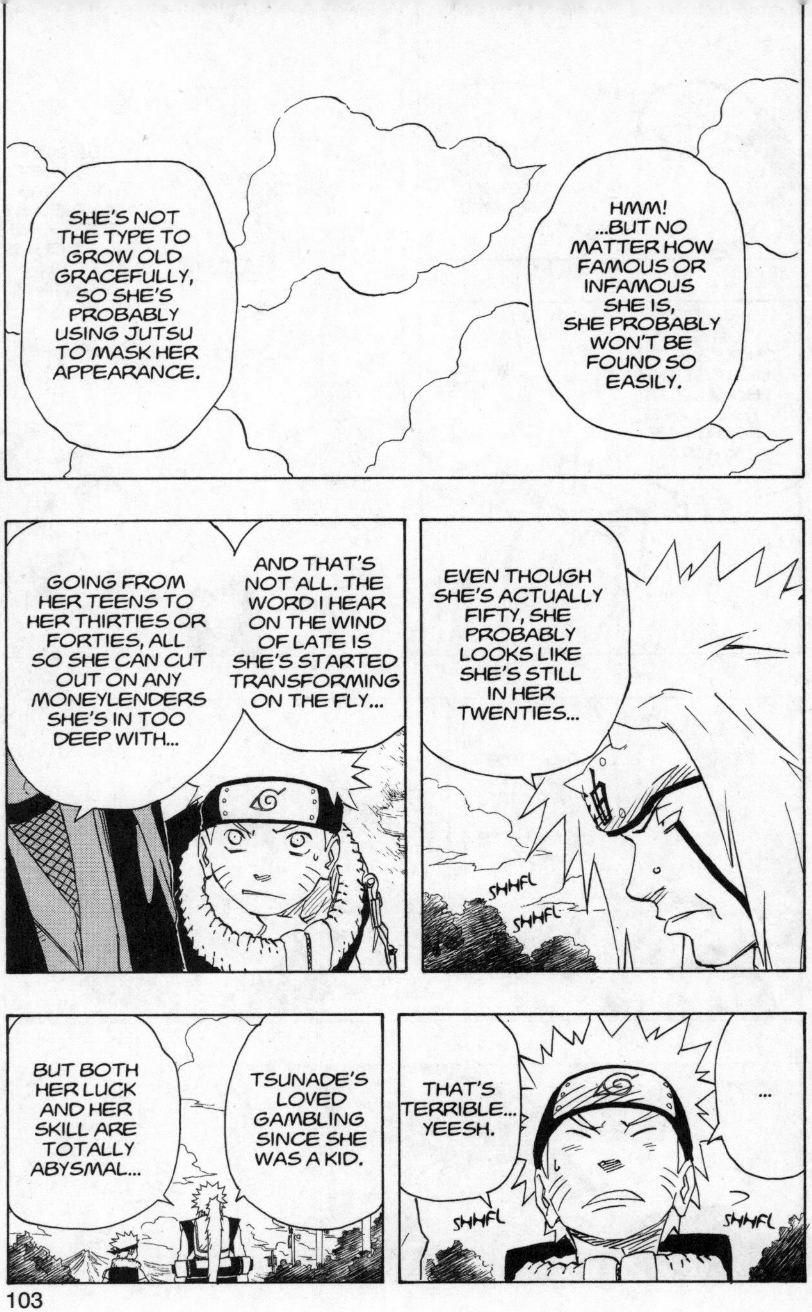
HMM! ...BUT NO MATTER HOW FAMOUS OR INFAMOUS SHE IS, SHE PROBABLY WON'T BE FOUND SO EASILY.
SHE'S NOT THE TYPE TO GROW OLD GRACEFULLY, SO SHE'S PROBABLY USING JUTSU TO MASK HER APPEARANCE.
EVEN THOUGH SHE'S ACTUALLY FIFTY, SHE PROBABLY LOOKS LIKE SHE'S STILL IN HER TWENTIES...
SHHFL
SHHFL
AND THAT'S NOT ALL. THE WORD I HEAR ON THE WIND OF LATE IS SHE'S STARTED TRANSFORMING ON THE FLY...
GOING FROM HER TEENS TO HER THIRTIES OR FORTIES, ALL SO SHE CAN CUT OUT ON ANY MONEYLENDERS SHE'S IN TOO DEEP WITH...
...
THAT'S TERRIBLE... YEESH.
SHHFL
SHHFL
TSUNADE'S LOVED GAMBLING SINCE SHE WAS A KID.
BUT BOTH HER LUCK AND HER SKILL ARE TOTALLY ABYSMAL...

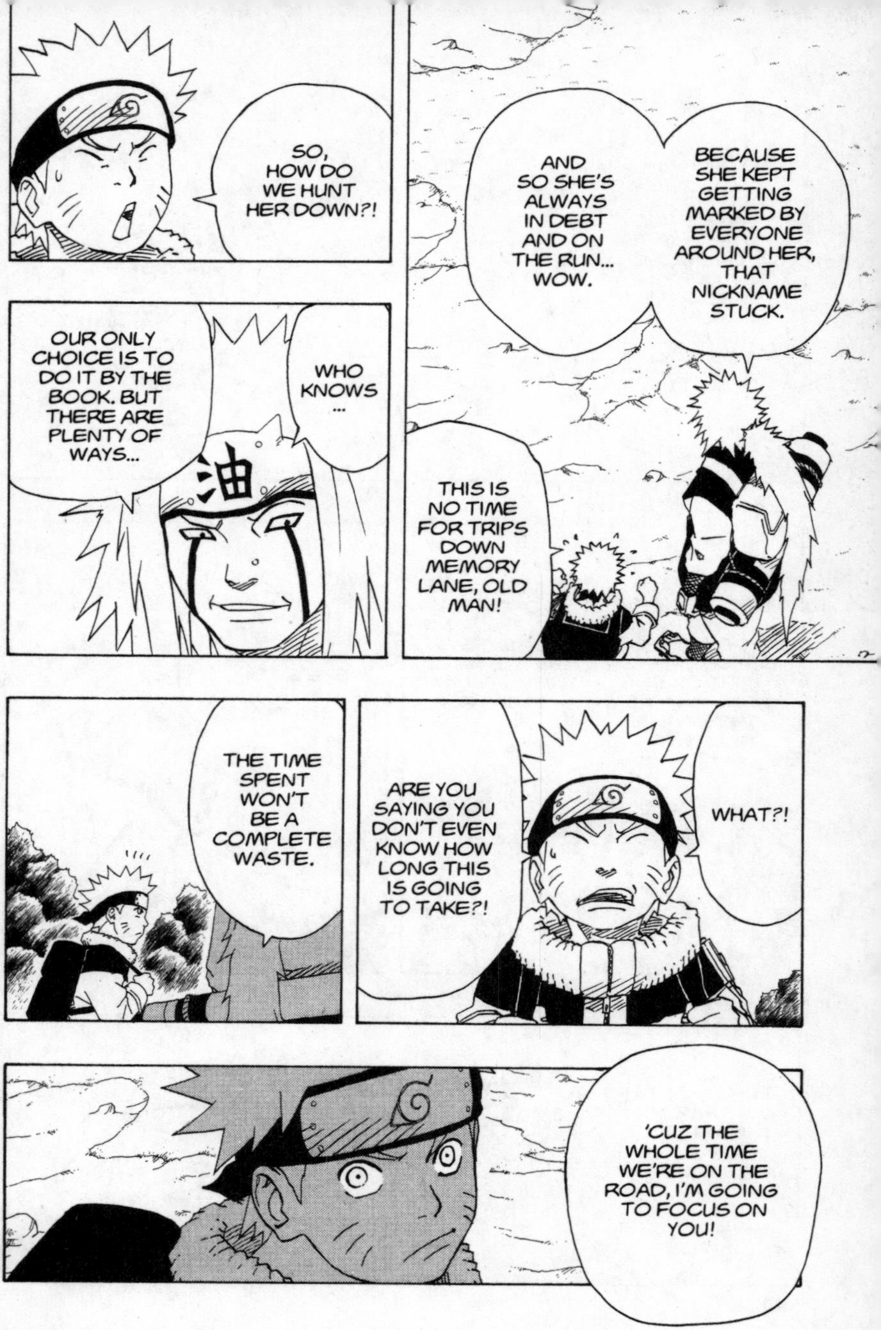
BECAUSE SHE KEPT GETTING MARKED BY EVERYONE AROUND HER, THAT NICKNAME STUCK.
AND SO SHE'S ALWAYS IN DEBT AND ON THE RUN... WOW.
THIS IS NO TIME FOR TRIPS DOWN MEMORY LANE, OLD MAN!
SO, HOW DO WE HUNT HER DOWN?!
WHO KNOWS ...
OUR ONLY CHOICE IS TO DO IT BY THE BOOK. BUT THERE ARE PLENTY OF WAYS...
油
WHAT?!
ARE YOU SAYING YOU DON'T EVEN KNOW HOW LONG THIS IS GOING TO TAKE?!
THE TIME SPENT WON'T BE A COMPLETE WASTE.
'CUZ THE WHOLE TIME WE'RE ON THE ROAD, I'M GOING TO FOCUS ON YOU!

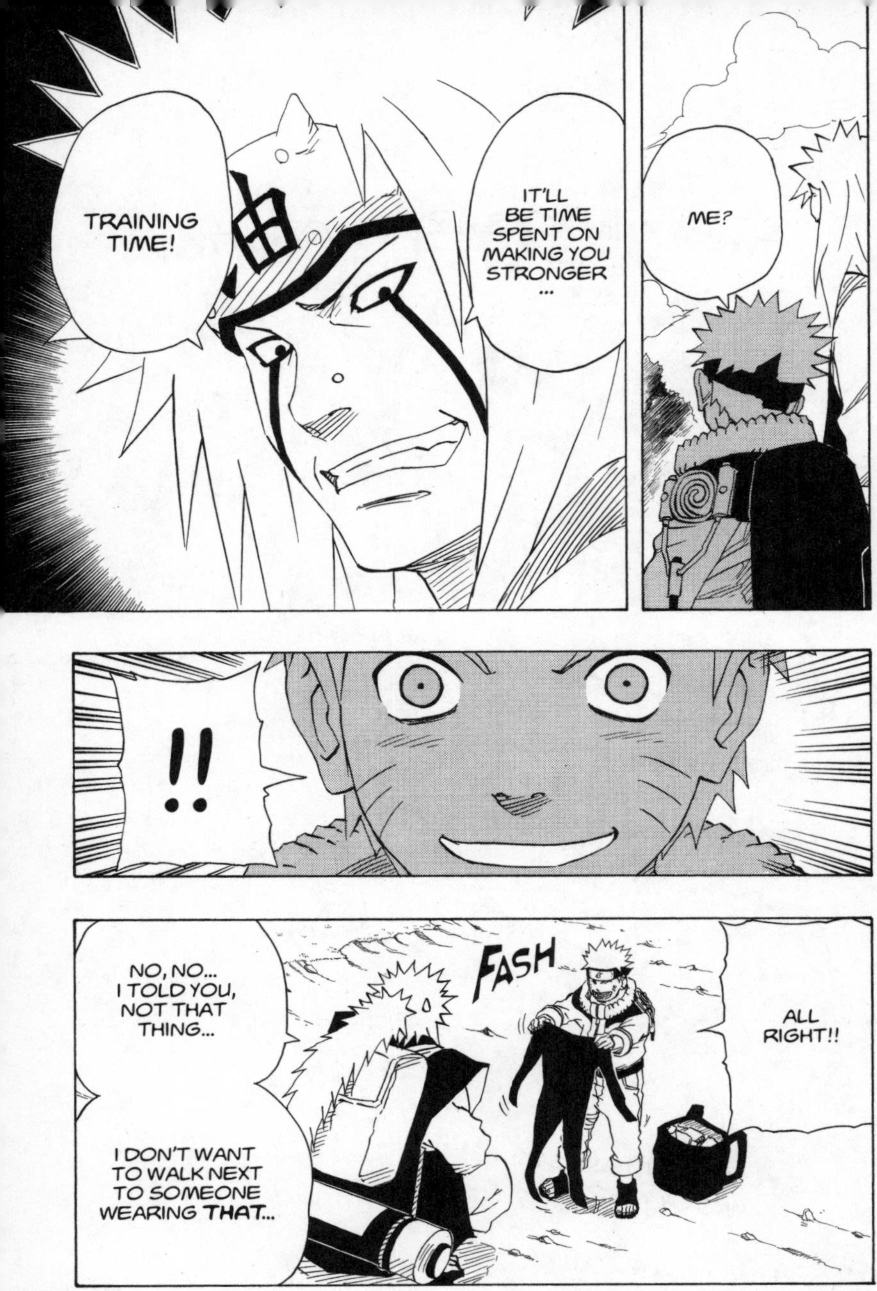
ME?
IT'LL BE TIME SPENT ON MAKING YOU STRONGER ...
TRAINING TIME!
!!
ALL RIGHT!!
FASH
NO, NO... I TOLD YOU, NOT THAT THING...
I DON'T WANT TO WALK NEXT TO SOMEONE WEARING THAT...

THIRD ANNIVERSARY CELEBRATION!

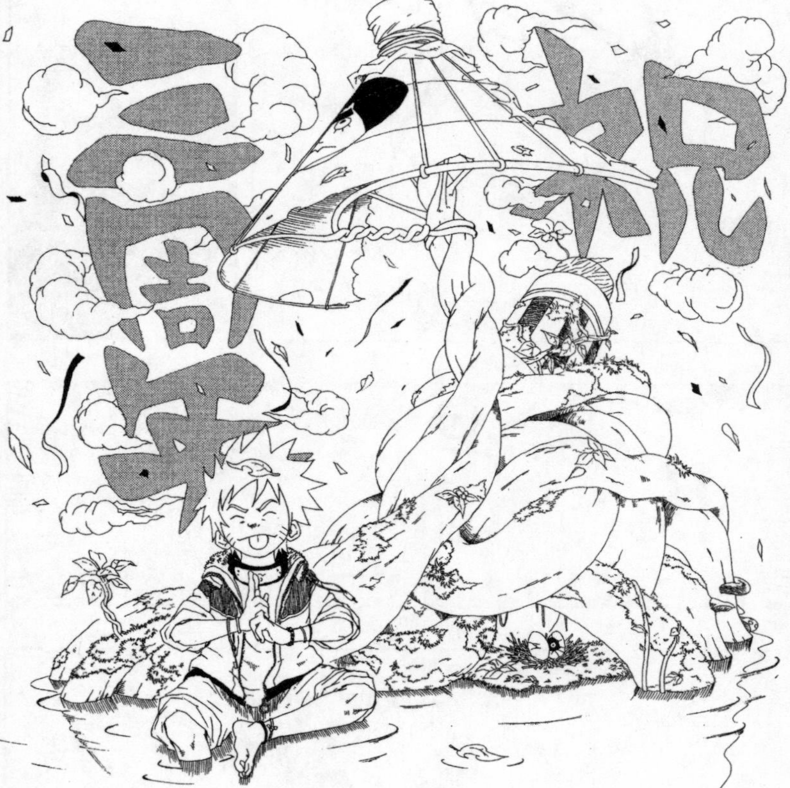
祝
三周年

KISHIMOTO-SAN, PLEASE STAY HEALTHY
AND KEEP WORKING HARD

大久保 彰

AKIRA OKUBO

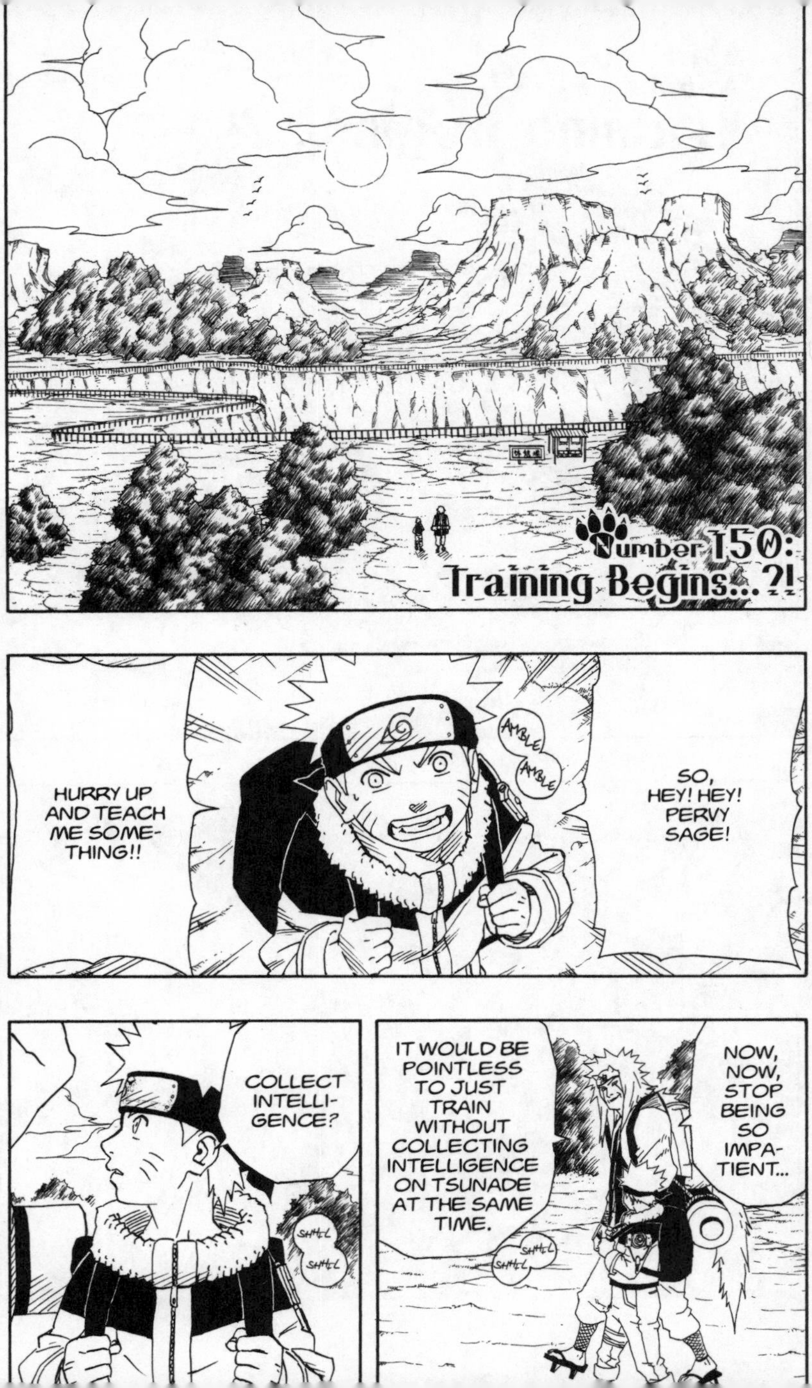
Number 150:
Training Begins...?!
SO, HEY! HEY! PERVY SAGE!
AMBLE
AMBLE
HURRY UP AND TEACH ME SOME-THING!!
NOW, NOW, STOP BEING SO IMPA-TIENT...
IT WOULD BE POINTLESS TO JUST TRAIN WITHOUT COLLECTING INTELLIGENCE ON TSUNADE AT THE SAME TIME.
COLLECT INTELLI-GENCE?

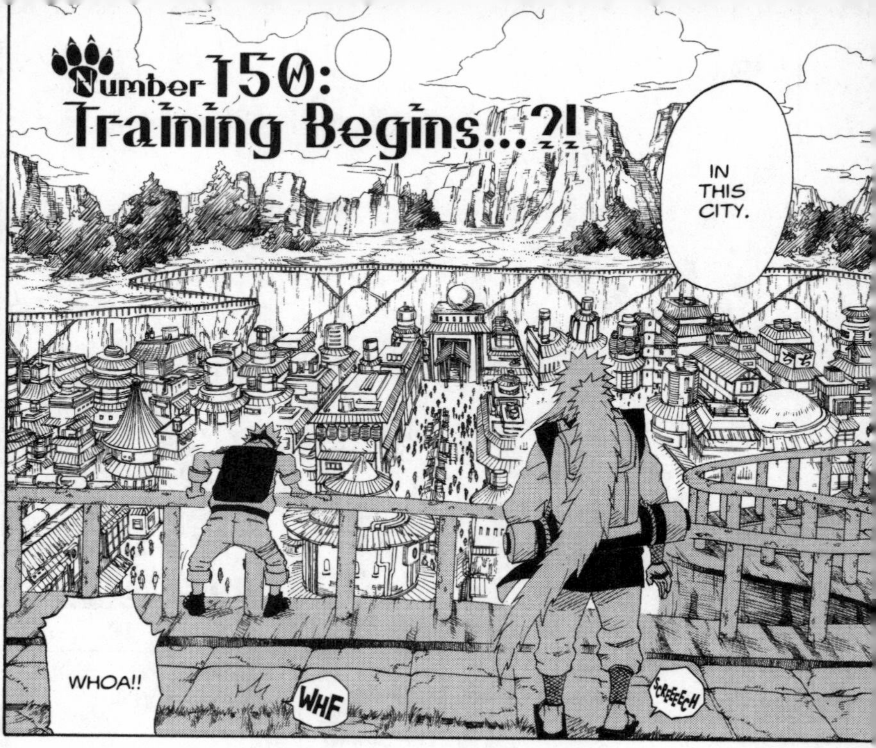
Number 150:
Training Begins...?!
IN THIS CITY.
SCREEECH
WHF
WHOA!!

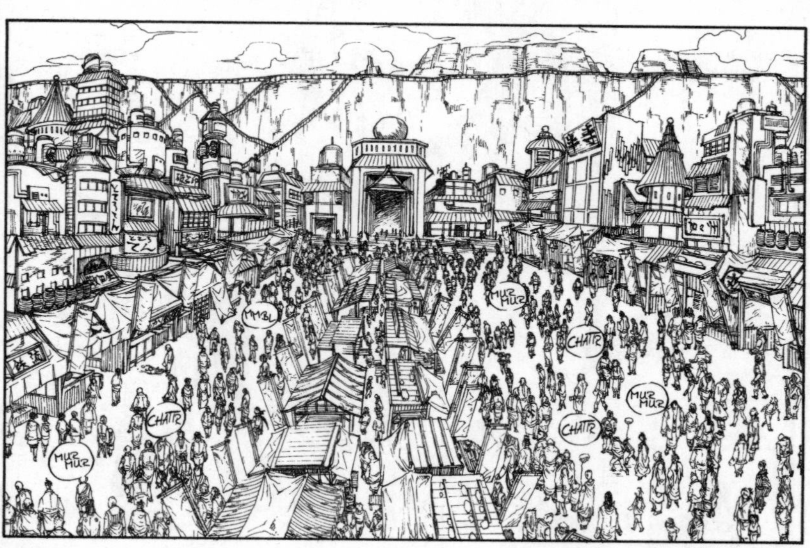
MUR MUR
CHATTR
MUR MUR
CHATTR
MMBL
CHATTR
MUR MUR

READ THIS WAY

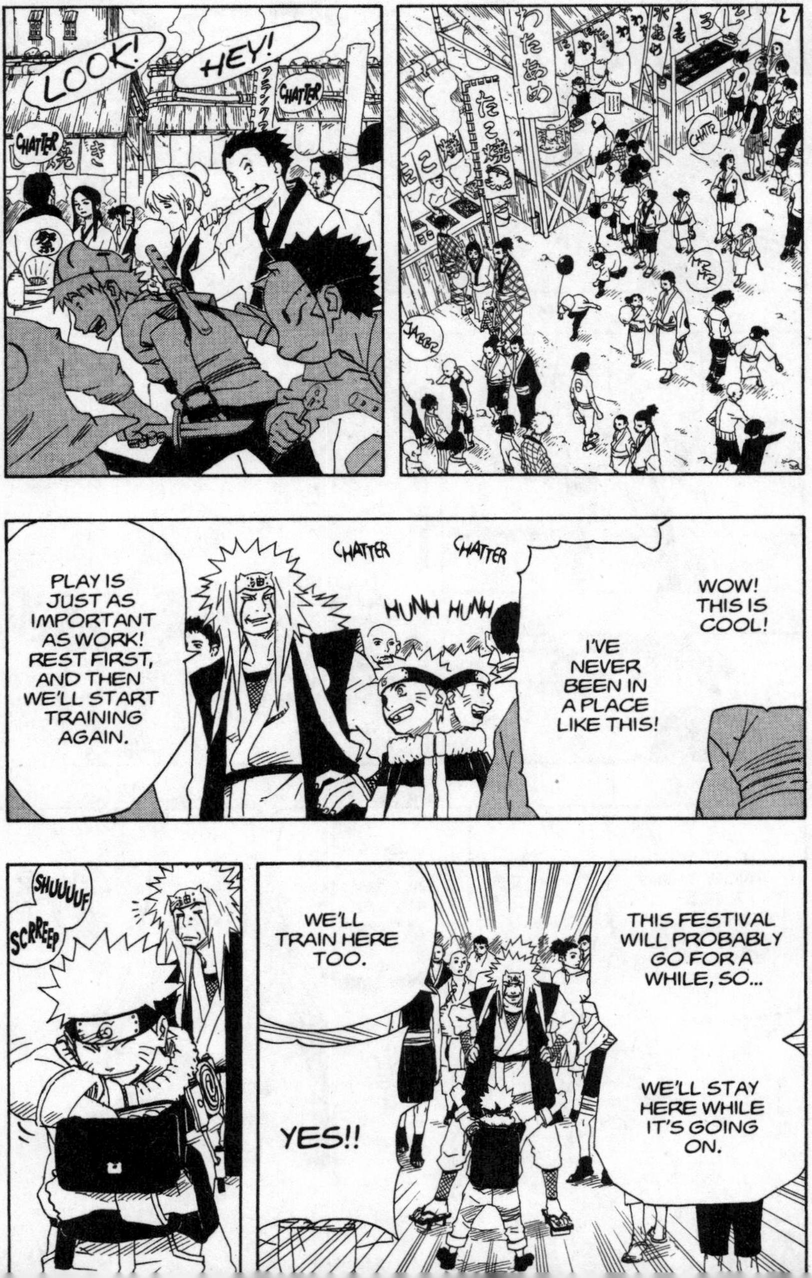
わたあめ
たこ焼
CHATR
JABBR
LOOK!
HEY!
CHATTER
CHATTER
WOW! THIS IS COOL!
I'VE NEVER BEEN IN A PLACE LIKE THIS!
CHATTER
CHATTER
HUNH HUNH
PLAY IS JUST AS IMPORTANT AS WORK! REST FIRST, AND THEN WE'LL START TRAINING AGAIN.
THIS FESTIVAL WILL PROBABLY GO FOR A WHILE, SO...
WE'LL TRAIN HERE TOO.
WE'LL STAY HERE WHILE IT'S GOING ON.
YES!!
SHUUUUF
SCRREEP

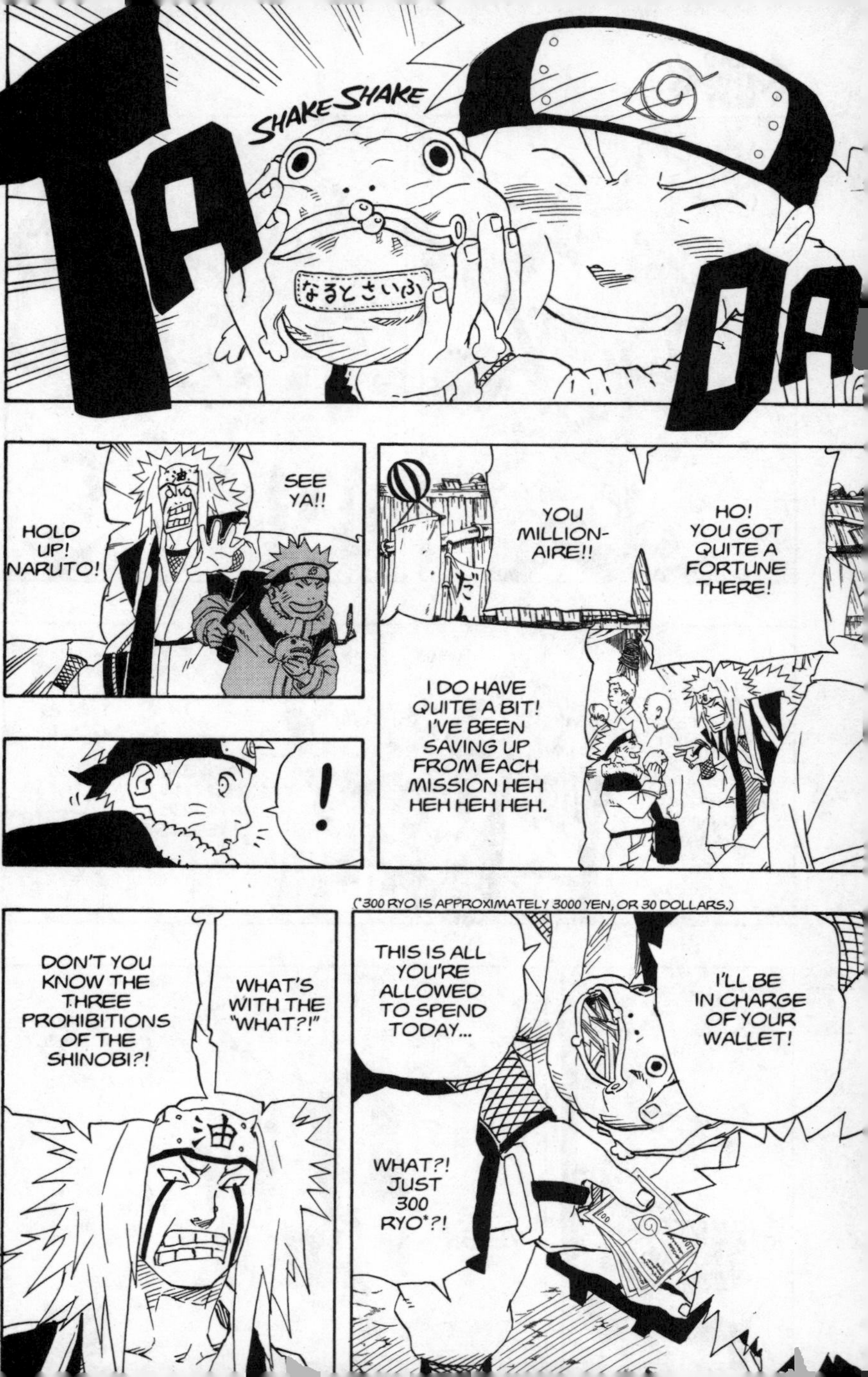
SHAKE SHAKE
TA DA
なるとさいふ
HO! YOU GOT QUITE A FORTUNE THERE!
YOU MILLION-AIRE!!
I DO HAVE QUITE A BIT! I'VE BEEN SAVING UP FROM EACH MISSION HEH HEH HEH HEH.
SEE YA!!
HOLD UP! NARUTO!
!
I'LL BE IN CHARGE OF YOUR WALLET!
THIS IS ALL YOU'RE ALLOWED TO SPEND TODAY...
WHAT?! JUST 300 RYO*?!
WHAT'S WITH THE "WHAT?!"
DON'T YOU KNOW THE THREE PROHIBITIONS OF THE SHINOBI?!
(*300 RYO IS APPROXIMATELY 3000 YEN, OR 30 DOLLARS.)

READ THIS WAY

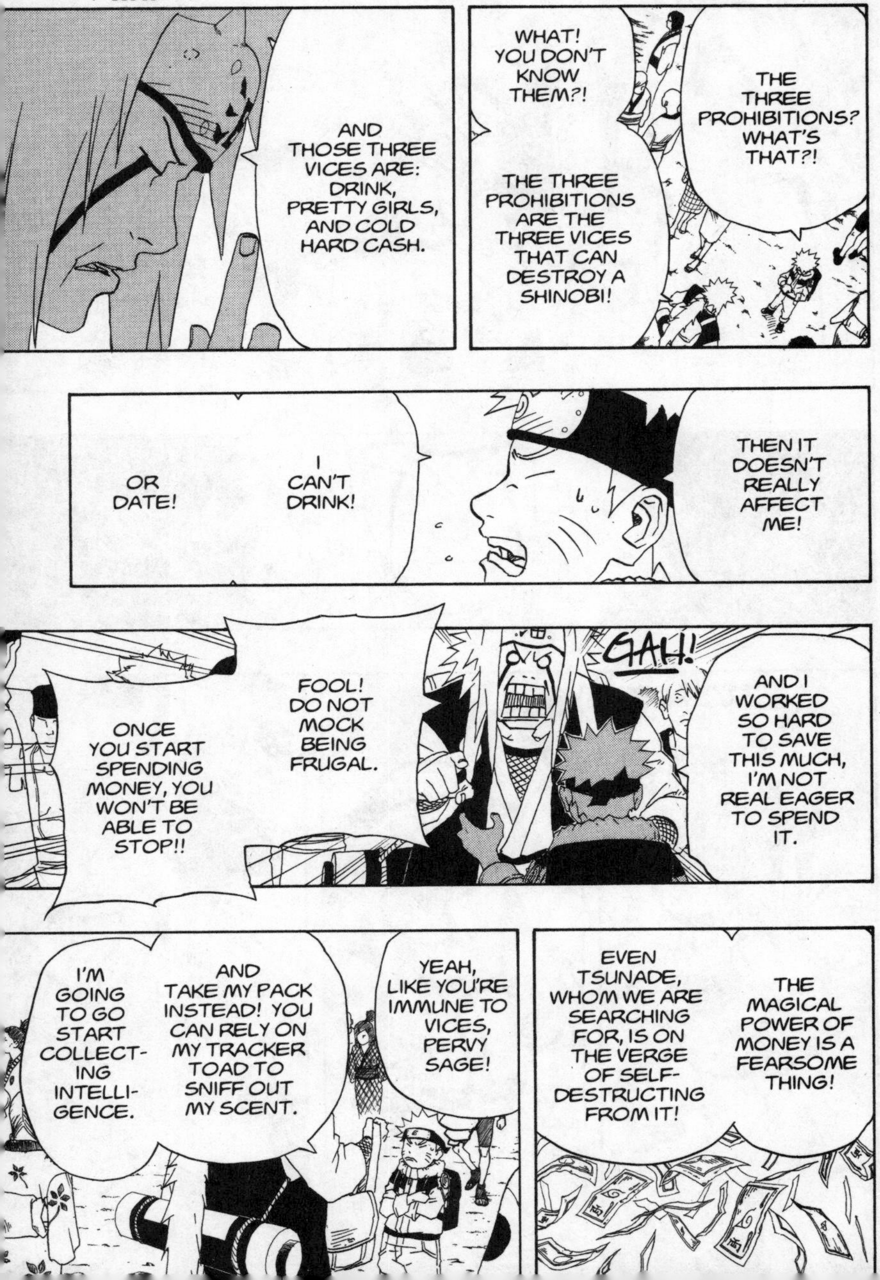
THE THREE PROHIBITIONS? WHAT'S THAT?!
WHAT! YOU DON'T KNOW THEM?!
THE THREE PROHIBITIONS ARE THE THREE VICES THAT CAN DESTROY A SHINOBI!
AND THOSE THREE VICES ARE: DRINK, PRETTY GIRLS, AND COLD HARD CASH.
THEN IT DOESN'T REALLY AFFECT ME!
I CAN'T DRINK!
OR DATE!
AND I WORKED SO HARD TO SAVE THIS MUCH, I'M NOT REAL EAGER TO SPEND IT.
GAH!
FOOL! DO NOT MOCK BEING FRUGAL.
ONCE YOU START SPENDING MONEY, YOU WON'T BE ABLE TO STOP!!
THE MAGICAL POWER OF MONEY IS A FEARSOME THING!
EVEN TSUNADE, WHOM WE ARE SEARCHING FOR, IS ON THE VERGE OF SELF-DESTRUCTING FROM IT!
YEAH, LIKE YOU'RE IMMUNE TO VICES, PERVY SAGE!
AND TAKE MY PACK INSTEAD! YOU CAN RELY ON MY TRACKER TOAD TO SNIFF OUT MY SCENT.
I'M GOING TO GO START COLLECTING INTELLIGENCE.

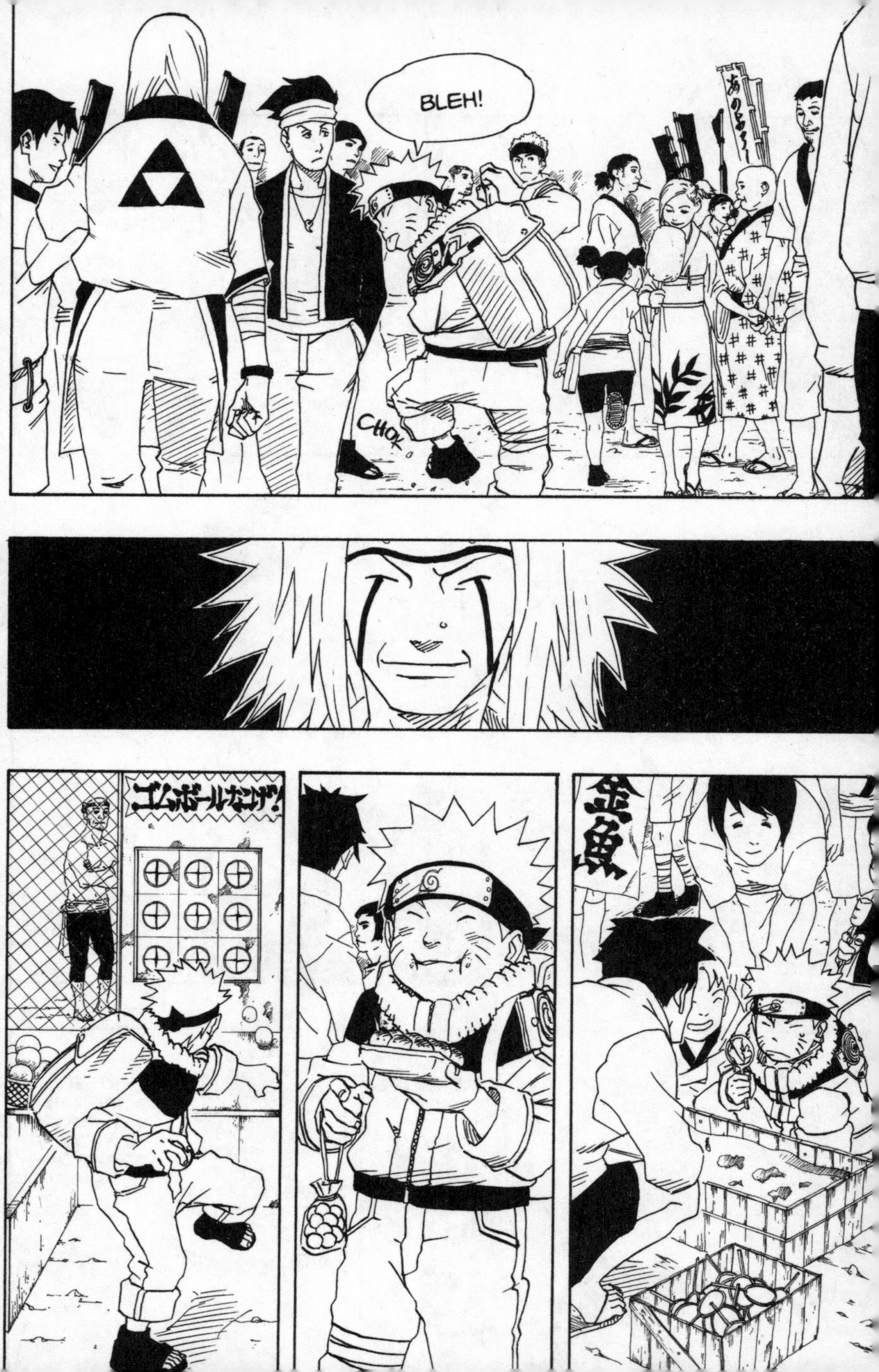
BLEH!
CHOK
金魚
ゴムボールなげ!

READ THIS WAY

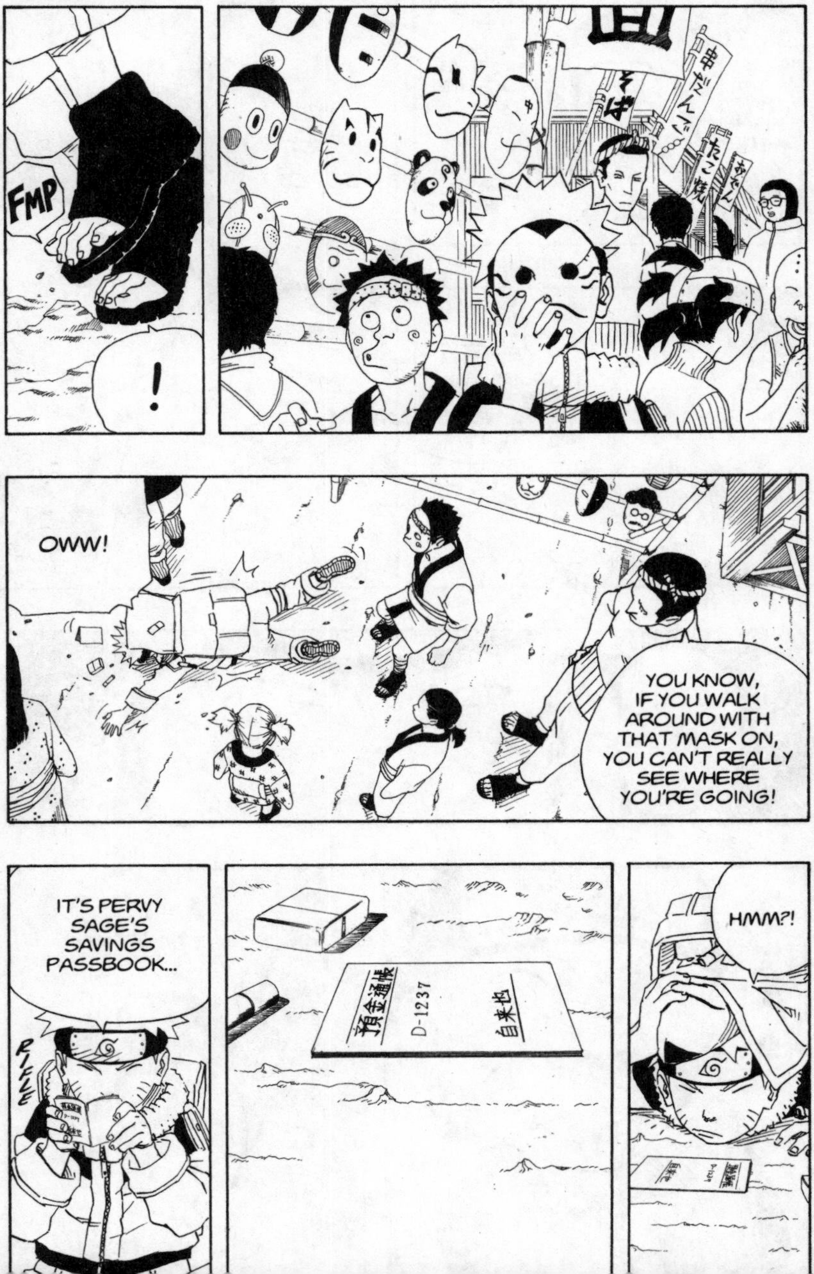
FMP
!
OWW!
YOU KNOW, IF YOU WALK AROUND WITH THAT MASK ON, YOU CAN'T REALLY SEE WHERE YOU'RE GOING!
HMM?!
預金通帳
D-1237
自来也
IT'S PERVY SAGE'S SAVINGS PASSBOOK...
RIFLE

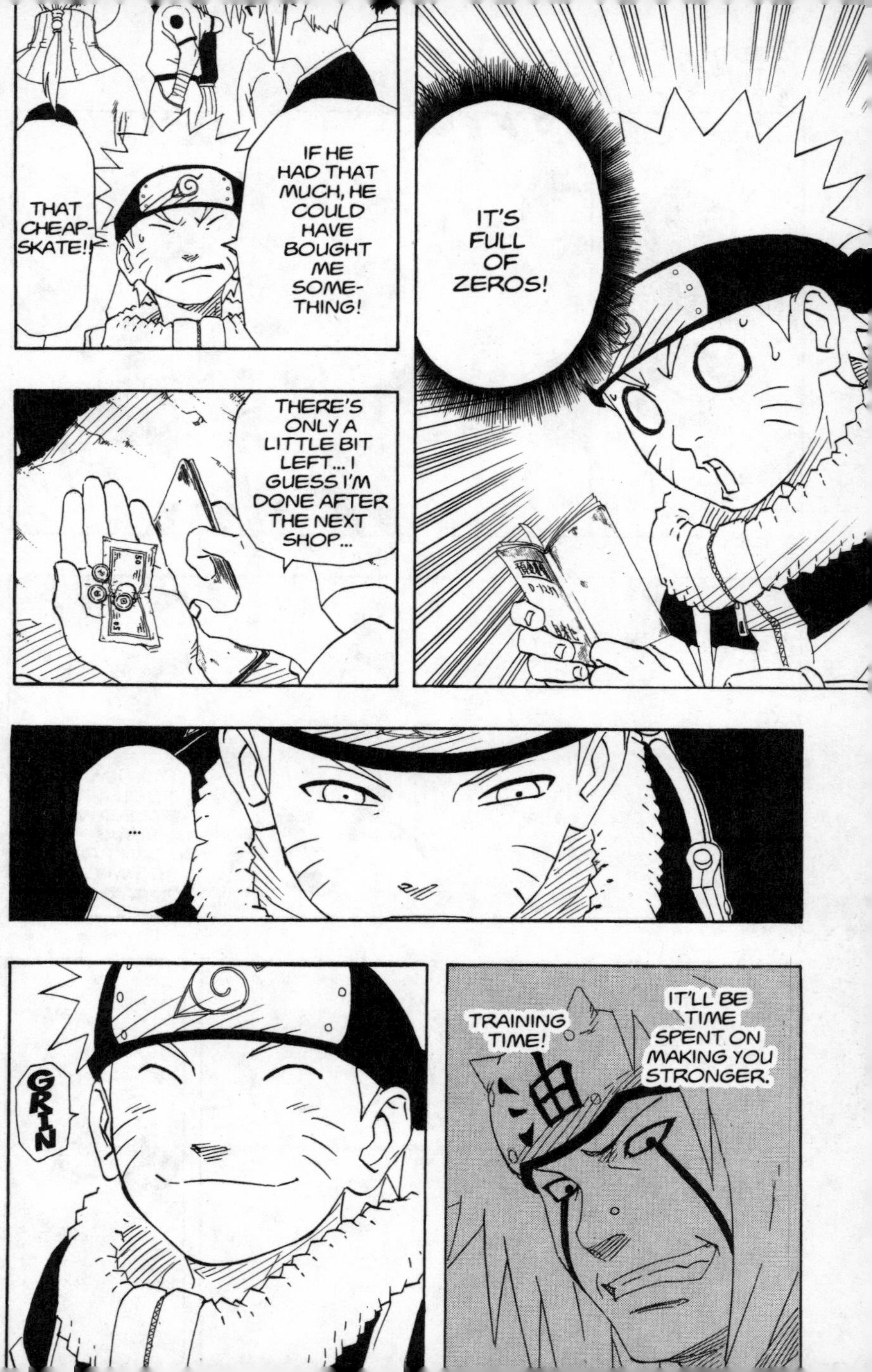
IT'S FULL OF ZEROS!
IF HE HAD THAT MUCH, HE COULD HAVE BOUGHT ME SOME-THING!
THAT CHEAP-SKATE!!
THERE'S ONLY A LITTLE BIT LEFT... I GUESS I'M DONE AFTER THE NEXT SHOP...
...
IT'LL BE TIME SPENT ON MAKING YOU STRONGER.
TRAINING TIME!
GRIN

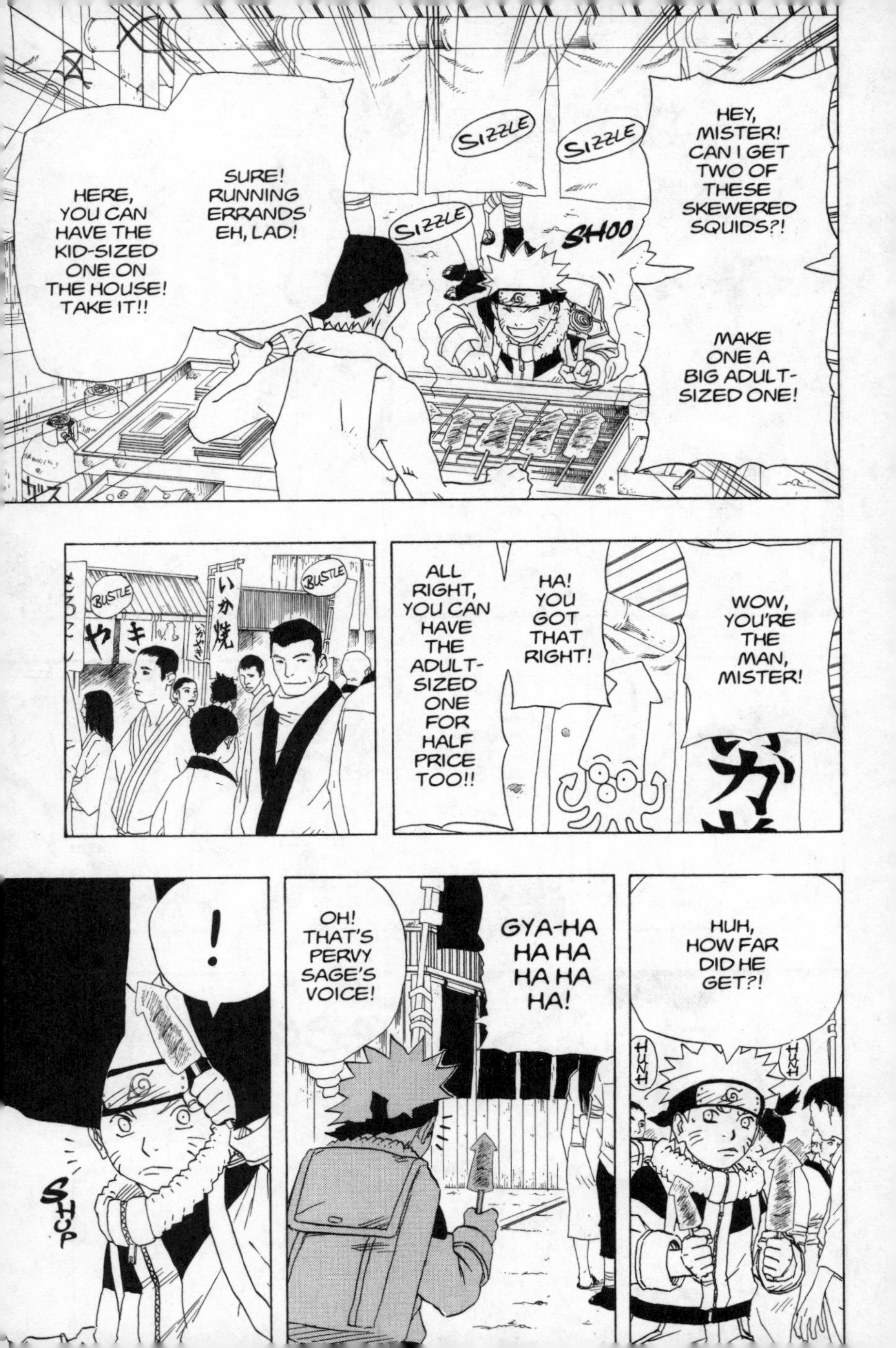
HEY, MISTER! CAN I GET TWO OF THESE SKEWERED SQUIDS?!
MAKE ONE A BIG ADULT-SIZED ONE!
SIZZLE
SIZZLE
SHOO
SIZZLE
SURE! RUNNING ERRANDS EH, LAD!
HERE, YOU CAN HAVE THE KID-SIZED ONE ON THE HOUSE! TAKE IT!!
WOW, YOU'RE THE MAN, MISTER!
HA! YOU GOT THAT RIGHT!
ALL RIGHT, YOU CAN HAVE THE ADULT-SIZED ONE FOR HALF PRICE TOO!!
BUSTLE
いか焼
いかやき
BUSTLE
HUNH
HUH, HOW FAR DID HE GET?!
HUNH
GYA-HA HA HA HA HA HA!
OH! THAT'S PERVY SAGE'S VOICE!
!
SHUP

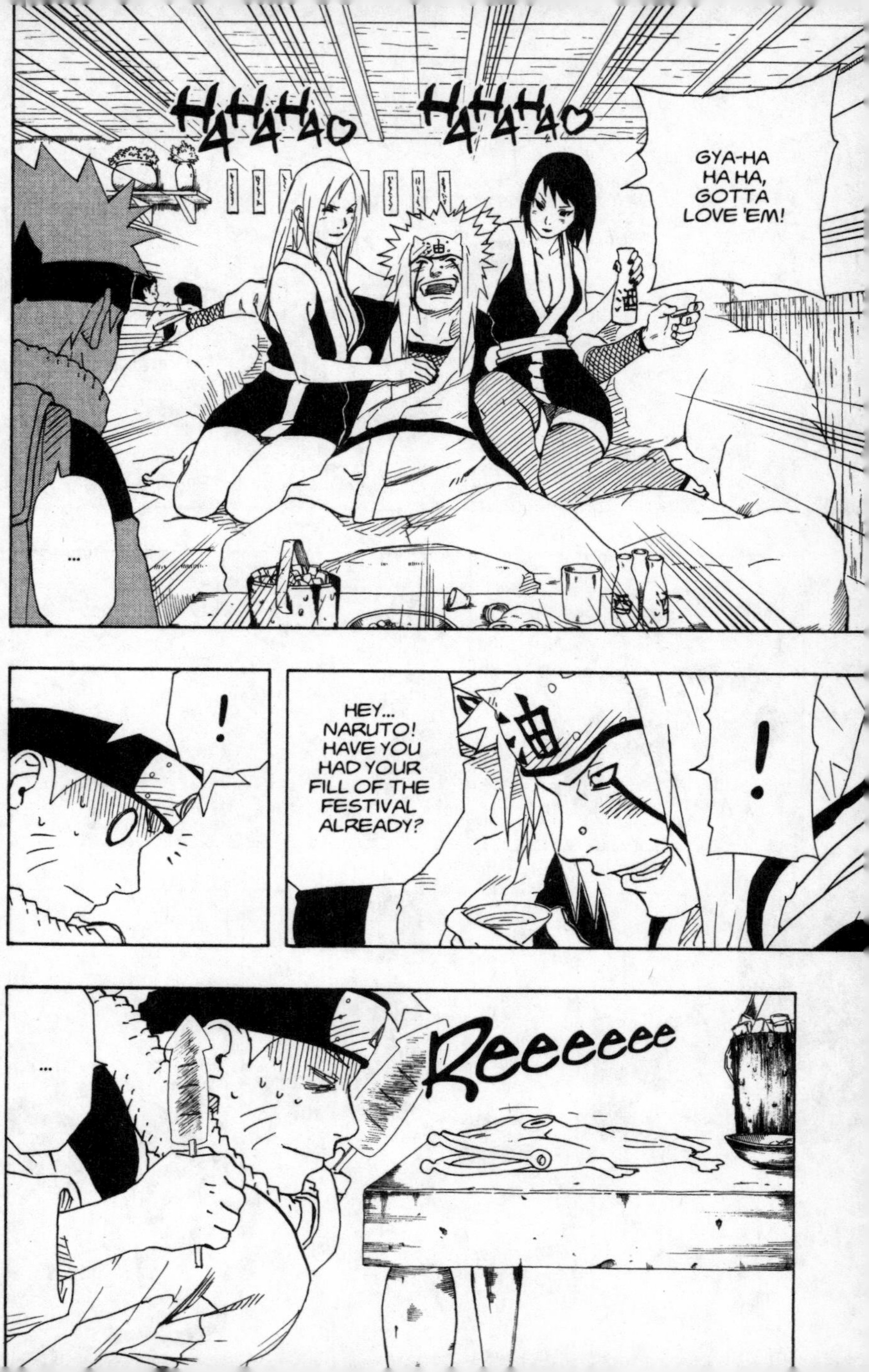
HAHAHAHO♡
GYA-HA HA HA, GOTTA LOVE 'EM!
HAHAHAHO
...
HEY... NARUTO! HAVE YOU HAD YOUR FILL OF THE FESTIVAL ALREADY?
!
!
Reeeeee
...

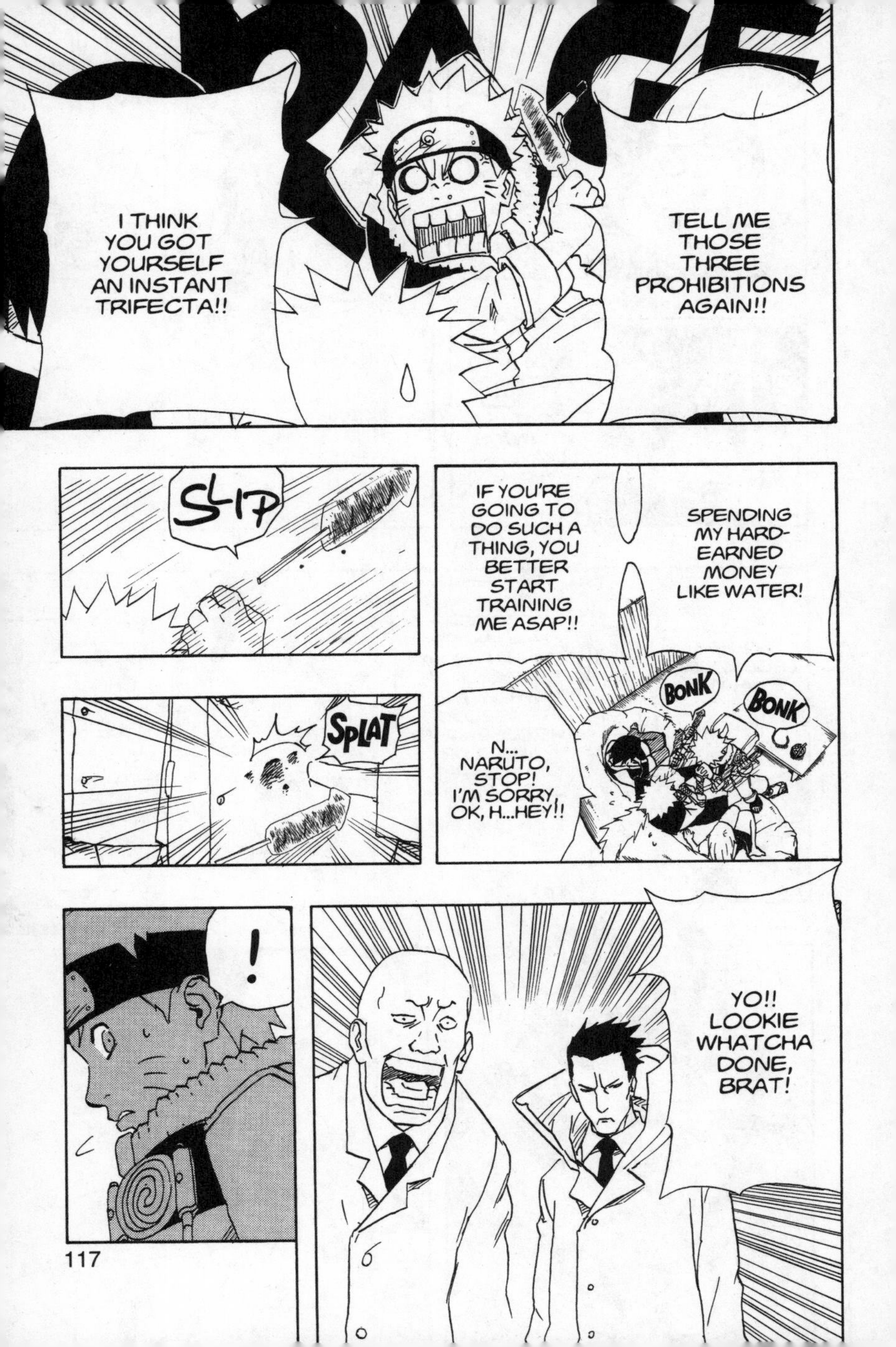
TELL ME THOSE THREE PROHIBITIONS AGAIN!!
I THINK YOU GOT YOURSELF AN INSTANT TRIFECTA!!
SPENDING MY HARD-EARNED MONEY LIKE WATER!
IF YOU'RE GOING TO DO SUCH A THING, YOU BETTER START TRAINING ME ASAP!!
BONK
BONK
N... NARUTO, STOP! I'M SORRY OK, H...HEY!!
SLIP
SPLAT
YO!! LOOKIE WHATCHA DONE, BRAT!
!

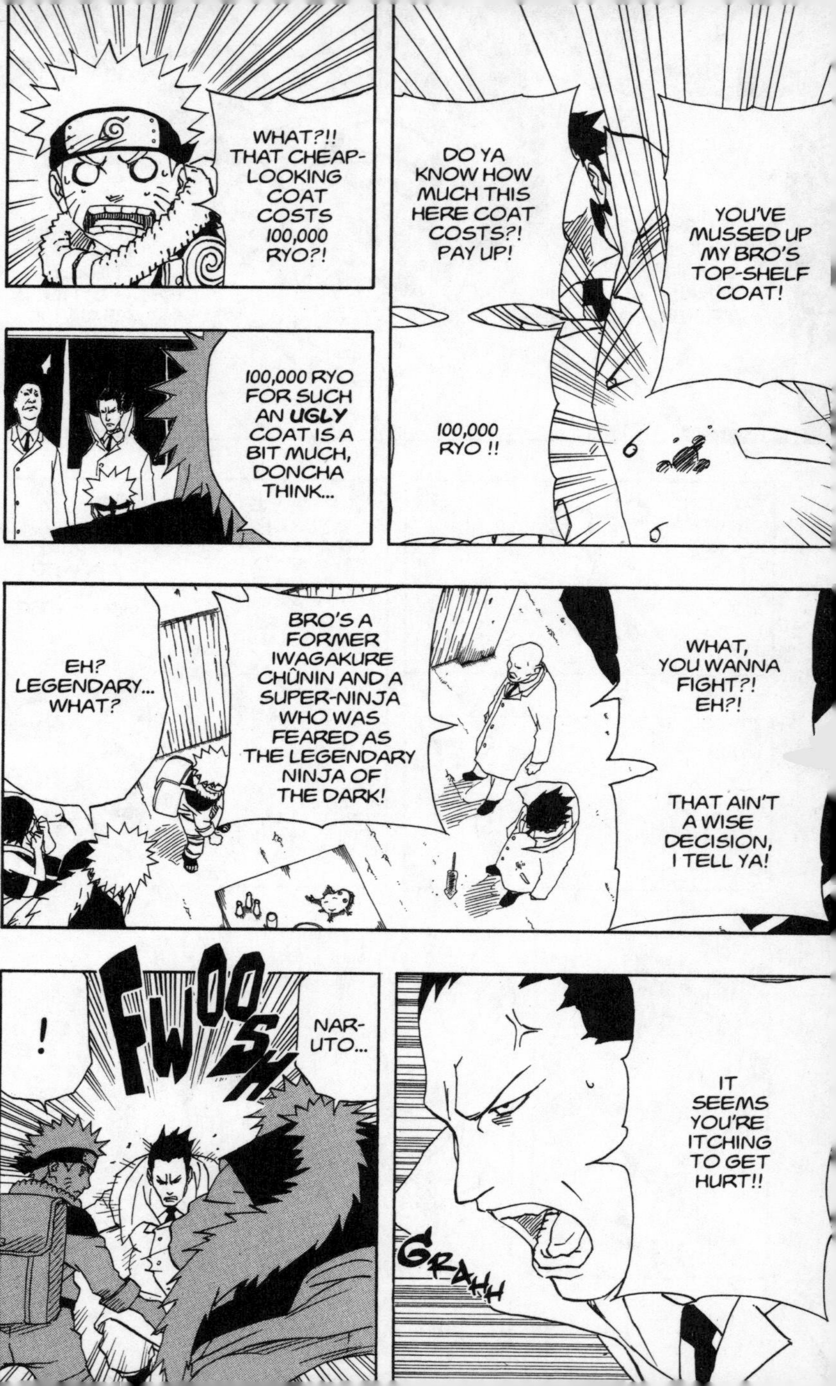

YOU'VE MUSSED UP MY BRO'S TOP-SHELF COAT!
DO YA KNOW HOW MUCH THIS HERE COAT COSTS?! PAY UP!
100,000 RYO !!
WHAT?!! THAT CHEAP-LOOKING COAT COSTS 100,000 RYO?!
100,000 RYO FOR SUCH AN **UGLY** COAT IS A BIT MUCH, DONCHA THINK...
WHAT, YOU WANNA FIGHT?! EH?!
THAT AIN'T A WISE DECISION, I TELL YA!
BRO'S A FORMER IWAGAKURE CHÛNIN AND A SUPER-NINJA WHO WAS FEARED AS THE LEGENDARY NINJA OF THE DARK!
EH? LEGENDARY... WHAT?
IT SEEMS YOU'RE ITCHING TO GET HURT!!
GRAHH
NAR-UTO...
FWOOSH
!

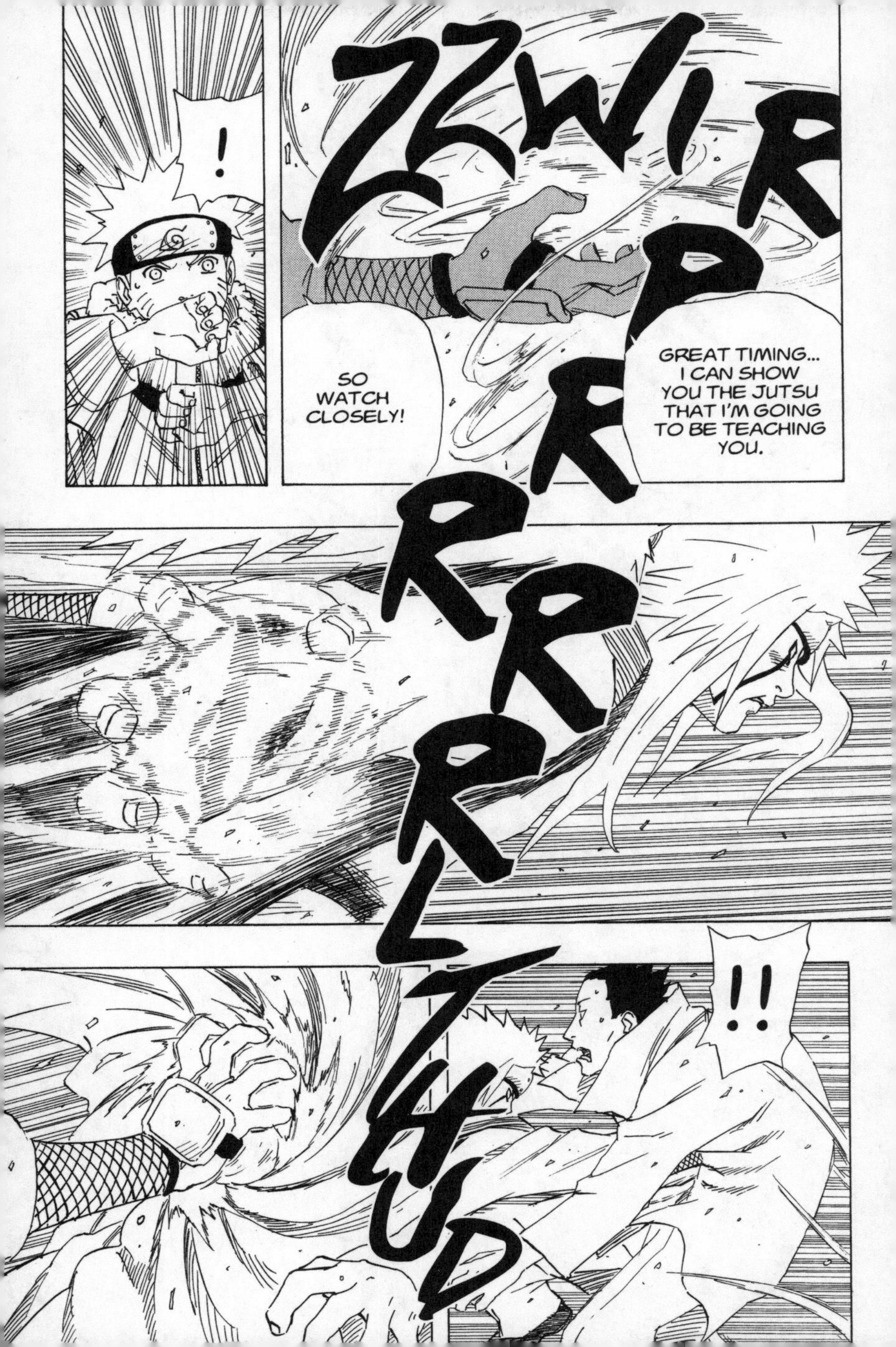
ZZWIRRRRRRRL
GREAT TIMING... I CAN SHOW YOU THE JUTSU THAT I'M GOING TO BE TEACHING YOU.
SO WATCH CLOSELY!
!
THUD
!!

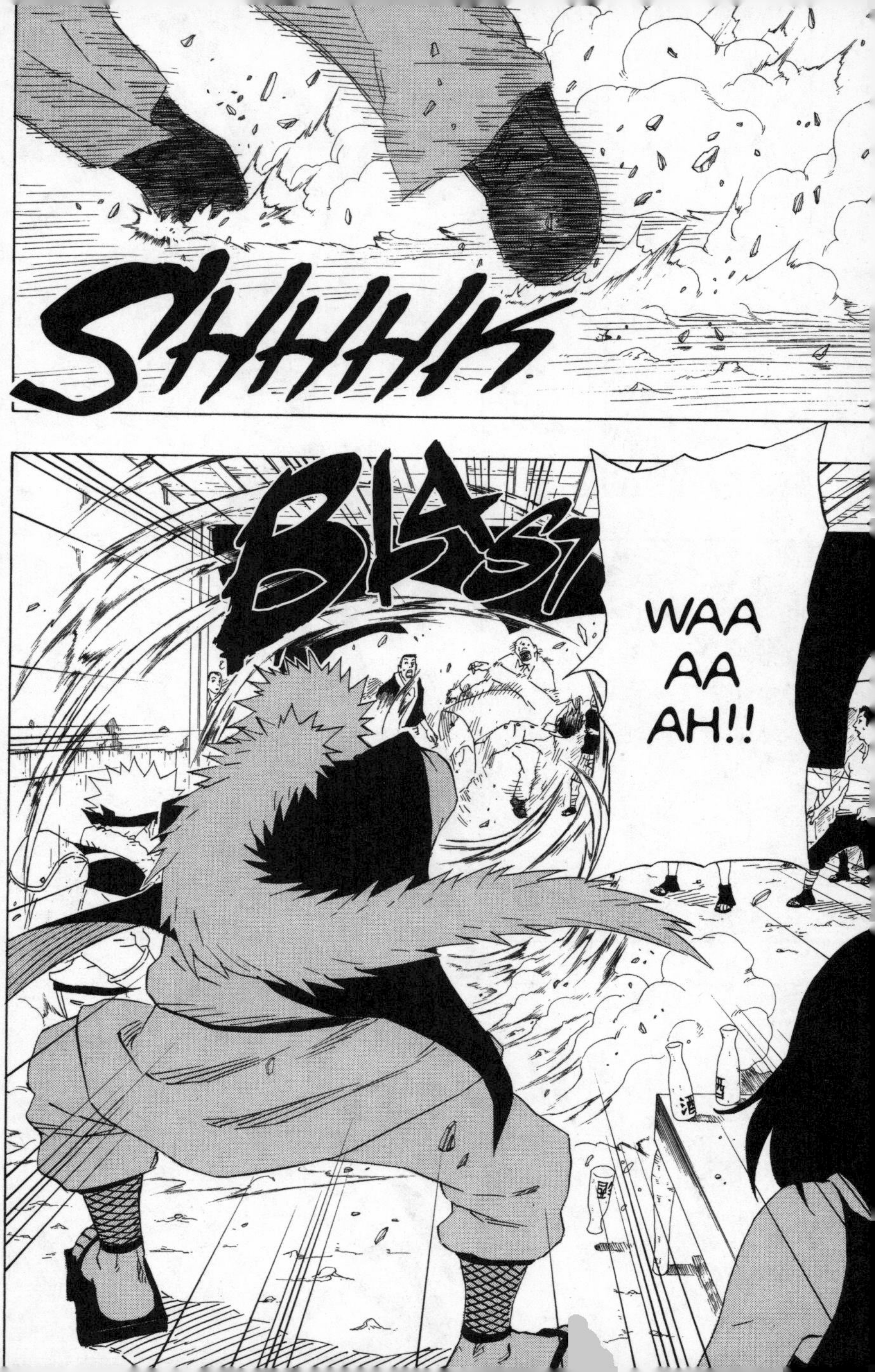
SHHHK
BLAST
WAA
AA
AH!!

READ THIS WAY

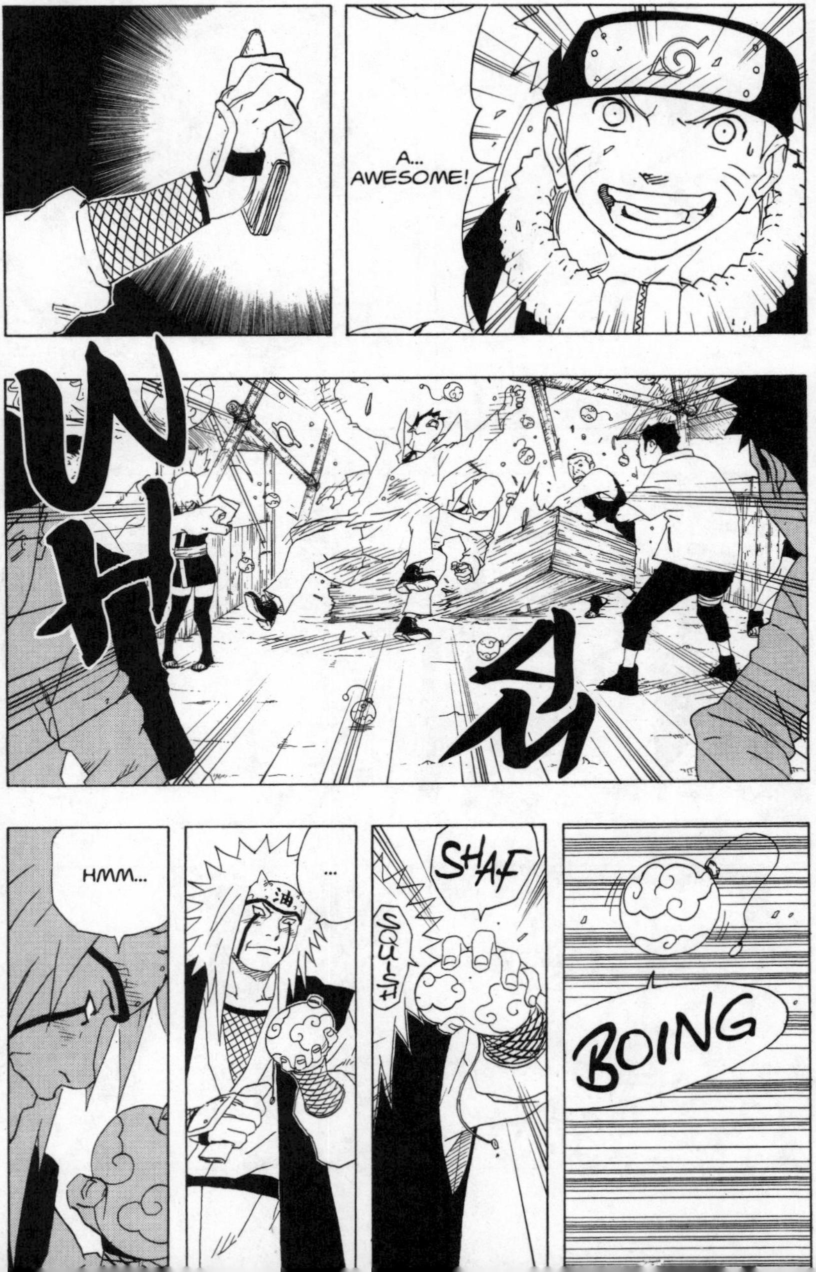
A... AWESOME!
BOING
SHAF
SQUISH
...
HMM...

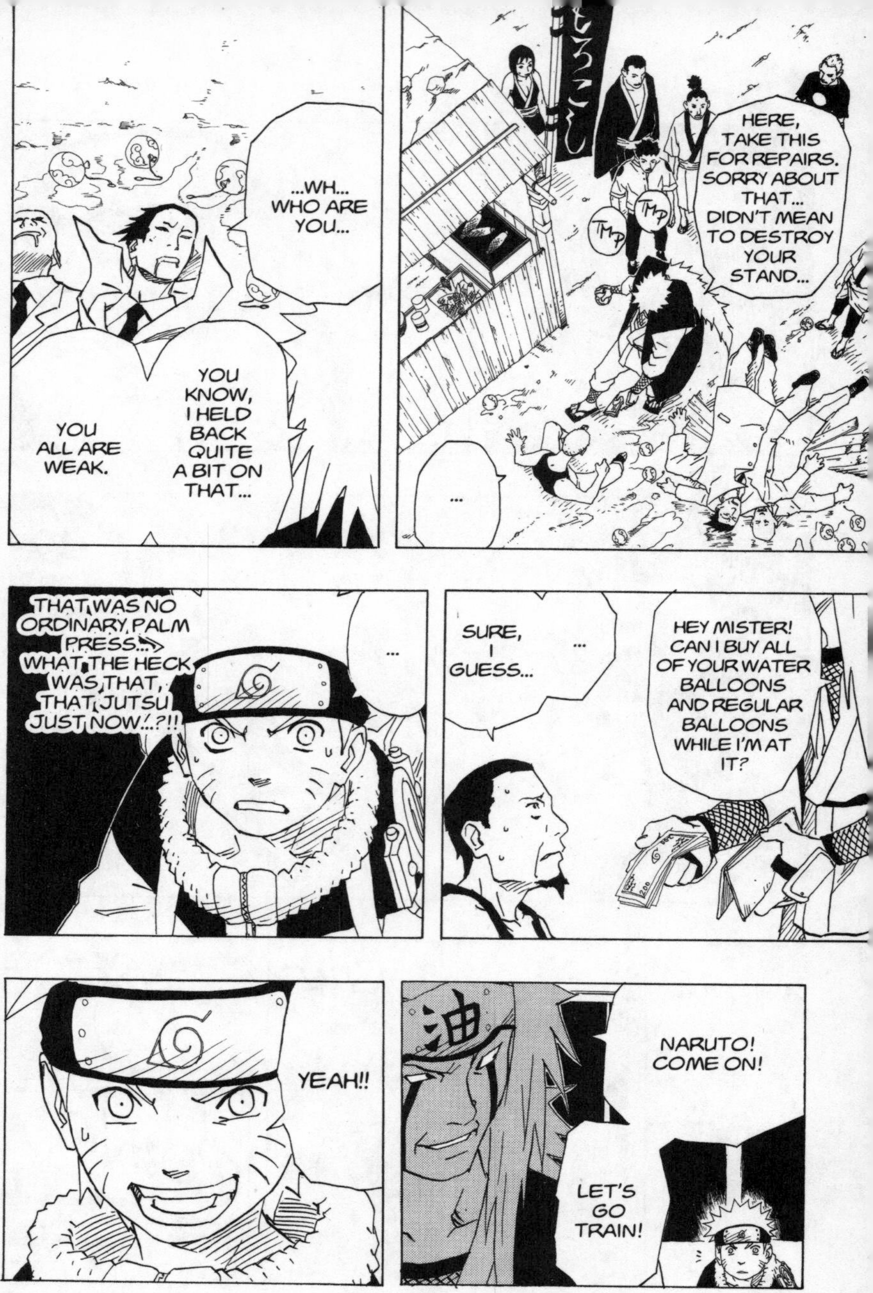
HERE, TAKE THIS FOR REPAIRS. SORRY ABOUT THAT... DIDN'T MEAN TO DESTROY YOUR STAND...
TMP
TMP
...
...WH... WHO ARE YOU...
YOU KNOW, I HELD BACK QUITE A BIT ON THAT...
YOU ALL ARE WEAK.
HEY MISTER! CAN I BUY ALL OF YOUR WATER BALLOONS AND REGULAR BALLOONS WHILE I'M AT IT?
...
SURE, I GUESS...
...
THAT WAS NO ORDINARY PALM PRESS...!! WHAT THE HECK WAS THAT, THAT JUTSU JUST NOW...?!!
NARUTO! COME ON!
LET'S GO TRAIN!
YEAH!!

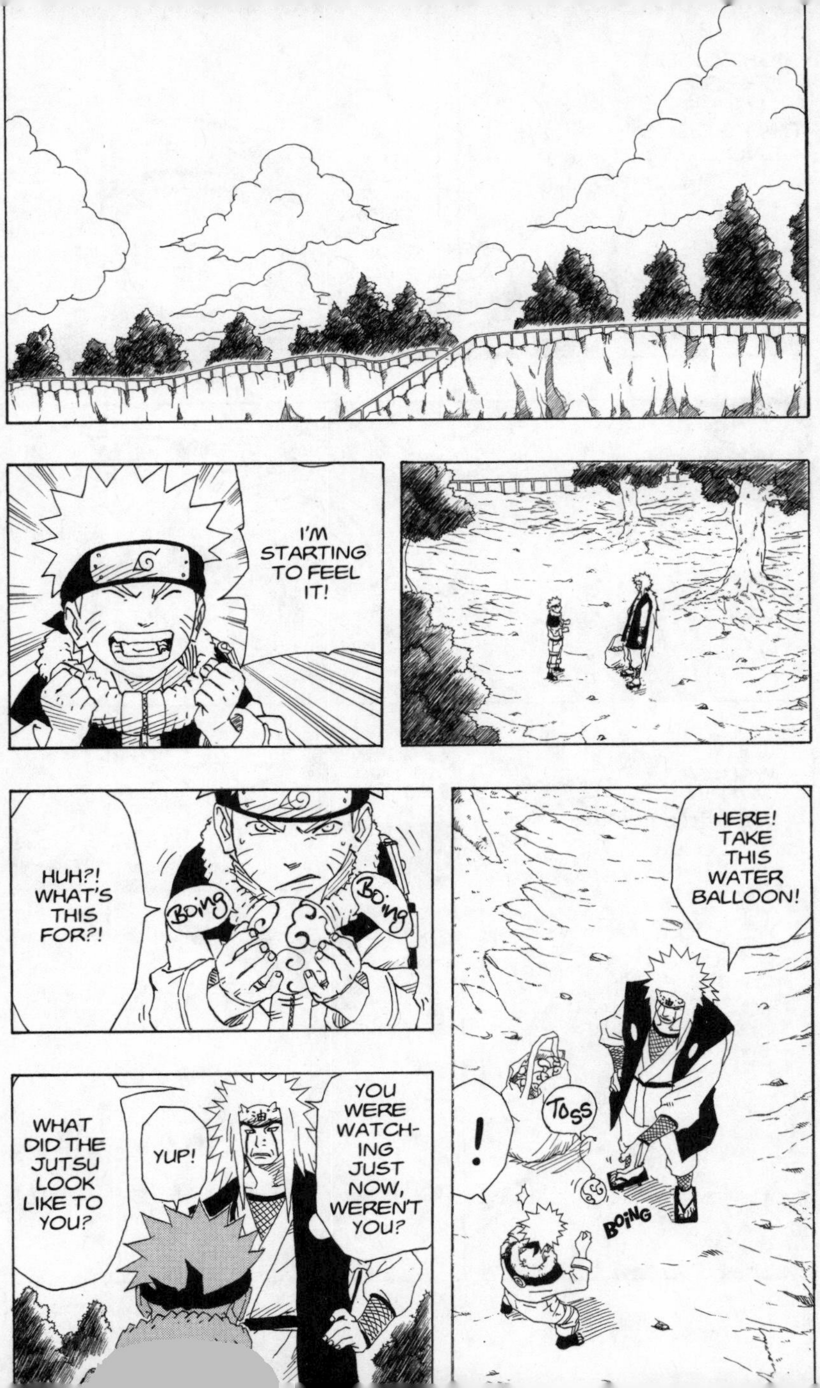
I'M STARTING TO FEEL IT!
HERE! TAKE THIS WATER BALLOON!
TOSS
!
BOING
HUH?! WHAT'S THIS FOR?!
Boing
Boing
YOU WERE WATCHING JUST NOW, WEREN'T YOU?
YUP!
WHAT DID THE JUTSU LOOK LIKE TO YOU?

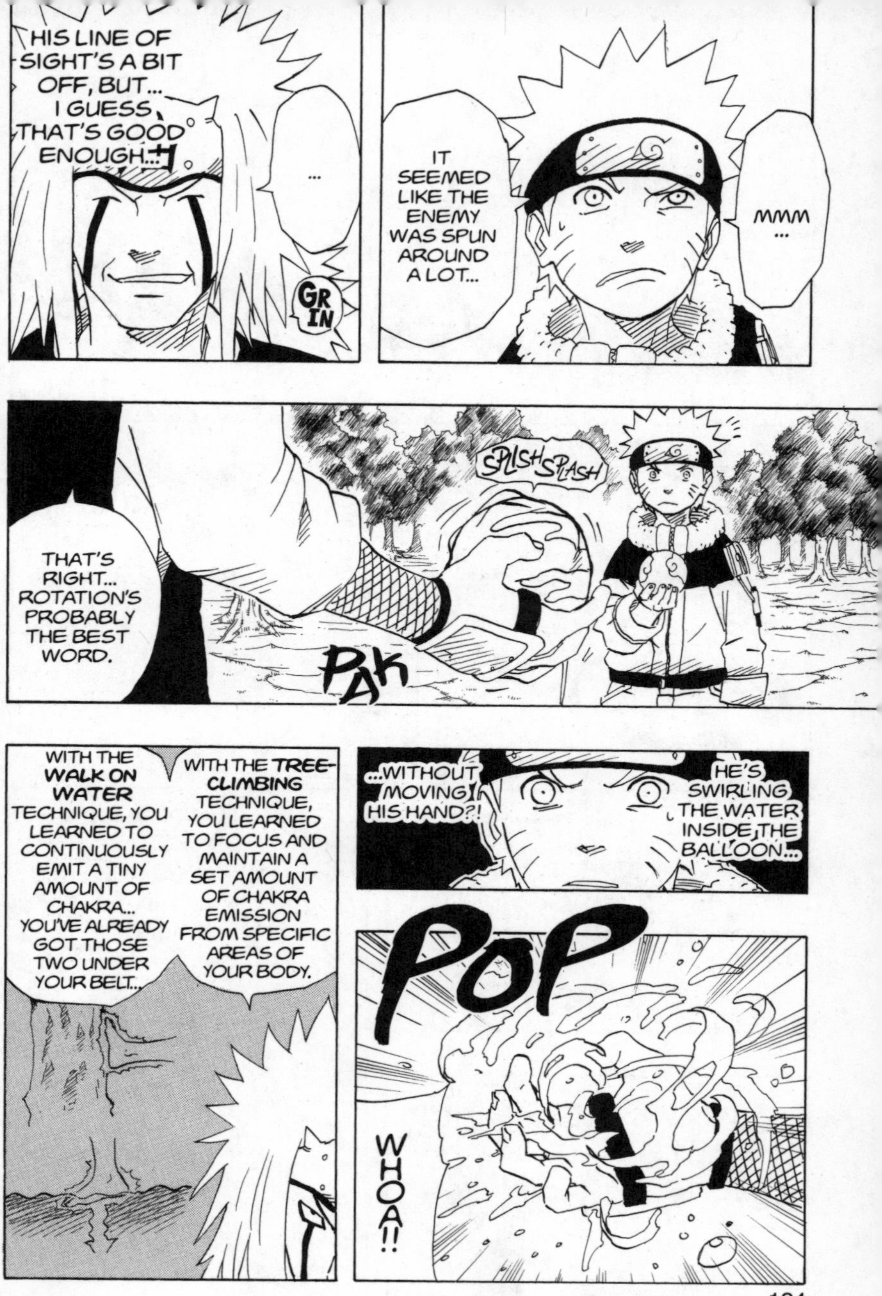
MMM...
IT SEEMED LIKE THE ENEMY WAS SPUN AROUND A LOT...
...
HIS LINE OF SIGHT'S A BIT OFF, BUT... I GUESS THAT'S GOOD ENOUGH...
GRIN
SPLISH SPLASH
THAT'S RIGHT... ROTATION'S PROBABLY THE BEST WORD.
PAK
HE'S SWIRLING THE WATER INSIDE THE BALLOON...
...WITHOUT MOVING HIS HAND?!
POP
WHOA!!
WITH THE TREE-CLIMBING TECHNIQUE, YOU LEARNED TO FOCUS AND MAINTAIN A SET AMOUNT OF CHAKRA EMISSION FROM SPECIFIC AREAS OF YOUR BODY.
WITH THE WALK ON WATER TECHNIQUE, YOU LEARNED TO CONTINUOUSLY EMIT A TINY AMOUNT OF CHAKRA... YOU'VE ALREADY GOT THOSE TWO UNDER YOUR BELT...

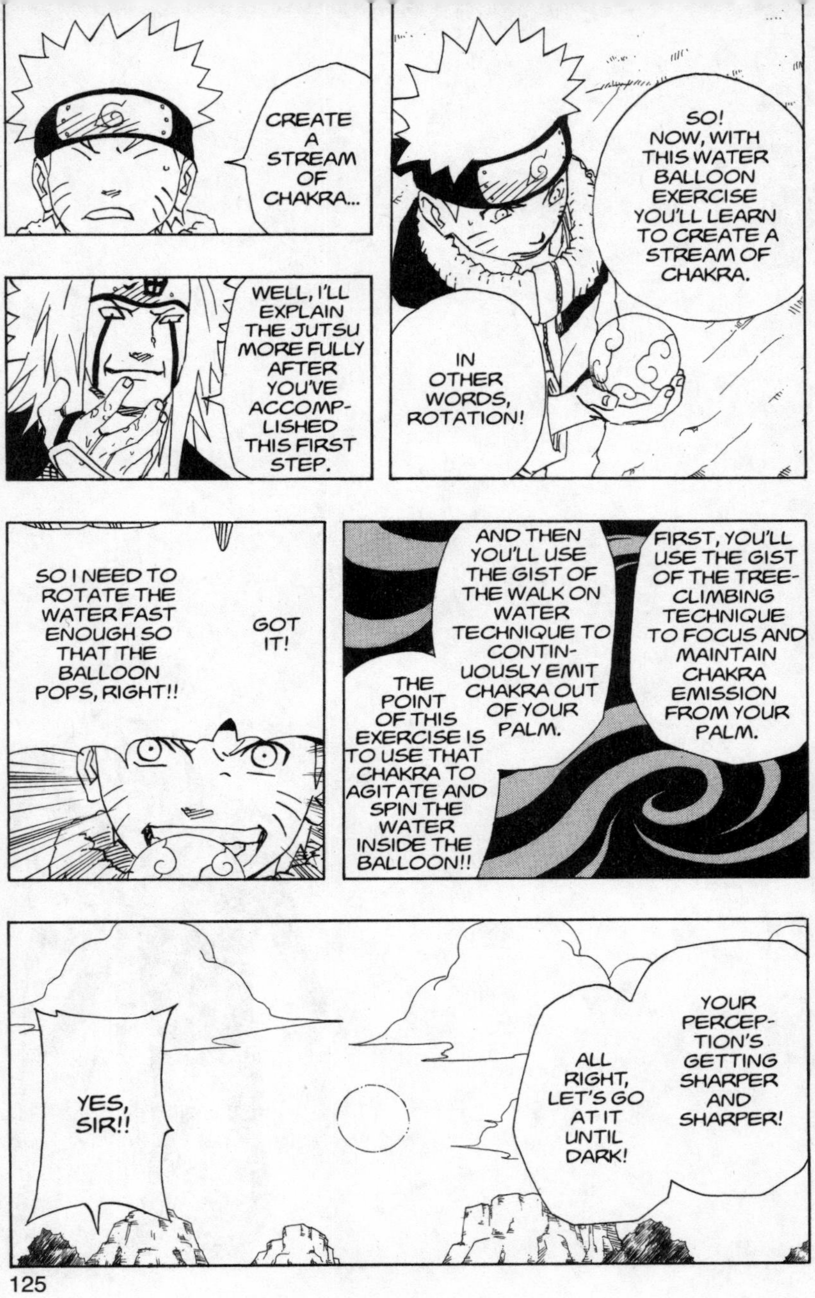
SO! NOW, WITH THIS WATER BALLOON EXERCISE YOU'LL LEARN TO CREATE A STREAM OF CHAKRA.
IN OTHER WORDS, ROTATION!
CREATE A STREAM OF CHAKRA...
WELL, I'LL EXPLAIN THE JUTSU MORE FULLY AFTER YOU'VE ACCOMP-LISHED THIS FIRST STEP.
FIRST, YOU'LL USE THE GIST OF THE TREE-CLIMBING TECHNIQUE TO FOCUS AND MAINTAIN CHAKRA EMISSION FROM YOUR PALM.
AND THEN YOU'LL USE THE GIST OF THE WALK ON WATER TECHNIQUE TO CONTIN-UOUSLY EMIT CHAKRA OUT OF YOUR PALM.
THE POINT OF THIS EXERCISE IS TO USE THAT CHAKRA TO AGITATE AND SPIN THE WATER INSIDE THE BALLOON!!
GOT IT!
SO I NEED TO ROTATE THE WATER FAST ENOUGH SO THAT THE BALLOON POPS, RIGHT!!
YOUR PERCEP-TION'S GETTING SHARPER AND SHARPER!
ALL RIGHT, LET'S GO AT IT UNTIL DARK!
YES, SIR!!

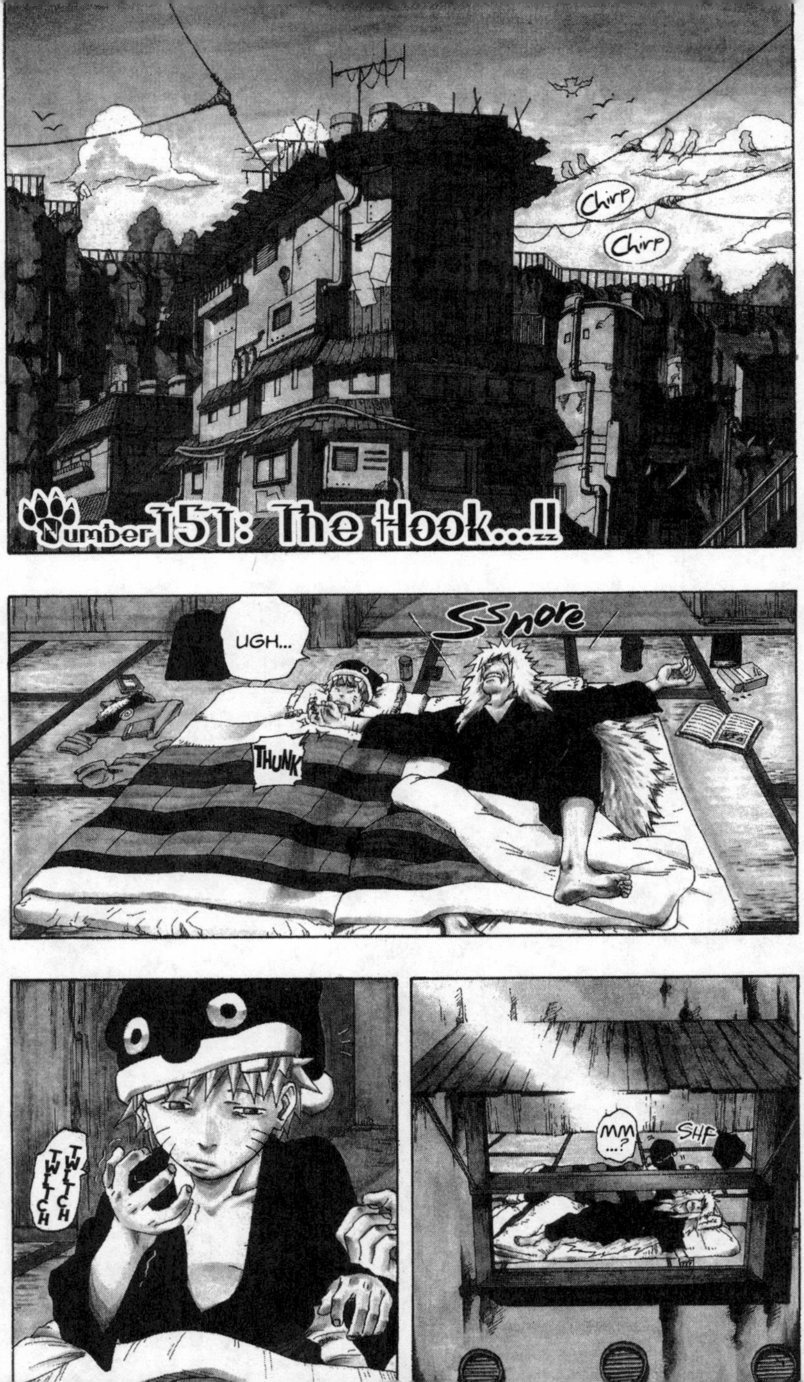
Number 151: The Hook...!!zz
Chirp
Chirp
SSnore
UGH...
THUNK
MM ...?
SHF
TWITCH TWITCH

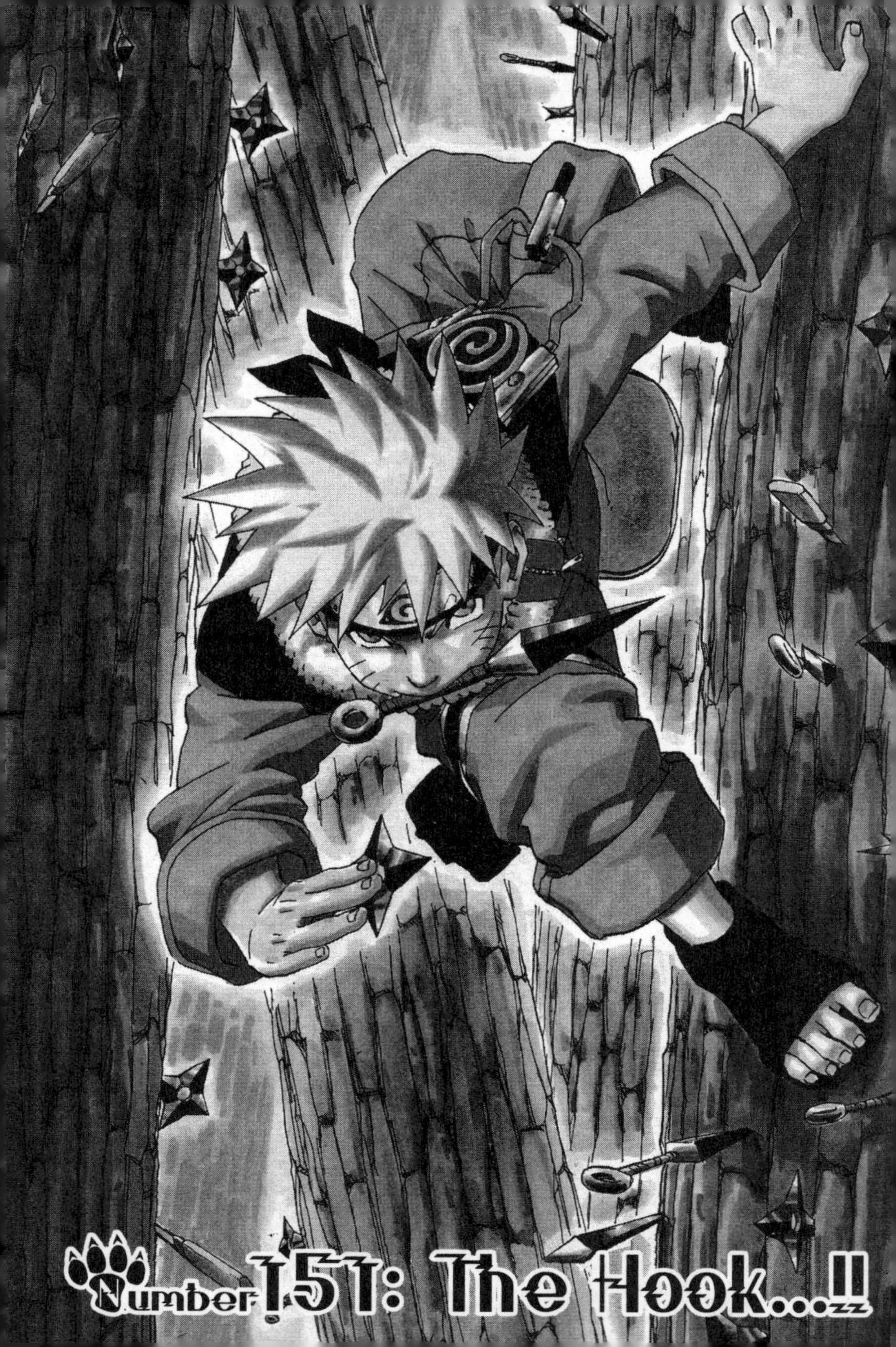
Number 151: The Hook...!!

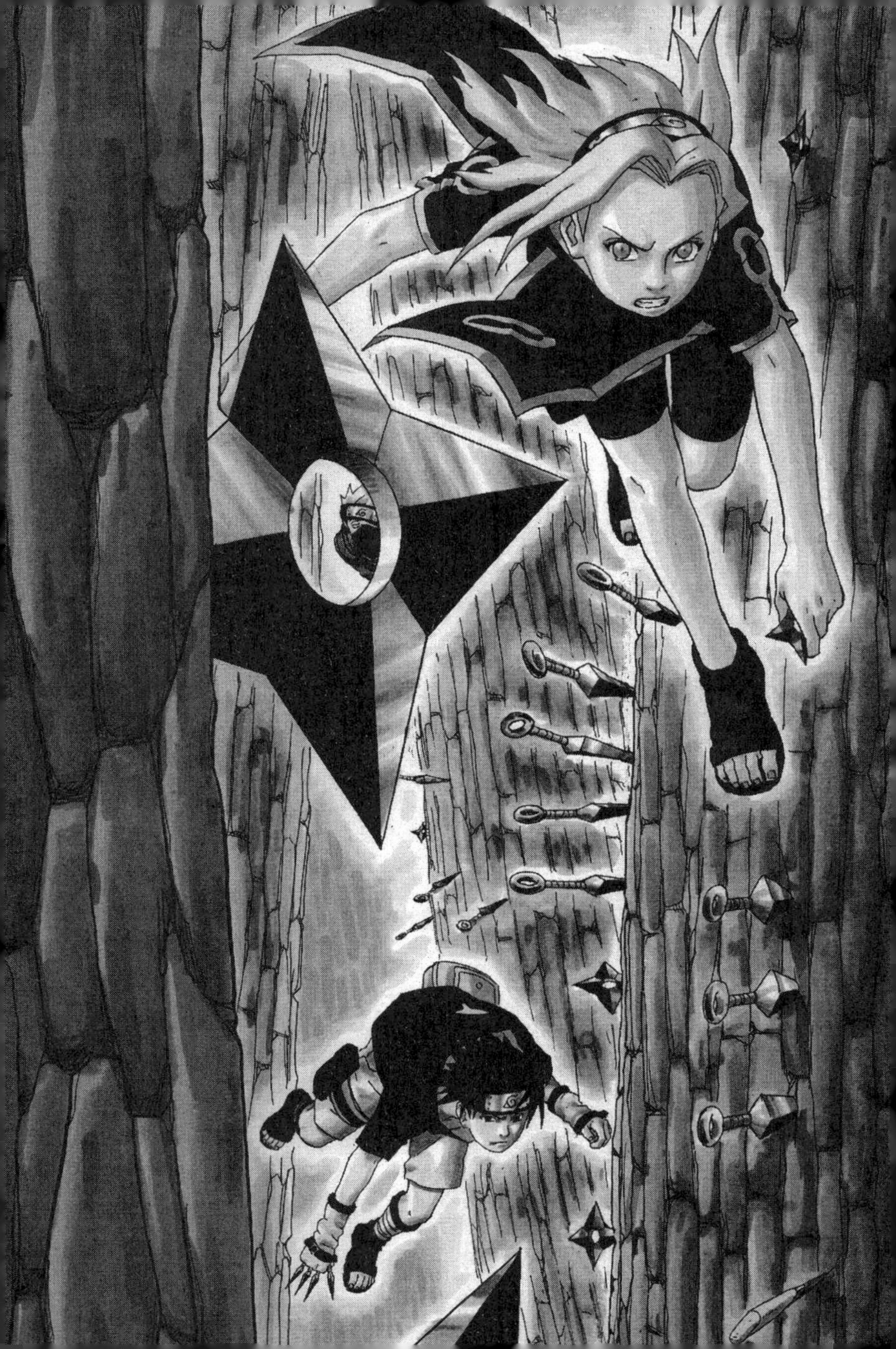

NARUTO
-ナルト-

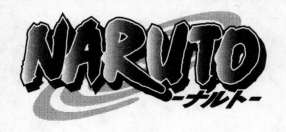

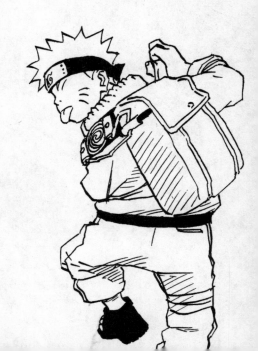

READ THIS WAY

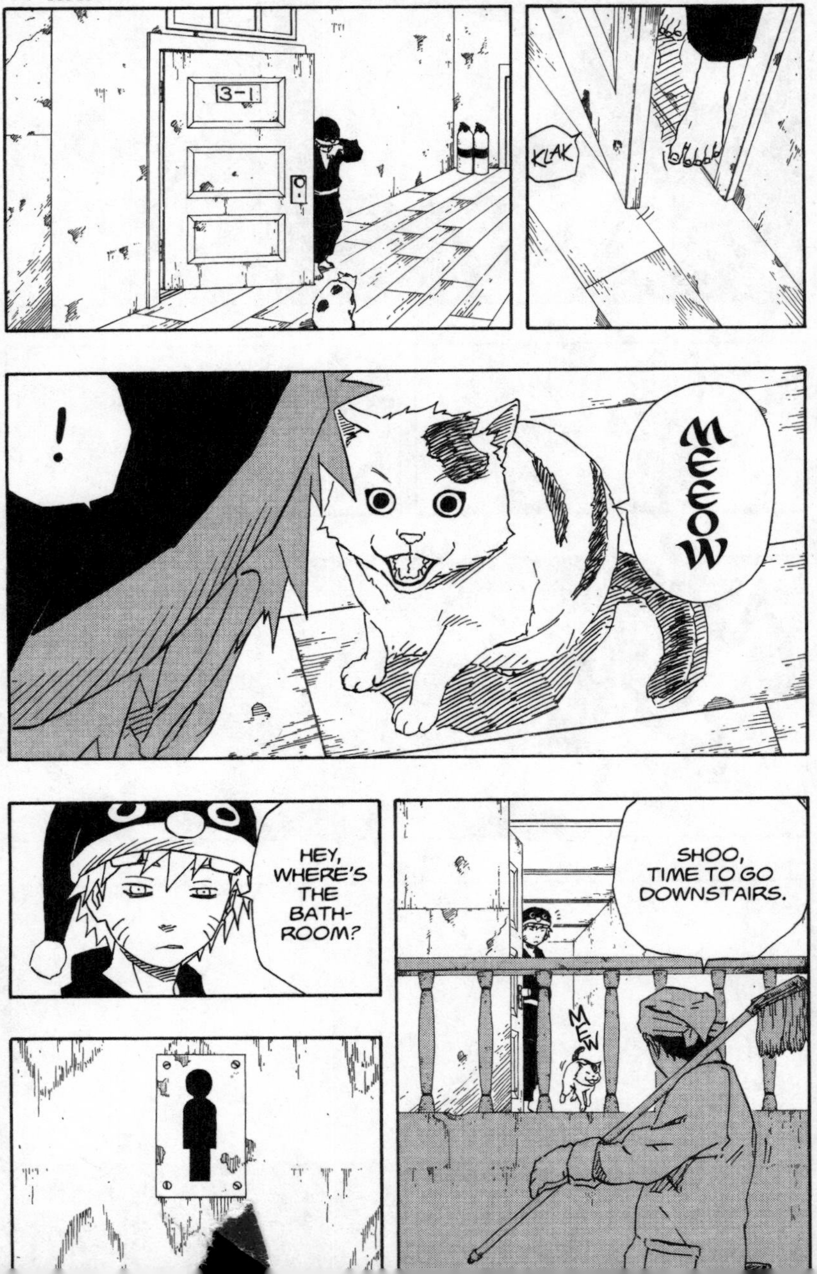
KLAK
MEEOW
!
SHOO, TIME TO GO DOWNSTAIRS.
MEW
HEY, WHERE'S THE BATH-ROOM?

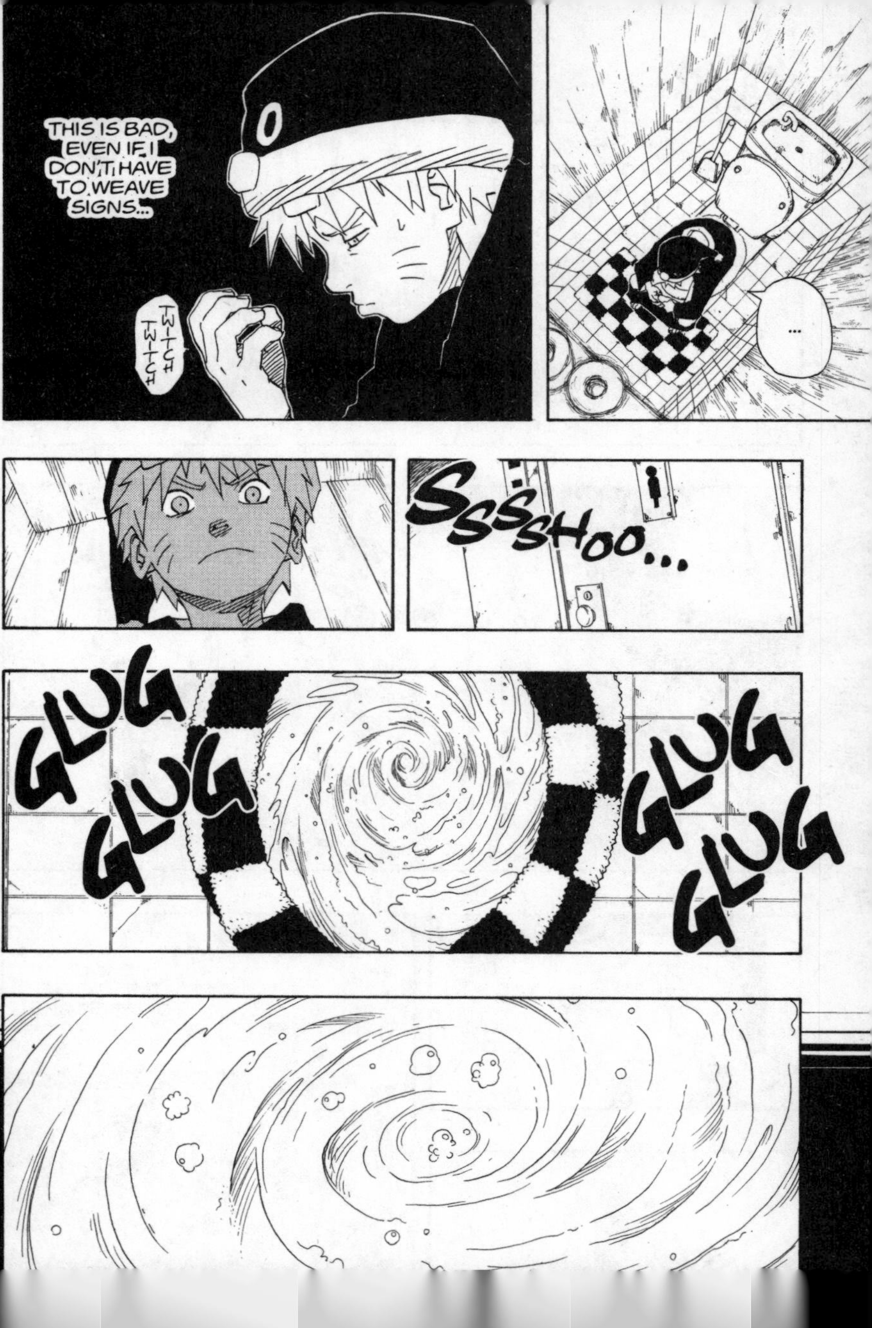
...
THIS IS BAD, EVEN IF I DON'T HAVE TO WEAVE SIGNS...
TWITCH TWITCH
SSSSHOO...
GLUG GLUG
GLUG GLUG

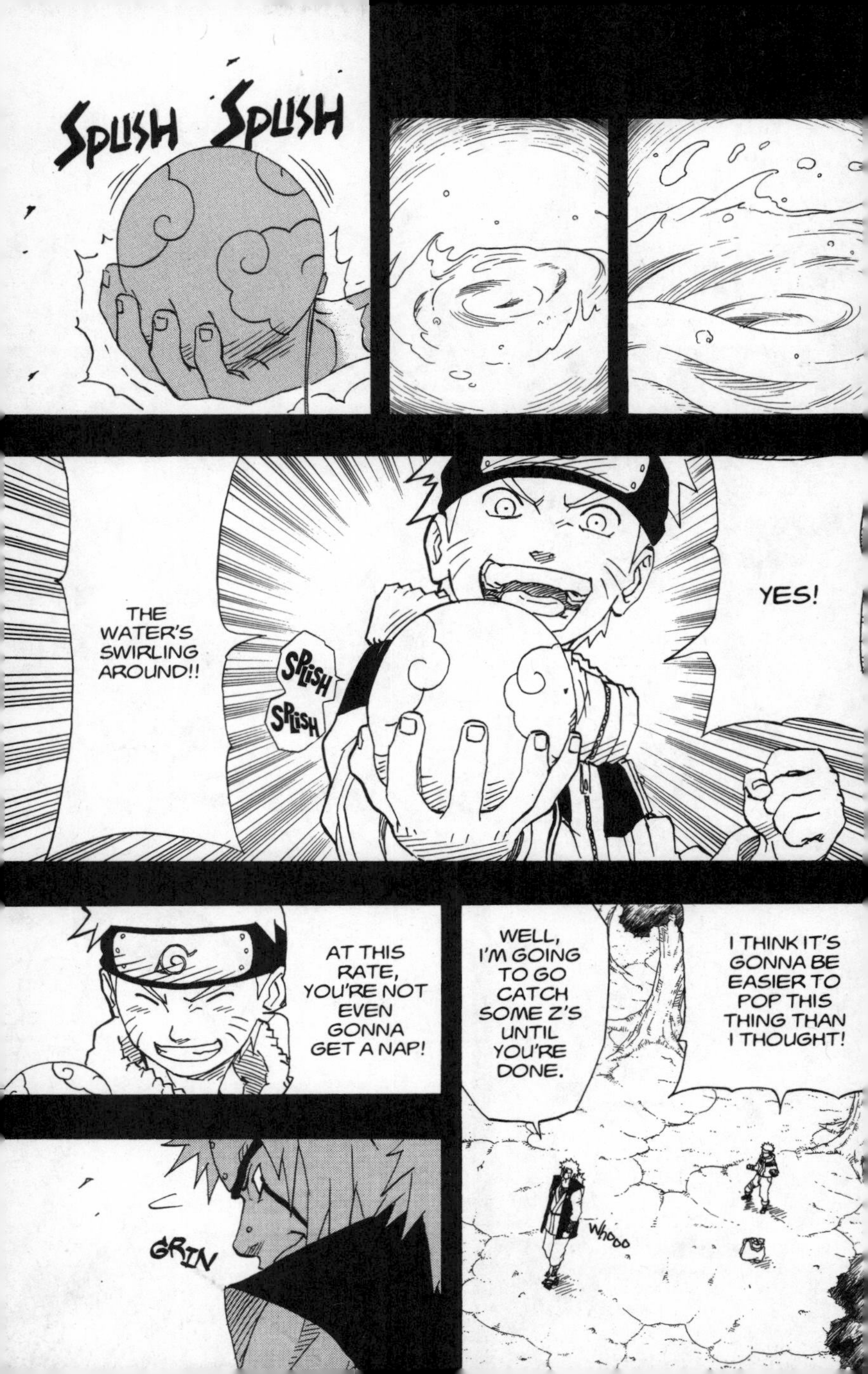
SPLISH SPLISH
YES!
SPLISH
SPLISH
THE WATER'S SWIRLING AROUND!!
I THINK IT'S GONNA BE EASIER TO POP THIS THING THAN I THOUGHT!
WELL, I'M GOING TO GO CATCH SOME Z'S UNTIL YOU'RE DONE.
Whooo
AT THIS RATE, YOU'RE NOT EVEN GONNA GET A NAP!
GRIN

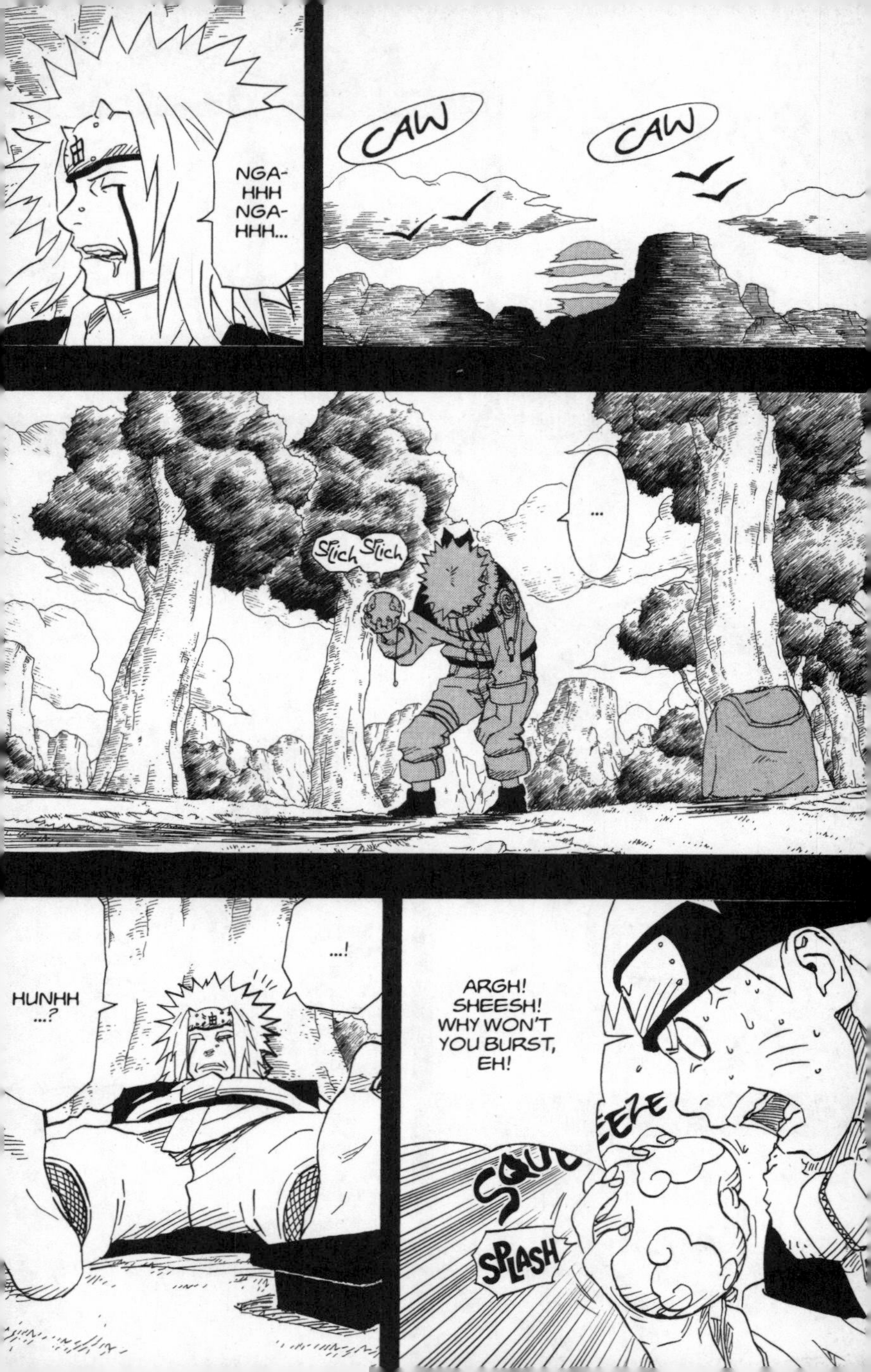

CAW
CAW
NGA-HHH NGA-HHH...
...
SPLICH SPLICH
ARGH! SHEESH! WHY WON'T YOU BURST, EH!
SQUEEZE
SPLASH
...!
HUNHH ...?

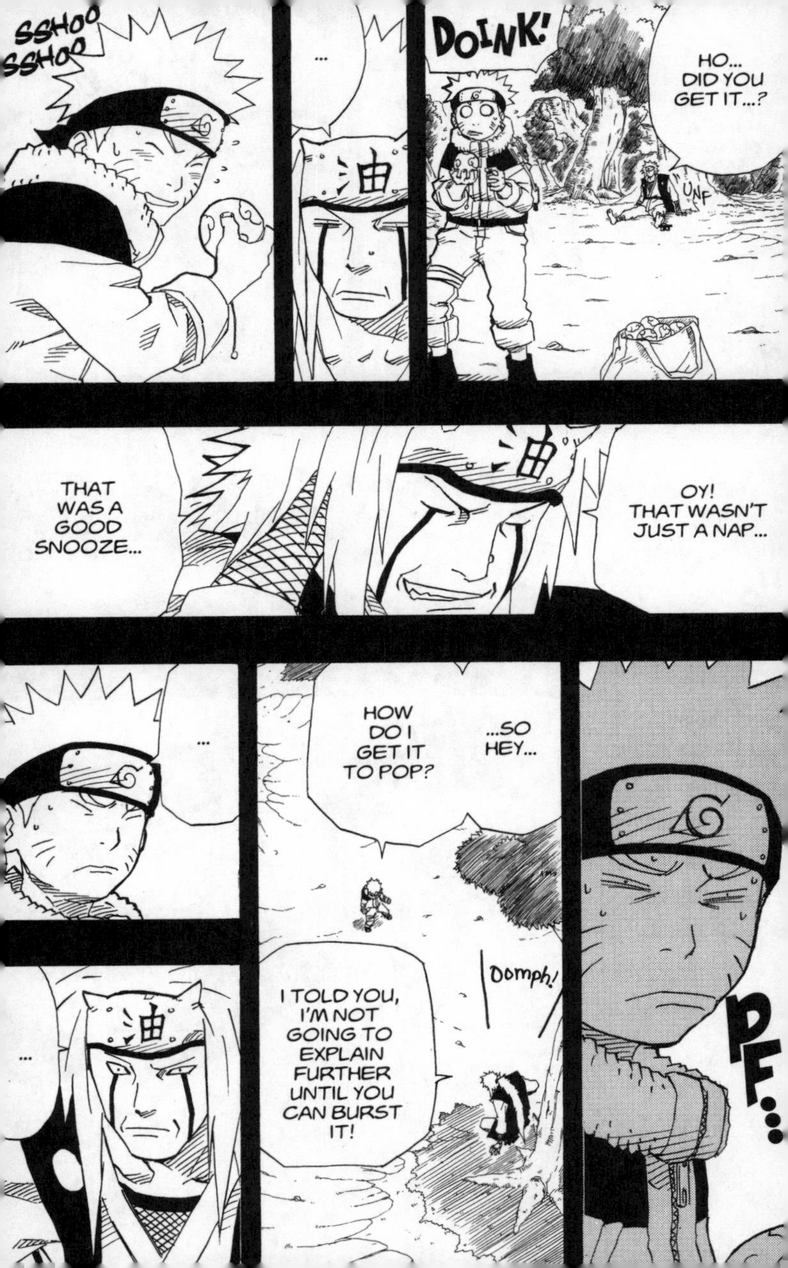
HO... DID YOU GET IT...?
DOINK!
UNF
...
SSHOO SSHOO
OY! THAT WASN'T JUST A NAP...
THAT WAS A GOOD SNOOZE...
PF...
...SO HEY...
HOW DO I GET IT TO POP?
Oomph!
I TOLD YOU, I'M NOT GOING TO EXPLAIN FURTHER UNTIL YOU CAN BURST IT!
...
...

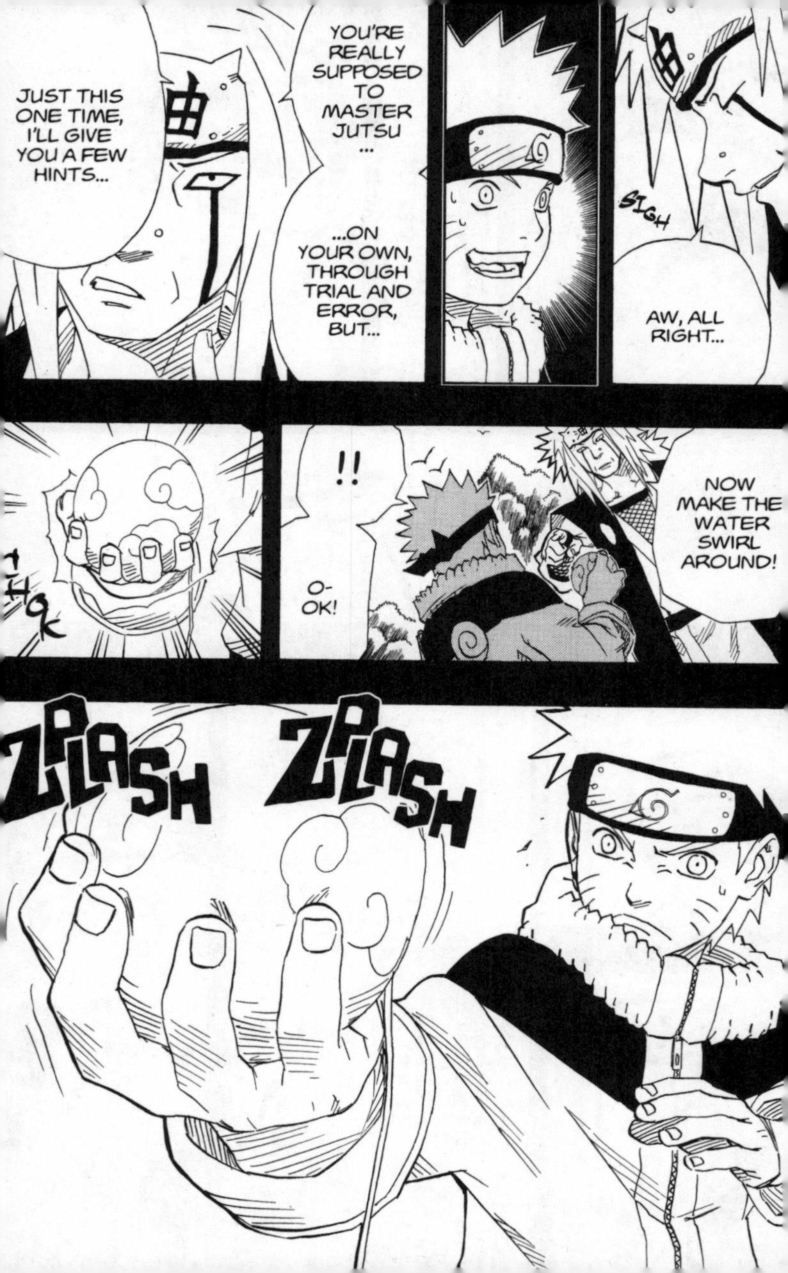
SIGH
AW, ALL RIGHT...
YOU'RE REALLY SUPPOSED TO MASTER JUTSU...
...ON YOUR OWN, THROUGH TRIAL AND ERROR, BUT...
JUST THIS ONE TIME, I'LL GIVE YOU A FEW HINTS...
NOW MAKE THE WATER SWIRL AROUND!
!!
O-OK!
THOK
ZPLASH
ZPLASH

READ THIS WAY

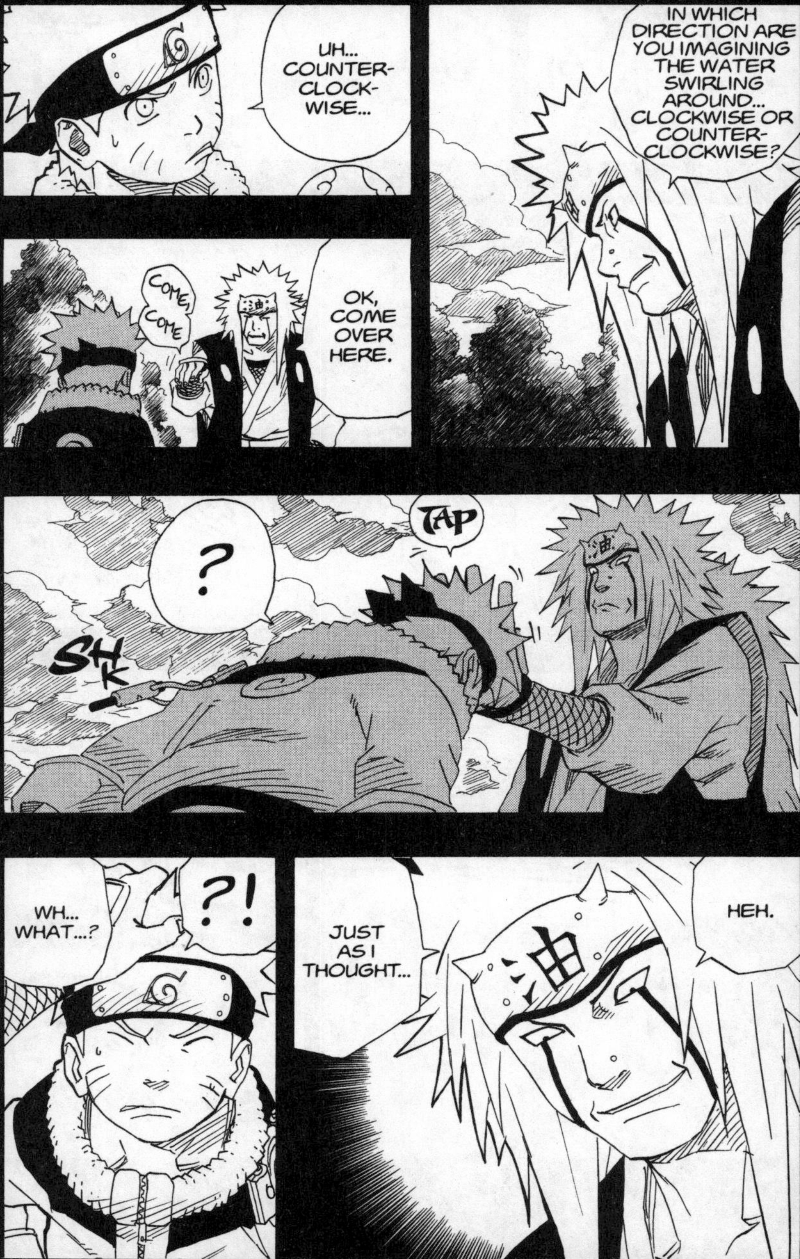

IN WHICH DIRECTION ARE YOU IMAGINING THE WATER SWIRLING AROUND... CLOCKWISE OR COUNTER-CLOCKWISE?
UH... COUNTER-CLOCKWISE...
OK, COME OVER HERE.
COME, COME
TAP
?
SHK
HEH.
JUST AS I THOUGHT...
?!
WH... WHAT...?

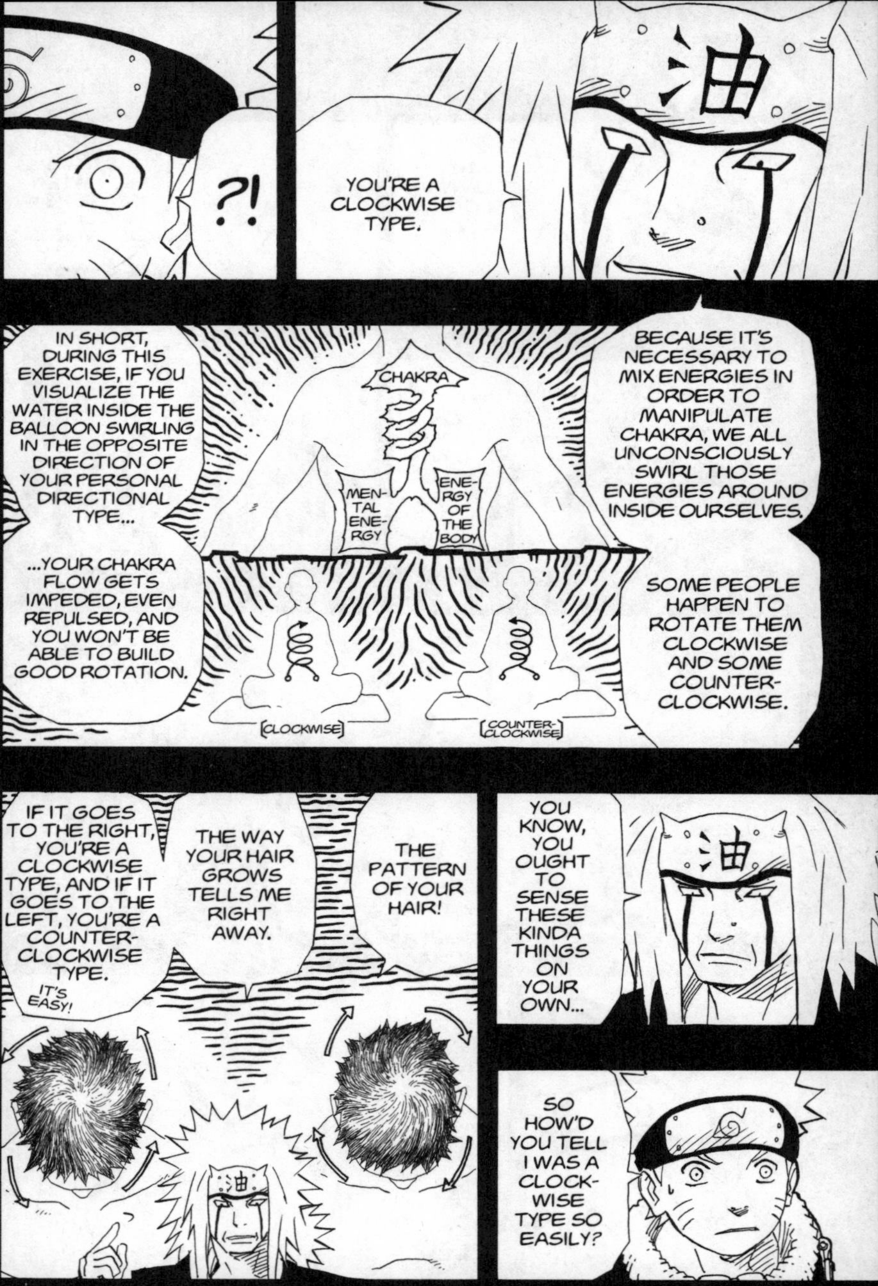
YOU'RE A CLOCKWISE TYPE.
?!
BECAUSE IT'S NECESSARY TO MIX ENERGIES IN ORDER TO MANIPULATE CHAKRA, WE ALL UNCONSCIOUSLY SWIRL THOSE ENERGIES AROUND INSIDE OURSELVES.
SOME PEOPLE HAPPEN TO ROTATE THEM CLOCKWISE AND SOME COUNTER-CLOCKWISE.
CHAKRA
ENERGY OF THE BODY
MENTAL ENERGY
COUNTER-CLOCKWISE
CLOCKWISE
IN SHORT, DURING THIS EXERCISE, IF YOU VISUALIZE THE WATER INSIDE THE BALLOON SWIRLING IN THE OPPOSITE DIRECTION OF YOUR PERSONAL DIRECTIONAL TYPE...
...YOUR CHAKRA FLOW GETS IMPEDED, EVEN REPULSED, AND YOU WON'T BE ABLE TO BUILD GOOD ROTATION.
YOU KNOW, YOU OUGHT TO SENSE THESE KINDA THINGS ON YOUR OWN...
SO HOW'D YOU TELL I WAS A CLOCKWISE TYPE SO EASILY?
THE PATTERN OF YOUR HAIR!
THE WAY YOUR HAIR GROWS TELLS ME RIGHT AWAY.
IF IT GOES TO THE RIGHT, YOU'RE A CLOCKWISE TYPE, AND IF IT GOES TO THE LEFT, YOU'RE A COUNTER-CLOCKWISE TYPE.
IT'S EASY!

READ THIS WAY

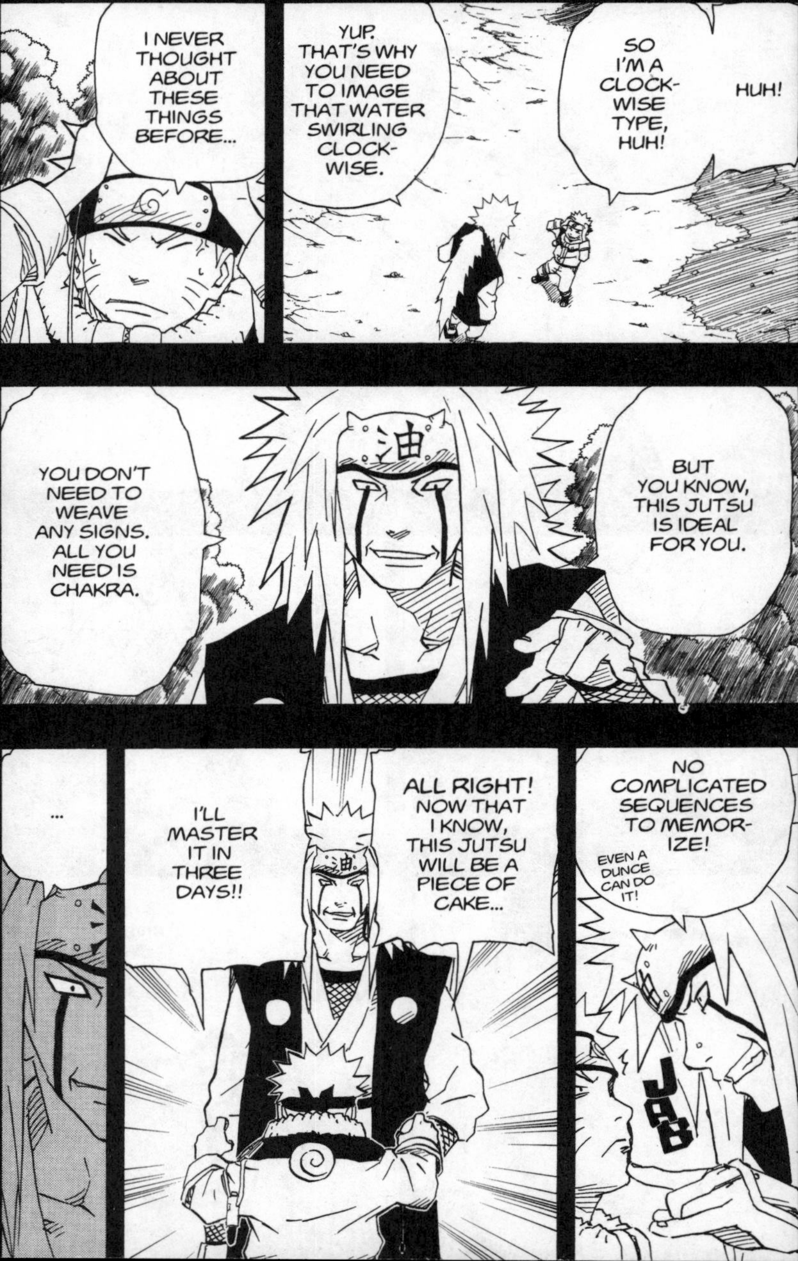
HUH!
SO I'M A CLOCKWISE TYPE, HUH!
YUP. THAT'S WHY YOU NEED TO IMAGE THAT WATER SWIRLING CLOCKWISE.
I NEVER THOUGHT ABOUT THESE THINGS BEFORE...
BUT YOU KNOW, THIS JUTSU IS IDEAL FOR YOU.
YOU DON'T NEED TO WEAVE ANY SIGNS. ALL YOU NEED IS CHAKRA.
NO COMPLICATED SEQUENCES TO MEMORIZE!
EVEN A DUNCE CAN DO IT!
ALL RIGHT! NOW THAT I KNOW, THIS JUTSU WILL BE A PIECE OF CAKE...
I'LL MASTER IT IN THREE DAYS!!
...

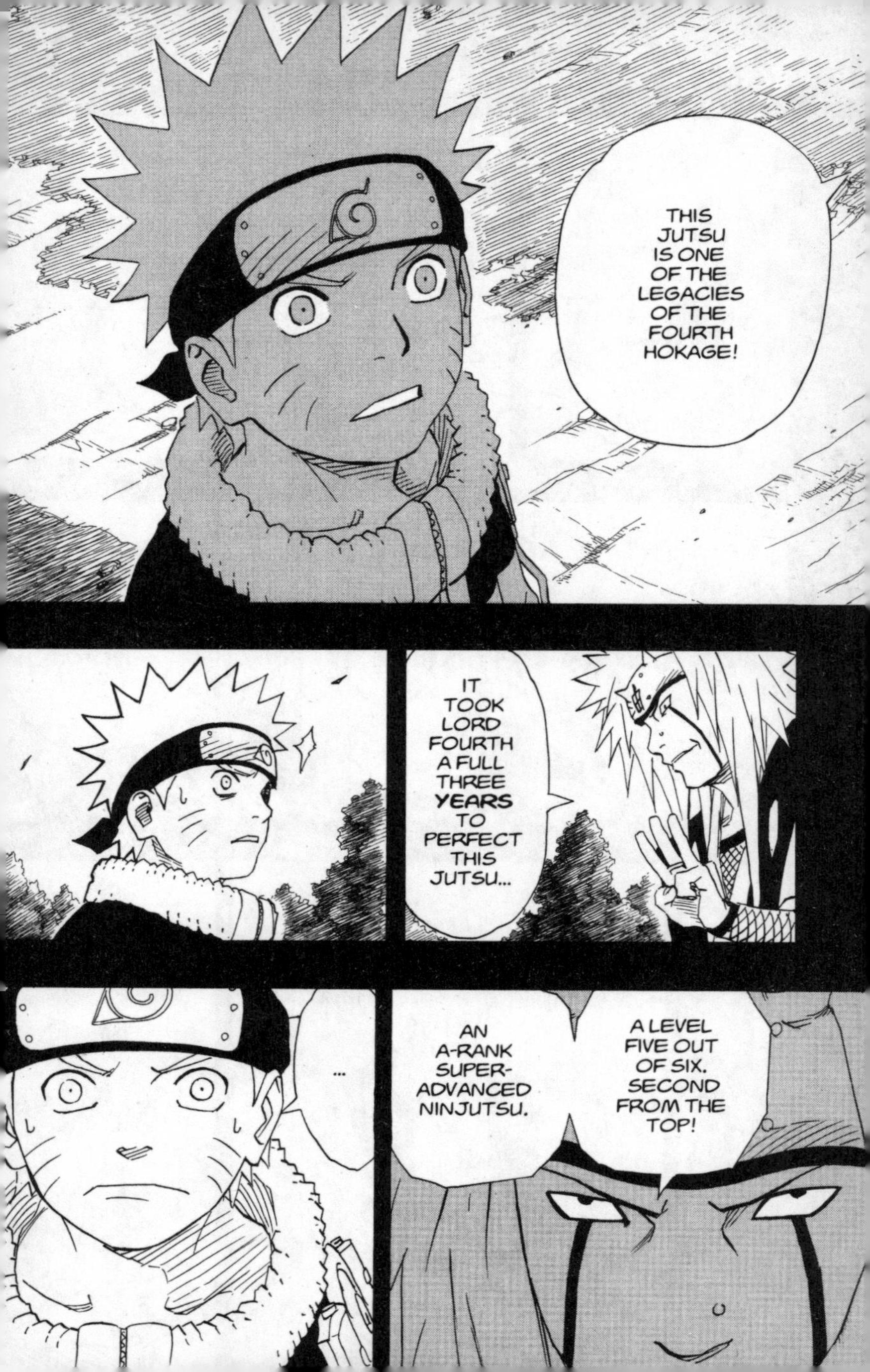
THIS JUTSU IS ONE OF THE LEGACIES OF THE FOURTH HOKAGE!
IT TOOK LORD FOURTH A FULL THREE **YEARS** TO PERFECT THIS JUTSU...
A LEVEL FIVE OUT OF SIX. SECOND FROM THE TOP!
AN A-RANK SUPER-ADVANCED NINJUTSU.
...

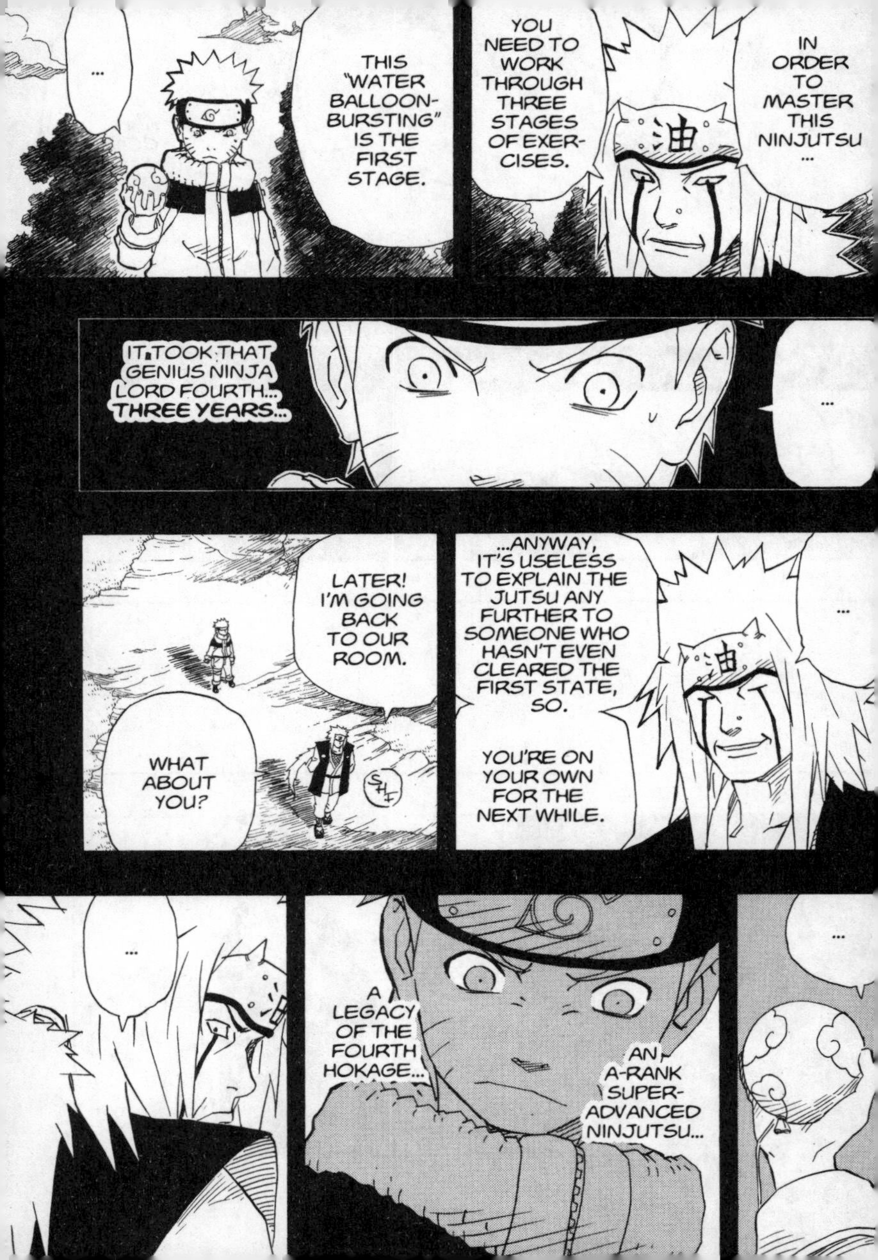
IN ORDER TO MASTER THIS NINJUTSU ...
YOU NEED TO WORK THROUGH THREE STAGES OF EXER-CISES.
THIS "WATER BALLOON-BURSTING" IS THE FIRST STAGE.
...
...
IT TOOK THAT GENIUS NINJA LORD FOURTH... THREE YEARS...
...
...ANYWAY, IT'S USELESS TO EXPLAIN THE JUTSU ANY FURTHER TO SOMEONE WHO HASN'T EVEN CLEARED THE FIRST STATE, SO.
YOU'RE ON YOUR OWN FOR THE NEXT WHILE.
LATER! I'M GOING BACK TO OUR ROOM.
WHAT ABOUT YOU?
...
A LEGACY OF THE FOURTH HOKAGE...
AN A-RANK SUPER-ADVANCED NINJUTSU...
...

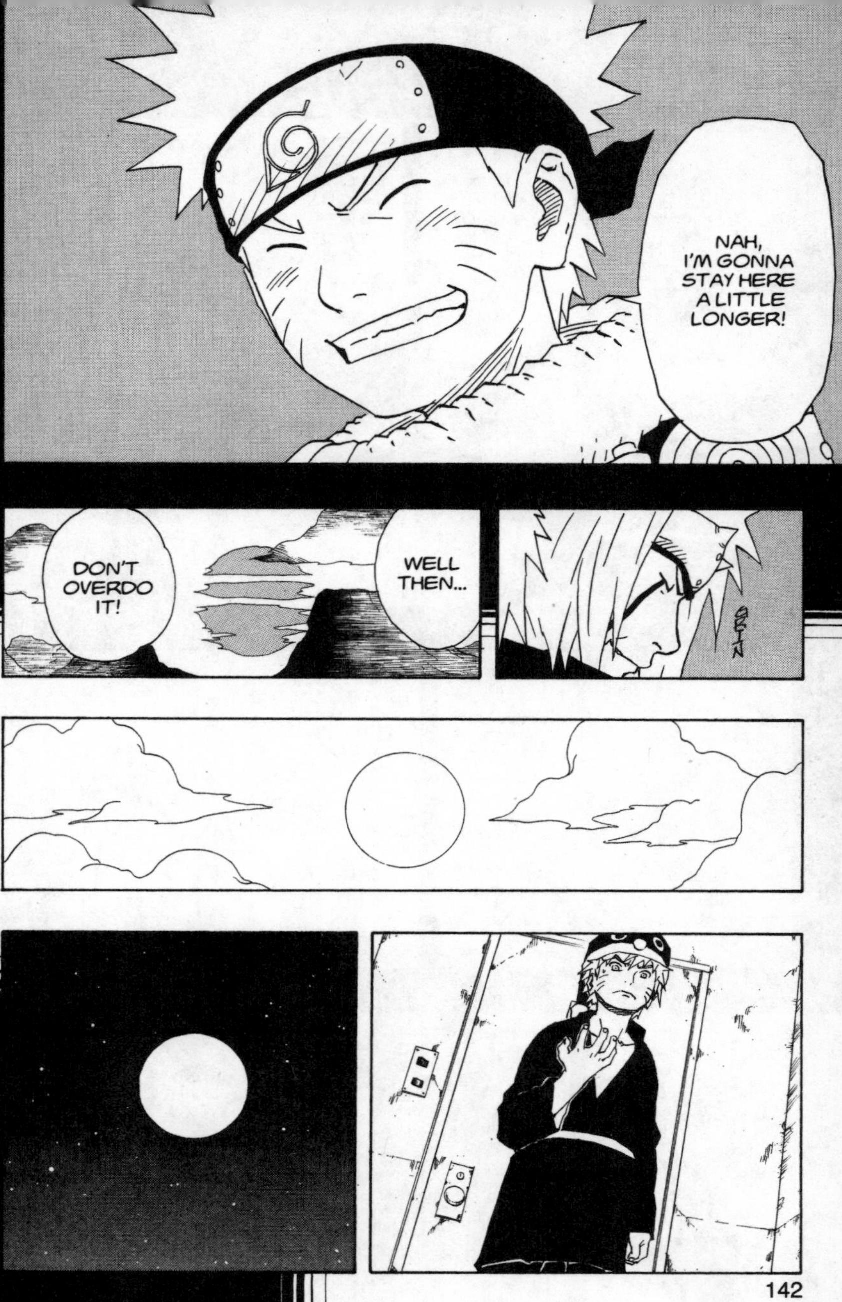
NAH, I'M GONNA STAY HERE A LITTLE LONGER!
GRIN
WELL THEN...
DON'T OVERDO IT!

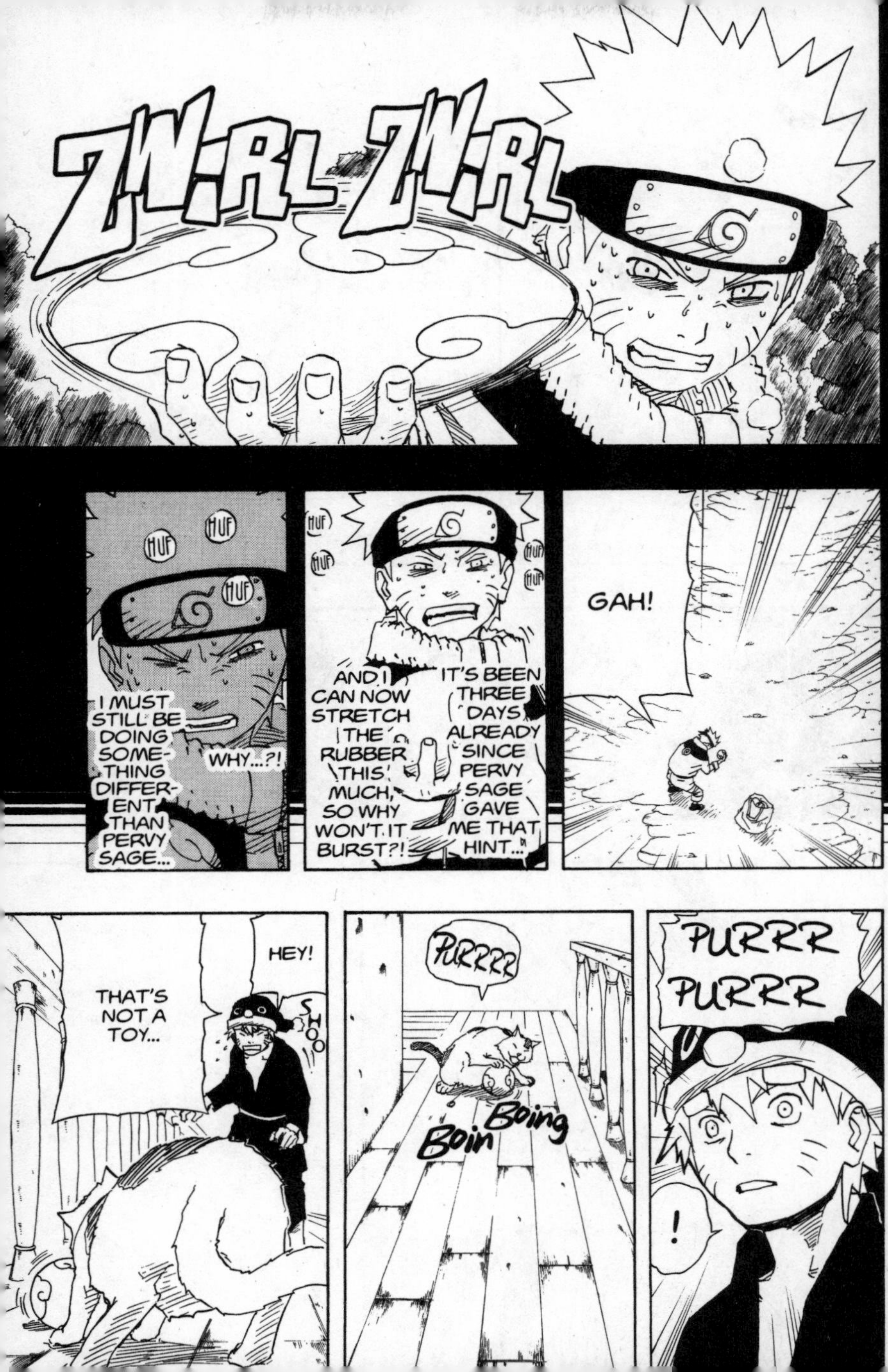
ZWIRL ZWIRL
GAH!
HUF HUF
HUF HUF
IT'S BEEN THREE DAYS ALREADY SINCE PERVY SAGE GAVE ME THAT HINT...
AND I CAN NOW STRETCH THE RUBBER THIS MUCH, SO WHY WON'T IT BURST?!
HUF HUF HUF
WHY...?!
I MUST STILL BE DOING SOMETHING DIFFERENT THAN PERVY SAGE...
PURRR PURRR
!
PURRRR
Boing
Boin
HEY!
SHOO
THAT'S NOT A TOY...

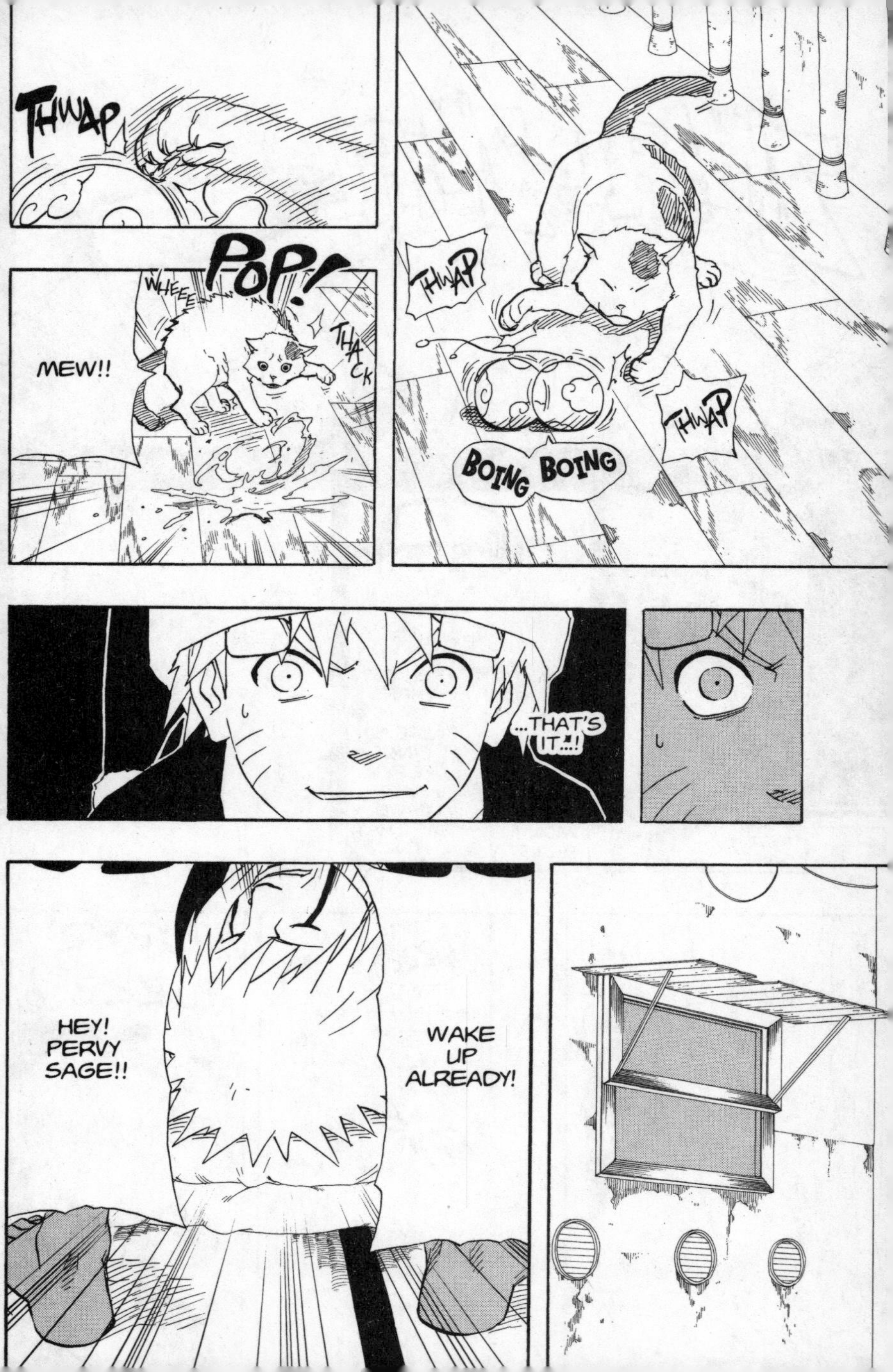
THWAP
THWAP
BOING BOING
THWAP
POP!
WHEEEE
THACK
MEW!!
...THAT'S IT...!
WAKE UP ALREADY!
HEY! PERVY SAGE!!

READ THIS WAY

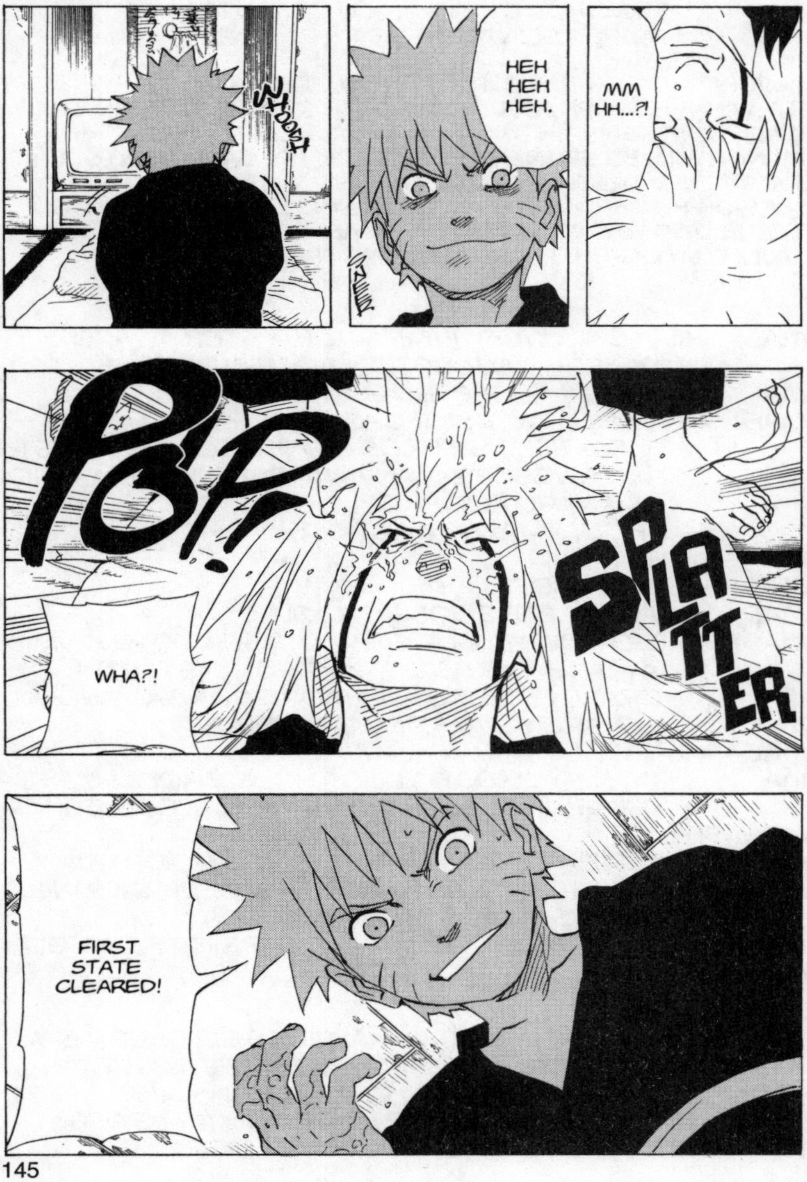
MM HH...?!
HEH HEH HEH.
POP!
SPLATTER
WHA?!
FIRST STATE CLEARED!

THE WORLD OF KISHIMOTO MASASHI
MY PERSONAL HISTORY, PART 25

ACCEPTED FOR THE HOP☆STEP AWARD! I HAD WON! THE WINNING WORK FOR THAT MONTH'S HOP☆STEP AWARD WAS PROMISED PRINTING IN *AKAMURU JUMP*. "FINALLY, MY MANGA WILL BE SEEN BY THE WORLD!" I RECALL BEING SO OVERJOYED THAT I PRANCED AROUND, TALKING TO MYSELF IN A HIGH-PITCHED VOICE AND LAUGHING AT HOME. I WANTED TO TELL SOMEONE HOW HAPPY I WAS! SO I IMMEDIATELY CALLED MY PARENTS' HOUSE. MY MOTHER ANSWERED.

MASASHI: "MOM! I WON JUMP'S HOP☆STEP AWARD! I'VE BEEN ACCEPTED! ACCEPTED!"

MA: "WHAT? ACCEPTED FOR WHAT?"

MASASHI: "...UH...! UM... JUMP CHOOSES FROM AMONG SUBMITTED ENTRIES OF NEWCOMER ARTISTS AND GIVES THEM AN AWARD. I GOT PICKED FOR AN AWARD FOR PEOPLE WHO WILL ONE DAY BECOME MANGA ARTISTS!"

MA: "WHO?"

MASASHI: "ME, I DID!"

MA: "AHH, I SEE! GOOD FOR YOU..."

MASASHI: "SO NOW I'M ONE STEP CLOSER TO BECOMING A MANGA ARTIST! I'M GOING TO START DRAWING MORE AND MORE MANGA... AND..."

MA: "SO, ARE YOU EATING PROPERLY?"

MASASHI: "...◊"

MA: "DON'T YOU BE EATING THOSE GROCERY STORE RAMEN! YOU HAVE TO EAT YOUR VEGGIES!"

MASASHI: "..."

MA: "AND EAT STEWED THINGS! IT'S GOOD FOR YOU!"

MASASHI: "...ALL RIGHT... HEY, I GOTTA GO... MY CALLING CARD'S ALMOST EMPTY..."

MA: "SURE! WELL THEN... TAKE CARE OF YOURSELF!"

MASASHI: "YEAH..."

SHE DIDN'T REALLY GET MY HAPPINESS... IT SEEMS MY MA WAS MORE CONCERNED ABOUT MY HEALTH THAN ABOUT A MANGA AWARD. SO I THOUGHT I WOULD START CHURNING OUT MANGA WHILE WATCHING MY HEALTH. THAT HELPED COOL ME OFF FROM MY HIGH.

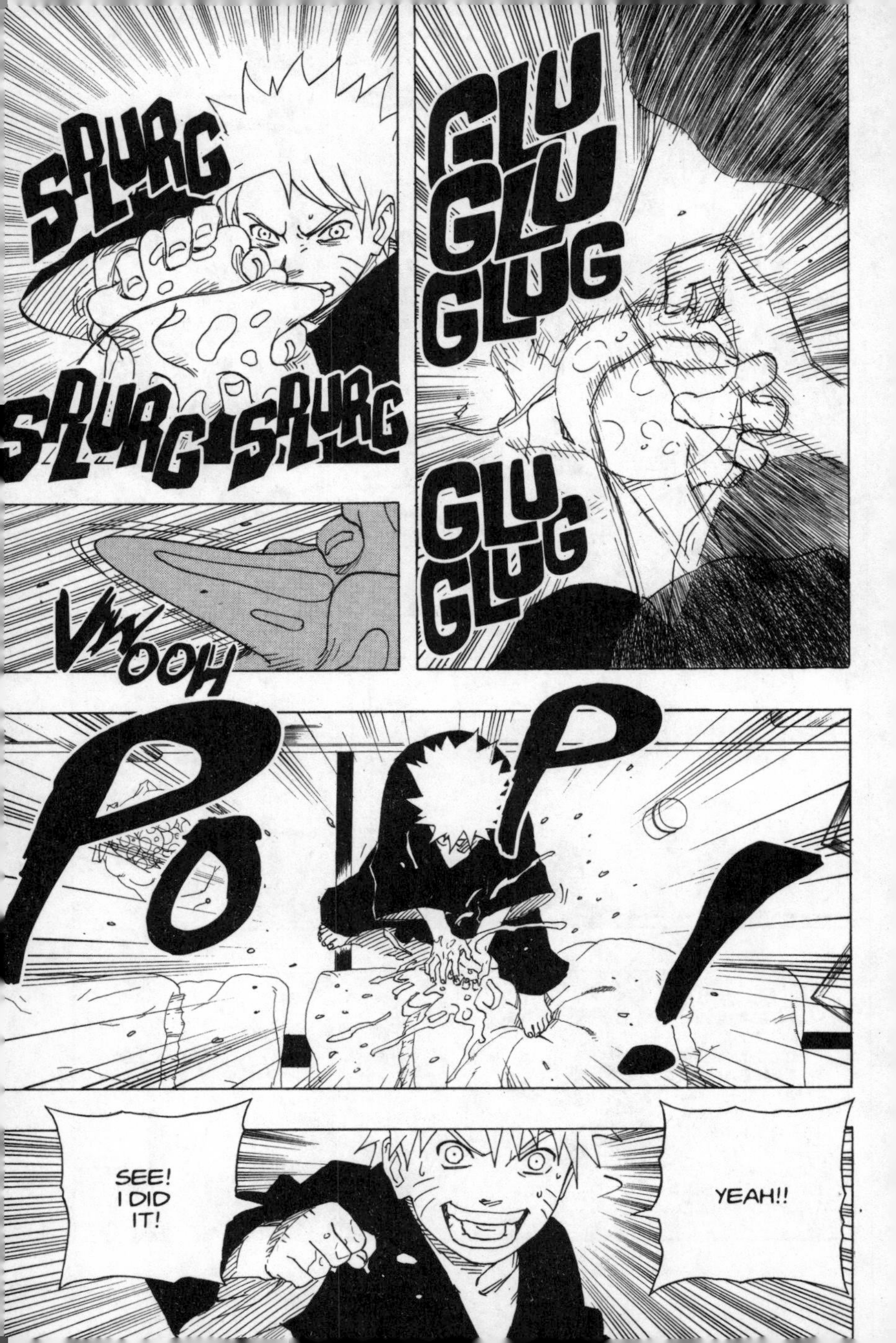
GLU GLU GLUG
GLU GLUG
SLURG
SLURG SLURG
VWOOH
POP!
YEAH!!
SEE! I DID IT!

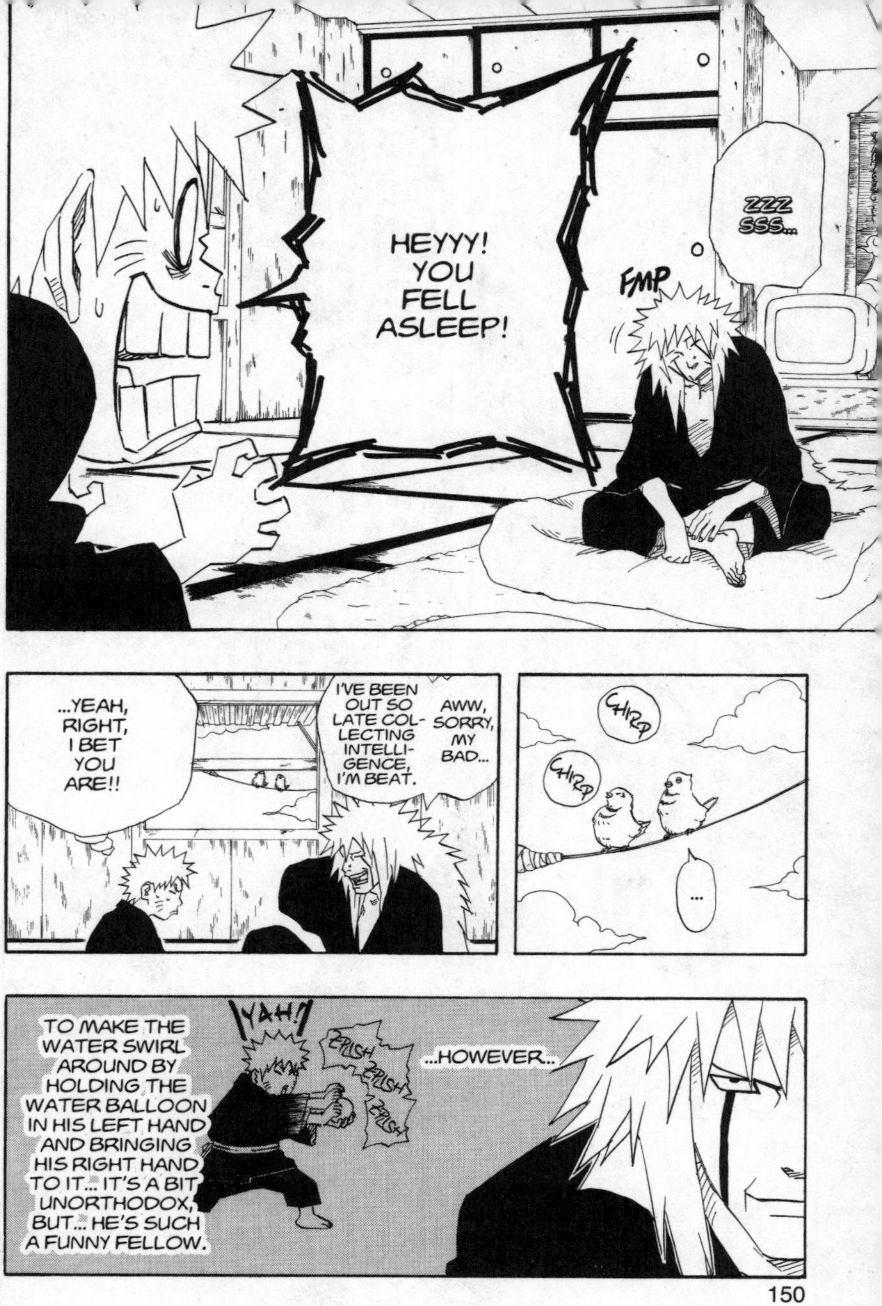
ZZZ SSS...
FMP
HEYYY! YOU FELL ASLEEP!
CHIRP
CHIRP
...
AWW, SORRY, MY BAD...
I'VE BEEN OUT SO LATE COLLECTING INTELLIGENCE, I'M BEAT.
...YEAH, RIGHT, I BET YOU ARE!!
...HOWEVER...
YAH!
ZPLISH ZPLISH ZPLISH
TO MAKE THE WATER SWIRL AROUND BY HOLDING THE WATER BALLOON IN HIS LEFT HAND AND BRINGING HIS RIGHT HAND TO IT... IT'S A BIT UNORTHODOX, BUT... HE'S SUCH A FUNNY FELLOW.

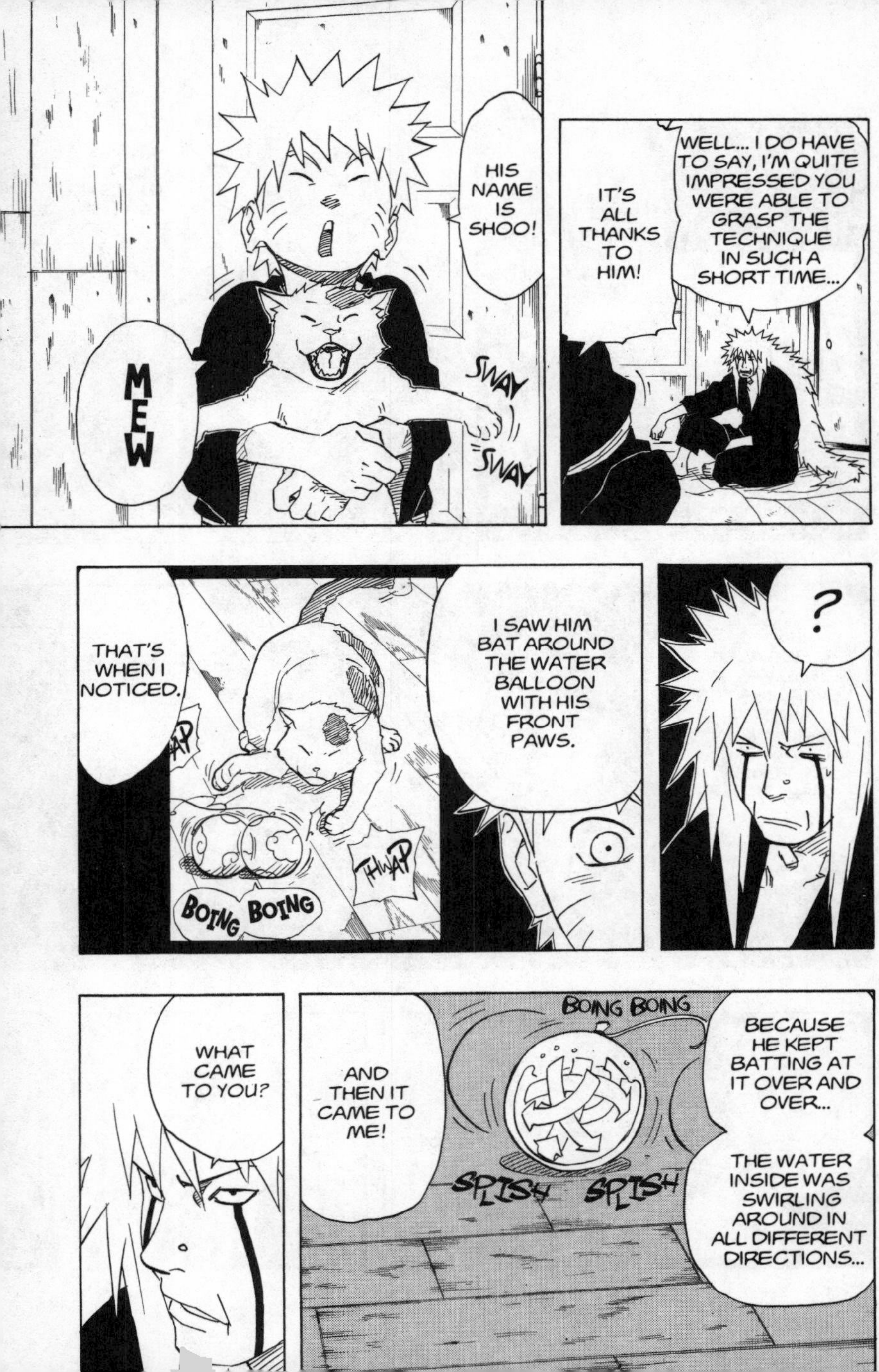
WELL... I DO HAVE TO SAY, I'M QUITE IMPRESSED YOU WERE ABLE TO GRASP THE TECHNIQUE IN SUCH A SHORT TIME...
IT'S ALL THANKS TO HIM!
HIS NAME IS SHOO!
SWAY
SWAY
MEW
?
I SAW HIM BAT AROUND THE WATER BALLOON WITH HIS FRONT PAWS.
THAT'S WHEN I NOTICED.
THWAP
BOING BOING
BOING BOING
BECAUSE HE KEPT BATTING AT IT OVER AND OVER...
THE WATER INSIDE WAS SWIRLING AROUND IN ALL DIFFERENT DIRECTIONS...
AND THEN IT CAME TO ME!
SPLISH SPLISH
WHAT CAME TO YOU?

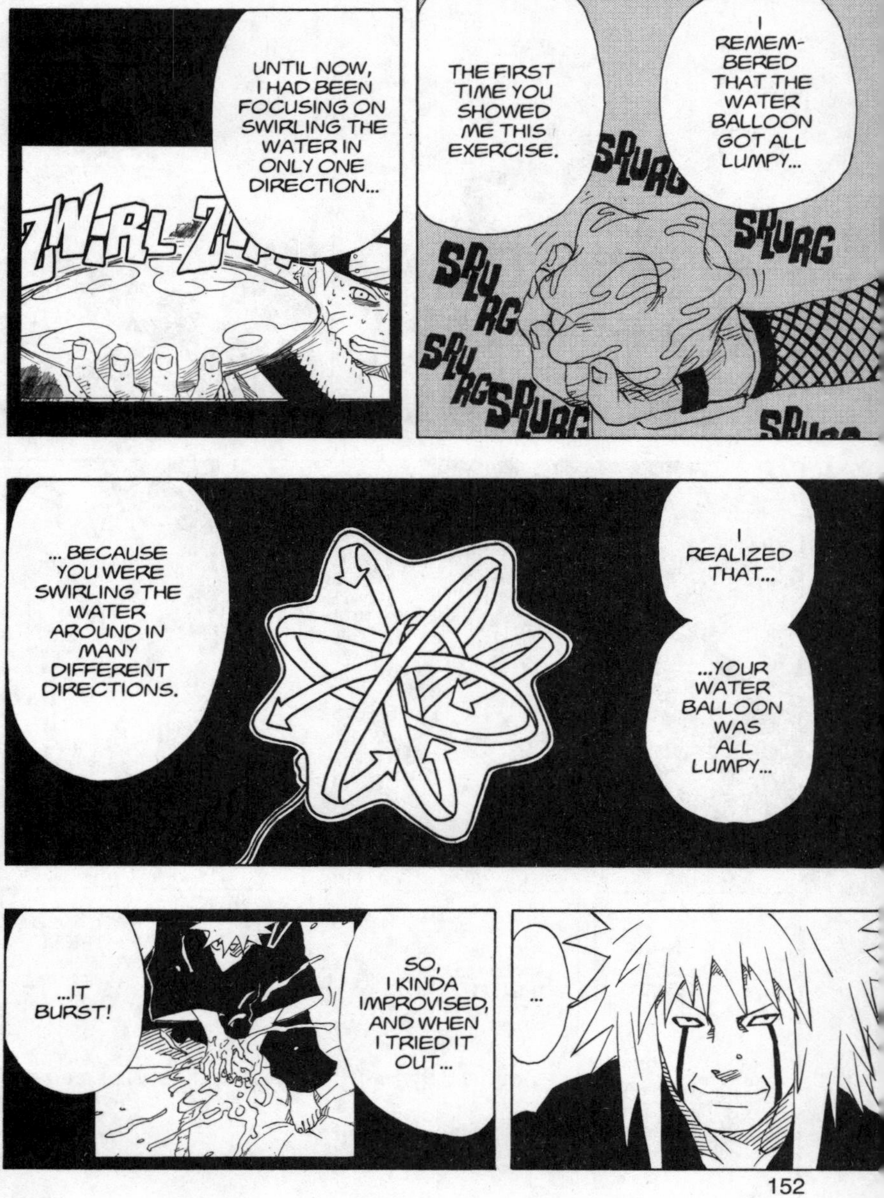

I REMEMBERED THAT THE WATER BALLOON GOT ALL LUMPY...
THE FIRST TIME YOU SHOWED ME THIS EXERCISE.
SPLURG
SPLURG
SPLURG
SPLURG
SPLURG
SPLURG
UNTIL NOW, I HAD BEEN FOCUSING ON SWIRLING THE WATER IN ONLY ONE DIRECTION...
ZWIRL
I REALIZED THAT...
...YOUR WATER BALLOON WAS ALL LUMPY...
... BECAUSE YOU WERE SWIRLING THE WATER AROUND IN MANY DIFFERENT DIRECTIONS.
...
SO, I KINDA IMPROVISED, AND WHEN I TRIED IT OUT...
...IT BURST!

READ THIS WAY

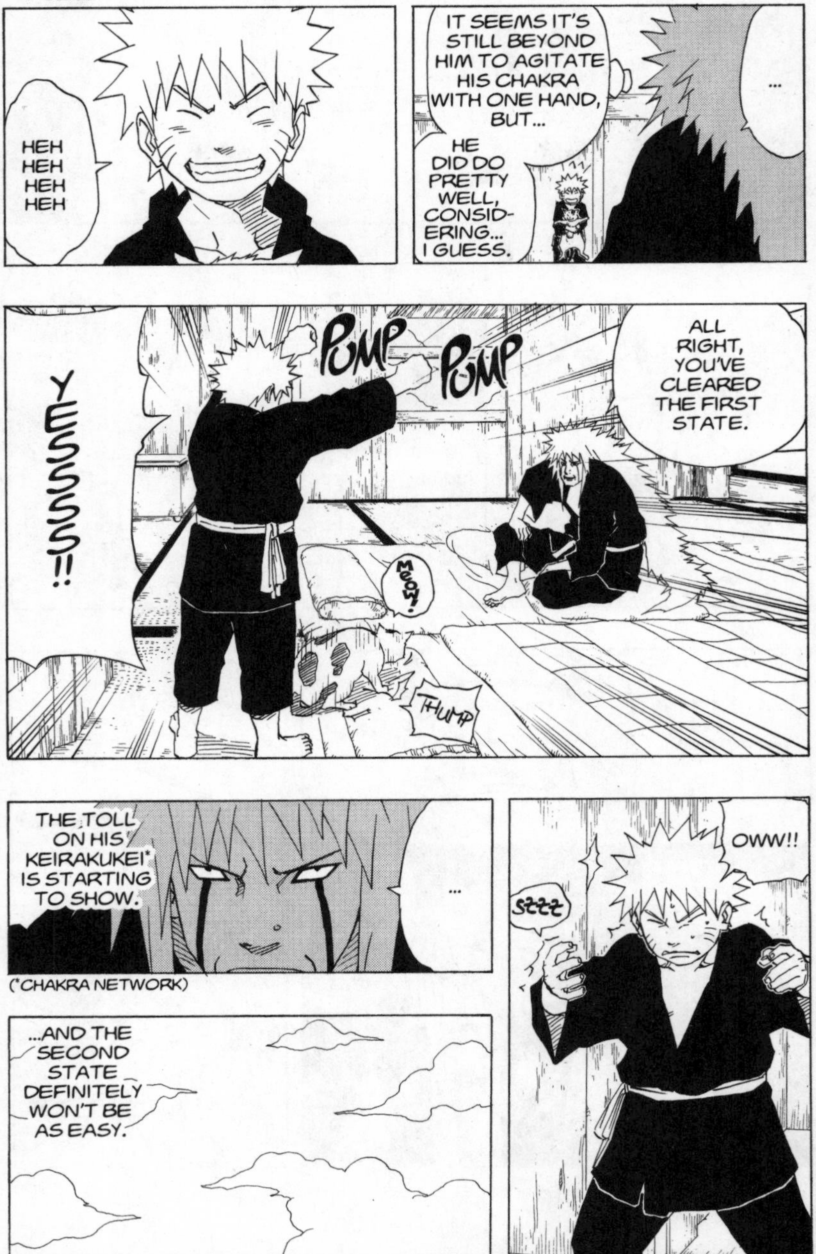
IT SEEMS IT'S STILL BEYOND HIM TO AGITATE HIS CHAKRA WITH ONE HAND, BUT...
HE DID DO PRETTY WELL, CONSID-ERING... I GUESS.
...
HEH HEH HEH HEH
ALL RIGHT, YOU'VE CLEARED THE FIRST STATE.
POMP
POMP
YESSSSS!!
MEOW!
THUMP
OWW!!
SZZZ
...
THE TOLL ON HIS KEIRAKUKEI* IS STARTING TO SHOW.
(*CHAKRA NETWORK)
...AND THE SECOND STATE DEFINITELY WON'T BE AS EASY.

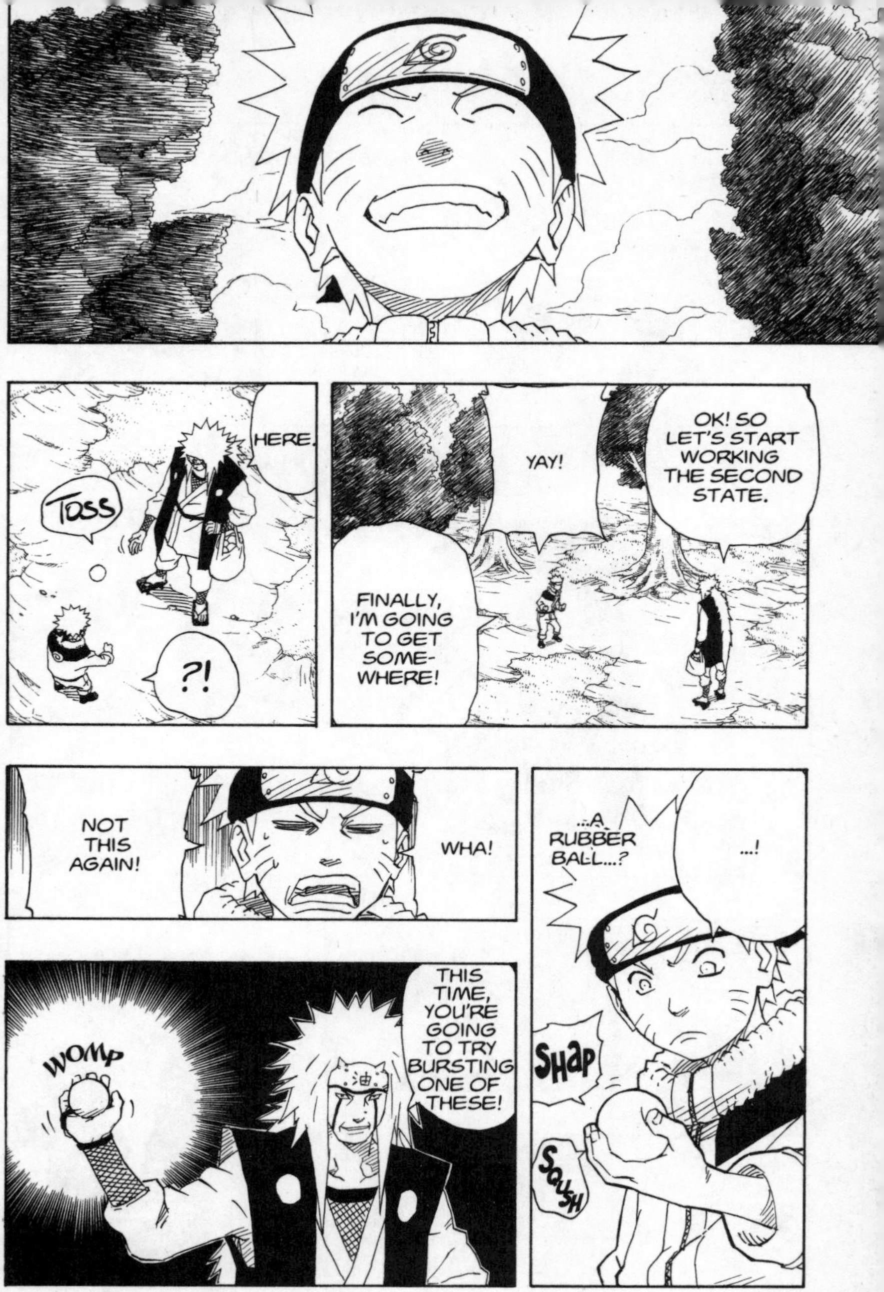
OK! SO LET'S START WORKING THE SECOND STATE.
YAY!
FINALLY, I'M GOING TO GET SOME-WHERE!
HERE.
TOSS
?!
...!
...A RUBBER BALL...?
SHAP
SQUSH
WHA!
NOT THIS AGAIN!
THIS TIME, YOU'RE GOING TO TRY BURSTING ONE OF THESE!
WOMP

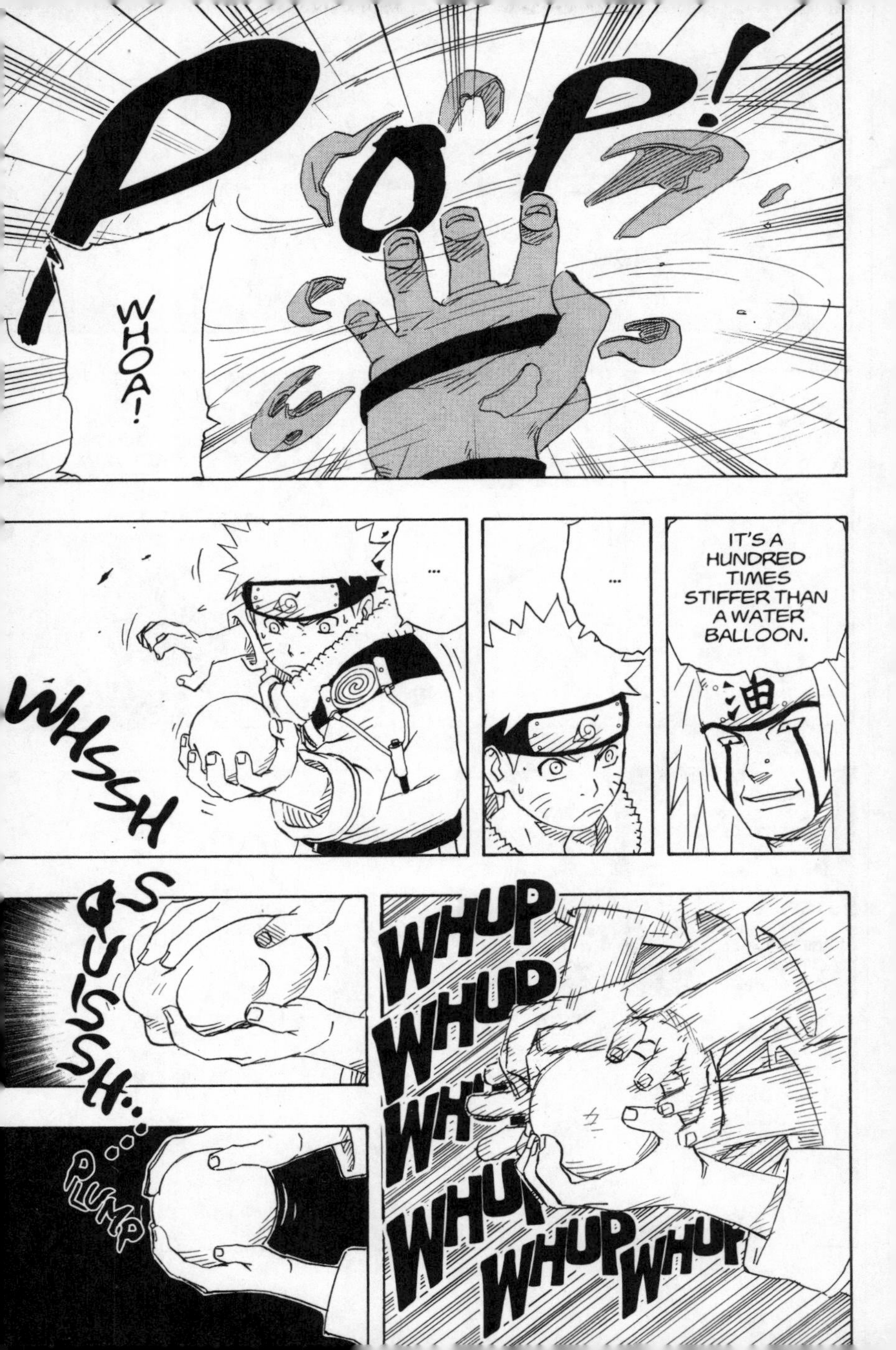
POP!
WHOA!
IT'S A HUNDRED TIMES STIFFER THAN A WATER BALLOON.
油
...
...
WHSSSH
WHUP
WHUP
WHUP
WHUP
SQUISSH...
PLUMP

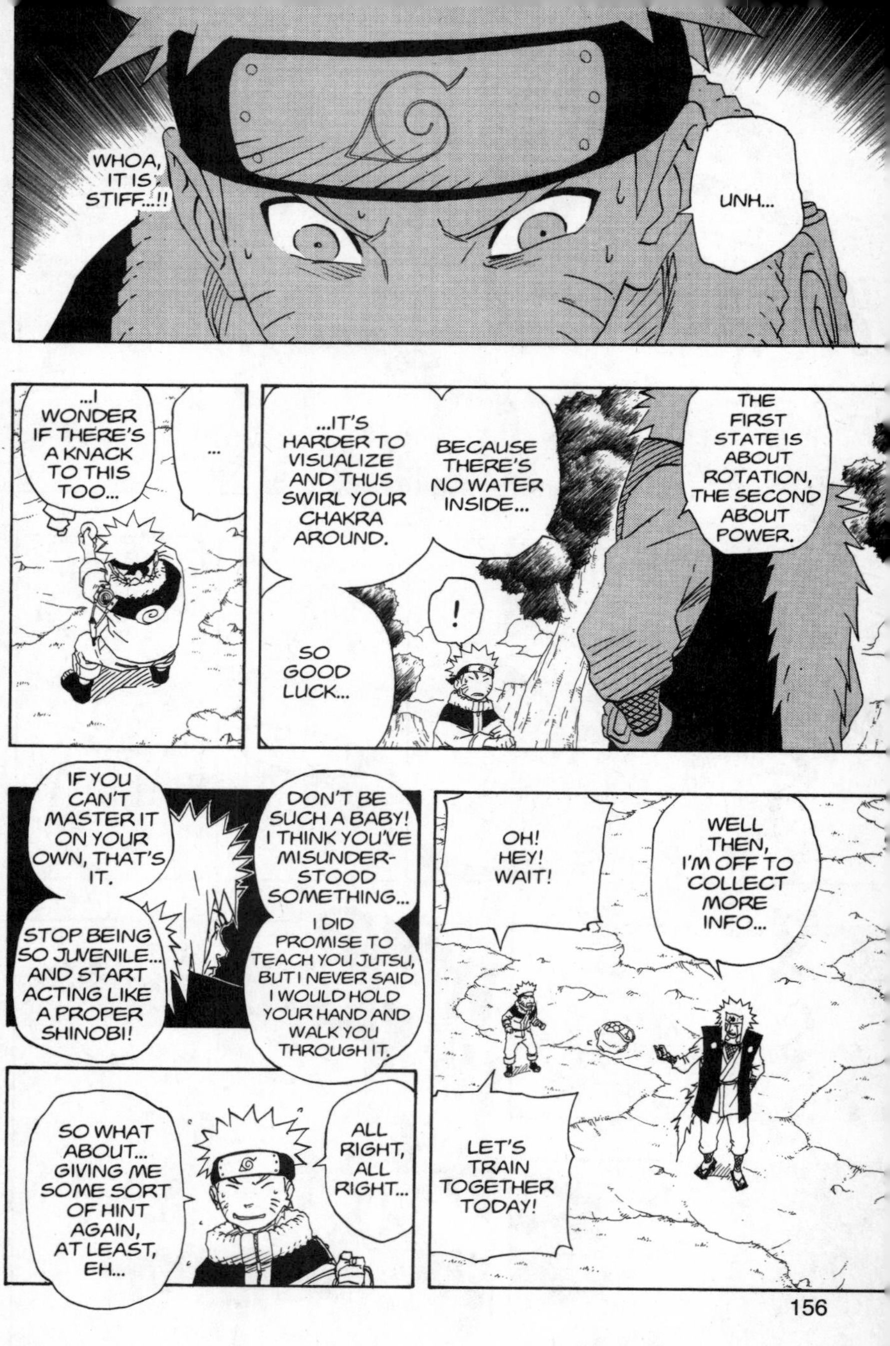
UNH...
WHOA, IT IS STIFF...!!
THE FIRST STATE IS ABOUT ROTATION, THE SECOND ABOUT POWER.
BECAUSE THERE'S NO WATER INSIDE...
...IT'S HARDER TO VISUALIZE AND THUS SWIRL YOUR CHAKRA AROUND.
!
SO GOOD LUCK...
...
...I WONDER IF THERE'S A KNACK TO THIS TOO...
WELL THEN, I'M OFF TO COLLECT MORE INFO...
OH! HEY! WAIT!
LET'S TRAIN TOGETHER TODAY!
DON'T BE SUCH A BABY! I THINK YOU'VE MISUNDER-STOOD SOMETHING...
I DID PROMISE TO TEACH YOU JUTSU, BUT I NEVER SAID I WOULD HOLD YOUR HAND AND WALK YOU THROUGH IT.
IF YOU CAN'T MASTER IT ON YOUR OWN, THAT'S IT.
STOP BEING SO JUVENILE... AND START ACTING LIKE A PROPER SHINOBI!
ALL RIGHT, ALL RIGHT...
SO WHAT ABOUT... GIVING ME SOME SORT OF HINT AGAIN, AT LEAST, EH...

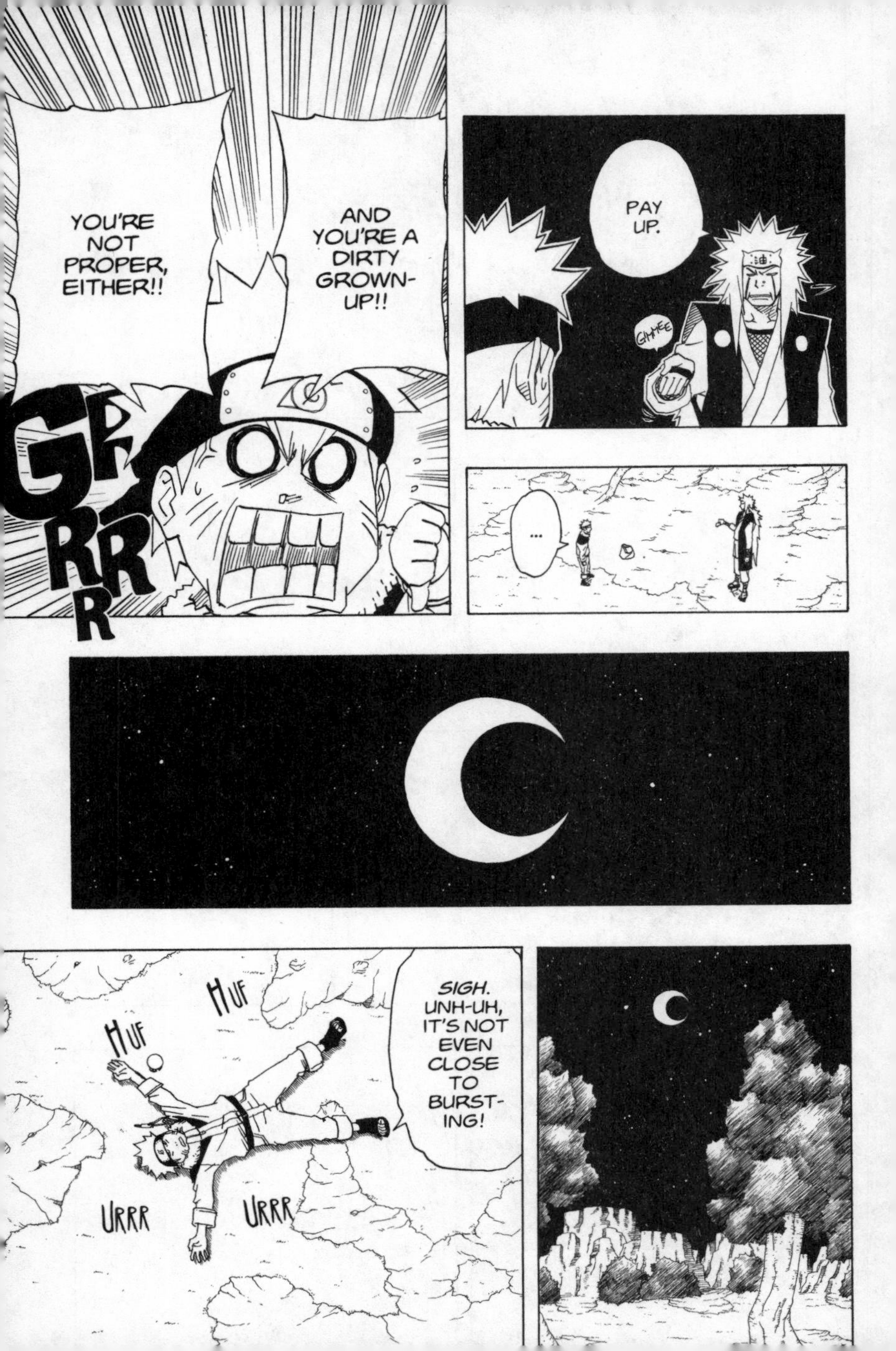
PAY UP.
GIMMEE
...
YOU'RE NOT PROPER, EITHER!!
AND YOU'RE A DIRTY GROWN-UP!!
GRRRR
SIGH. UNH-UH, IT'S NOT EVEN CLOSE TO BURST-ING!
HUF
HUF
URRR
URRR

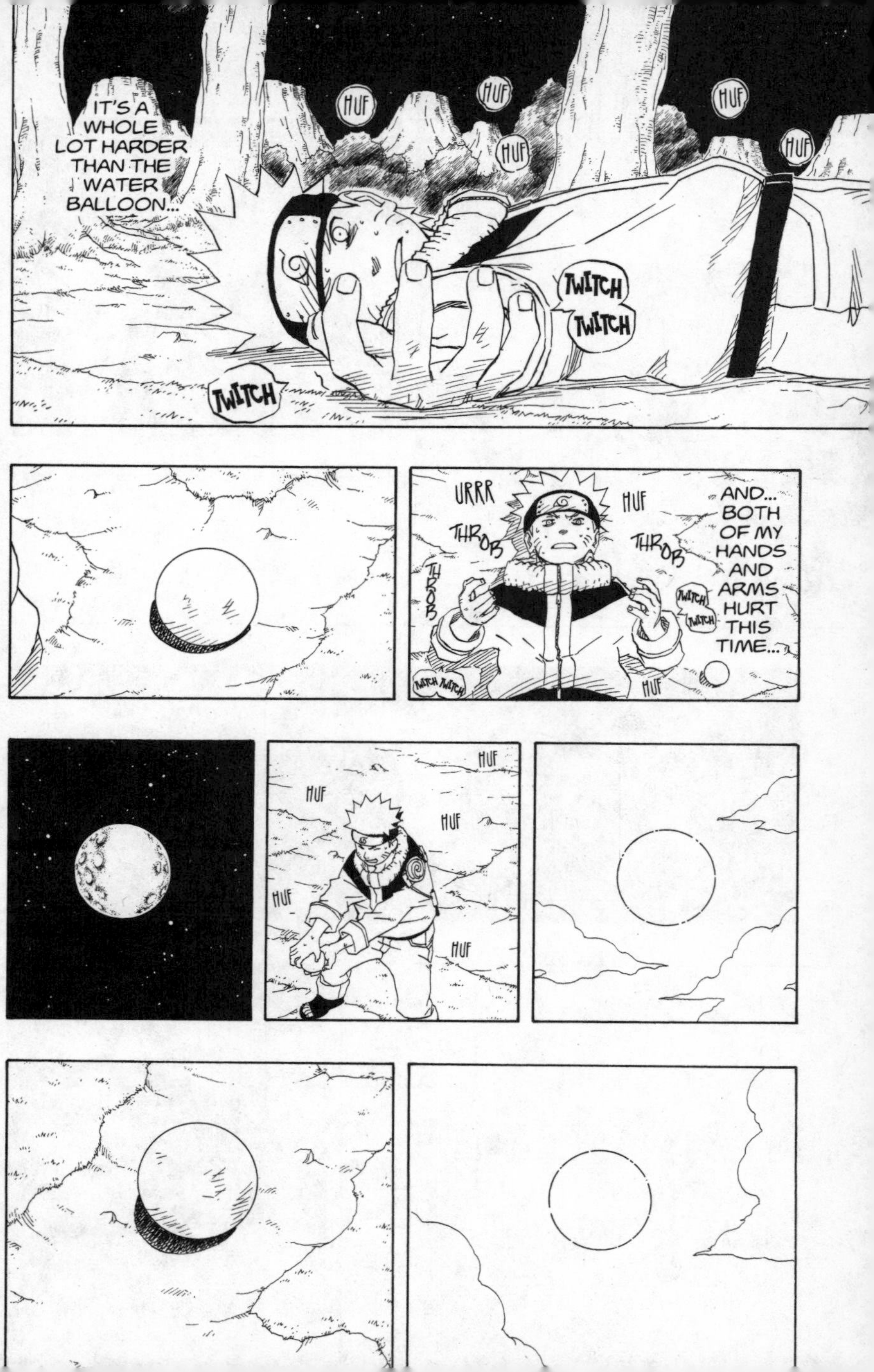
HUF
HUF
HUF
HUF
HUF
IT'S A WHOLE LOT HARDER THAN THE WATER BALLOON...
TWITCH
TWITCH
TWITCH
AND... BOTH OF MY HANDS AND ARMS HURT THIS TIME...
HUF
URRR
THROB
THROB
THROB
TWITCH
TWITCH
TWITCH TWITCH
HUF
HUF
HUF
HUF
HUF

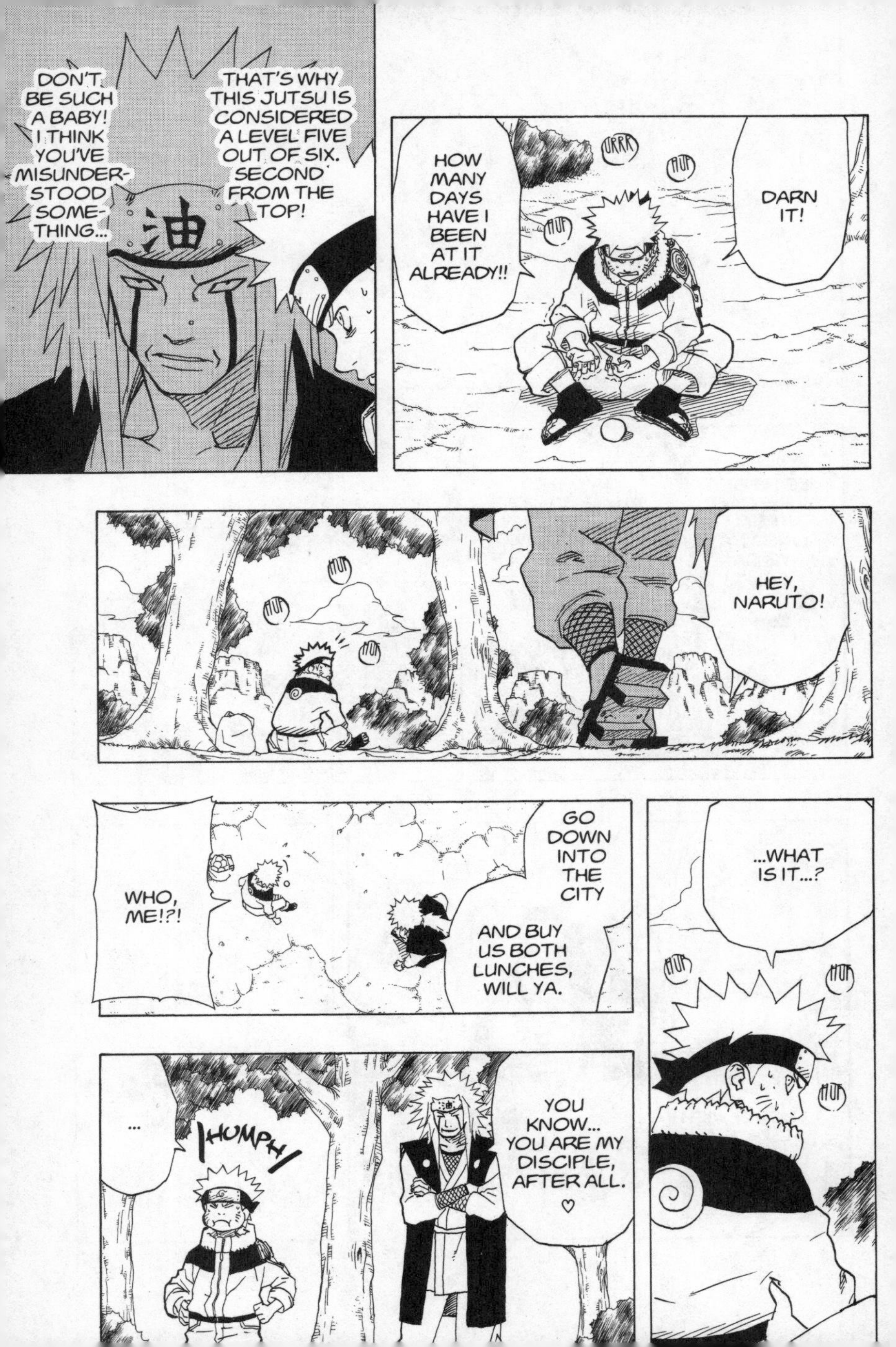
DARN IT!
URRR
HUF
HUF
HOW MANY DAYS HAVE I BEEN AT IT ALREADY!!
THAT'S WHY THIS JUTSU IS CONSIDERED A LEVEL FIVE OUT OF SIX. SECOND FROM THE TOP!
DON'T BE SUCH A BABY! I THINK YOU'VE MISUNDERSTOOD SOME-THING...
HEY, NARUTO!
HUF
HUF
HUF
...WHAT IS IT...?
HUF
HUF
HUF
GO DOWN INTO THE CITY
AND BUY US BOTH LUNCHES, WILL YA.
WHO, ME!?!
YOU KNOW... YOU ARE MY DISCIPLE, AFTER ALL. ♡
HUMPH!
...

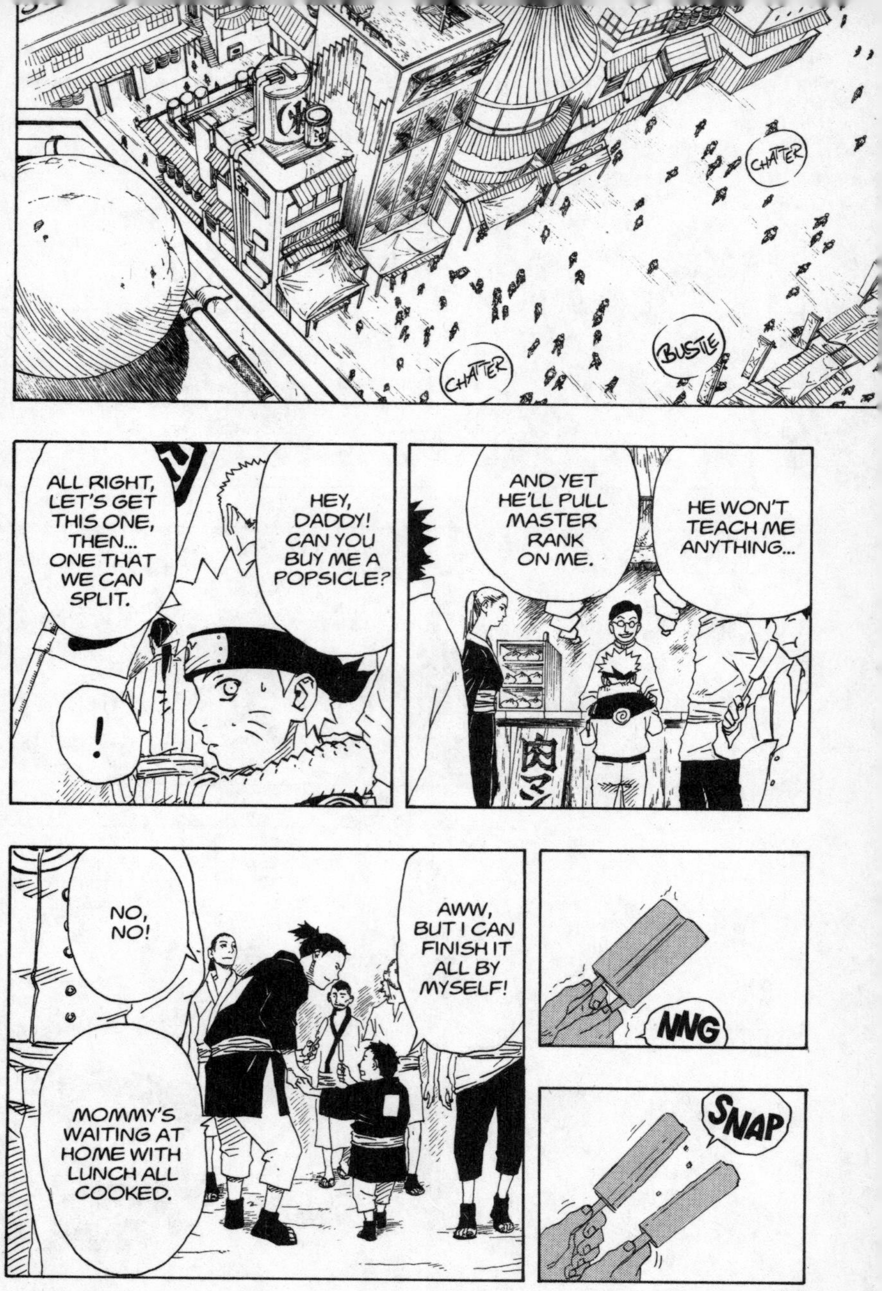
CHATTER
BUSTLE
CHATTER
HE WON'T TEACH ME ANYTHING...
AND YET HE'LL PULL MASTER RANK ON ME.
HEY, DADDY! CAN YOU BUY ME A POPSICLE?
ALL RIGHT, LET'S GET THIS ONE, THEN... ONE THAT WE CAN SPLIT.
!
NNG
SNAP
AWW, BUT I CAN FINISH IT ALL BY MYSELF!
NO, NO!
MOMMY'S WAITING AT HOME WITH LUNCH ALL COOKED.

READ THIS WAY

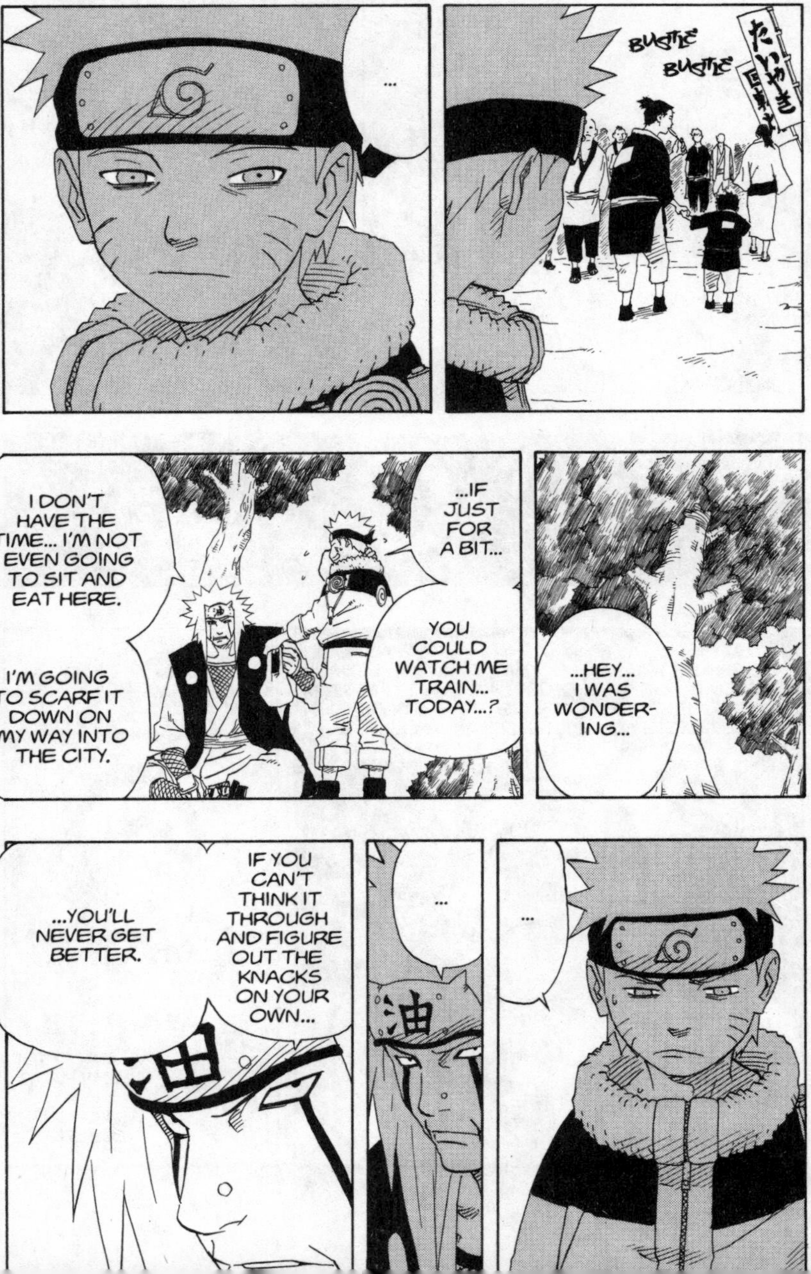

BUSTLE
BUSTLE
たいやき
...
...HEY... I WAS WONDERING...
...IF JUST FOR A BIT...
YOU COULD WATCH ME TRAIN... TODAY...?
I DON'T HAVE THE TIME... I'M NOT EVEN GOING TO SIT AND EAT HERE.
I'M GOING TO SCARF IT DOWN ON MY WAY INTO THE CITY.
...
...
IF YOU CAN'T THINK IT THROUGH AND FIGURE OUT THE KNACKS ON YOUR OWN...
...YOU'LL NEVER GET BETTER.

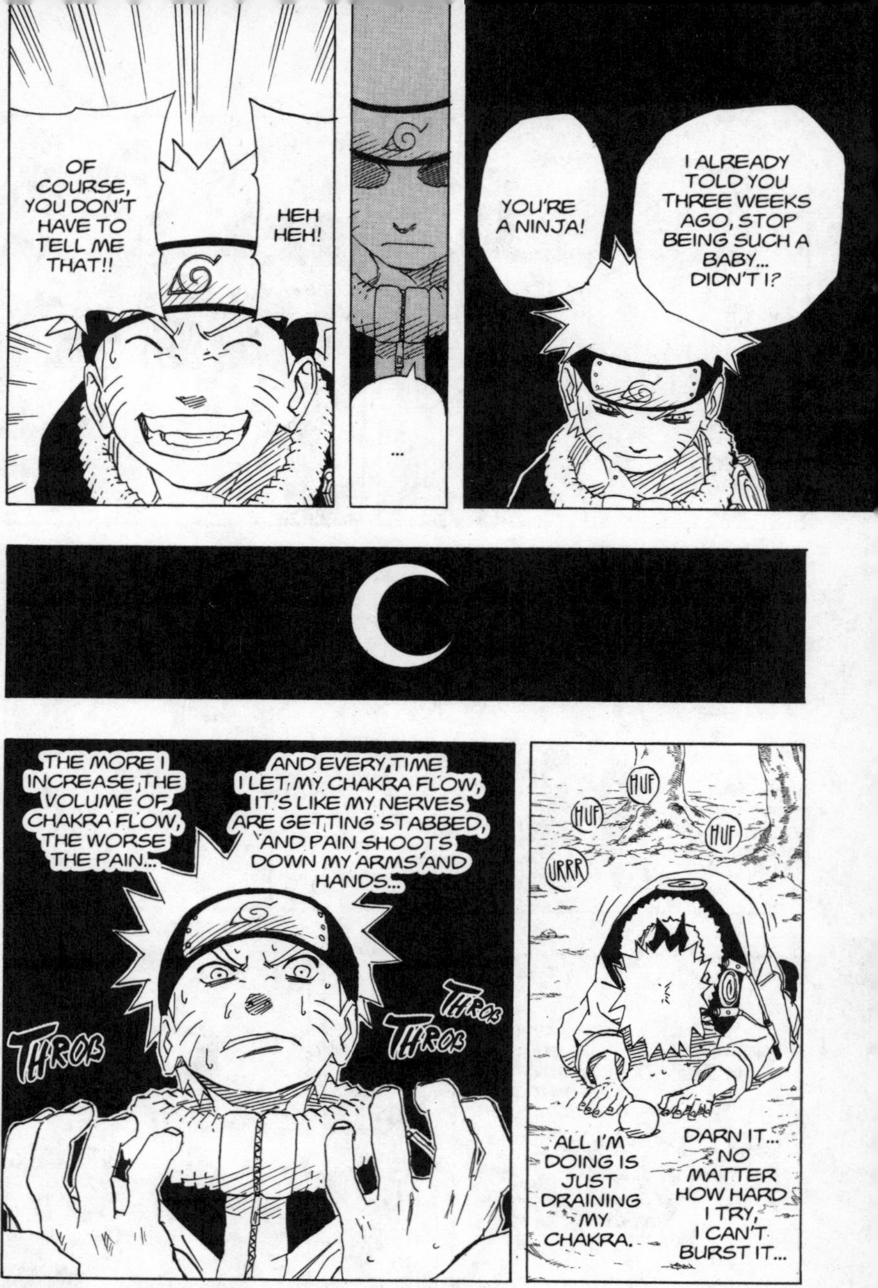
I ALREADY TOLD YOU THREE WEEKS AGO, STOP BEING SUCH A BABY... DIDN'T I?
YOU'RE A NINJA!
...
HEH HEH!
OF COURSE, YOU DON'T HAVE TO TELL ME THAT!!
HUF
HUF
HUF
URRR
DARN IT... NO MATTER HOW HARD I TRY, I CAN'T BURST IT...
ALL I'M DOING IS JUST DRAINING MY CHAKRA.
AND EVERY TIME I LET MY CHAKRA FLOW, IT'S LIKE MY NERVES ARE GETTING STABBED, AND PAIN SHOOTS DOWN MY ARMS AND HANDS...
THE MORE I INCREASE THE VOLUME OF CHAKRA FLOW, THE WORSE THE PAIN...
THROB
THROB
THROB

THAT'S IT!!

...

!

I GET THIS FEELING THAT... UNLESS I MAKE MY CHAKRA EXPLODE...

BUT... SOME-HOW...

(HUF)

LIKE IN A SINGLE BLAST, IT WON'T BURST...

(HUF)

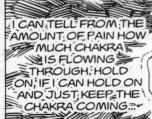

I CAN TELL FROM THE AMOUNT OF PAIN HOW MUCH CHAKRA IS FLOWING THROUGH. HOLD ON, IF I CAN HOLD ON AND JUST KEEP THE CHAKRA COMING...

UNNG

WHUP WHUP WHUP WHUP

NOW!!

UGGH!

THROB THROB THROB

NOT YET... NO, NOT YET. J-JUST A... LITTLE BIT MORE...

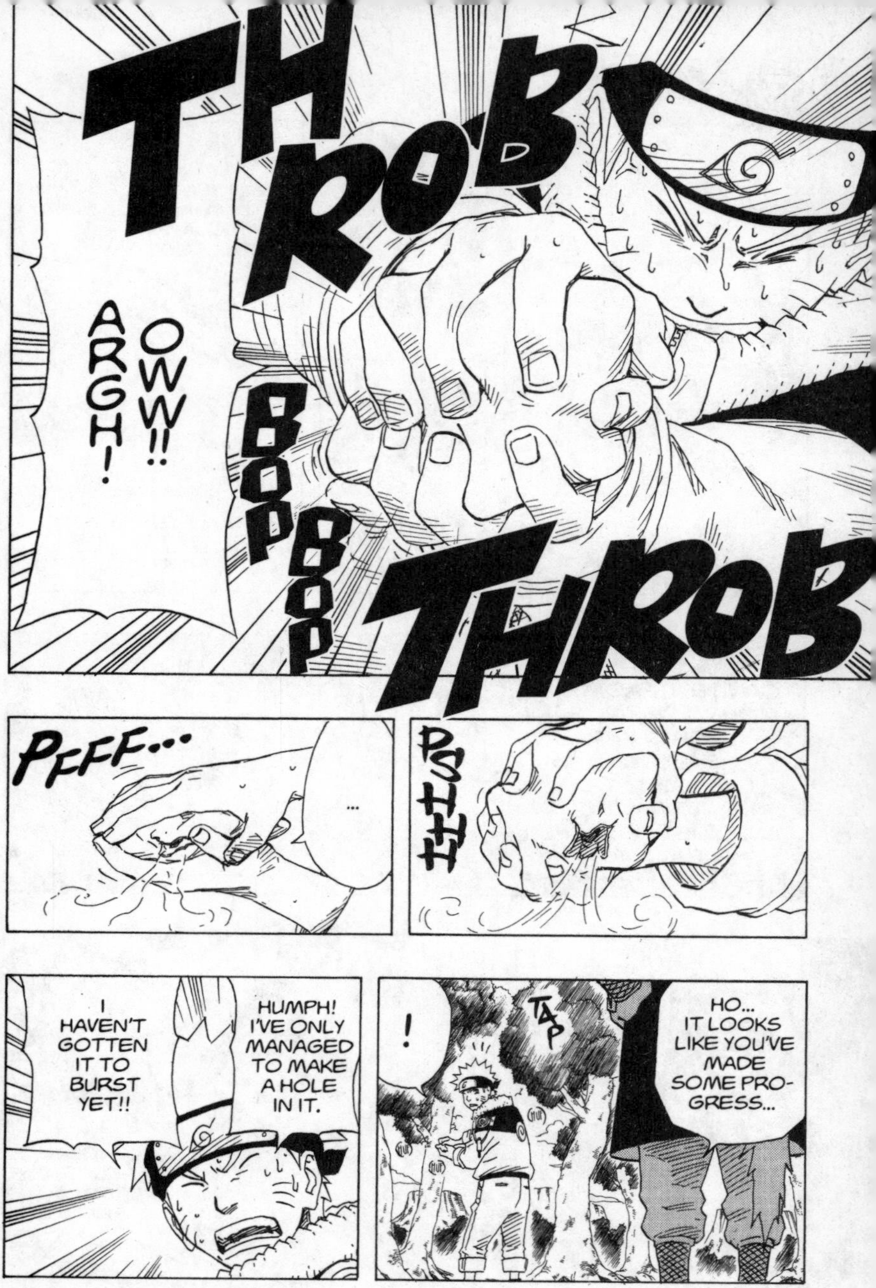
THROB
OWW!! ARGH!
BOP BOP
THROB
PSHHH
PFFF...
...
HO... IT LOOKS LIKE YOU'VE MADE SOME PROGRESS...
TAP
!
HUMPH! I'VE ONLY MANAGED TO MAKE A HOLE IN IT.
I HAVEN'T GOTTEN IT TO BURST YET!!

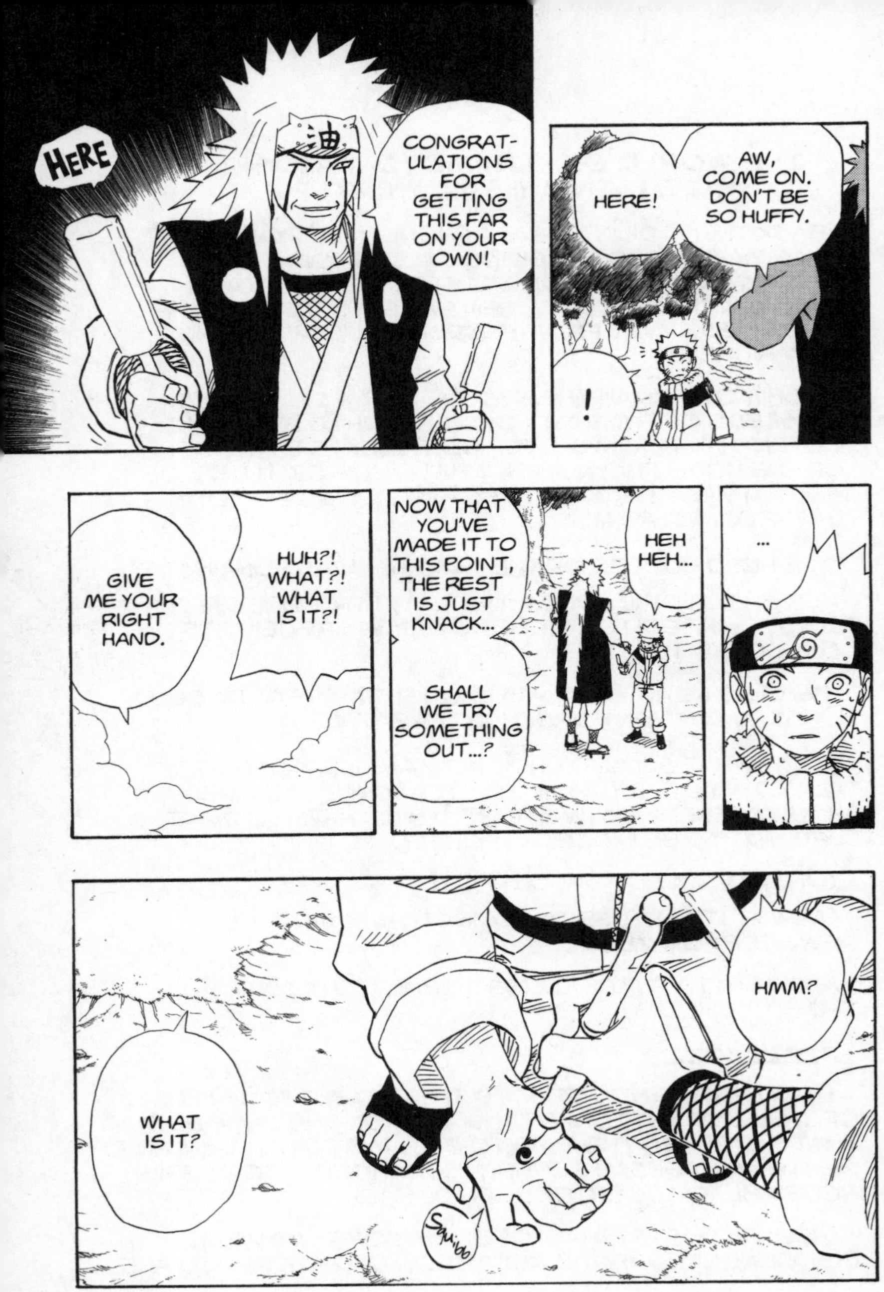
AW, COME ON. DON'T BE SO HUFFY.
HERE!
!
CONGRAT-ULATIONS FOR GETTING THIS FAR ON YOUR OWN!
HERE
...
HEH HEH...
NOW THAT YOU'VE MADE IT TO THIS POINT, THE REST IS JUST KNACK...
SHALL WE TRY SOMETHING OUT...?
HUH?! WHAT?! WHAT IS IT?!
GIVE ME YOUR RIGHT HAND.
HMM?
Squibb
WHAT IS IT?

THE WORLD OF KISHIMOTO MASASHI
MY PERSONAL HISTORY, PART 26

BACK THEN, I DIDN'T HAVE A PHONE IN MY ROOM, SO I WAS MAKING AND RECEIVING CALLS FROM MY BOARDINGHOUSE LANDLORD'S PHONE. THE NIGHT THE AWARDS ANNOUNCEMENT WAS PRINTED IN *JUMP*, I RECEIVED A CALL FROM SHUEISHA'S *JUMP* EDITING DEPARTMENT.

"KISHIMOTO-KUN! I THINK YOU'VE GOT A CALL FROM A *JUMP* EDITOR," MY LANDLORD SAID WHILE STANDING OUTSIDE MY ROOM CLUTCHING THE EXTRA HANDSET OF THE HOME PHONE. (WH...WHAT?!) "UH, OK! I'LL BE RIGHT THERE!" I KICKED OUT OF MY ROOM AND TOOK THE RECEIVER AWAY.

THE HOLD BUTTON OF THE HANDSET WAS BLINKING.

(SH-SHOOT! ARE YOU SAYING THAT I'M CONNECTED TO A J...JUMP EDITOR RIGHT NOW?! THIS RECEIVER'S CONNECTED TO *JUMP!*)

I WAS SO NERVOUS THAT I THOUGHT MY HEART WOULD BURST, AND I EVEN FORGOT TO BREATHE.

(...UM, WHAT SHOULD I SAY? HOW AM I SUPPOSED TO TALK TO HIM... U...UH... I-I'VE GOT TO PICK UP THE LINE... I SHOULDN'T KEEP HIM WAITING!) (...BUT I HAVE TO MAKE SURE NOT TO BE DISCOURTEOUS!...)

(OH, MAN, I'M SO NERVOUS! 'CUZ IT'S *JUMP!*)

(AARGH! IT'S NO USE DAWDLING! ONE GIANT NEW STEP FOR MEEE!)

AND WITH THAT, THE YOUNG KISHIMOTO PRESSED THE BUTTON...

BZZZZZZZZZ...

I HAD MISTAKENLY PRESSED THE END BUTTON INSTEAD OF THE HOLD BUTTON, AND HUNG UP ON THE *JUMP* EDITOR THAT HAD TAKEN THE TIME TO CALL ME. BUT THE KIND AND GENTLE YAHAGI-SAN GENEROUSLY CHOSE TO CALL THIS INCREDIBLY DISCOURTEOUS FOOL BACK...

"HELLO? THIS IS YAHAGI OF *JUMP*. SORRY WE WERE DISCONNECTED. IS THE RECEPTION BAD WHERE YOU ARE...?"

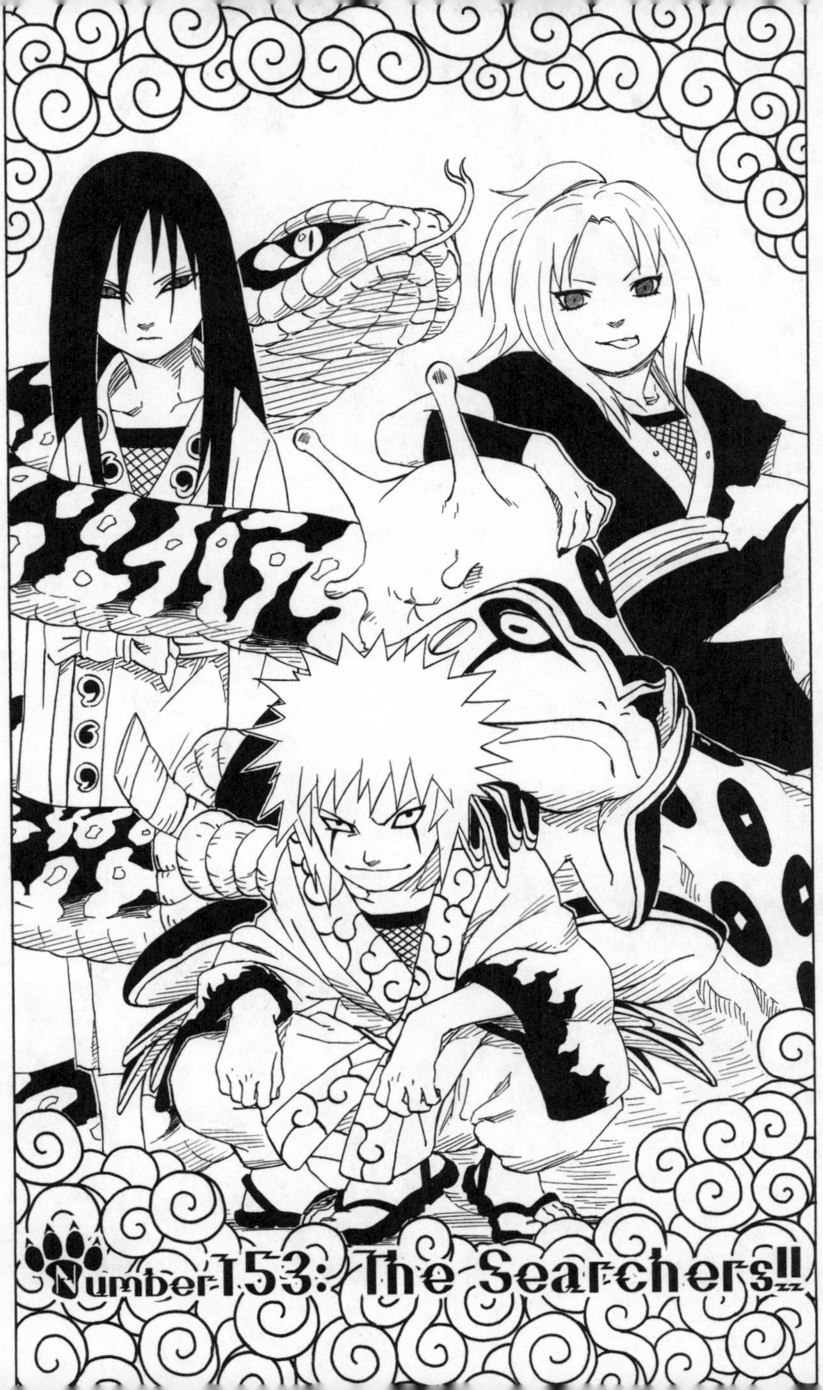
Number 153: The Searchers!!

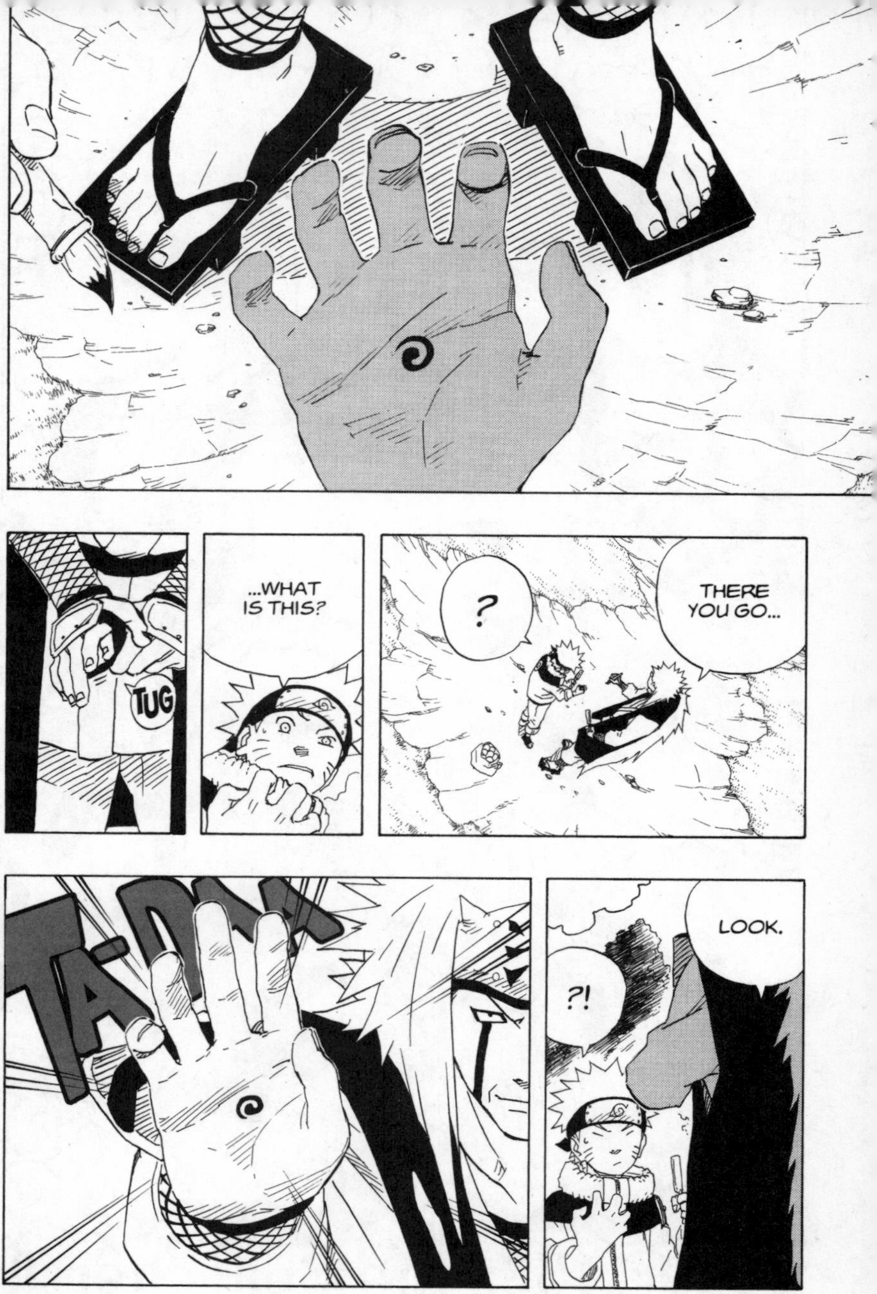
THERE YOU GO...
?
...WHAT IS THIS?
TUG
LOOK.
?!
TA-DA

READ THIS WAY

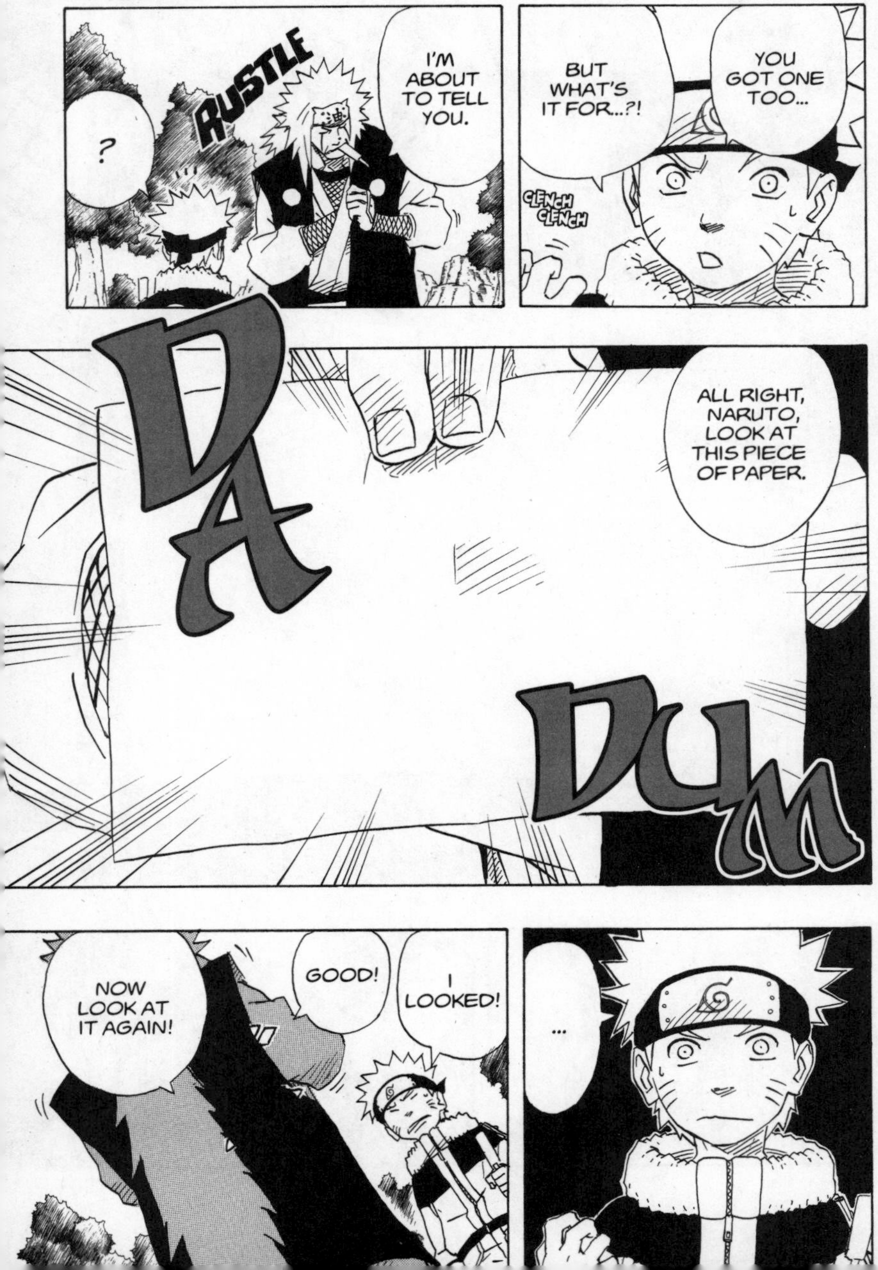
YOU GOT ONE TOO...
BUT WHAT'S IT FOR...?!
CLENCH CLENCH
I'M ABOUT TO TELL YOU.
RUSTLE
?
ALL RIGHT, NARUTO, LOOK AT THIS PIECE OF PAPER.
DA
DUM
...
I LOOKED!
GOOD!
NOW LOOK AT IT AGAIN!

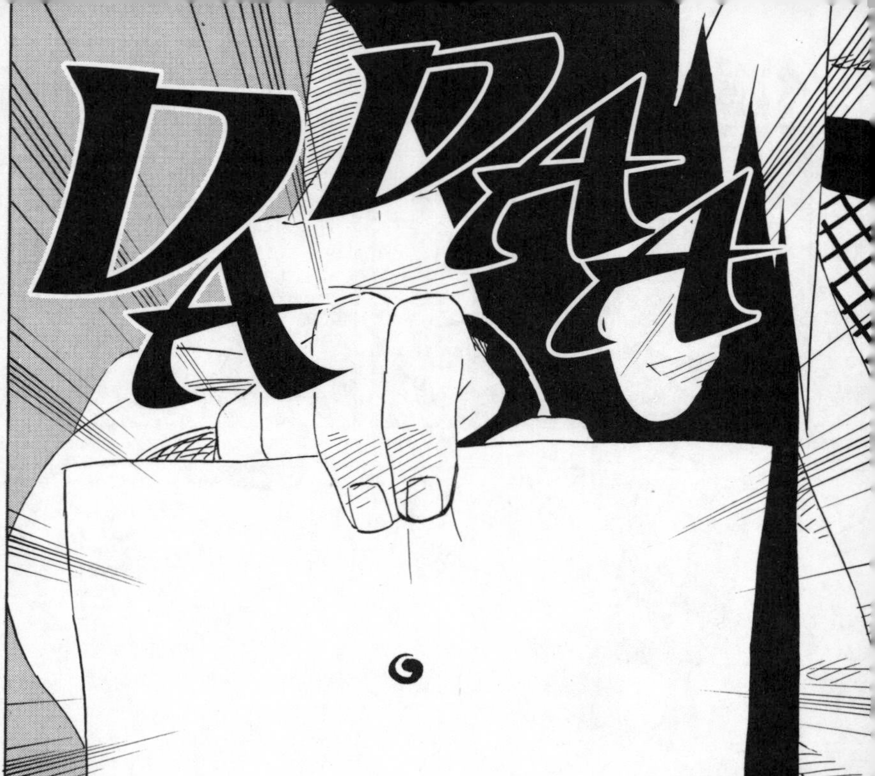
DADAA
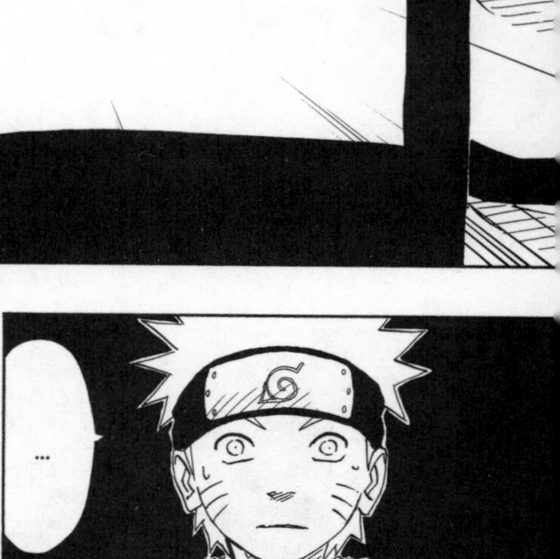
...
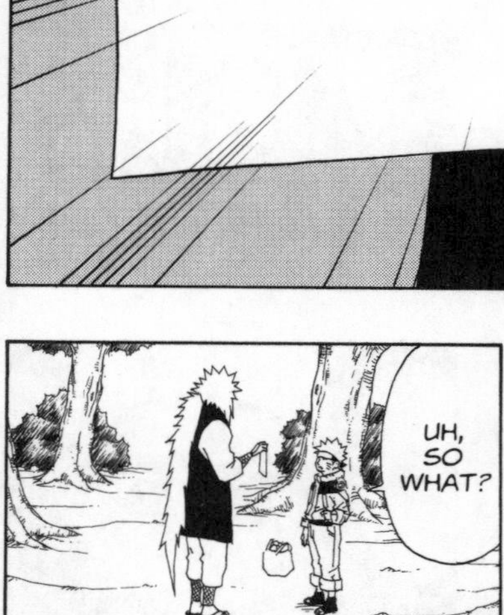
UH, SO WHAT?

READ THIS WAY

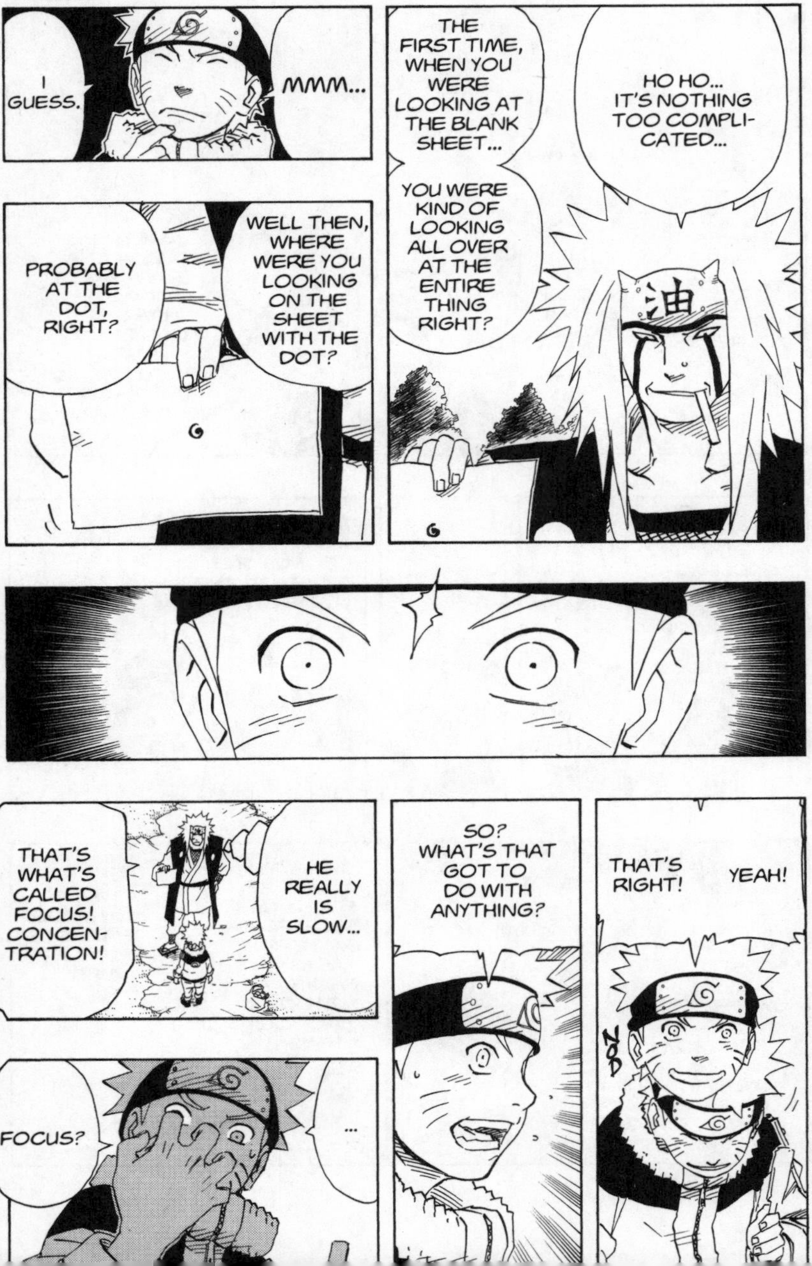

HO HO... IT'S NOTHING TOO COMPLICATED...
THE FIRST TIME, WHEN YOU WERE LOOKING AT THE BLANK SHEET...
YOU WERE KIND OF LOOKING ALL OVER AT THE ENTIRE THING RIGHT?
MMM...
I GUESS.
WELL THEN, WHERE WERE YOU LOOKING ON THE SHEET WITH THE DOT?
PROBABLY AT THE DOT, RIGHT?
YEAH!
THAT'S RIGHT!
NOD
SO? WHAT'S THAT GOT TO DO WITH ANYTHING?
HE REALLY IS SLOW...
THAT'S WHAT'S CALLED FOCUS! CONCENTRATION!
...
FOCUS?

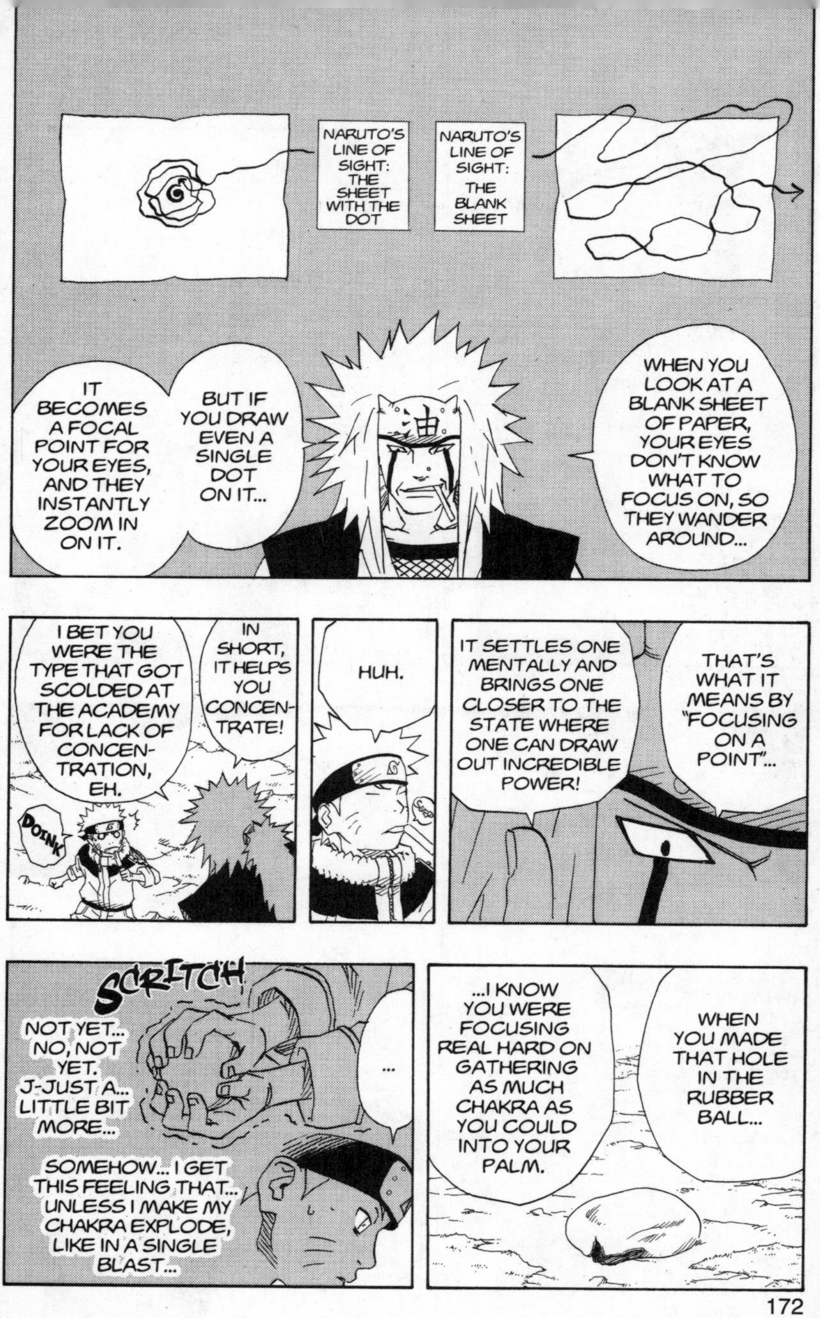
NARUTO'S LINE OF SIGHT: THE BLANK SHEET
NARUTO'S LINE OF SIGHT: THE SHEET WITH THE DOT
WHEN YOU LOOK AT A BLANK SHEET OF PAPER, YOUR EYES DON'T KNOW WHAT TO FOCUS ON, SO THEY WANDER AROUND...
BUT IF YOU DRAW EVEN A SINGLE DOT ON IT...
IT BECOMES A FOCAL POINT FOR YOUR EYES, AND THEY INSTANTLY ZOOM IN ON IT.
THAT'S WHAT IT MEANS BY "FOCUSING ON A POINT"...
IT SETTLES ONE MENTALLY AND BRINGS ONE CLOSER TO THE STATE WHERE ONE CAN DRAW OUT INCREDIBLE POWER!
HUH.
IN SHORT, IT HELPS YOU CONCEN-TRATE!
I BET YOU WERE THE TYPE THAT GOT SCOLDED AT THE ACADEMY FOR LACK OF CONCEN-TRATION, EH.
DOINK
WHEN YOU MADE THAT HOLE IN THE RUBBER BALL...
...I KNOW YOU WERE FOCUSING REAL HARD ON GATHERING AS MUCH CHAKRA AS YOU COULD INTO YOUR PALM.
...
SCRITCH
NOT YET... NO, NOT YET. J-JUST A... LITTLE BIT MORE...
SOMEHOW... I GET THIS FEELING THAT... UNLESS I MAKE MY CHAKRA EXPLODE, LIKE IN A SINGLE BLAST...

READ THIS WAY

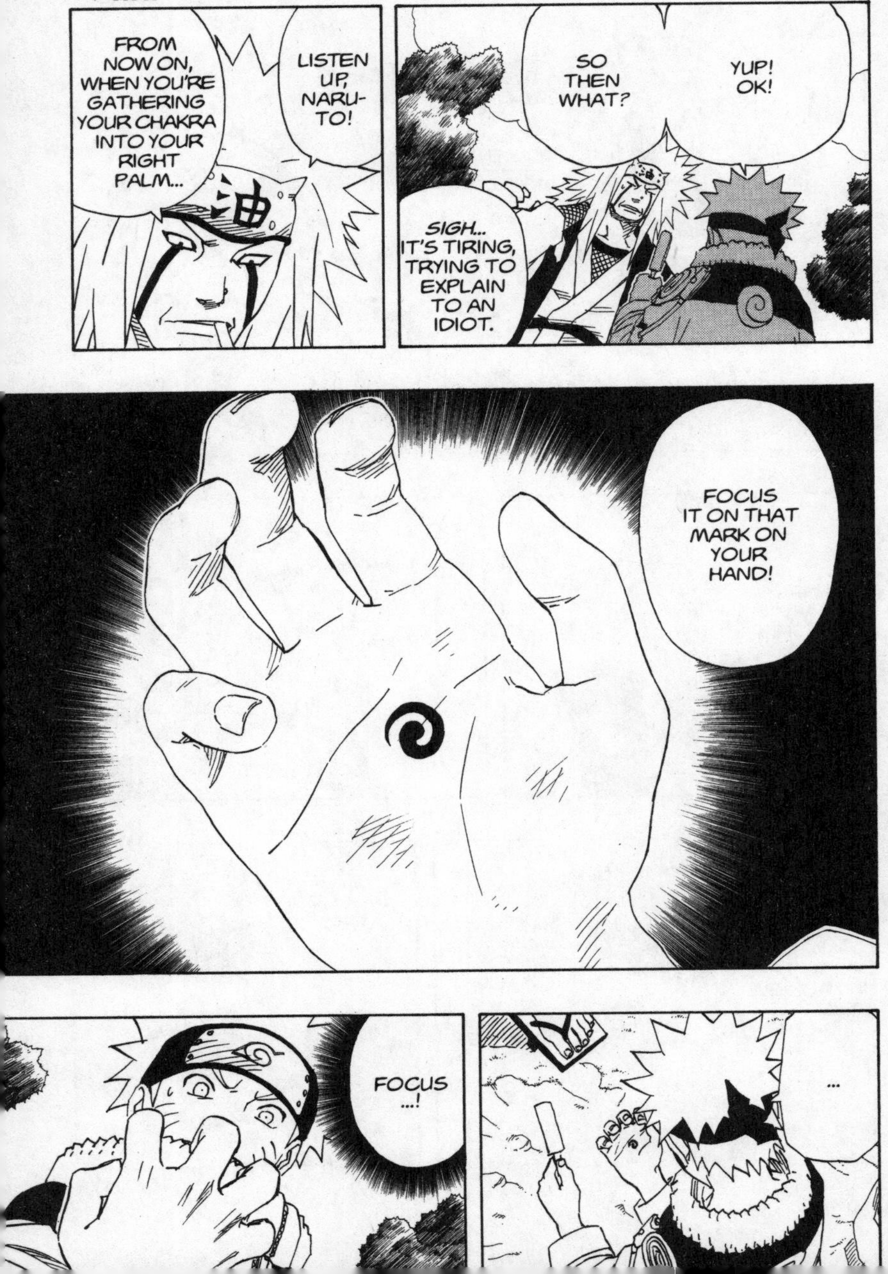
YUP! OK!
SO THEN WHAT?
SIGH... IT'S TIRING, TRYING TO EXPLAIN TO AN IDIOT.
LISTEN UP, NARU-TO!
FROM NOW ON, WHEN YOU'RE GATHERING YOUR CHAKRA INTO YOUR RIGHT PALM...
FOCUS IT ON THAT MARK ON YOUR HAND!
...
FOCUS ...!

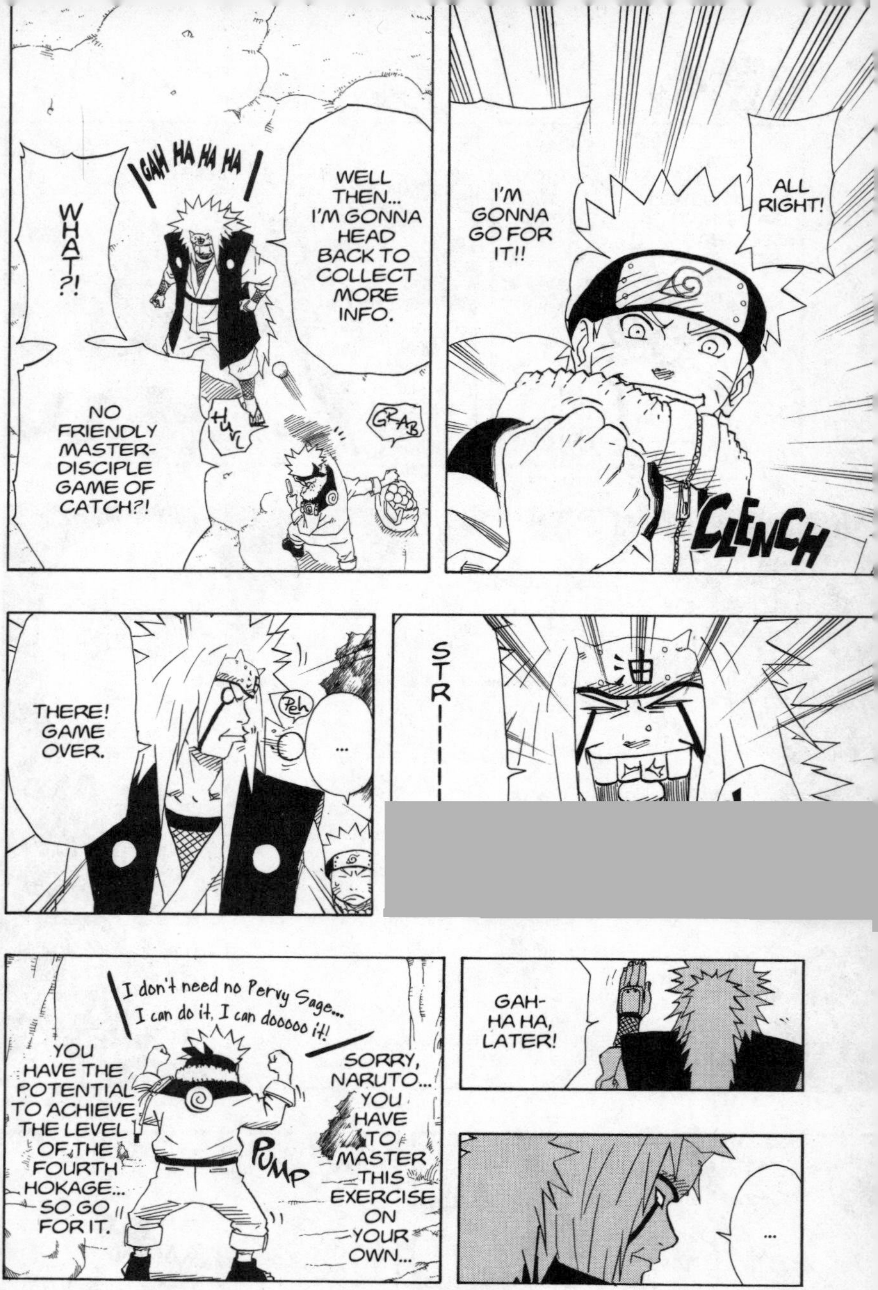
ALL RIGHT!
I'M GONNA GO FOR IT!!
CLENCH
WELL THEN... I'M GONNA HEAD BACK TO COLLECT MORE INFO.
GAH HA HA HA
WHAT?!
GRAB
HURL
NO FRIENDLY MASTER-DISCIPLE GAME OF CATCH?!
STR
...
Peh
THERE! GAME OVER.
GAH-HA HA, LATER!
...
SORRY, NARUTO... YOU HAVE TO MASTER THIS EXERCISE ON YOUR OWN...
I don't need no Pervy Sage... I can do it, I can dooooo it!
PUMP
YOU HAVE THE POTENTIAL TO ACHIEVE THE LEVEL OF THE FOURTH HOKAGE... SO GO FOR IT.

READ THIS WAY

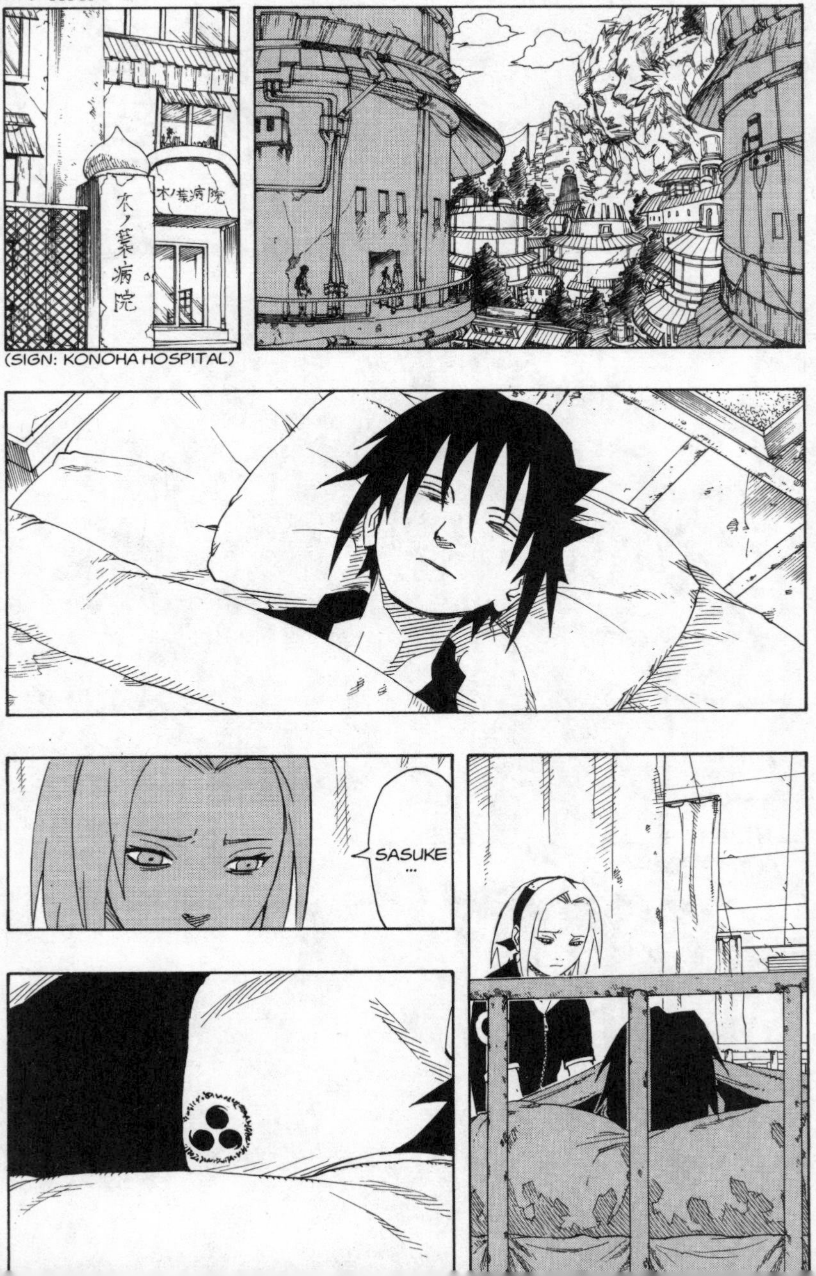

木ノ葉病院
木ノ葉病院
(SIGN: KONOHA HOSPITAL)
SASUKE ...

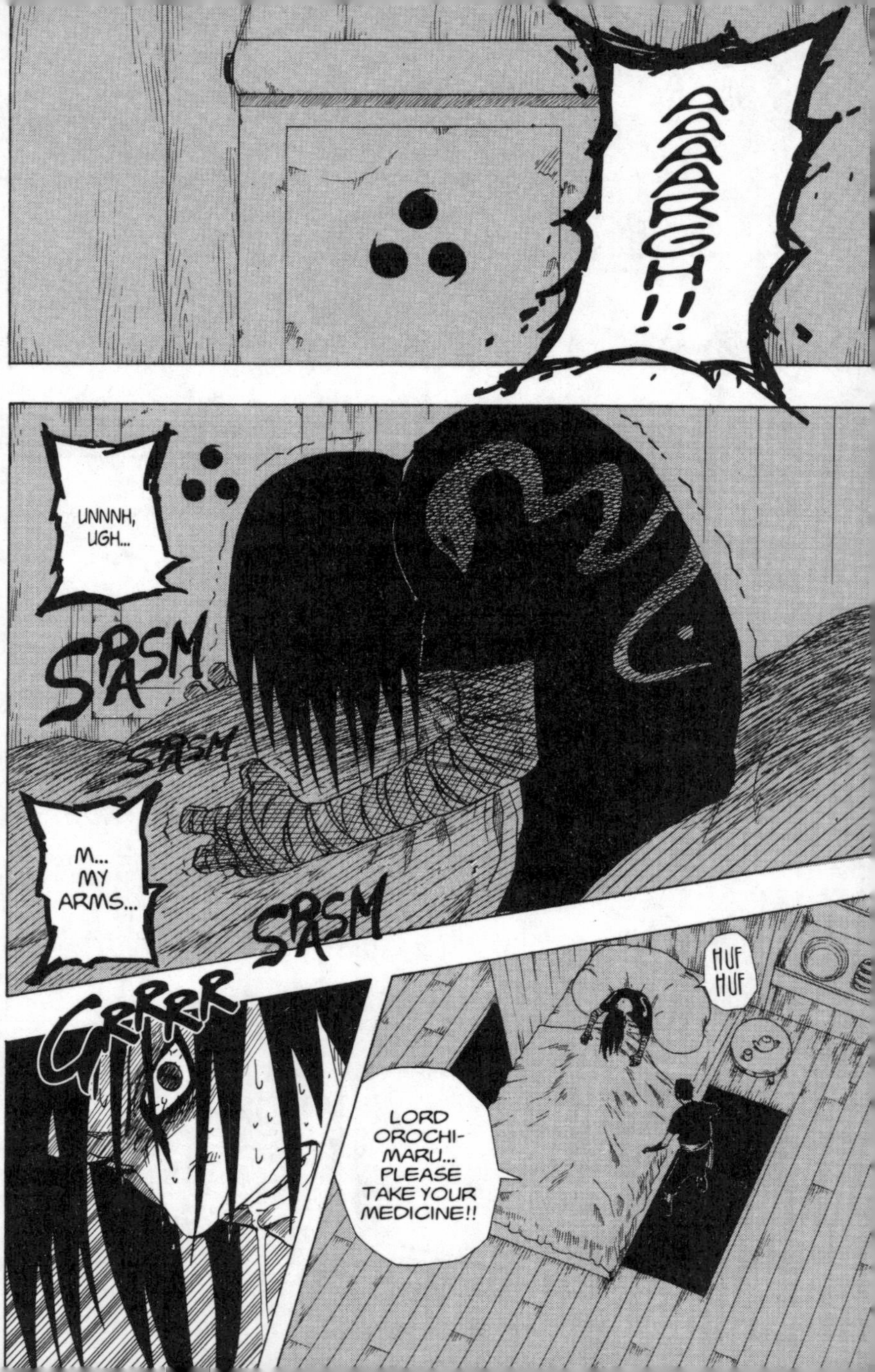
AAAARGH!!
UNNNH, UGH...
SRASM
SRASM
M... MY ARMS...
SRASM
HUF HUF
LORD OROCHI-MARU... PLEASE TAKE YOUR MEDICINE!!
GRRRR

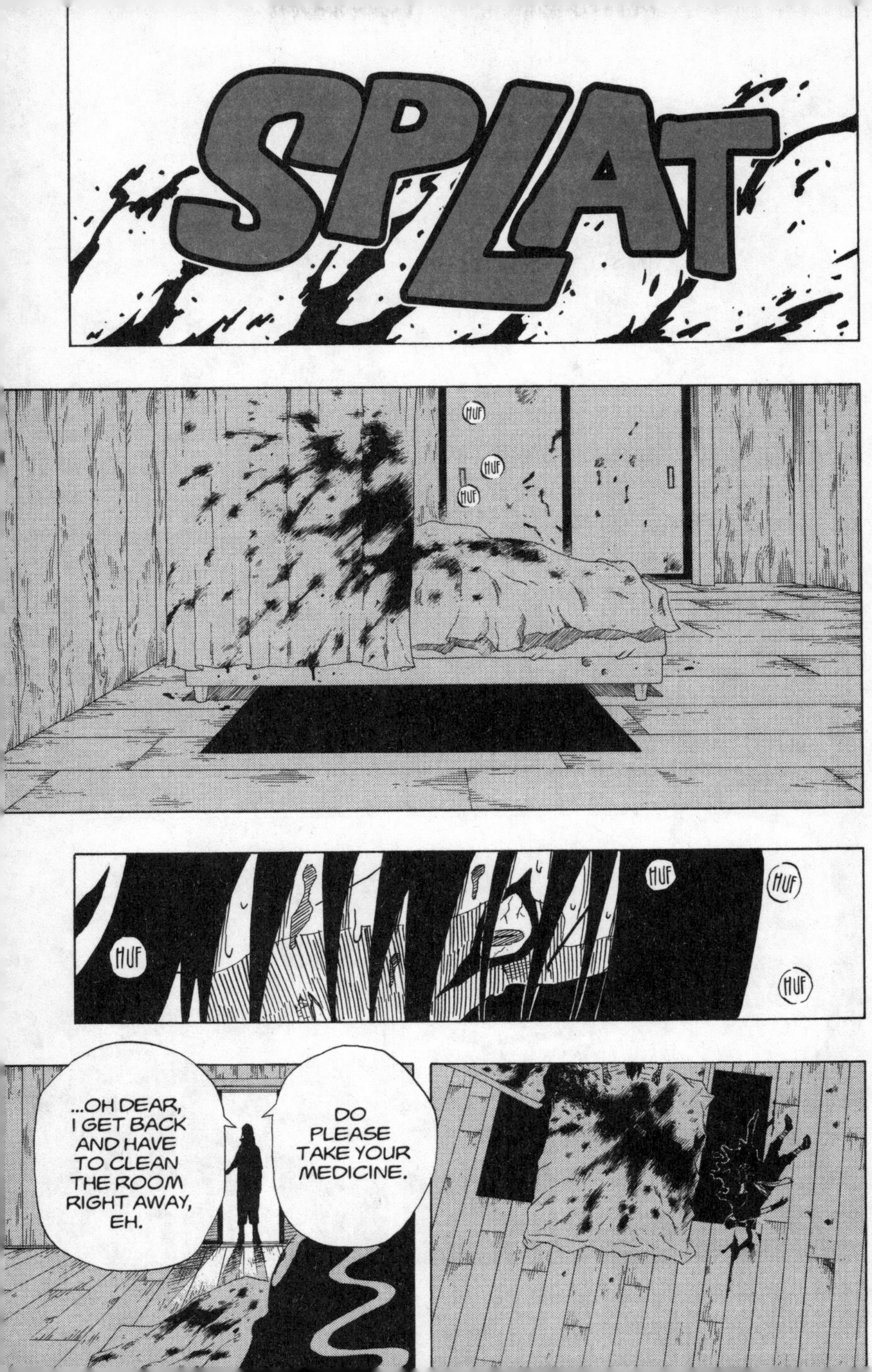
SPLAT
HUF
HUF
HUF
HUF
HUF
HUF
HUF
DO PLEASE TAKE YOUR MEDICINE.
...OH DEAR, I GET BACK AND HAVE TO CLEAN THE ROOM RIGHT AWAY, EH.

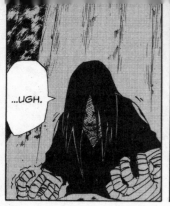

...I DON'T NEED YOUR USELESS MEDS...
BUT I MADE THEM FOR YOU ALONE!
THEY SHOULD RELIEVE AT LEAST A LITTLE OF THE PAIN...
...UGH.
...I FEEL LIKE MY ARMS ARE BURNING UP...
...I DIDN'T THINK IT WOULD BE THIS PAINFUL...
HUF
HUF
HUF
TAP
WELL, THEY ARE THE CURSED WOUNDS OF SARUTOBI...
IT'S THE THIRD HOKAGE'S FINAL ACT...
...CAN THE TEDIOUS SPEECH...
HUF
HUF
HUF
UGH... MORE TO THE POINT...
HAVE... YOU LOCATED HER?
...YES.
IT SEEMS SHE IS HANGING AROUND A TOWN CALLED TANZAKU.

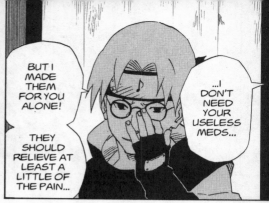

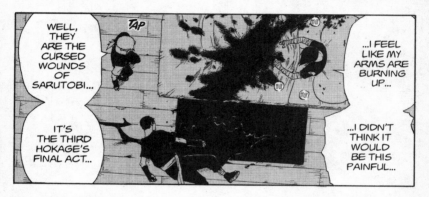

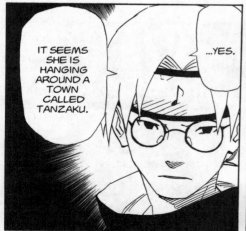

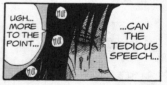

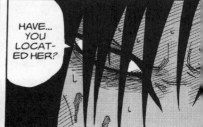

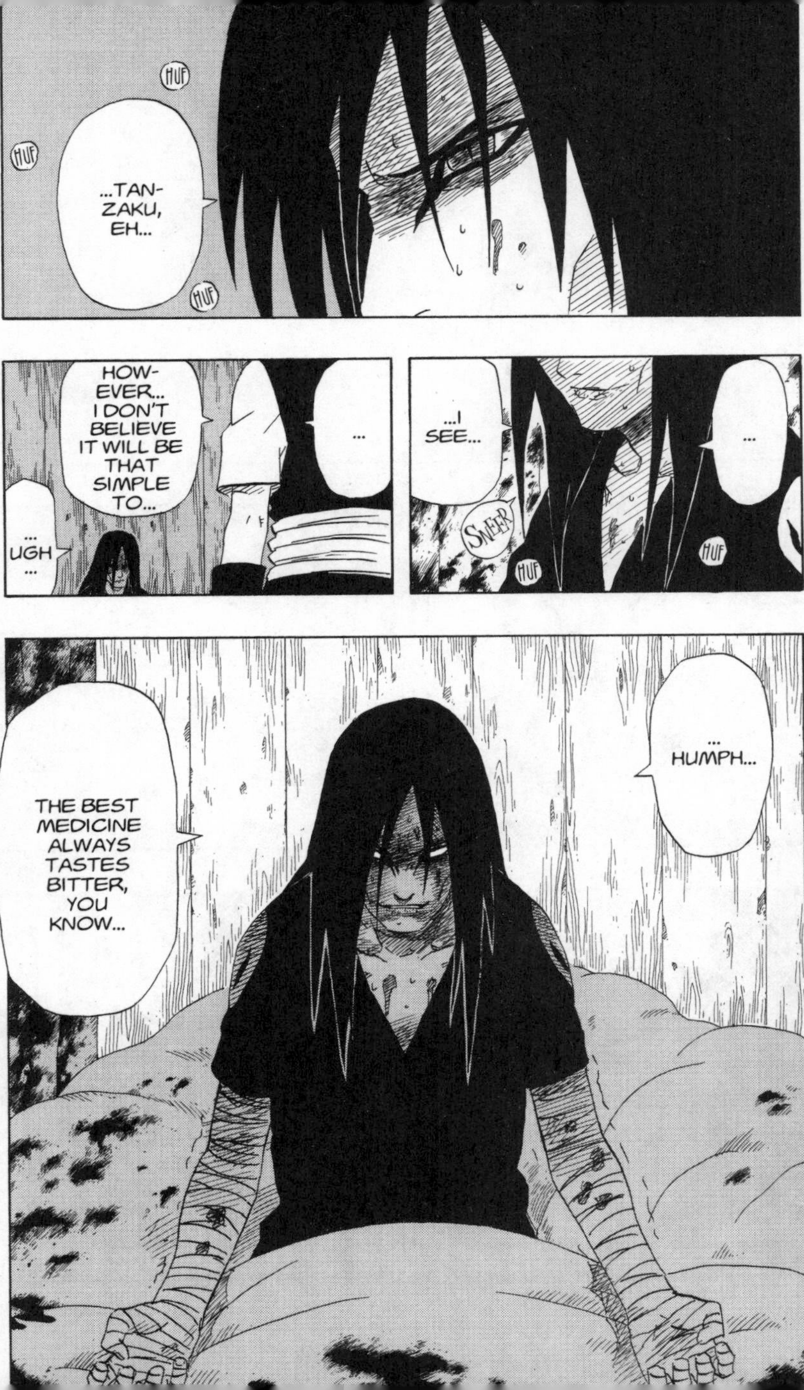
HUF
HUF
...TAN-ZAKU, EH...
HUF
...
...I SEE...
HUF
SNEER
HUF
...
HOW-EVER... I DON'T BELIEVE IT WILL BE THAT SIMPLE TO...
... UGH ...
... HUMPH...
THE BEST MEDICINE ALWAYS TASTES BITTER, YOU KNOW...

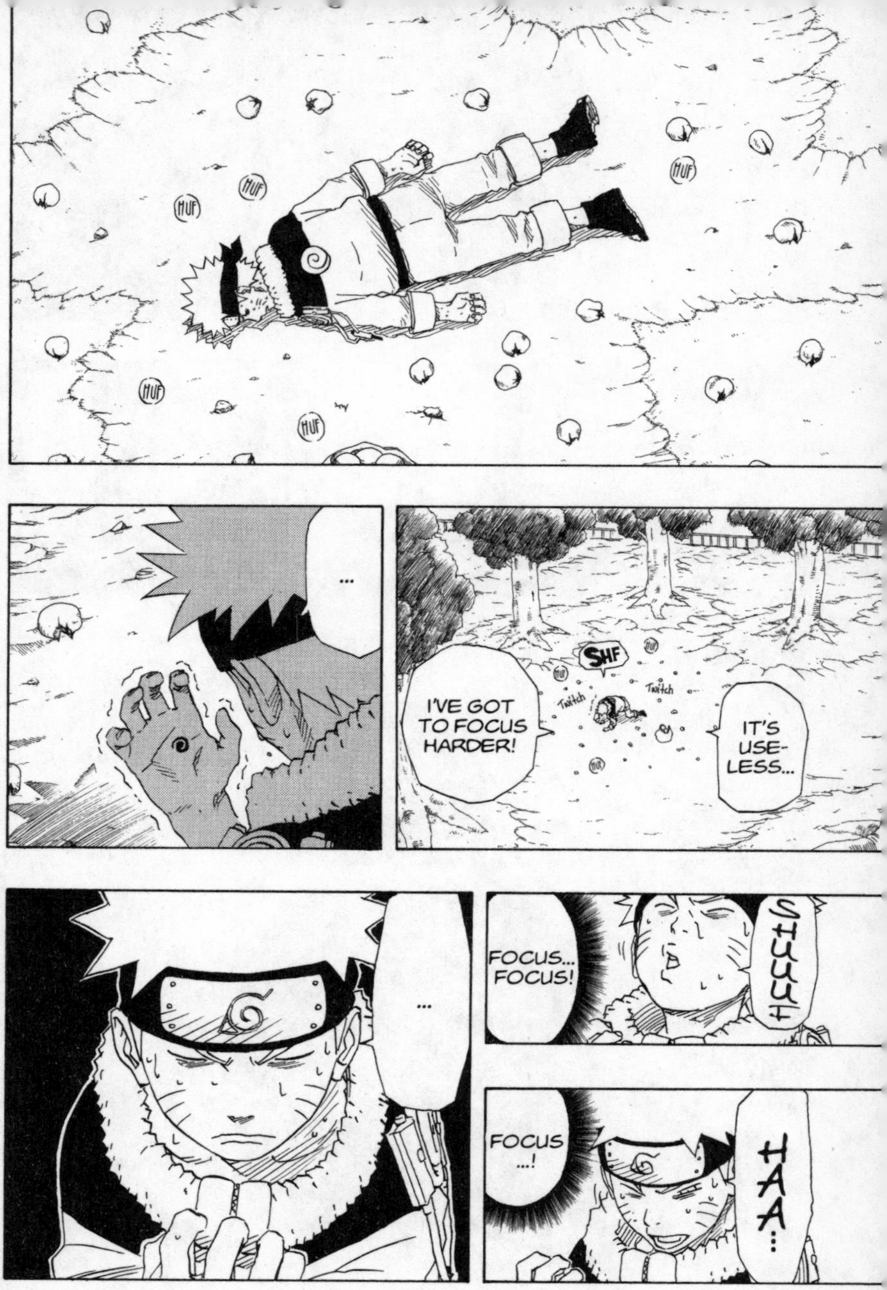
HUF
HUF
HUF
HUF
HUF
IT'S USE-LESS...
SHF
HUF
Twitch
Twitch
HUF
HUF
I'VE GOT TO FOCUS HARDER!
...
SHUUUF
FOCUS... FOCUS!
HAA...
FOCUS ...!
...

READ THIS WAY

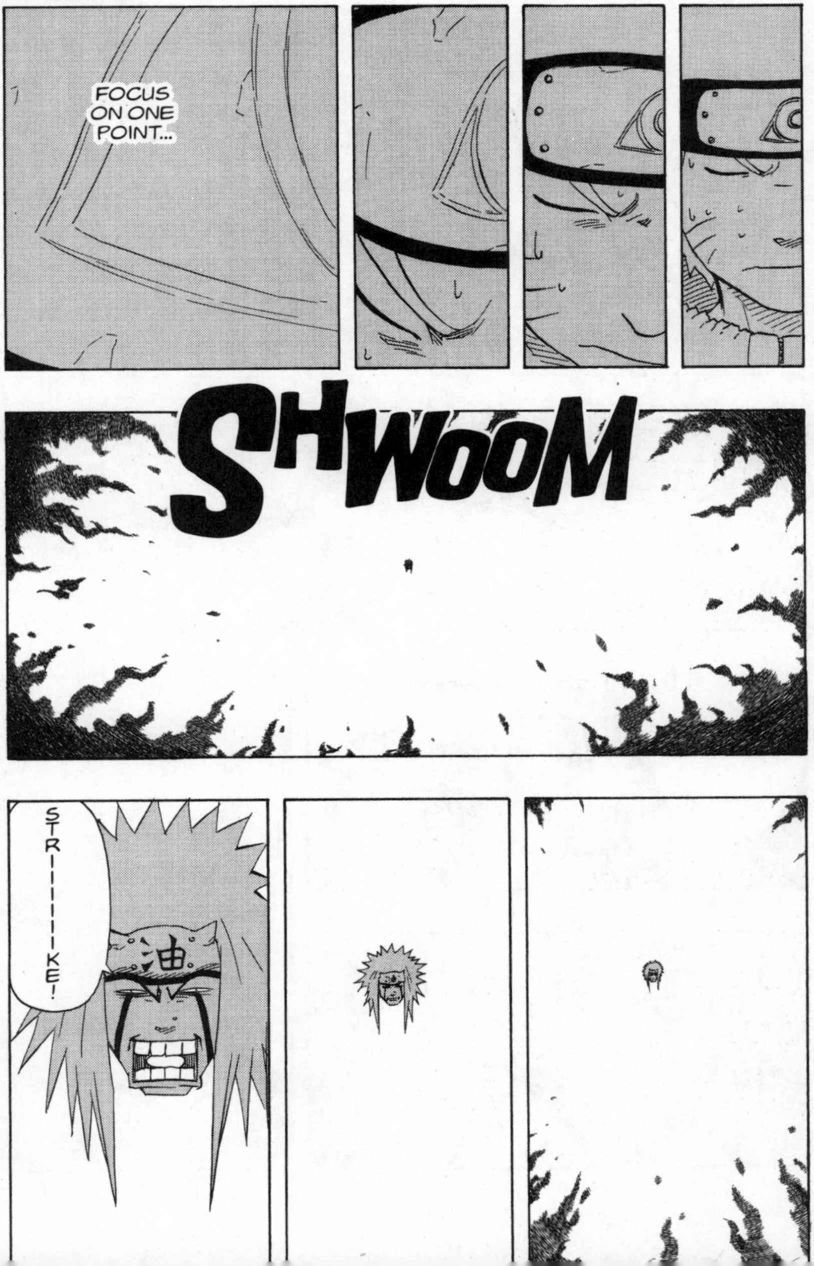
FOCUS ON ONE POINT...
SHWOOM
STRIIIIIIKE!

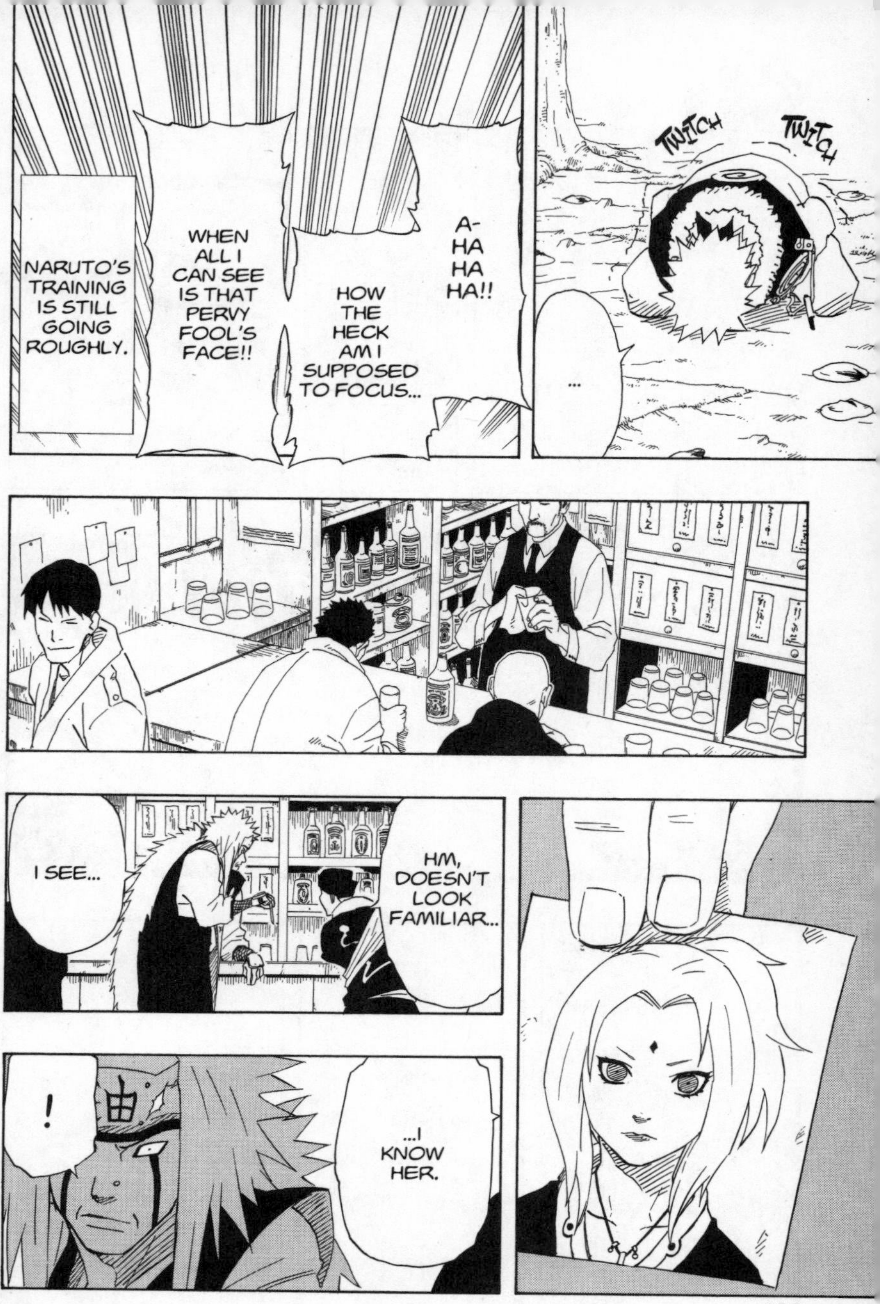

TWITCH
TWITCH
...
A-HA HA HA!!
HOW THE HECK AM I SUPPOSED TO FOCUS...
WHEN ALL I CAN SEE IS THAT PERVY FOOL'S FACE!!
NARUTO'S TRAINING IS STILL GOING ROUGHLY.
HM, DOESN'T LOOK FAMILIAR...
I SEE...
...I KNOW HER.
!

READ THIS WAY

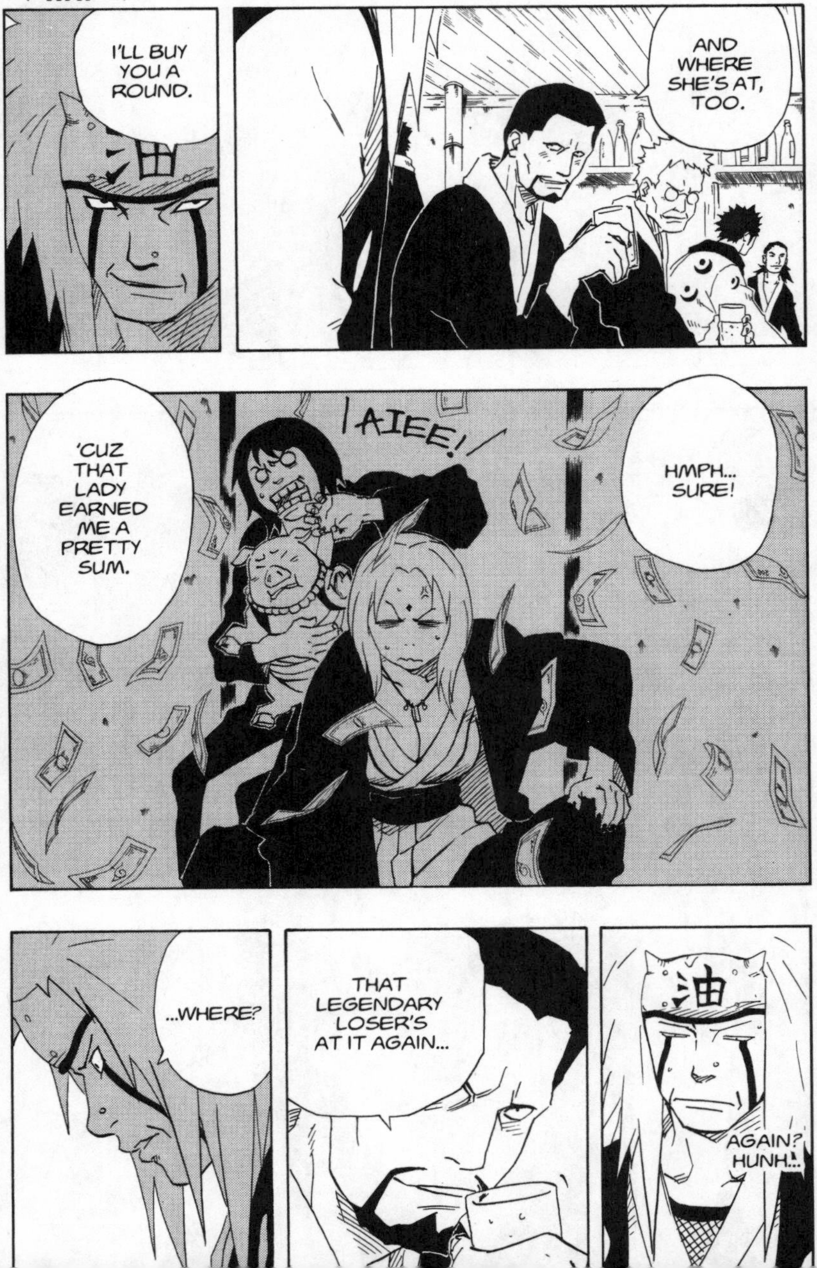
AND WHERE SHE'S AT, TOO.
I'LL BUY YOU A ROUND.
HMPH... SURE!
AIEE!
'CUZ THAT LADY EARNED ME A PRETTY SUM.
AGAIN? HUNH...
THAT LEGENDARY LOSER'S AT IT AGAIN...
...WHERE?

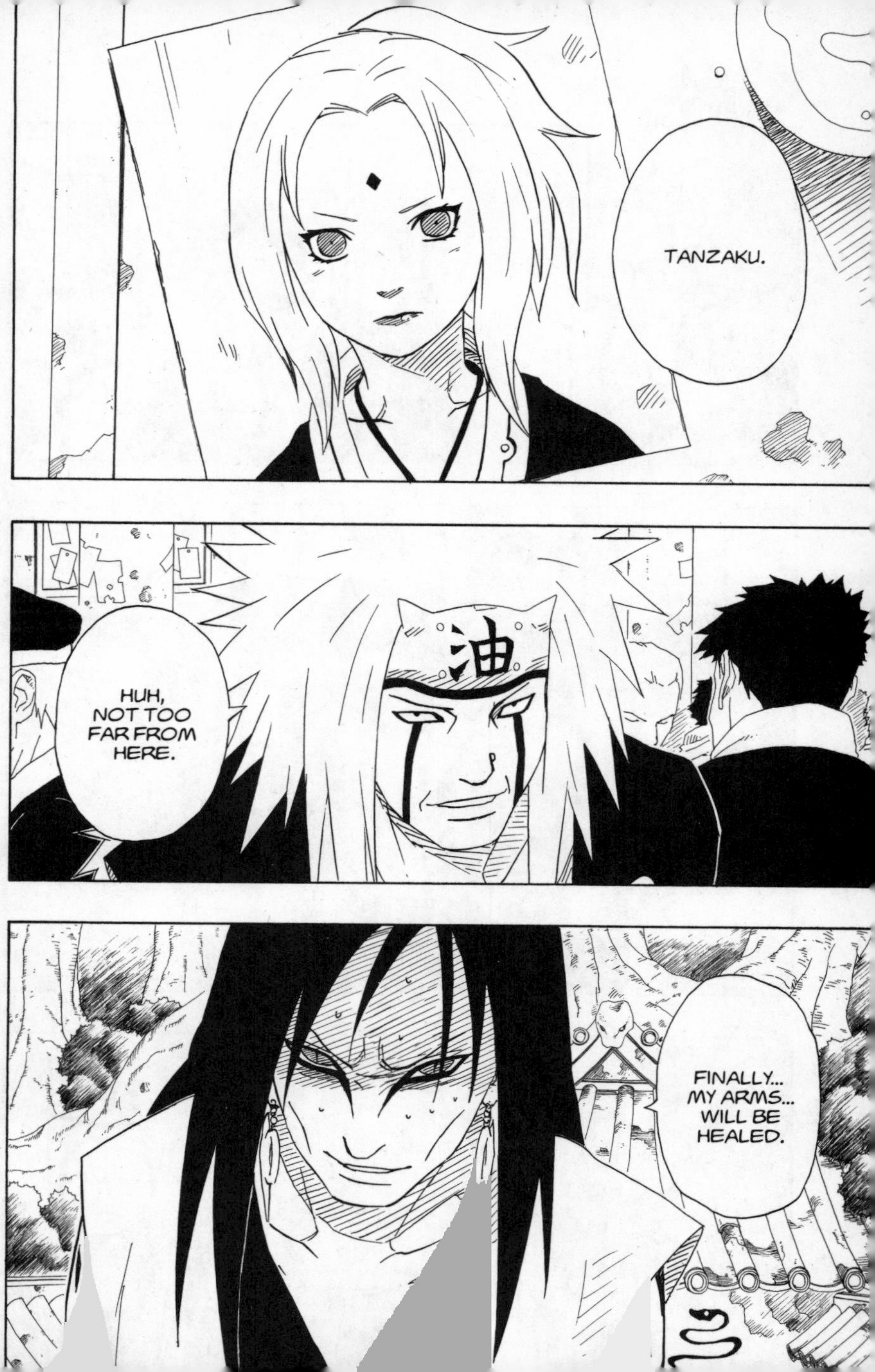
TANZAKU.
HUH, NOT TOO FAR FROM HERE.
FINALLY... MY ARMS... WILL BE HEALED.

READ THIS WAY

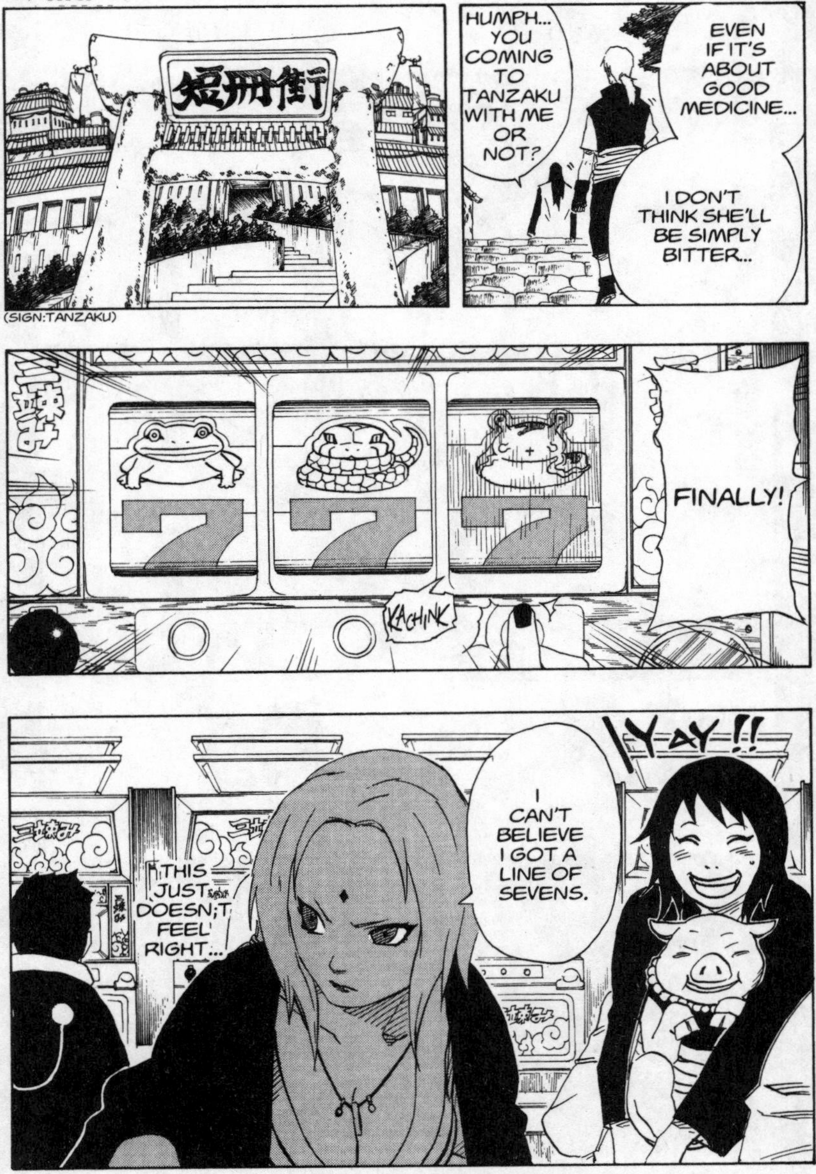
EVEN IF IT'S ABOUT GOOD MEDICINE...
I DON'T THINK SHE'LL BE SIMPLY BITTER...
HUMPH... YOU COMING TO TANZAKU WITH ME OR NOT?
短冊街
(SIGN:TANZAKU)
FINALLY!
KACHINK
YAY!!
I CAN'T BELIEVE I GOT A LINE OF SEVENS.
THIS JUST DOESN;T FEEL RIGHT...

TO BE CONTINUED IN *NARUTO* VOL. 18!

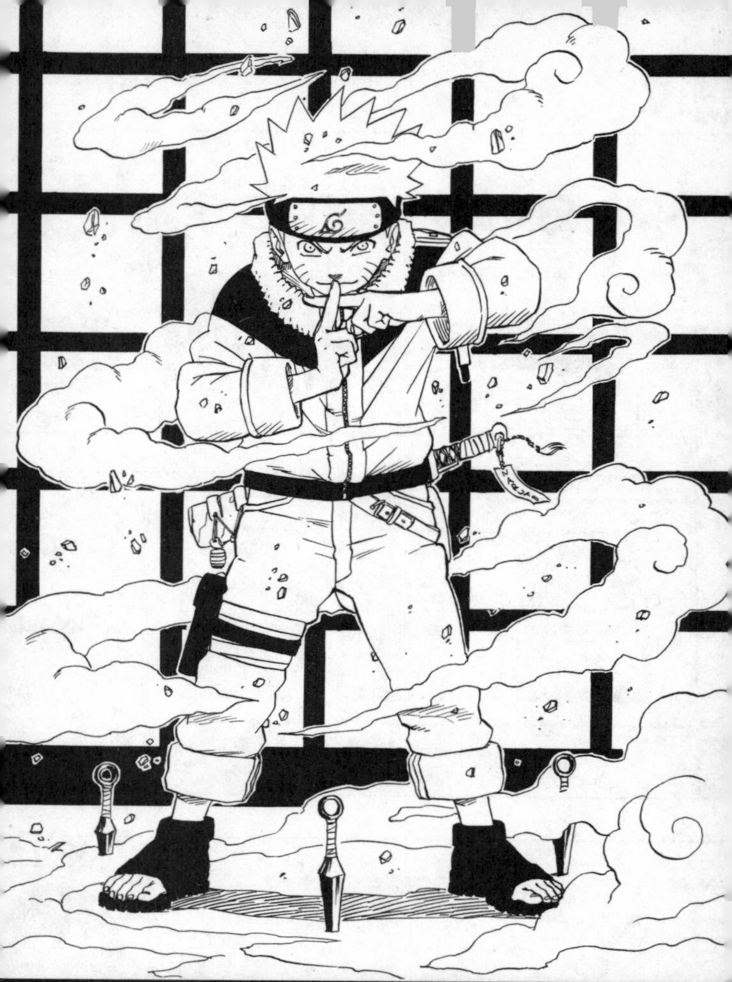

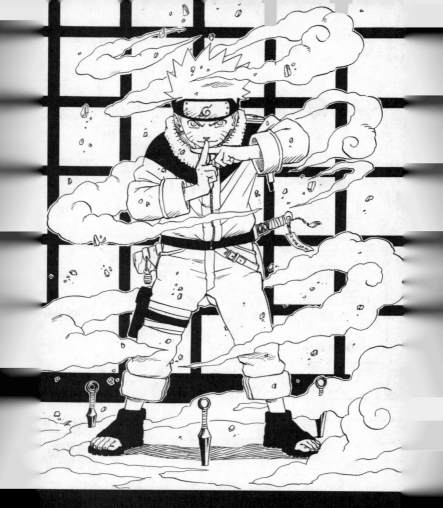

IN THE NEXT VOLUME...

TSUNADE'S CHOICE

Naruto's training with Jiraiya intensifies, while Orochimaru uses threats to coerce a legendary kunoichi into helping him. But will her tragic past play a part in destroying Naruto's future?

AVAILABLE NOW!

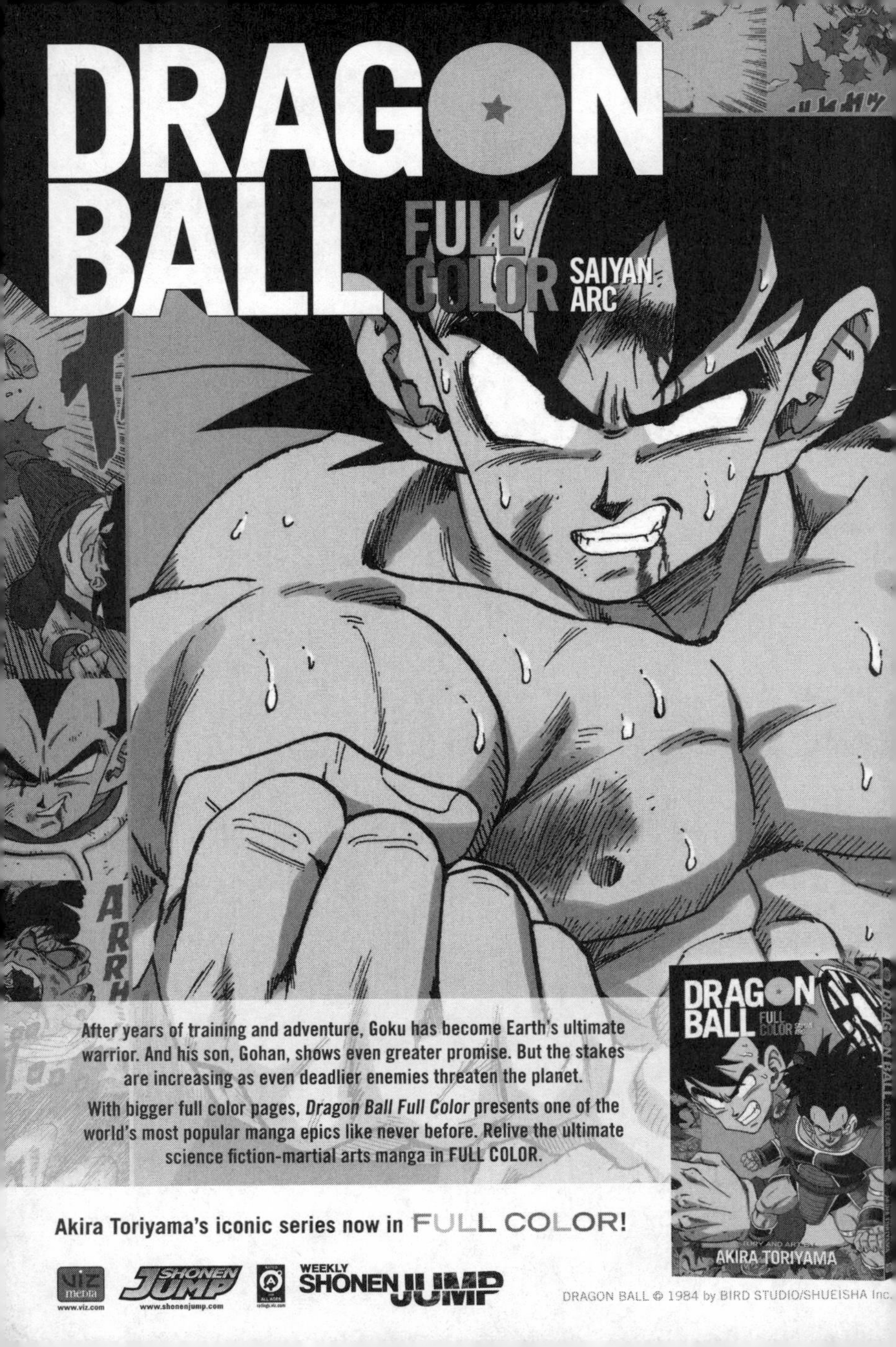
DRAGON BALL
FULL COLOR
SAIYAN ARC
After years of training and adventure, Goku has become Earth's ultimate warrior. And his son, Gohan, shows even greater promise. But the stakes are increasing as even deadlier enemies threaten the planet.
With bigger full color pages, *Dragon Ball Full Color* presents one of the world's most popular manga epics like never before. Relive the ultimate science fiction-martial arts manga in FULL COLOR.
Akira Toriyama's iconic series now in FULL COLOR!
DRAGON BALL FULL COLOR
AKIRA TORIYAMA
viz media
www.viz.com
SHONEN JUMP
www.shonenjump.com
WEEKLY SHONEN JUMP
DRAGON BALL © 1984 by BIRD STUDIO/SHUEISHA Inc.

Dr.STONE

STORY BY
RIICHIRO INAGAKI

ART BY
BOICHI

One fateful day, all of humanity turned to stone. Many millennia later, Taiju frees himself from petrification and finds himself surrounded by statues. The situation looks grim—until he runs into his science-loving friend Senku! Together they plan to restart

DEMON SLAYER
KIMETSU NO YAIBA

Story and Art by
KOYOHARU GOTOUGE

In Taisho-era Japan, kindhearted Tanjiro
Kamado makes a living selling charcoal. But
his peaceful life is shattered when a demon
slaughters his entire family. His little sister
Nezuko is the only survivor, but she has
been transformed into a demon herself!
Tanjiro sets out on a dangerous journey to
find a way to return his sister to normal and
destroy the demon who ruined his life.

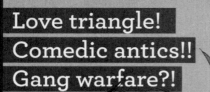

ASTRA
LOST IN SPACE

CAN EIGHT TEENAGERS FIND THEIR WAY HOME FROM 5,000 LIGHT-YEARS AWAY?

It's the year 2063, and interstellar space travel has become the norm. Eight students from Caird High School and one child set out on a routine planet camp excursion. While there, the students are mysteriously transported 5,000 light-years away to the middle of nowhere! Will they ever make it back home?!

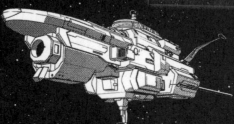

You're Reading in the Wrong Direction!!

Whoops! Guess what? You're starting at the wrong end of the comic!

...It's true! In keeping with the original Japanese format, **Naruto** is meant to be read from right to left, starting in the upper-right corner.

Unlike English, which is read from left to right, Japanese is read from right to left, meaning that action, sound effects and word-balloon order are completely reversed...something which can make readers unfamiliar with Japanese feel pretty backwards themselves. For this reason, manga or Japanese comics published in the U.S. in English have sometimes been published "flopped"—that is, printed in exact reverse order, as though seen from the other side of a mirror.

By flopping pages, U.S. publishers can avoid confusing readers, but the compromise is not without its downside. For one thing, a character in a flopped manga series who once wore in the original Japanese version a T-shirt emblazoned with "M A Y" (as in "the merry month of") now wears one which reads "Y A M"! Additionally, many manga creators in Japan are themselves unhappy with the process, as some feel the mirror-imaging of their art alters their original intentions.

We are proud to bring you Masashi Kishimoto's **Naruto** in the original unflopped format. For now, though, turn to the other side of the book and let the ninjutsu begin...!

—Editor

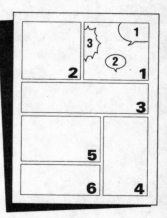